Cyber Litigation: The Legal Principles

Dedications

This book is dedicated to my son, Frederick Armstrong, who is the most wonderful human being. Also to my mum and dad, Merle and Paul, whose wise counsel continues to guide me. For Paula Cooke, my sister, and for Oliver and Anna Cooke, whose help and support means the world.

To my wife, Pip, and my children Finn and Ellie, to my mother Janine, and to my father Paul, who passed away on 8 November 2020. Without their love and support, and without the encouragement of my father in particular, this book would not have been written.

This book is dedicated to my husband, Kristian Glass, who is my person, my always and forever, my inspiration, and without whom this book would not have been possible; my parents, Lynne and Phil Davis, for everything, especially for always being there; and my grandmother, Meg, for always believing.

Cyber Litigation: The Legal Principles

Dean Armstrong QC
Fergus McCombie
Ceri Davis

Bloomsbury Professional

LONDON • DUBLIN • EDINBURGH • NEW YORK • NEW DELHI • SYDNEY

BLOOMSBURY PROFESSIONAL

Bloomsbury Publishing Plc
50 Bedford Square, London, WC1B 3DP, UK
1385 Broadway, New York, NY 10018, USA
29 Earlsfort Terrace, Dublin 2, Ireland

British Library Cataloguing-in-Publication Data

A catalogue record for this book is available from the British Library.

ISBN: PB 978 1 52651 359 5
ePDF 978 1 52651 361 8
ePub 978 1 52651 360 1

Typeset by Evolution Design and Digital Ltd (Kent)
Printed and bound by CPI Group (UK) Ltd, Croydon, CR0 4YY

To find out more about our authors and books, visit www.bloomsburyprofessional.com. Here you will find extracts, author information, details of forthcoming events and the option to sign up for our newsletters.

Preface

Is cyber litigation simply classic litigation with a computer wrapping, or is it a completely novel area?

Whilst the words 'technology' and 'cyber' have a tendency to denote the new and unprecedented, we do not claim that this subject is a total departure from traditional actions, rights and remedies. What we do claim is that there are aspects of cyber litigation that require special consideration.

One of the biggest challenges is the ability of courts and tribunals to react to the instantaneous nature of actions and the need for remedies in a digital age. The law also needs to respond to new technological developments, and, when it does so, to be prepared to depart from traditional norms and analysis.

This work concentrates on those challenges and looks at how traditional rules and remedies are being adapted, refined and replaced altogether in order to meet new and increased demands.

The cyber world is fast-paced and ever-changing. Although much of the black letter law and many of the legal concepts in this book will be familiar to legal practitioners and other professionals in the information technology and data sectors, it is inevitable that we will not have anticipated every development. We have sought to provide an overview and discussion of those areas that we believe will become most prominent in the burgeoning field of cyber litigation.

The law quoted in this work is up to date as of 31 October 2020.

Dean Armstrong QC, Fergus McCombie and Ceri Davis
The 36 Group
November 2020

Contents

Table of statutes

[All references are to paragraph numbers]

Table of statutory instruments

[All references are to paragraph numbers]

Table of cases

[All references are to paragraph numbers]

O

P

R

Part I

Introduction

Chapter 1

What is Cyber Litigation?

This chapter outlines:

- what cyber litigation is;
- the technologies that affect litigation;
- the areas of society that are affected by cyber litigation;
- the current areas of cyber litigation; and
- cyber litigation in practice.

WHAT IS CYBER LITIGATION?

1.1 Cyber litigation is a very broad concept. It means any litigation or case that is affected or impacted (in any way) by computers or technology.

As such, cyber litigation is not new. Computers and technology have been making their way into the justice system for years. For example:

- parties, practitioners and judges alike are assisted by computers in the preparation and hearing of cases;
- service can be effected by electronic means;
- parties correspond by email;
- witnesses can appear and give evidence via video link;
- evidence is now often held in electronic form as opposed to in hardcopy;
- disclosure can be carried out by way of e-Discovery software platforms rather than having to look through hardcopy material; and
- technology forms the subject matter of cases, such as copyright and trade mark infringement.

The list goes on.

However, advances in technological spheres mean that technology has become ubiquitous and now touches on almost every aspect of daily life. Consequently, technology now also affects or impacts on almost all cases and forms of litigation in some form or another, and is doing so at an increasing rate and in new areas.

Take, for example, cryptoassets. Originally a niche interest of libertarian, anti-establishment, anti-regulatory futurists of the technical persuasion, they are now a worldwide trading commodity used by millions of people each day. In England and Wales, they have been deemed property by the UK Jurisdiction Taskforce's Legal Statement on Cryptoassets and Smart Contracts.[1] The Legal Statement has been adopted by the High Court in a decision which is innovative and highly significant: *AA v Persons Unknown & Ors* [2019] EWHC 3556 (Comm) (13 December 2019). The consequences of this are enormous. Suddenly, cryptoassets are something that can be included in matrimonial financial settlements; they can be protected through proprietary and freezing injunctions; and they can form part of, and be considered in, restraint and confiscation proceedings. They are even being used as incentives in dispute resolution.

Another example is the General Data Protection Regulation[2] ('GDPR'), where technology led to legislative intervention which, in turn, has the potential to lead to an explosion in cyber litigation. Although the protection of personal data was always something that data controllers had to heed, it was, until the introduction of the GDPR in May 2018, something that the general public did not generally think much about. The cookie banner on websites was an annoyance that people just clicked 'Accept' to get rid of. The introduction of the GDPR was a watershed moment and heralded an increased public awareness of the importance and value of personal data. In a similar way to cryptoassets, it was suddenly realised that personal data was a commodity. People became aware of cookies and what they do; AdTech industry practices were exposed; obtaining and selling and/or revealing and/or ransoming personal data became a much bigger target for criminals; and data controllers went into overdrive to protect personal data and avoid the eye-watering fines provided for in the GDPR.

Therefore, although cyber litigation is not new, it is a fast-developing and dynamic area, and one that almost every party and practitioner will be involved in.

WHAT ARE THE TECHNOLOGIES THAT AFFECT LITIGATION?

1.2 Name any piece of technology and it will, more likely than not, have an effect or impact on litigation in some way and thus make the litigation 'cyber litigation'.

Data, for example, can be considered 'a technology' in the broadest sense of the word. It can be the subject matter of litigation (in terms of civil breach of confidence or misuse of private information claims), the basis of a criminal offence, or the subject of regulatory action. It is also the core of any case because data underpins all cases. It is the details of the case, the names of the parties, the material held, the documentation disclosed, corporate documentation, emails

1 https://35z8e83m1ih83drye280o9d1-wpengine.netdna-ssl.com/wp-content/uploads/2019/11/6.6056_JO_Cryptocurrencies_Statement_FINAL_WEB_111119-1.pdf.

2 Regulation (EU) 2016/679.

between parties or lawyers, etc. Adequate procedural and technological measures must be in place to ensure its security and confidentiality.

Artificial intelligence is a developing area of technology that is increasingly making its presence felt in litigation. It is being used to:

- conduct disclosure and legal professional privilege reviews;
- review contracts;
- draft contract terms;
- decide cases;
- determine sentences;
- create fake evidence; and
- predict 'hot-spot' areas of criminality.

The following technologies are also having a significant impact on litigation and cases:

- databases;
- blockchains;
- cryptoassets;
- smart contracts;
- e-communications (e-filing, e-signatures, e-contracts, etc.);
- smart devices; and
- malware, ransomware and spyware/stalkerware.

Taking a step back from specific technologies, the internet plays a huge role in all types of case, from facilitating e-filing and the establishment of contractual relationships, to the posting of illegal or abusive content and being the means of acquiring and deploying malware. It is also the means by which litigation can be conducted remotely: cyber litigation in the purest sense.

Other technologies also have an effect on litigation, but those outlined above are the focus of this book.

WHAT AREAS OF SOCIETY ARE AFFECTED BY CYBER LITIGATION?

1.3 All areas of society are affected by cyber litigation. Individuals, consumers, businesses, the Government, criminals and the criminal justice system all interact with, and use, computers and technology. Exactly how each of these is affected by cyber litigation is outside the remit of this chapter, as this is discussed in detail in the other chapters of this book. However, many cases in this day and age will, almost inevitably, have a 'cyber' or 'technology' aspect to them and thus be capable of being classified as cyber litigation.

WHAT ARE THE CURRENT AREAS OF CYBER LITIGATION?

1.4 The natural consequence of the above is that cyber litigation is present in all areas of law and is relevant to all parties and practitioners, not just those where technology is the subject matter of the case (for example, cases involving copyright and trade mark infringement).

In the criminal sphere, technology can assist the commission of established criminal offences in new ways ('cyber-assisted crimes') – for example, blackmail being perpetrated through the use of ransomware, or domestic abuse being committed through smart devices. It can also be the sole means by which offences are committed ('cyber-dependent crimes') – for example, the development and deployment of malware or data destruction. Technology is also used in the investigation and prosecution stages of criminal proceedings. It is used to obtain evidence, interrogate and analyse information, conduct disclosure exercises and in the presentation of cases. Thus, cyber litigation has a wide reach in the world of criminal justice (see **Chapter 2**).

It has an equally long reach in the civil and regulatory spheres. The development outlined above, which recognised cryptoassets as property, has widespread significance. Now, pieces of computer code can be property; they can therefore be the subject of asset seizure, preservation and forfeiture orders; and they can be divisible, if appropriate, on divorce. Smart contracts found exclusively in blockchains can theoretically govern multi-million pound contracts. None of this could have been envisaged even a few years ago.

'Data as a commodity' is becoming an increasingly well-known mantra and is already giving rise to cases that are, perhaps, the real shape of cyber litigation to come. Both the *Morrisons* case[3] and *Lloyd v Google*[4] have seen group actions brought in respect of breaches of data obligations (see **Chapter 6**) and, although the Supreme Court reversed the Court of Appeal's decision on the facts of the *Morrisons* case, breaches of data obligations can attract vicarious liability (see **Chapter 7**). Although, at the time of writing, the *Lloyd v Google* appeal to the Supreme Court is outstanding, if the Court of Appeal's decision is affirmed, it will be possible for damages to be awarded for loss of control of data without there being a need to prove pecuniary loss or distress. This is a monumental development and opens the door for other claims based on the inherent value of data. The true value of data is only just beginning to be realised, but these emerging areas of cyber litigation (group actions, vicarious liability and damages for loss of control of data and/or in respect of the inherent value of data) are, in the authors' opinion, the sign of things to come.

Another current area of cyber litigation that is a sign of things to come is the international transfer of data. Not only is the UK's future in respect of receiving

3 *Various Claimants v Wm Morrison Supermarkets plc* [2017] EWHC 3113 (QB); *Wm Morrison Supermarkets plc v Various Claimants* [2018] EWCA Civ 2339 and [2020] UKSC 12.

4 [2018] EWHC 2599 (QB) and [2019] EWCA Civ 1599.

data transfers from the EU currently unclear but, at the time of writing, a decision of the European Court of Justice ('CJEU') has invalidated the EU-US Privacy Shield[5] (see **Chapter 5**). This does not mean that transatlantic data transfers can no longer occur, as the CJEU validated Standard Contractual Clauses ('SCC') as a mechanism that ensures appropriate safeguards and compliance with the GDPR. However, many will have to re-draft contracts to include SCC and, if there are any concerns about compliance with the SCC – for example, if the law of a third country overrides contractual provisions – transfers under the contracts will have to cease. Thus, SCC are going to be subject to close scrutiny, both in terms of drafting and compliance, and so international transfers of data look set to become a cornerstone of cyber litigation.

CYBER LITIGATION IN PRACTICE

1.5 Some technological advances mean that legislative and regulatory changes and intervention will be necessary. For example, Her Majesty's Revenue and Customs ('HMRC') has introduced guidance on cryptoasset taxation for individuals,[6] and the advent of driverless cars will likely lead to the introduction of specific legislation and regulatory regimes.

However, not all technological advances require such intervention. Where technology affects traditional causes of action, or traditional remedies are sought in respect of technology or cases with cyber aspects, the courts are showing themselves willing to extend and adapt current legislation, processes, procedures and remedies to such cyber litigation. The current common law and legislative framework underpinning the criminal justice system also provides investigative agencies and prosecutors with the means to investigate and prosecute cyber-dependent and cyber-assisted crimes. Additionally, although 'cyber' and technology remove boundaries and borders, there are no special jurisdictional or evidential rules relating to cyber litigation.

Therefore, unless new technologies give rise to questions, damage or harm not seen before and not capable of being answered, addressed or remedied by existing means, cyber litigation is likely to fall within existing causes of action and offences, without the need for legislative and regulatory changes. In the criminal sphere this means that, as more individuals use technology to commit crimes in new ways, investigative agencies, prosecution authorities, practitioners, courts and judges will have to recognise the need for technical expertise in the investigation, prosecution and defence of such crimes, and readjust how such cases are presented to juries.

In the civil sphere, recent and forthcoming legislation generally seeks to extend and clarify existing rights and liabilities. As noted above, although the law of

5 Schrems II (C-3111/18).

6 www.gov.uk/government/publications/tax-on-cryptoassets/cryptoassets-for-individuals#other-considerations.

data protection is not new as a concept, the GDPR is a more powerful tool in the hands of individuals with data rights than has been available previously. The UK Government, in common with many around the world, is actively considering regulation of online platforms of various kinds. The UK Government's White Paper on Online Harms[7] proposes legislating to create a new statutory duty of care to have regard to the risk of a range of actual and potential harms arising from unregulated use of the internet. The Automated and Electric Vehicles Act 2018 clarifies how existing legal rules would apply, for example, insurance liability and contributory negligence in the event of a road traffic accident involving a self-driving vehicle. Financial technology, such as crowdfunding platforms, have been brought within the scope of the existing regulatory regime of the Financial Services and Markets Act 2000.

These examples – and there are many others to discover in this book – illustrate that the legal concepts which emerge from the developing law ought to be familiar to practitioners, even if the subject matter is not.

All parties and practitioners need to be aware of the increasing impact of technology in all areas of the legal sector, and the increasing reach of cyber litigation.

7 April 2019; Home Office and Department for Digital, Culture, Media and Sport.

Part II

Causes of Action

Chapter 2

Cyber Litigation and Criminal Law

This chapter considers:

- traditional crimes where technology and software are giving rise to new ways of committing them ('cyber-assisted crimes');
- offences that can only be committed by technological means ('cyber-dependent crimes');
- how the criminal justice system can deal with cyber-assisted and cyber-dependent crimes within its current framework;
- how the criminal justice system can develop and adapt in order to be better placed to engage with the developing cyber world; and
- the impact that new technologies may have on criminal investigations and prosecutions.

INTRODUCTION

2.1 At first blush, cyber litigation and the criminal law looks like a very narrow concept. For a lot of people, the combination of 'cyber' and criminal law means cybercrime in the form of hacking.

However, the relationship between 'cyber' and the criminal law is much broader than this, as technology gives rise to two closely linked, but distinct, areas of criminal activity:

- cyber-dependent crimes, which are offences that can only be committed technologically, ie by using a computer, computer networks or other forms of information communications technology, with computing being both the means and ends of a crime (for example, developing and deploying ransomware, malware etc, hacking, data destruction etc); and
- cyber-enabled crimes, which are traditional crimes that can be increased in scale and reach by the use of digital technologies (for example, drug dealing, fraud and money laundering).

As long as there are software developers, there will always be a steady increase in cyber-dependent crimes. Meanwhile, the development of new and better technologies will potentially lead to an exponential increase in cyber-enabled crimes: technology enables us to do things faster, more cheaply, more efficiently and on a larger scale, and so technology also enables individuals to commit traditional crimes in new ways, faster, more cheaply, more efficiently and on a larger scale.

This chapter considers both traditional crimes where technology (and the software that underpins the concept of cyber-dependent crimes) is giving rise to new ways of committing them, and cyber-dependent crimes, and looks at not only how the criminal justice system can deal with them within its current framework, but also how it can develop and adapt in order to be better placed to engage with the developing cyber world. This chapter also considers the impact that new technologies may have upon criminal investigations and prosecutions.

Before considering these matters, it is important to first address some of the terminology that is currently being used, and how some of it is unhelpful and, indeed, potentially misleading.

CYBER-ENABLED OR CYBER-ASSISTED?

2.2 The current use of the phrases 'cyber-enabled' and 'cyber-dependent' is, in the author's opinion, unhelpful and misleading, as they do not truly reflect what they are intended to mean.

2.3 For example, the Cambridge English Dictionary defines 'enabled' as:

> 'operated or made possible by the use of a particular thing.'

Based on this definition, 'cyber-enabled crime' would appear to mean a crime that is operated or made possible by cyber/technology. This, as can be seen from the above (at para **2.1**), is not what is meant by 'cyber-enabled crime' and seems more akin to the definition of a 'cyber-dependent crime'.

2.4 'Dependent' is defined as:

> 'needing the support of something or someone in order to continue existing or operating.'

Although this does accord with the definition of 'cyber-dependent crime' – they are crimes that require the support of cyber/technology in order to be carried out – it does not seem like the best description; and, as indicated above, 'cyber-enabled' seems like a much more appropriate phrase to describe a crime that is made possible by cyber/technology, as opposed to a traditional crime that cyber/technology helps to facilitate.

Would it, therefore, be better to re-name 'cyber-enabled crime' as 'cyber-assisted crime'?

The Cambridge English Dictionary defines 'assist' as 'to help'. This seems a much more appropriate way to describe traditional crimes that can be increased in scale and reach by the use of digital technologies. As such, throughout this chapter (and throughout this book), what have been known as 'cyber-enabled crimes' will be referred to as 'cyber-assisted crimes'. It is also encouraged that this phrase be adopted outside the confines of this book in order to establish a rigid distinction between crimes that can only be committed technologically, and traditional crimes that can be increased in scale and reach by the use of digital technologies.

Even though re-naming 'cyber-dependent crime' as 'cyber-enabled crime' seems sensible, given the definition of 'enabled', it is likely to lead to confusion, given the current categorisation. Therefore, provided that 'cyber-assisted crime' is adopted, 'cyber-dependent crime' could continue to be used to refer to crimes that can only be committed technologically, and will continue to be used to refer to such crimes in the rest of this chapter (and this book).

WHAT CYBER-ASSISTED CRIMES IS TECHNOLOGY GIVING RISE TO?

Domestic violence and domestic abuse

2.5 Technology, particularly the Internet of Things ('IoT'), allows people to commit domestic violence and domestic abuse offences in new and different ways. Consequently, the criminal justice system will need to adjust its way of thinking about what constitutes domestic violence and/or abuse in order to combat these offences being committed by technology.

What is 'smart abuse'?

2.6 The IoT is an umbrella term for smart devices which connect to the internet and/or make up an interconnected system of automation.

In order to assist us with our everyday lives, our homes are being filled with smart devices (for example, smart TVs, fridges, washing machines and lights). These devices are enhanced with additional remote sensor/control functionalities, and these enhanced functionalities provide the opportunity to expand the reach of controlling and coercive behaviour, such that home automation devices may be used to control a partner's behaviour.[1] For example:

- a fridge that only unlocks at certain times, so that a person is able to control when someone is able to eat or drink;
- lights that only switch on at certain times; or
- doors that only unlock at certain times, thereby controlling someone's movements.

1 '"Gender and IoT": The Implications of smart technologies on victims and survivors of domestic and sexual violence and abuse', Leonie Tanczer, University College London, presented at the Cambridge Cybercrime Conference, 11 July 2019. The attribution to Ms Tanczer is from the author's own notes of the event rather than an official transcript. Any mistakes or omissions are entirely the fault of the author.

These are somewhat extreme examples, but consider the 'Find My' iPhone application. This application allows a person to track someone all day, every day, and there is spyware and stalkerware that will allow a person to track all communications to and from someone's smartphone.

Using home automation devices to control someone's behaviour is 'smart abuse' and, much like the 'traditional methods' of committing domestic violence and domestic abuse, there may not be any visible signs of it. Consequently, the police and support services need to be alert to the possibility of smart abuse, they need to start thinking about and asking about smart technologies at the initial point of contact with complainants, and they need to consider how they keep in contact with complainants. For example, if a complainant has had spyware placed on their smartphone, and does not volunteer that information (or they do not know about it), and the police and/or support services do not ask about it, then if the police and/or support services contact the complainant on that smartphone, they may unwittingly be putting that complainant in a very dangerous position.

How to prosecute smart abuse

2.7 Think about the IoT and all the smart devices in people's homes that are used on a daily basis, and the realisation of how easy it is for people to commit smart abuse soon dawns. The next question is whether current common law and/or legislation can be used to prosecute individuals for smart abuse.

The traditional means used to prosecute cases of domestic abuse are the common law offences of assault and battery, and the offences contained within the Offences Against the Person Act 1861:

- assault occasioning actual bodily harm;[2]
- unlawful wounding;[3] and
- wounding with intent.[4]

With the exception of assault, all of the above-mentioned offences require the unlawful application of force. Therefore, these tried and tested methods of prosecuting individuals for domestic abuse are clearly not capable of prosecuting smart abuse.

Serious Crime Act 2015

2.8 The Serious Crime Act 2015 ('SCA 2015') introduced a new offence of controlling or coercive behaviour in an intimate or family relationship,[5] which came into force on 29 December 2015.

2 Offences Against the Person Act 1861, s 47.
3 Offences Against the Person Act 1861, s 20.
4 Offences Against the Person Act 1861, s 18.
5 SCA 2015, s 76.

Under section 76(1) of the SCA 2015, a person commits an offence if:

- they repeatedly or continuously engage in behaviour towards another person that is controlling or coercive;
- at the time of the behaviour, they and that other person are personally connected;
- the behaviour has a serious effect on that other person; and
- the person knows or ought to know that their behaviour will have a serious effect on the other person.

Individuals are 'personally connected' if they are in an intimate relationship, or they live together and are members of the same family or have previously been in an intimate personal relationship with each other.[6]

Behaviour is defined as having a 'serious effect' on a person if:[7]

- it causes them to fear, on at least two occasions, that violence will be used against them; or
- it causes them serious alarm or distress which has a substantial adverse effect on their usual day-to-day activities.

There is no statutory definition of what constitutes 'controlling or coercive behaviour', but the Home Office published a Statutory Guidance Framework on Controlling or Coercive Behaviour in an Intimate or Family Relationship in December 2015.[8] Paragraph 12 provides a non-exhaustive list of types of behaviour associated with coercion or control, which include:

- isolating a person from their friends and family;
- depriving them of their basic needs;
- monitoring their time;
- monitoring a person via online communication tools or using spyware; and
- taking control over aspects of their everyday life, such as where they can go, who they can see, what to wear and when they can sleep.

This list is supplemented by a non-exhaustive list on the CPS website.[9]

The Statutory Framework also notes that controlling or coercive behaviour does not only happen in the home, and states that individuals can be monitored by telephone or social media from a distance and can be made to fear violence on at

6 SCA 2015, s 76(2) and (6).

7 SCA 2015, s 76(4).

8 https://assets.publishing.service.gov.uk/government/uploads/system/uploads/attachment_data/file/482528/Controlling_or_coercive_behaviour_-_statutory_guidance.pdf.

9 www.cps.gov.uk/legal-guidance/controlling-or-coercive-behaviour-intimate-or-family-relationship.

least two occasions or adapt their everyday behaviour as a result of serious alarm or distress.[10]

Therefore, the section 76 offence catches smart abuse committed by the constant tracking of a partner, the control of a partner's movements or activities through technology, and the monitoring of a partner's use of the internet, email or any other form of electronic communication, provided that such behaviour causes the partner serious alarm or distress and has a substantial adverse effect on their usual day-to-day activities.

A person guilty of an offence under section 76 is liable on conviction on indictment to imprisonment for a term not exceeding five years, or a fine, or both; and, on summary conviction, to imprisonment for a term not exceeding 12 months, or a fine, or both.[11]

It should be noted that, other than in a case relating to behaviour that causes another person to fear that violence will be used against them,[12] a defendant will have a defence to the section 76 offence if they show that they believed that they were acting in the other person's best interests and the behaviour was, in all the circumstances, reasonable.[13] A defendant will be taken to have shown that they were acting in the other person's best interests and that the behaviour was reasonable if sufficient evidence of the facts is adduced to raise an issue with respect to them and the contrary is not proved beyond reasonable doubt.[14]

It should also be noted that, as per section 76(1)(b) and (2), it is the status of the relationship and the living arrangements at the time of the offending behaviour that are relevant to the appropriate charge to be brought. Where, therefore, the status of the relationship or the living arrangements change during the course of the offending behaviour, it might be appropriate to bring charges of both controlling or coercive behaviour and harassment or stalking, to cover the different periods.

Protection from Harassment Act 1997

2.9 Section 1 of the Protection from Harassment Act 1997 ('PHA 1997') prohibits harassment, which is a course of conduct which amounts to harassment of another.[15] A 'course of conduct' is defined as conduct on at least two occasions,[16] and harassment includes alarming a person or causing a person distress.[17] Thus, the PHA 1997 is concerned with conduct targeted at an individual

10 Statutory Guidance Framework on Controlling or Coercive Behaviour in an Intimate or Family Relationship, para 13.
11 SCA 2015, s 76(11).
12 SCA 2015, s 76(10).
13 SCA 2015, s 76(8).
14 SCA 2015, s 76(9).
15 PHA 1997, s 1(1).
16 PHA 1997, s 7(3)(a).
17 PHA 1997, s 7(2).

which is calculated to produce alarm and distress, and which is oppressive and unreasonable.[18] This would seem to be able to encompass smart abuse.

A person who pursues a course of conduct which harasses another person commits an offence under section 2 of the PHA 1997[19] and will be liable on summary conviction to imprisonment for a term not exceeding six months, or a level 5 fine,[20] or both.[21] The court may also make a restraining order,[22] and an actual or apprehended breach of section 1(1) (the prohibition of harassment) may be the subject of a civil claim for damages or an injunction by the person who is or may be the victim of the course of conduct in question.[23]

Section 2A of the PHA 1997 provides for the offence of stalking.[24] Monitoring a person's use of the internet, email or any other form of electronic communication, and watching or spying on a person, are both acts associated with stalking.[25] Therefore, section 2A of the PHA 1997 could be used to prosecute an individual for smart abuse by way of spyware or stalkerware on their partner's smartphone, or the constant tracking of their partner.

A person who is guilty of an offence under section 2A of the PHA 1997 is liable on summary conviction to imprisonment for a term not exceeding 51 weeks, or a level 5 fine,[26] or both.[27] The court may also make a restraining order.[28]

In addition to sections 2 and 2A, sections 4 and 4A of the PHA 1997 could also be used to prosecute an individual for smart abuse by way of spyware or stalkerware on their partner's smartphone, or the constant tracking of their partner, as they provide for the offences of putting people in fear of violence[29] and stalking involving fear of violence or serious alarm or distress[30] (respectively). In respect of a section 4A offence, for a course of conduct to amount to stalking involving

18 *Thomas v News Group Newspapers Ltd* [2001] EWCA Civ 1233 at [30].
19 PHA 1997, s 2(1).
20 For offences committed before 13 March 2015, the maximum statutory limit for a level 5 fine is GBP 5,000. For offences committed after 13 March 2015, the maximum statutory limit for a level 5 fine is unlimited: www.sentencingcouncil.org.uk/explanatory-material/magistrates-court/item/fines-and-financial-orders/approach-to-the-assessment-of-fines-2/9-maximum-fines/.
21 PHA 1997, s 2(2).
22 PHA 1997, s 5.
23 PHA 1997, s 3(1)–(2).
24 PHA 1997, s 2A(1).
25 PHA 1997, s 2A(3)(d) and (g).
26 For offences committed before 13 March 2015, the maximum level 5 fine that can be imposed is GBP 5,000. For offences committed after 13 March 2015, a level 5 fine is unlimited: www.sentencingcouncil.org.uk/explanatory-material/magistrates-court/item/fines-and-financial-orders/approach-to-the-assessment-of-fines-2/9-maximum-fines/.
27 PHA 1997, s 2A(4). Note: In relation to an offence committed before the commencement of s 281(5) of the Criminal Justice Act 2003, the reference in subs (4) to 51 weeks is to be read as a reference to six months: PHA 1997, s 2A(5).
28 PHA 1997, s 5.
29 PHA 1997, s 4(1).
30 PHA 1997, s 4A(1).

serious alarm of distress, the serious alarm or distress must have a substantial adverse effect on the complainant's usual day-to-day activities.[31] Again, this would seem to be able to encompass smart abuse.

A person who is guilty of an offence under section 4 of the PHA 1997 is liable on summary conviction to imprisonment for a term not exceeding six months, or a fine, or both; and, on conviction on indictment, to imprisonment for a term not exceeding ten years, or a fine, or both.[32] In respect of an offence under section 4A of the PHA 1997, a person will be liable on summary conviction to imprisonment for a term not exceeding 12 months, or a fine, or both; and, on conviction on indictment, to imprisonment for a term not exceeding ten years, or a fine, or both.[33] As with offences under sections 2 and 2A, if a person is convicted of an offence under section 4 or 4A of the PHA 1997, the court may also make a restraining order.[34]

It should also be noted that, on a trial on indictment for a section 4 or 4A offence, if the jury finds a defendant not guilty of the offence charged, they may still find the defendant guilty of an offence under section 2 or 2A of the PHA 1997 instead.[35]

False imprisonment

2.10 In addition to the above, the common law offence of false imprisonment – the unlawful and intentional or reckless restraint of a person's freedom of movement from a particular place – might provide a method of prosecuting smart abuse which involves controlling someone's movements.[36]

Modern Slavery Act 2015

2.11 The Modern Slavery Act 2015 ('MSA 2015') might also provide a method of prosecuting some instances of smart abuse. Section 1 of the MSA 2015 provides that a person commits an offence if they hold another person in slavery or servitude and they know or ought to know that the other person is held in slavery or servitude.[37] 'Holding a person in slavery or servitude' is to be construed in accordance with Article 4 of the Human Rights Convention.[38]

31 PHA 1997, s 4A(1)(b)(ii).

32 PHA 1997, s 4(4).

33 PHA 1997, s 4A(5). Note: In relation to an offence committed before the commencement of s 154(1) of the Criminal Justice Act 2003, the reference in subs (5)(b) to 12 months is to be read as a reference to six months: PHA 1997, s 4A(6).

34 PHA 1997, s 5.

35 PHA 1997, ss 4(5) and 4A(7).

36 For general guidance on sentencing in cases of false imprisonment, see *R v Spence and Thomas* (1983) 5 Cr App R (S) 413, CA.

37 MSA 2015, s 1(1)(a).

38 MSA 2015, s 1(2).

In *R v K*,[39] the Court of Appeal said that 'slavery', 'servitude' and 'forced or compulsory labour' were 'crisply defined' in *Siliadin v France*,[40] and that they form a hierarchy of a denial of personal autonomy: the essence of 'slavery' is treating someone as belonging to oneself, by exercising some power over that person as one might over an animal or an object; the essence of 'servitude' is one person's obligation to provide services to another, an obligation imposed by the use of coercion; and the essence of 'forced or compulsory labour' is work exacted under the menace of a penalty and performed against the will of the person concerned.

From the above definitions, it appears as though some forms of smart abuse (for example, controlling a person's movements, or when they eat) might fall under the definition of 'slavery', these actions being a denial of personal autonomy and exercising power over someone as one might over an animal.

A person guilty of an offence under section 1 of the MSA 2015 is liable on conviction on indictment to imprisonment for life or, on summary conviction, to imprisonment for a term not exceeding 12 months, or a fine, or both.[41]

What offences are committed by using spyware or stalkerware to commit smart abuse?

2.12 The above focuses on prosecuting an offender for the harm caused by smart abuse – false imprisonment, distress, loss of personal autonomy etc – but, if someone commits smart abuse by way of spyware or stalkerware, they may also be guilty of offences under the Computer Misuse Act 1990 ('CMA 1990') and the Investigatory Powers Act 2016 ('IPA 2016').

Computer Misuse Act 1990

2.13 Unauthorised access to computer material is an offence under section 1 of the CMA 1990.[42] This offence does not merely apply to cases of gaining unauthorised access to computer programs or data held on a computer which, among lay persons, is commonly referred to as 'hacking'. (It is important to note that, within the technical community, 'hacking' has a much broader and more positive definition.[43] This chapter will, however, use the term 'hacking' in the lay sense ('hacking simpliciter'), rather than the technical sense.) Section 1 of the CMA 1990 provides that it is an offence to use a computer *in any way* to secure unauthorised access to *any* program or data held in *any* computer.[44]

39 [2011] EWCA Crim 1691 at [39].
40 (2006) 43 EHRR 16.
41 MSA 2015, s 5(1). Note: In relation to an offence committed before the commencement of s 154(1) of the Criminal Justice Act 2003, the reference in subs (1)(b) to 12 months is to be read as a reference to six months: MSA 2015, s 5(4).
42 CMA 1990, s 1(1).
43 www.rfc-editor.org/rfc/rfc1392.txt.
44 CMA 1990, s 1(1)(a)–(b).

Thus, by deploying stalkerware or spyware onto a partner's smartphone in order to monitor their communications and internet usage, with that deployment and monitoring not having been consented to or authorised by the partner, a person would commit an offence of unauthorised access to computer material under section 1 of the CMA 1990.

A person guilty of an offence under section 1 of the CMA 1990 is liable on summary conviction to imprisonment for a term not exceeding 12 months (six months prior to the commencement of section 154(1) of the Criminal Justice Act 2003), or a fine, or both; and, on conviction on indictment, to imprisonment for a term not exceeding two years, or a fine, or both.[45]

The obtaining of the stalkerware or spyware would also be an offence under section 3A of the CMA 1990, which provides that a person is guilty of an offence if they obtain any article (which includes any program or data held in electronic form)[46] intending to use it to commit, or assist in the commission of, an offence under section 1 of the CMA 1990.[47]

A person guilty of an offence under section 3A of the CMA 1990 is liable on summary conviction to imprisonment for a term not exceeding 12 months (six months prior to the commencement of section 154(1) of the Criminal Justice Act 2003), or a fine, or both; and, on conviction on indictment, to imprisonment for a term not exceeding two years, or a fine, or both.[48]

Investigatory Powers Act 2016

2.14 If the spyware or stalkerware would allow a person to view messages, emails and internet browsing, that person would also commit an offence under section 3 of the IPA 2016, which provides for the commission of an offence where a person intentionally, and without lawful authority, intercepts a communication in the course of its transmission by means of a telecommunication system.[49]

A person intercepts a communication in the course of its transmission by means of a telecommunication system if the person does a relevant act in relation to the system and the effect of the relevant act is to make any content of the communication available, at a relevant time, to a person who is not the sender or intended recipient of the communication.[50] A 'telecommunication system' is a system (including the apparatus comprised in it) that exists (whether wholly or partly in the United Kingdom ('UK') or elsewhere) for the purpose of facilitating the transmission of communications by any means involving the use of electrical

45 CMA 1990, s 1(3)(a) and (c).
46 CMA 1990, s 3A(4).
47 CMA 1990, s 3A(3)(a).
48 CMA 1990, s 3A(5)(a) and (c).
49 IPA 2016, s 3(1).
50 IPA 2016, s 4(1).

or electromagnetic energy,[51] and a 'relevant act' in relation to a telecommunication system means:[52]

> '(a) modifying, or interfering with, the system or its operation;
>
> (b) monitoring transmissions made by the means of the system;
>
> (c) monitoring transmissions made by wireless telegraphy to or from apparatus that is part of the system.'

Although the offence relates to intercepting communications in the course of the transmission, that does not mean that the content of the communication must be available in real time to the person who has deployed the spyware or stalkerware. Although section 4(4)(a) of the IPA 2016 provides that 'relevant time' means any time while the communication is being transmitted, section 4(4)(b) provides that it also means 'any time when the communication is stored in or by the system (whether before or after its transmission)'. Therefore, interception includes obtaining stored communications, such as messages stored on phones, tablets and other individual devices, whether before or after they are sent.[53]

A person guilty of an offence under section 3 of the IPA 2016 is liable on summary conviction to a fine; and, on conviction on indictment, to imprisonment for a term not exceeding two years, or a fine, or both.[54]

Conclusions on smart abuse

2.15 The above shows that the current common law and legislative framework provide the means to prosecute perpetrators of smart abuse. It may be that, over time, as technology develops further, even more specific legislation will be brought in to address the technology angle in smart abuse. However, as matters currently stand, the law provides a number of ways in which offenders may be prosecuted.

What is important now is that the police and support services become alive to the concept of smart abuse, and are trained in not only how to recognise it, but also how to investigate it and support complainants.

Harassment and public order

2.16 There was a TV advert where a little boy sat on his bed, rocking back and forth, repeating 'Sticks and stones may break my bones', as a smartphone on his desk kept lighting up and vibrating.

51 IPA 2016, s 261(13).
52 IPA 2016, s 4(2).
53 Explanatory Notes to the IPA 2016, para 41: www.legislation.gov.uk/ukpga/2016/25/pdfs/ukpgaen_20160025_en.pdf.
54 IPA 2016, s 3(6).

Smartphones and tablets, together with the proliferation of social networking sites, messaging applications, gaming sites and chat rooms, mean that bullying and stalking are easier than ever before, and it can happen no matter where someone is or what time it is.

Bullying which takes place online or through smartphones and tablets is known as 'cyber bullying'.

What are the different types of cyber bullying?

2.17 Cyber bullying can take many forms and, according to www.bullying.co.uk, can be categorised (and defined) as follows:[55]

- **Harassment** – This includes the act of sending offensive, rude and insulting messages and being abusive. For example, making nasty or humiliating comments on posts, photos and in chat rooms and/or being explicitly offensive on gaming sites.
- **Denigration** – This is when a person may send fake, damaging and/or untrue information about someone else. For example, sharing photos of someone for the purpose of ridicule, and spreading fake rumours and gossip. This can be on any site online or on applications, and people sometimes alter photos of others and post them online for the purpose of bullying. With the advance of technology, people are now also able to alter videos and create 'deepfakes', which people may also post online for the purposes of bullying or revenge pornography.
- **Flaming** – This is when a person purposely uses really extreme and offensive language in order to cause reactions or distress.
- **Impersonation** – This is when a person uses another person's online identity to send or post vicious or embarrassing material to/about others. This could be by compromising someone's existing accounts, or by creating new accounts in that other person's name/using that other person's details.
- **Outing and trickery** – This is when a person shares personal information about another or tricks someone into revealing secrets and forwards it to others. They may also do this with private images and videos, for example, through posting revenge pornography.
- **Cyber stalking** – This is the act of repeatedly sending messages that include threats of harm, harassment, intimidating messages, or engaging in other online activities that make someone afraid for their safety.
- **Exclusion** – This is when others intentionally leave someone out of a group, such as group messages, online applications, gaming sites and other online engagement.

55 www.bullying.co.uk/cyberbullying/what-is-cyberbullying/.

How to prosecute cyber bullying?

2.18 What can the criminal law do to protect people from, and prosecute people who conduct, cyber bullying?

Where the individuals carrying out cyber bullying are located outside England and Wales, there may be little that can be done, other than reporting them to the service administrator and request that posts etc be taken down (see para **9.27**), as the courts of England and Wales may not have jurisdiction over such individuals (see **Chapter 5**).

However, where the individuals are located within the jurisdiction, in addition to reporting them to service administrators and requesting that posts etc be taken down, the criminal law can also afford some protection in respect of all forms of cyber bullying other than exclusion.

Protection from Harassment Act 1997 – harassment, denigration, impersonation, outing and cyber stalking

2.19 As outlined at paragraph **2.9** above, section 1 of the PHA 1997 prohibits harassment, and harassment is an offence under section 2(1) of the PHA 1997.

Where a person sends threats or nasty, humiliating or abusive messages etc, spreads false information, or posts altered photographs and/or 'deepfake' videos on at least two occasions[56] and the recipient/subject is caused oppressive and unreasonable[57] alarm or distress, the person sending the messages, spreading the misinformation and posting the photographs/videos may be guilty of an offence under section 2(1) of the PHA 1997 and liable on summary conviction to imprisonment for a term not exceeding six months, or a level 5 fine,[58] or both.[59] The court may also make a restraining order,[60] and an actual or apprehended breach of section 1(1) of the PHA 1997 (the prohibition of harassment) may be the subject of a civil claim for damages or an injunction by the person who is or may be the victim of the course of conduct in question.[61]

Where messages and/or posts cause another to fear, on at least two occasions, that violence will be used against them, and the person sending the messages/ making the posts knows or ought to know that their actions will cause the other so to fear on each of those occasions, the person will be guilty of an offence

56 PHA 1997, s 7(3)(a).

57 *Thomas v News Group Newspapers Ltd* [2001] EWCA Civ 1233 at [30].

58 For offences committed before 13 March 2015, the maximum statutory limit for a level 5 fine is GBP 5,000. For offences committed after 13 March 2015, the maximum statutory limit for a level 5 fine is unlimited: www.sentencingcouncil.org.uk/explanatory-material/magistrates-court/item/fines-and-financial-orders/approach-to-the-assessment-of-fines-2/9-maximum-fines/.

59 PHA 1997, s 2.

60 PHA 1997, s 5.

61 PHA 1997, s 3(1)–(2).

under section 4(1) of the PHA 1997 (putting people in fear of violence). A person guilty of an offence under this section is liable on conviction on indictment to imprisonment for a term not exceeding ten years, or a fine, or both; and, on summary conviction, to imprisonment for a term not exceeding six months, or a fine, or both.[62]

Additionally, where conduct amounts to stalking, the person may be guilty of an offence under section 2A(1) of the PHA 1997. Contacting, or attempting or contact, a person by any means, and publishing any statement or other material relating or purporting to relate to a person, or purporting to originate from a person, are all acts associated with stalking,[63] and ones for which criminal liability would attach. This would appear to capture cyber bullying committed through repeated contact, threats and/or nasty, humiliating and/or abusive messages, and the spreading of false, vicious or embarrassing information, either by an individual directly or through impersonation. Indeed, it would also appear to capture the spreading of truthful information (ie outing), by an individual directly or through impersonation.

A person who is guilty of an offence under section 2A(1) of the PHA 1997 is liable on summary conviction to imprisonment for a term not exceeding 51 weeks, or a level 5 fine,[64] or both.[65] The court may also make a restraining order.[66]

As a parallel provision to section 4 of the PHA 1997, section 4A provides that, where a person's conduct amounts to stalking and it either causes another to fear, on at least two occasions, that violence will be used against them, or causes them serious alarm or distress which has a substantial adverse effect on their usual day-to-day activities, the person undertaking the course of conduct will be guilty of an offence if they know or ought to know that their actions will cause the other person to so fear on each of those occasions or (as the case may be) will cause such alarm or distress.[67]

Note that, although parallel to section 4, section 4A goes further and provides for 'causing serious alarm or distress which has a substantial adverse effect on their usual day-to-day activities'.[68] Thinking back to that little boy rocking back and forth on his bed, section 4A would appear to be a method of pursuing his tormentors.

62 PHA 1997, s 4(4).

63 PHA 1997, s 2A(3)(b) and (c).

64 For offences committed before 13 March 2015, the maximum level 5 fine that can be imposed is GBP 5,000. For offences committed after 13 March 2015, a level 5 fine is unlimited: www.sentencingcouncil.org.uk/explanatory-material/magistrates-court/item/fines-and-financial-orders/approach-to-the-assessment-of-fines-2/9-maximum-fines/.

65 PHA 1997, s 2A(4). Note: In relation to an offence committed before the commencement of s 281(5) of the Criminal Justice Act 2003, the reference in subs (4) to 51 weeks is to be read as a reference to six months: PHA 1997, s 2A(5).

66 PHA 1997, s 5.

67 PHA 1997, s 4A(1).

68 PHA 1997, s 4A(1)(b)(ii).

A person guilty of an offence under section 4A is liable, on conviction on indictment, to imprisonment for a term not exceeding ten years, or a fine, or both; or, on summary conviction, to imprisonment for a term not exceeding 12 months, or a fine, or both.[69] Again, the court may also make a restraining order.[70]

Despite affording some protection from cyber bullying, the obvious limiting factor in relation to the PHA 1997 offences is that, in order to constitute a course of conduct, the conduct must have occurred on at least two occasions. Whilst proving this element of the offence is likely to be less problematic where cyber bullying takes the form of messages being sent – because such messages are usually sent repeatedly – it is likely to be the stumbling block in the posting of photographs and/or deepfakes, and also the spreading of false or 'outing' information, as these events may only happen on one occasion. Therefore, in these situations, complainants may have to look to other areas of the criminal law for assistance.

Computer Misuse Act 1990 – impersonation

2.20 The CMA 1990 is not only able to address the actual sending or posting of vicious or embarrassing material to others, it is also able to address the means by which individuals do this.

Section 1 of the CMA 1990 can be used to prosecute individuals who hack into someone's email or social networking account, as it provides that gaining unauthorised access to any program or data held in any computer is an offence.[71] A person guilty of such an offence is liable on summary conviction to imprisonment for a term not exceeding 12 months (six months prior to the commencement of section 154(1) of the Criminal Justice Act 2003), or a fine, or both; and, on conviction on indictment, to imprisonment for a term not exceeding two years, or a fine, or both.[72]

In the situation where a person hacks into someone's social networking account and that person then writes/posts untrue vicious or embarrassing things about the individual whose account it is, that might constitute unauthorised access intending to impair the reliability of the data on the account. Consequently, it might be an offence under section 3 of the CMA 1990, which provides that it is an offence to do any unauthorised act in relation to a computer where, by doing the act, the person intends to impair the operation of any such program or the reliability of any such data.[73]

69 PHA 1997, s 4A(5). Note: in relation to an offence committed before the commencement of s 154(1) of the Criminal Justice Act 2003, the reference in subs 5(b) to 12 months is to be read as a reference to six months (PHA 1997, s 4A(6)).

70 PHA 1997, s 5.

71 CMA 1990, s 1(1).

72 CMA 1990, s 1(3)(a) and (c).

73 CMA 1990, s 3(1) and (2)(c).

A person guilty of an offence under section 3 of the CMA 1990 is liable on summary conviction to imprisonment for a term not exceeding 12 months (six months prior to the commencement of section 154(1) of the Criminal Justice Act 2003), or to a fine, or both; and, on conviction on indictment, to imprisonment for a term not exceeding ten years, or to a fine, or both.[74]

Where, however, the vicious or embarrassing things that are posted are true, that might form a defence to a section 3 offence, as it would be arguable that posting such truths was not impairing the reliability of the data. In which case, recourse might need to be had to section 2A(3)(c) of the PHA 1997 instead (publishing any statement or other material relating or purporting to relate to a person, or purporting to originate from a person) (see para **2.19** above) or section 4A of the Public Order Act 1986 ('POA 1986') (intentional harassment, alarm or distress) (see para **2.22** below).

Outraging public decency – denigration and flaming

2.21 As flaming involves the use of really extreme and offensive language, it is possible that, in some extreme circumstances, it may fall under the common law offence of outraging public decency. This offence might also capture the posting of altered photographs or 'deepfake' videos.

For an individual to be guilty of an offence of outraging public decency, it must first be proved that the act complained of was committed in public, which means that it must be committed in a place, public or private, where at least two people were able to witness the act and where there existed a real possibility that a member of the general public might witness it.[75] There is, however, no requirement that someone actually saw the act.[76]

The internet is, arguably, either the biggest public space that there is or, conversely, given the need to have an internet service provider ('ISP') and 'sign up to the internet', the biggest private space that there is. The 'act' being complained of is the act of posting inflammatory, extreme and offensive comments etc, or altered photographs and videos, on the internet. Although two people may not be able to witness the actual physical act of pressing the relevant buttons to publish the post itself, provided that it is not a direct message to the recipient,[77] at least two people will be able to witness the post and, provided that it is not posted to a 'members only' website, there is a real possibility that a member of the general public might witness the post. Note that the Hong Kong Court of Final Appeal has held that the public element of the offence requires the act to be committed in a physical, tangible place, and that the internet is not a place for this purpose; whereas, in

74 CMA 1990, s 3(6)(a) and (c).

75 *R v Walker (S)* [1996] 1 Cr App R 111.

76 *R v Hamilton* [2007] EWCA Crim 2062.

77 *R v Mayling* [1963] 2 QB 717 and *Knuller (Publishing, Printing and Promotions) Ltd v DPP* [1973] AC 435.

England and Wales, the courts have held that any person who posts material on the internet puts that material within the public ambit.[78]

Secondly, it must be proved that the act is of such a lewd, obscene or disgusting character as constitutes an outrage on public decency, but it is not necessary to prove that the act in fact disgusted or annoyed the persons within whose purview it was committed.[79] Whether an act is obscene, lewd or disgusting is a question of fact,[80] but 'outraging public decency' goes considerably further than offending the susceptibilities of, or even shocking, reasonable people. The offence is concerned with minimum standards which are likely to vary from time to time and, in a plural society with a tradition of toleration towards minorities, that atmosphere is part of public decency.[81]

Although it is not necessary that the act itself is of a sexual nature or is inherently lewd, obscene or disgusting,[82] one can envisage circumstances where revenge pornography or altered photographs or 'deepfake' videos might meet this requirement. Flaming is likely to have to be particularly extreme to meet this requirement, but there may be circumstances in which proceeding with a prosecution under this offence is appropriate.

On conviction on indictment, this offence is punishable by a fine, or imprisonment, or both, and there is no limit on what might be imposed, provided that the sentence is not inordinate.[83]

Public Order Act 1986 – denigration and flaming

2.22 Given that so many people now live much of their lives online, the internet is considered to be a 'public place', and flaming and posting altered photographs and 'deepfake' videos can constitute public order offences.

Section 4 of the POA 1986 (fear or provocation of violence) requires a person to intend to cause another to believe that immediate unlawful violence will be used against them or another, or intend to provoke the immediate use of unlawful violence by that person or another, or the other is likely to believe that such violence will be used or it is likely that such violence will be provoked. Given the distancing factor of the internet, cyber bullying in the form of denigration and flaming is unlikely to result in a person fearing that they will be subjected to immediate unlawful violence, so section 4 of the POA 1986 is unlikely to provide assistance in prosecuting cyber bullying.

Section 5 of the POA 1986 provides for the offence of harassment, alarm or distress, and it is for when someone uses threatening or abusive words or

78 See *HKSAR v Chan Yau Hei* [2014] HKCFA 18 and *S v CPS* [2008] EWHC 438 (Admin).

79 *R v Hamilton* [2007] EWCA Crim 2062.

80 *R v Choi* [1999] 8 Archbold News 3, CA.

81 *Knuller (Publishing, Printing and Promotions) Ltd v DPP* [1973] AC 435.

82 *R v Choi* [1999] 8 Archbold News 3, CA.

83 *R v Morris* (1950) 34 Cr App R 210, CCA.

behaviour, or disorderly behaviour, or displays any writing, sign or other visible representation which is threatening or abusive, within the hearing or sight or a person likely to be caused harassment, alarm or distress thereby. Whilst this may capture some of what people post on the internet generally, there are the considerations of Article 10 of the European Convention on Human Rights ('ECHR') (right to freedom of expression) to be taken into account in respect of prosecutions under section 5 of the POA 1986; and, in any event, section 5 of the POA 1986 does not address the intent behind cyber bullying – someone wanting to harass, alarm, distress or upset a particular person. Therefore, whilst section 5 of the POA 1986 may be a fall-back option for prosecutors, it does not adequately address the criminality involved in cyber bullying, which is represented by the fact that a person guilty of an offence under section 5 is only liable on summary conviction to a fine not exceeding level 3.[84]

However, section 4A of the POA 1986 provides that a person will be guilty of an offence if, with intent to cause a person harassment, alarm or distress, they use threatening, abusive or insulting words or behaviour, or disorderly behaviour, or display any writing, sign or other visible representation which is threatening, abusive or insulting, and cause that or another person harassment, alarm or distress.[85] What constitutes 'threatening, abusive or insulting' is a question of fact.[86]

Therefore, a person who posts threatening, abusive or insulting messages, or posts an insulting altered photograph or a deepfake video, intending to cause the recipient/subject harassment, alarm or distress, and that subject/recipient is harassed, alarmed or distressed, would be guilty of an offence under section 4A of the POA 1986, and would be liable on summary conviction to imprisonment for a term not exceeding six months, or a level 5 fine,[87] or both.[88]

There is a potential limiting factor to potential prosecutions under section 4A of the POA 1986, which is found in section 4A(2):

> '(2) An offence under this section may be committed in a public or private place, except that no offence is committed where the words or behaviour are used, or the writing, sign or other visible representation is displayed, by a person inside a dwelling and the person who is harassed, alarmed or distressed is also inside that or another dwelling.'

84 POA 1986, s 5(6). A level 3 fine has a maximum statutory limit of GBP 1,000: www.sentencingcouncil.org.uk/explanatory-material/magistrates-court/item/fines-and-financial-orders/approach-to-the-assessment-of-fines-2/9-maximum-fines/.

85 POA 1986, s 4A(1).

86 *Brutus v Cozens* [1973] AC 854.

87 For offences committed before 13 March 2015, the maximum statutory limit for a level 5 fine is GBP 5,000. For offences committed after 13 March 2015, the maximum statutory limit for a level 5 fine is unlimited: www.sentencingcouncil.org.uk/explanatory-material/magistrates-court/item/fines-and-financial-orders/approach-to-the-assessment-of-fines-2/9-maximum-fines/.

88 POA 1986, s 4A(5).

On one reading, this could be taken to mean that, if individuals are located within their own homes whilst posting threatening, abusive or insulting messages, and the individuals who are harassed, alarmed or distressed are also within their own homes, no offence would be committed.

However, this would be an incorrect interpretation of section 4A(2). Although the person who is harassed, alarmed or distressed may be inside their own home, the writing, sign or other visible representation, although posted from another person's own home, would not only be displayed in that person's home: it would be displayed on the internet for, potentially, the entire world (or at least the entirety of the world's population with internet access) to see. Given the proliferation of computers, smartphones and tablets, the internet is, arguably, the biggest public space that there is (or conversely, given the need to have an ISP and 'sign up to the internet', the biggest private space that there is) and a website can have many thousands, if not millions, of viewers/onlookers. Therefore, the internet is a public/private space, and section 4A(2) should not affect the consideration of whether internet posts can constitute an offence under section 4A(1).

Indeed, the courts have held that posting to a website puts material within the public ambit and can constitute an offence contrary to section 4A of the POA 1986. In *S v CPS*[89] the defendant, an animal rights activist, took a photograph of a security guard for an animal-testing company and posted it on the website run by the activists, with a message implying that the security guard had been convicted of violence in the past. The district judge 'was of the view that any person who posts material on the Internet puts that material within the public ambit'.

Therefore, when someone is flaming and purposely using really extreme and offensive language, or posting altered photographs and videos, in order to cause reactions and cause a particular person alarm or distress, it is open to the courts to conclude that they have committed an offence contrary to section 4A of the POA 1986.

Procuring – outing and trickery

2.23 Posting someone's personal information online is not a criminal offence in England and Wales if you are acting in a personal capacity, and provided that you are not pursuing a course of conduct (for which, see the section on the PHA 1997 at paras **2.9** and **2.19** above). Therefore, the criminal law does not afford protection for cyber bullying when it takes the form of pure 'outing'.

Given the value of personal data, the criminalisation of the unauthorised publishing of personal data when acting in a personal capacity might be something that the courts and the Government seek to address in the future. That said, imposing such regulation on individuals in their personal capacity is likely to be too onerous a burden to be able to monitor, be too onerous on individuals to comply with (will the Government really legislate that people need to get consent from all

89 [2008] EWHC 438 (Admin) at [4], [13] and [15].

data subjects before posting photos on Facebook?), constitute a disproportionate response to the need to protect personal information, and be a disproportionate interference with people's personal lives. Therefore, such criminalisation and/or regulation may not be realistic or practical.

However, where the outing of personal information is for a particular purpose, the criminal law may be able to provide some protection. As we have seen above, in some circumstances it may fall under the PHA 1997. Additionally, where, for example, the personal details of a suspected murderer are 'outed' to a vigilante group, and someone from that group goes on to attack the suspected murderer, it may well be that the person 'outing' the information would be liable for having procured the offence.

In *Attorney-General's Reference (No 1 of 1975)*[90] it was said that:

> 'To procure means to produce by endeavour. You procure a thing by setting out to see that it happens and taking the appropriate steps to produce that happening. We think that there are plenty of instances in which a person may be said to procure the commission of a crime by another even though there is no sort of conspiracy between the two, even though there is no attempt at agreement or discussion as to the form which the offence should take.'

An offence cannot, however, be said to have been procured unless there is a causal link between what the alleged procurer did and the commission of the offence. Therefore, whether or not an 'outer' would be liable for having procured an offence which resulted from the 'outing' of information would depend on the circumstances of each case.

Section 8 of the Accessories and Abettors Act 1861 provides that a procurer of an indictable offence is liable to be punished as though they were the principal offender. Similar provision is made in respect of summary offences by virtue of section 44 of the Magistrates' Courts Act 1980.

Conclusions on cyber bullying

2.24 As with smart abuse, the current common law and legislative framework provide methods for addressing cyber bullying. Most are likely to fall under the PHA 1997, but the CMA 1990 and the POA 1986 will also have a role to play.

However, people, specifically children, will likely not know that their actions online might make them criminally liable. Think back to the little boy rocking back and forth on his bed, afraid of his phone and what was being sent to him. The people sending those messages were most likely children, oblivious of the criminal offences that they were committing. Schools need to educate children, not only about staying safe online, but also about how they should behave online and the criminal offences that they might be committing with certain actions.

90 [1975] QB 773.

Children should also be taught, and encouraged, to speak to someone should they find themselves a target of cyber bullying. That is much easier said than done but, if children are taught that particular behaviours are not acceptable and are, in fact, criminal, it might give some the confidence to speak out and seek help.

Teaching adults about what is and is not acceptable online is much harder. Perhaps the answer is better awareness training, or a Code of Conduct that has to be clicked through (rather than just accepted without reading) when signing up to Facebook or Twitter etc, or a system that reminds people that there is an actual person with feelings behind the account. Human beings will always be horrible to each other, but an awareness of where that crosses into criminality, or a reminder that their actions are directed at, and have an effect upon, a real person, might make people think twice before acting, and will hopefully make people more likely to stand up to it and hold people to account.

It is only if people are aware of when actions cross into the criminal, and have the confidence to stand up to people and hold them to account, that they will report them; and it is only then that the police and prosecuting authority will be able to intervene and pursue people under the common law and legislative framework.

Voyeurism

2.25 Technology and smart devices have increased the ways in which individuals can commit voyeurism, which was traditionally envisaged as a peeping-Tom looking in through the window.

Section 67 of the Sexual Offences Act 2003 ('SOA 2003') defines voyeurism as:[91]

- for the purpose of obtaining sexual gratification, observing another person doing a private act, knowing that the subject does not consent to being observed for that purpose;
- operating equipment with the intention of enabling another person to observe, for the purposes of obtaining sexual gratification, an individual doing a private act, knowing that the subject does not consent to their operating of equipment with that intention; or
- recording an individual doing a private act with the intention that they or another person will, for the purposes of obtaining sexual gratification, look at an image of the subject doing the act, knowing that the subject does not consent to their recording the action with that intention.

Observation includes both direct observation and looking at an image,[92] and an image is a moving or still image and includes an image produced by any means

91 SOA 2003, s 67(1)–(3).
92 SOA 2003, s 79(7).

and, where the context permits, a three-dimensional image.[93] A person is doing a private act if:[94]

- the person is in a place which, in the circumstances, would reasonably be expected to provide privacy, and the person's genitals, buttocks or breasts are exposed or covered only with underwear;
- the person is using a lavatory; or
- the person is doing a sexual act that is not of a kind ordinarily done in public.

A person guilty of an offence under section 67 is liable on summary conviction to imprisonment for a term not exceeding six months, or a fine not exceeding the statutory maximum, or both; and is liable, on conviction on indictment, to imprisonment for a term not exceeding two years.[95]

Easily accessible and user-friendly spyware can be placed on people's smartphones and computers without their knowledge or consent, thereby enabling others to remotely access and control the phone's and/or computer's cameras and observe their targets as they go about their daily lives. The acquisition and installation of spyware on a smartphone or computer may, in itself, constitute offences under sections 1 and 3A of the CMA 1990 (see para **2.13** above).

Smart home devices also have similar observational capabilities. For example, smart televisions that are connected to the internet can also have their cameras and microphones turned on remotely, meaning that people have the ability to see and hear everything that is going on in their target's home. Again, the remote accessing of a smart television's camera function could constitute an offence under section 1 of the CMA 1990.

Therefore, the increased use of the IoT and smart devices means that homes no longer afford the sanctuary of privacy that people expect, as they give individuals the opportunity to commit voyeurism by observing people when they are getting ready for work in the morning, having a shower, getting ready to go out in the evening, engaging in sexual acts etc. And it is not only adults who can be observed through smart devices – children could also be the observational target.

How, then, can people tell whether or not they are being observed through their phones, computers or smart devices? The short answer is that, unless there are helpful LEDs indicating that cameras and microphones are switched on, many people will not be able to tell. The only possible indicator might be a noticeable change in the phone's, computer's or device's performance, thereby suggesting that something is running in the background. However, poorer performance can be caused by lots of other factors, and so it is not a reliable indicator.

93 SOA 2003, s 79(4).
94 SOA 2003, s 68(1).
95 SOA 2003, s 67(5).

What can people do in order to ensure that they are not observed through their phones, computers and other smart devices? Again, the short answer is, very little. To mitigate the risk, people can use camera covers on their laptops, smartphones etc and, rather than connecting smart devices directly to the internet, connect them to a home network so that it is the home network that then accesses the internet. The latter is, however, likely to be beyond the technological capabilities of most consumers. Therefore, there is very little that consumers are able to do to protect themselves from voyeurism through their smart devices.

In addition to the above, smartphones have increased people's ability to 'upskirt': the act, usually performed in a public place, of taking a sexually intrusive photograph up someone's skirt without their permission. Although the posting of such images could, in some circumstances, be addressed under the PHA 1997, there was no legislative means of prosecuting the specific act of 'upskirting' – it was prosecuted under either the offence of outraging public decency or the traditional voyeurism offence. As can be seen from the discussions above, both of these offences have their limitations in prosecuting an act of upskirting.

Consequently, on 12 April 2019, additional voyeurism offences were brought into force by the Voyeurism (Offences) Act 2019 to combat 'upskirting'. The Voyeurism (Offences) Act 2019 inserted section 67A into the SOA 2003, which provides that a person commits an offence if they, without the subject's consent, and with the intention of obtaining sexual gratification or humiliating, alarming or distressing the subject:[96]

- operate equipment beneath the clothing of the subject in order to observe that person's genitals, buttocks or underwear in circumstances where they would not otherwise be visible; or
- record an image beneath the clothing of the subject of that person's genitals, buttocks or underwear in circumstances where they would not otherwise be visible.

A person guilty of an offence under section 67A is liable on summary conviction to imprisonment for a term not exceeding 12 months,[97] or a fine not exceeding the statutory maximum, or both; and is liable, on conviction on indictment, to imprisonment for a term not exceeding two years.[98]

As with voyeurism through smart devices, it is not always easy to detect, and therefore prosecute, voyeurism through upskirting. It is likely that individuals would need to be caught in the act or be caught through boasting about it, or such actions would need to be discovered as part of an investigation into a separate matter. On that view, one can see the most likely defendants of a section 67A

96 SOA 2003, s 67A(1)–(3).

97 In relation to an offence committed before the coming into force of s 154(1) of the Criminal Justice Act 2003 (increased maximum term that may be imposed on summary conviction of offence triable either way), the reference to 12 months is to be read as a reference to six months: SOA 2003, s 67A(5).

98 SOA 2003, s 67A(4).

charge being children and teenagers who are using upskirting to bully by causing humiliation, alarm and distress. As with cyber bullying, do children and teenagers realise that their actions may, in fact, constitute criminal offences? Should more be done to educate children and young people about the crimes that they may be committing through the use of their smartphones?

Indecent photographs and prohibited images of children, and extreme pornographic images

2.26 What comes to mind when thinking about the cyber-assisted crimes that cryptocurrencies and blockchain technology can perpetuate? Fraud? Bribery and corruption? Money laundering and terrorist financing? All of these answers are correct and will be addressed below. But, how about the possession and distribution of indecent photographs of children? Or the possession of prohibited images of children? Or the possession of extreme pornographic images?

Blockchain technology is such that images can be embedded within the blockchain (as raw bytes) and, because blockchains are immutable, these images/raw bytes exist in the blockchain forever. This means that images embedded within the transactions that form part of the next block mined will be distributed when that block is circulated for inclusion on the blockchain ledger, and that they will be present when an individual and/or wallet software downloads a copy of the blockchain.[99]

If these embedded images are indecent photographs of children, prohibited images of children and/or extreme pornographic images, what does that mean for miners, individuals downloading the blockchain, and the individuals seeking to have these images embedded?

Indecent photographs of children

Protection of Children Act 1978

2.27 Section 1 of the Protection of Children Act 1978 ('PCA 1978') provides that it is an offence to take, permit to be taken, make, distribute, show or possess with a view to their being distributed or shown, an indecent photograph or pseudo-photograph of a child (defined as a person under the age of 18).[100]

In terms of what constitutes an indecent photograph or pseudo-photograph:

- a photograph includes:
  - data stored on a computer disc or other electronic means which is capable of conversion into a photograph;[101] and

99 See the CoinMarketCap Crypto Glossary for a definition of cryptoasset and blockchain terminology: https://coinmarketcap.com/alexandria/glossary.
100 PCA 1978, ss 1(1) and 7(6).
101 PCA 1978, s 7(4)(b).

  - a tracing or other image, whether made by electronic or other means, which is not itself a photograph or pseudo-photograph, but which is derived from the whole or part of a photograph and/or a pseudo-photograph;[102]

- an indecent photograph includes an indecent film, a copy of an indecent photograph or film, and an indecent photograph comprised in a film;[103]
- a pseudo-photograph means an image, whether made by computer-graphics or otherwise howsoever, which appears to be a photograph;[104] and
- an indecent pseudo-photograph includes a copy of an indecent pseudo-photograph and data stored on a computer disc or by other electronic means which is capable of conversion into an indecent pseudo-photograph.[105]

If the impression conveyed by a pseudo-photograph is that the person shown is a child, the pseudo-photograph is treated as showing a child, as will a pseudo-photograph where the predominant impression conveyed is that the person shown is a child, notwithstanding that some of the physical characteristics shown are those of an adult.[106]

2.28 As a small aside, it may have been more helpful if the legislation (section 7(4)(b) of the PCA 1978 and the other subsections referring to a photograph and pseudo-photographs including stored data) had been drafted so as to read: 'data stored on a computer disc or by other electronic means which is capable of conversion into ***or being viewed as*** a photograph'. 'Conversion' suggests a process of changing or causing something to change from one form to another. Whilst conversion in this sense may be true in respect of .zip files (a discussion of which is beyond the scope of this text), in the case of single file data, the data does not change into a photograph: it merely appears as a photograph when viewed with particular software. Data is not changed from one form to another: it is the software through which the data is being viewed (or, if you will, interpreted) that determines what someone sees. For example, viewing image data in a text editor such as Notepad will mean that it appears as an incomprehensible jumble of characters and symbols, and viewing it as a hexdump will mean that it appears as hexadecimal digits. It is only when the data is viewed through appropriate image viewing software that the data will appear as a photograph. As a completely different non-technology example, if there is a piece of paper with 'B' 'A' 'D' 'G' 'E' written on it, a writer will view these as letters making up the word 'BADGE'; a musician, on the other hand, will go to the piano and play a melody. It is the same data, but it is viewed and interpreted differently. This is a fundamental principle to remember when considering data: the raw bytes are always the same, but it is how these bytes are interpreted by software that determines what we see.

102 PCA 1978, s 7(4A)(b).
103 PCA 1978, s 7(2).
104 PCA 1978, s 7(7). The definition of pseudo-photograph in s 7(7) covers instances of 'deepfakes', which are discussed in greater detail at para **2.61** below.
105 PCA 1978, s 7(9).
106 PCA 1978, s 7(8).

Downloading a blockchain

2.29 Turning then to the consideration of the PCA 1978 in the context of blockchain technology, in *R v Smith; R v Jayson*[107] the Court of Appeal held that 'the act of downloading an image from the internet to a computer monitor' was an act of making a photograph or pseudo-photograph. When someone downloads a blockchain which contains an embedded image, they are downloading the raw bytes. As outlined above and in section 7(4)(b) of the PCA 1978, this is an image/photograph and, as such, by downloading the blockchain they are making a photograph; and, if the embedded image is an indecent photograph of a child, they will be making an indecent photograph of a child contrary to section 1(1)(a) of the PCA 1978.

However, the court in *R v Smith; R v Jayson* also held that it was only if the person downloading the image did so intentionally and with the knowledge that the image was, or was likely to be, an indecent image of a child that the person would be guilty of an offence under section 1(1)(a) of the PCA 1978. Whilst someone downloading the blockchain would be doing so intentionally and, thereby, intentionally downloading any embedded images, the argument would be in respect of whether they knew that any embedded images were, or were likely to be, indecent images of a child.

The Court of Appeal's considerations in *R v Harrison*[108] are likely to be pertinent to any such argument. In this case it was held that, where the appellant had accessed legal pornographic websites in which indecent photographs had appeared by way of an automatic 'pop-up' mechanism, it was the appellant, and not the web-designer, who was the maker of the image. In terms of *mens rea*, the jury had to be sure that the appellant knew about the 'pop-up' activity when he accessed the adult pornographic sites and that, in accessing those sites, there was a likelihood that the pop-ups would include illegal images.

Thus, if someone were to be prosecuted under section 1(1)(a) for downloading the blockchain with embedded indecent images of children, the prosecution would need to prove that the individual knew that images could be embedded within the blockchain and that, in downloading the blockchain, there was a likelihood that the blockchain would include illegal images. The possibility of embedding sensitive, unlawful or malicious material on a blockchain has been a concern and the subject of discussion in the Bitcoin technical community for years, and articles have been written about it.[109] Additionally, a paper has been published on the arbitrary content on the Bitcoin blockchain,[110] and the researchers identified 59 files containing links to unlawful images of child exploitation, politically sensitive content, or privacy violations. Given this, and the fairly limited pool

107 [2002] EWCA Crim 683.

108 [2007] EWCA Crim 2976.

109 www.theregister.co.uk/2018/03/19/ability_to_dump_illegal_content_in_bitcoins_blockchain_puts_participants_in_peril/.

110 https://fc18.ifca.ai/preproceedings/6.pdf.

of users of cryptoassets and blockchains (ie they are still, generally, the purview of those with a more technical disposition), it may be hard for an individual to persuade a jury that they did not know that images could be embedded within a blockchain and that there was a likelihood that the blockchain included illegal images. Indeed, anyone who has now read this section has such knowledge. It is only a matter of time before such a prosecution is brought, and it will be interesting to see how these arguments play out in front of a jury. It is likely that much will turn on the character of the particular defendant and how technically minded they are.

The miner

2.30 It is important to note that the term 'miner' is generally used interchangeably to refer to both the computer that is running mining software and the human and/or corporate who owns that computer. In this section, 'miner' is used to refer to the human and/or corporate controlling the computer that is running mining software.

Turning then to the miner who successfully mines the next block: if that block contains an embedded indecent image of a child, would the circulation of that block to others for inclusion on the blockchain ledger be distribution under section 1(1)(b)? Given that the miner would not be parting with possession of the image (they would be keeping it on their ledger), and that they had not exposed or offered it for acquisition,[111] it is arguable that such circulation would not be distribution. The circulation of the block and the raw bytes could, however, be said to be showing the image to others, and so an offence under section 1(1)(b) on that basis.

Additionally, there could also be an offence under section 1(1)(c), as the miner would have an indecent photograph in their possession with a view to it being shown by them to others if/when they successfully mine the next block.

However, section 1(4) of the PCA 1978 might provide a defence for miners charged with offences under section 1(1)(b) or (c):

> '(4) Where a person is charged with an offence under subsection (1)(b) or (c), it shall be a defence for him to prove–
>
> (a) that he had a legitimate reason for distributing or showing the photographs or pseudo-photographs or (as the case may be) having them in his possession; or
>
> (b) that he had not himself seen the photographs or pseudo-photographs and did not know, nor had any cause to suspect, them to be indecent.'

The defence of 'legitimate reason' is an issue of fact and will be for a jury to decide. Will a jury find that being a blockchain miner is a legitimate reason?

111 PCA 1978, s 1(2).

In terms of the section 1(4)(b) defence, a miner is unlikely to have seen the particulars of individual transactions and so would be able to say that they had not seen the photograph or pseudo-photograph (be that the raw bytes or the image through viewing software). Further, the number of bytes in a transaction, or the number of outputs, may indicate that a transaction includes embedded data. However, not having seen the particulars of the transaction, a miner would be able to argue that they did not know, nor had any cause to suspect, that the transaction contained embedded data, let alone an indecent image of a child. Therefore, in most cases, section 1(4)(b) will afford miners a defence.

However, if it could be shown that a miner had viewed the particulars of individual transactions, they might be hard pressed to argue that they had not seen the photograph: they would, potentially, have seen the raw bytes and so technically seen the photograph as per the definition of 'photograph' in section 7(4)(b). Therefore, it would appear that the section 1(4)(b) defence would not be available to them. However, if it could be argued that the 'and' in section 1(4)(b) should be read as 'or' in the case of raw bytes, or that it should be read as not having seen the photograph in image viewer software, then the defence might be available, and the issue would again be whether a miner knew or had cause to suspect the photograph to be indecent. As outlined above, the number of bytes in a transaction, or the number of outputs, may indicate that a transaction includes embedded data. However, would this be enough to establish suspicion that raw bytes are indecent images? Should miners have to check/verify each transaction to ensure that they do not contain illegal content? Would this create an excessive burden on miners? Imposing the requirement to check the content of transactions would also, presumably, mean that miners would take on liability for the content of the blockchain. What effect would the risk of liability have on the blockchain community and technology?

These are all questions that, currently, do not have clear answers. On one hand, the answer is that miners should not view the particulars of individual transactions. However, on the other, the questions in themselves may provoke the blockchain community to introduce countermeasures, such as mandatory minimum fees for transactions with various number of outputs. This would, perhaps, prevent some individuals from embedding images into the blockchain, but it would not eliminate the risk of others doing so.

Sentencing

2.31 In terms of the sentence for an offence under the PCA 1978, a person convicted on indictment of an offence under section 1 of the PCA 1978 is liable to imprisonment for a term of not more than ten years, or a fine, or both. A person convicted summarily of an offence under the PCA 1978 is liable to imprisonment for a term not exceeding six months, or a fine, or both.[112]

112 PCA 1978, s 6(2)–(3).

The Schedule to the PCA 1978 provides for the forfeiture of indecent photographs of a child. An interesting question applies in respect of how this would, or could, apply in respect of an image embedded in a blockchain. Paragraph 1(2)(b) of the Schedule provides that any property which it is not reasonably practicable to separate from any indecent photograph or pseudo-photograph of a child is forfeitable property. Given that a blockchain is a linked record of all transactions, there is no way to separate a single block from it. On that basis, the entire blockchain would fall to be forfeitable property. Does this mean that, if a blockchain contained an embedded indecent image of a child, the entire blockchain could be 'shut down'?

It should be noted that proceedings for an offence under the PCA 1978 cannot be instituted except by or with the consent of the Director of Public Prosecutions.[113]

Criminal Justice Act 1988

2.32 In addition to the PCA 1978, section 160 of the Criminal Justice Act 1988 ('CJA 1988') provides that it is an offence for a person to have any indecent photograph or pseudo-photograph of a child in their possession.[114] A person guilty of this offence is liable on summary conviction to imprisonment for a term not exceeding six months, a level 5 fine,[115] or both; and, on conviction on indictment, to imprisonment for a term not exceeding five years, or a fine, or both.[116]

Whilst, at first blush, this would appear to be a strict liability offence and criminalise anyone who downloads a blockchain within which an indecent image is embedded, the case law suggests that this is not, in fact, the case.

In *Atkins v DPP* and *Goodland v DPP*[117] the High Court held that knowledge is an essential element of the offence under section 160, so an accused cannot be convicted where it cannot be shown that they were aware of the existence of the photographs in the first place. In *R v Porter*[118] the Court of Appeal held that a person would have possession of indecent images if they had custody or control of them. Where, therefore, the images had been deleted from a person's computer, whether or not they had possession of them would depend on whether or not they had the know-how and the software to allow them to retrieve them, so that it could be said, as a matter of fact, that they had control over them.

113 PCA 1978, s 1(3).

114 CJA 1988, s 160(1).

115 For offences committed before 13 March 2015, the maximum statutory limit for a level 5 fine is GBP 5,000. For offences committed after 13 March 2015, the maximum statutory limit for a level 5 fine is unlimited: www.sentencingcouncil.org.uk/explanatory-material/magistrates-court/item/fines-and-financial-orders/approach-to-the-assessment-of-fines-2/9-maximum-fines/.

116 CJA 1988, s 160(2A)–(3).

117 [2000] 2 Cr App R 248.

118 [2006] EWCA Crim 560.

This position was reaffirmed by the Court of Appeal in *R v Leonard,*[119] where it was held that, in respect of an offence under section 160, the prosecution had to prove that the defendant was capable of retrieving, or in a position to retrieve, the image.

Taking knowledge first, whilst a technologically aware/competent miner may have difficulty in arguing that they were not aware of the existence of embedded photographs in the blockchain, an individual simply downloading a blockchain may be able to make such an argument. As outlined above in relation to offences under the PCA 1978, it is likely that much will turn on the character of the particular defendant and how technically minded they are.

Turning then to possession requiring an individual to have custody or control over the images, the cases outlined above are concerned with the deletion of images and subsequent retrieval, but a similar retrieval argument could be made in respect of a person's ability to view embedded raw bytes. Thus, where a person downloads a blockchain with embedded indecent images, whether or not they had possession of them could depend on whether they have the know-how and the software to allow them to view the raw bytes in a pictorial form. Whilst this argument might assist individuals who download a blockchain, again, it is unlikely to afford much assistance to technologically competent miners.

Such miners, therefore, might need to look to make an argument based on the decision of the Supreme Court of Canada in *Morelli v The Queen.*[120] In this case, it was held that merely viewing an image stored in a remote location on the internet through a web browser does not involve the level of control necessary to establish possession of that image; and that, in order to commit the offence of possession of child pornography, a person must knowingly acquire an image's underlying data file and store it in a place under their possession, whether on a hard drive or otherwise. Thus, the argument would come back to one about knowledge, and whether a miner, who downloaded and stored a blockchain with an embedded image, knowingly acquired the underlying data file of the indecent image.

If these arguments fail, recourse may be had to the defences outlined in section 160(2):

> '(2) Where a person is charged with an offence under subsection (1) above, it shall be a defence for him to prove–
>
> (a) that he had a legitimate reason for having the photograph or pseudo-photograph in his possession;
>
> (b) that he had not himself seen the photograph or pseudo-photograph and did not know, nor had any cause to suspect, it to be indecent; or
>
> (c) that the photograph or pseudo-photograph was sent to him without any prior request made by him or on his behalf and that he did not keep it for an unreasonable time.'

119 [2012] EWCA Crim 277.
120 252 CCC (3d) 273.

As above in relation to the defences under section 1(4) of the PCA 1978, the defence of 'legitimate reason' will be an issue of fact for a jury to decide and, in terms of the section 160(2)(b) defence, individuals and miners who download and store a blockchain might be hard pressed to argue that they had not seen the photograph (they would, potentially, have seen the raw bytes). Therefore, the matter is likely to turn on arguments as to the construction of this subsection, and whether they knew or had cause to suspect the photograph to be indecent. Until there is case law on this point, it is unclear how this subsection will be interpreted by the courts and unclear when individuals and miners will be thought to have cause to suspect that photographs are indecent.

Also, as in relation to the PCA 1978, proceedings for an offence under section 160 of the CJA 1988 cannot be instigated except by or with the consent of the Director of Public Prosecutions.[121]

Prohibited images of children

2.33 Whilst the PCA 1978 and CJA 1988 are concerned with indecent photographs and pseudo-photographs, section 62(1) of the Coroners and Justice Act 2009 ('CaJA 2009') makes it an offence to be in possession of a prohibited image of a child.

To be a prohibited image and fall within the offence, an image (including a moving or still image (produced by any means)) or data (stored by any means and which is capable of conversion into an image) other than an indecent photograph or pseudo-photograph[122] must be:[123]

(a) pornographic (ie it is of such a nature that it must reasonably be assumed to have been produced solely or principally for the purpose of sexual arousal, which, if it is part of a series of images, must be determined by reference to the context in which it appears);

(b) an image which focuses solely or principally on a child's genitals or anal region, or be an image which portrays:

   (i) the performance by a person of an act of intercourse or oral sex with or in the presence of a child;

   (ii) an act of masturbation by, of, involving or in the presence of a child;

   (iii) an act which involves penetration of the vagina or anus of a child with a part of a person's body or with anything else;

   (iv) an act of penetration, in the presence of a child, of the vagina or anus of a person with a part of a person's body or with anything else;

121 CJA 1988, s 160(4) and PCA 1978, s 1(3).
122 CaJA 2009, s 65(2)–(3).
123 CaJA 2009, s 62(2)–(7).

(v) the performance by a child of an act of intercourse or oral sex with an animal (whether dead or alive or imaginary);

(vi) the performance by a person of an act of intercourse or oral sex with an animal (whether dead or alive or imaginary) in the presence of child; and

(c) grossly offensive, disgusting or otherwise of an obscene character.

Note that images which form part of a series of images contained in a recording of the whole or part of a 'classified work' (ie a video work in respect of which a classification certificate has been issued) do not fall within the section 62 offence.[124] Therefore, there may be arguments about whether the images form part of a classified work. However, if the image is contained in a recording of an extract from a classified work and it is of such a nature that it must reasonably be assumed to have been extracted (whether with or without other images) solely or principally for the purpose of sexual arousal, then it will still fall within the ambit of the section 62 offence.[125]

Proceedings for an offence under section 62 may not be instituted except by or with the consent of the Director of Public Prosecutions,[126] and the offence is triable either way, with the maximum penalty on conviction on indictment being three years' imprisonment, a fine, or both.[127]

Section 64 outlines the defences available to the section 62 offence:

> '(1) Where a person is charged with an offence under section 62(1), it is a defence for the person to prove any of the following matters–
>
> (a) that the person had a legitimate reason for being in possession of the image concerned;
>
> (b) that the person had not seen the image concerned and did not know, nor had any cause to suspect, it to be a prohibited image of a child;
>
> (c) that the person–
>
> (i) was sent the image concerned without any prior request having been made by or on behalf of the person, and
>
> (ii) did not keep it for an unreasonable time.'

Section 67 provides that the Schedule to the PCA 1978 (forfeiture of photographs) applies in relation to prohibited images of children.

Given the similarities between the offences under the CaJA 2009, PCA 1978 and CJA 1988, similar considerations and concerns will apply in respect of all of them, and the arguments and issues outlined above should be considered if

124 CaJA 2009, s 63(2).
125 CaJA 2009, s 63(3).
126 CaJA 2009, s 62(9)(a).
127 CaJA 2009, s 66.

an offence under the CaJA 2009 has allegedly been committed by way of an embedded image in a blockchain.

Extreme pornographic images

2.34 Section 63(1) of the Criminal Justice and Immigration Act 2008 ('CJIA 2008') makes provision for the offence of possession of extreme pornographic images. As with indecent photographs and prohibited images of children, extreme pornographic images can also be embedded into a blockchain.

To be an extreme pornographic image, an image (meaning a moving or still image (produced by any means)) or data (stored by any means and which is capable of conversion into an image)[128] must be:[129]

(a) pornographic (ie it is of such a nature that it must reasonably be assumed to have been produced solely or principally for the purpose of sexual arousal, which, if it is part of a series of images, must be determined by reference to the context in which it appears);

(b) an extreme image which portrays, in an explicit and realistic way:

  (i) an act which threatens a person's life;

  (ii) an act which results, or is likely to result, in serious injury to a person's anus, breasts or genitals;

  (iii) an act which involves sexual interference with a human corpse;

  (iv) a person performing an act of intercourse or oral sex with an animal (whether dead or alive);

  (v) an act which involves the non-consensual penetration of a person's vagina, anus or mouth by another with the other person's penis; or

  (vi) an act which involves the non-consensual sexual penetration of a person's vagina or anus by another with a part of the other person's body or anything else;

  and a reasonable person looking at the image would think that the persons or animals were real;

  and the image is grossly offensive, disgusting or otherwise of an obscene character.

Note, again, that images which form part of a series of images contained in a recording of the whole or part of a 'classified work' (ie a video work in respect of which a classification certificate has been issued) do not fall within the section 63 offence.[130] Therefore, there may be arguments about whether the images form part of a classified work. However, if the image is contained in a recording of an

128 CJIA 2008, s 63(8).
129 CJIA 2008, s 63(2)–(5A) and (7)–(7A).
130 CJIA 2008, s 64(2).

extract from a classified work and it is of such a nature that it must reasonably be assumed to have been extracted (whether with or without other images) solely or principally for the purpose of sexual arousal, then it will still fall within the ambit of the section 63 offence.[131]

Proceedings for an offence under section 63 may not be instituted except by or with the consent of the Director of Public Prosecutions.[132] The offence is triable either way, with the maximum penalty on conviction on indictment for an image portraying the acts outlined at (i), (ii), (v) and (vi) above being three years' imprisonment, a fine, or both; whereas the maximum penalty on conviction on indictment for an image portraying the acts outlined at (iii) and (iv) above is two years' imprisonment, a fine, or both.[133]

The defences to a section 63 offence are outlined in sections 65 and 66. Section 66 provides the defence of 'participation in consensual acts', which is not relevant to the present consideration of criminal liability arising out of the downloading of a blockchain or being a miner. Section 65, however, provides the same defence as that under the CaJA 2009, namely:

> '(1) Where a person is charged with an offence under section 63, it is a defence for the person to prove any of the following matters–
>
> (a) that the person had a legitimate reason for being in possession of the image concerned;
>
> (b) that the person had not seen the image concerned and did not know, nor had any cause to suspect, it to be an extreme pornographic image;
>
> (c) that the person–
>
> (i) was sent the image concerned without any prior request having been made by or on behalf of the person, and
>
> (ii) did not keep it for an unreasonable time.'

As with the other offences considered above, the issue is likely to be whether the individual knew or had any cause to suspect that the image was extreme pornography, and the same considerations and concerns apply.

Conclusions on indecent photographs and prohibited images of children, and extreme pornographic images

2.35 Offences of making, possessing, distributing and showing indecent, prohibited and extreme pornographic images as a result of raw bytes being embedded into blockchains have not yet been tested before the courts. It is, however, only a matter of time before such prosecutions are brought, and the arguments and considerations may well take lawyers, judges and jurors outside

131 CJIA 2008, s 64(3).
132 CJIA 2008, s 63(10)(a).
133 CJIA 2008, s 67(2)–(3) and (5)(a).

of their comfort zones. However, as can be seen from the case law above, the courts have shown themselves able to grapple with such issues in the past, and the fact that blockchain technology is a significant feature in these offences should pose no problems: as with embedded data on a blockchain, these are the same issues that have arisen in the past, but they are now just being seen in a different scenario/context.

Financial crime: fraud, bribery and corruption, money laundering, terrorist financing and financial sanctions

Phishing emails

2.36 Phishing emails, which trick people into installing malware on their device/s or trick people into using a website that requires the input of their credentials or installs malware on their device/s, are a means by which individuals can gain access to sensitive personal data. This, in turn, allows them to commit identity theft and fraud. Thus, whilst they might be able to be pursued in respect of the substantive theft or fraud offences, the initial phishing attacks could also be pursued under the CMA 1990 (see para **2.13** above and paras **2.49–2.51** below).

Cryptoassets

2.37 Cryptoassets provide a veritable playground for fraudsters, those paying bribes, money launderers, financiers of terrorism and those seeking a way to circumvent financial sanctions. Although public immutable ledgers exist, the cryptoasset environment: has traditionally lacked Know-Your-Customer ('KYC') requirements in respect of the creation of wallets or exchange platforms (see below for how this has now changed); provides pseudonymity (or almost anonymity in the case of Monero) through public keys; provides invisibility in respect of off-chain transfers (ie within an exchange or custodian wallet provider); provides the ability to create as many wallets (public and private keys) as desired and the ability to create 'cold' wallets (ie ones not connected to the internet that individuals manage themselves without the assistance of an exchange or custodian wallet provider); and there are no restrictions on the type of transactions that can be made.

By setting up many wallets through which transactions can flow, setting up their own mining teams, setting up their own exchanges, and off-ramping cryptoassets for fiat currency[134] in less regulated jurisdictions etc, individuals can conduct transactions that cannot be traced, and that cannot be traced back to them.

134 Fiat currency is government-issued currency that is not backed by a physical commodity, such as gold or silver, but by the government that issued it. Its value is derived from the relationship between supply and demand, and the stability of the issuing government. Most modern currencies, including USD, EUR, GBP, are fiat currencies.

There is also fraud potential from Initial Coin Offerings ('ICOs'), and one notorious example of an ICO fraud is OneCoin.[135]

> Case Study
>
> In 2014, Ruja Ignatova launched OneCoin. It claimed to work like any other cryptocurrency, where coins are generated through mining and can then be used to make global payments. It claimed that it would have a private blockchain that would be audited monthly and that its value would be determined by market supply and demand. OneCoin was to rival Bitcoin. It operated as a multi-level marketing structure, with its organisers selling various levels of educational 'trader packages', which included new education material and tokens that could be used to mine OneCoins. Users were also enticed with referral rewards to urge more users to join: they would receive a commission of the value of the trader packages purchased by the individuals they recruited. OneCoin secured investments from around the world of approximately EUR 3.5 billion.
>
> From the end of September 2015, there were worldwide concerns about OneCoin, and the FBI began an investigation. This discovered that the OneCoin business seemed to be built to defraud investors as, not only was their ability to convert OneCoins into fiat currency through the OneCoin exchange – xcoinx – limited by a daily selling limit based on the package obtained, but it was dependent upon the continued flow of revenues from the sale of trader packages to new members. Additionally, a substantial part of USD 1.2 billion of investor funds had been laundered through financial institutions in 21 different countries, and multiple transactions directly benefited Igantova and her co-founder, Sebastian Greenwood. The investigation also discovered that the value of OneCoin is determined internally and not based on market supply and demand, and that OneCoins are not mined but rather auto-generated through software and distributed to members on an as-needed basis.
>
> There is an indictment charging Ignatova with wire fraud, securities fraud and money laundering offences. However, in October 2017, just as a US warrant was filed for her arrest, Ignatova disappeared following a Ryanair flight to Athens and has not been seen since. Greenwood was extradited from Thailand to the US in November 2018.

135 Complaint in the matter of the United States of America v Konstantin Ignatov: www.justice.gov/usao-sdny/press-release/file/1141986/download#:~:targetText=OneCoin%20Ltd.,others%20to%20purchase%20cryptocurrency%20packages.&targetText=OneCoin%20continues%20to%20operate%20to%20this%20day; Press Release from the US Attorney's Office, Southern District of New York, 8 March 2019: www.justice.gov/usao-sdny/pr/manhattan-us-attorney-announces-charges-against-leaders-onecoin-multibillion-dollar; '2019's juiciest crypto drama: The saga of OneCoin's $4B "cryptocurrency" scam', Yessi Bello Perez, TNW, 23 December 2019: https://thenextweb.com/hardfork/2019/12/23/onecoin-cryptocurrency-scam-need-to-know/.

Ignatova's brother, Konstantin Ignatov, who was Ignatova's personal assistant before ascending to OneCoin's leadership following his sister's disappearance, was charged with conspiracy to commit wire fraud. He was arrested at Los Angeles International Airport in March 2019. He pleaded guilty to money laundering and fraud charges in respect of the cryptocurrency scam, and signed a plea deal on 4 October 2019.

Mark Scott, formerly a partner at the US legal firm Locke Lord, was charged with conspiracy to commit money laundering. It was alleged that he registered fake companies, offshore accounts and fraudulent vehicles to launder USD 400 million from the scam, and that he made USD 50 million from doing so. Scott was found guilty in November 2019 and was due to be sentenced in February 2020. His sentencing was postponed several times, and the latest information is that it was postponed until 14 July 2020 due to Scott's 'need to undergo further medical testing'.[136] However, at the time of writing, Scott's sentencing hearing has not yet been held.

And OneCoin is not the only instance of cryptoassets being used in fraud and money laundering: the collapse of Mt.Gox is an infamous tale of theft, fraud and money laundering.

Case Study

Mt.Gox was a Bitcoin exchange based in Shibuya, Tokyo, Japan. It was launched in July 2010, and by 2013/2014 it was handling over 80% of all Bitcoin transactions worldwide. It was the largest Bitcoin intermediary and the world's leading Bitcoin exchange. Then, in early 2014, it collapsed and declared bankruptcy, claiming that it had been hacked and had lost approximately 850,000 Bitcoins (then worth around USD 0.5 billion) and USD 28 million. 200,000 Bitcoins of the 'missing' Bitcoins were then discovered in an online wallet, bringing the 'missing' total to approximately 650,000 Bitcoins.

Following its collapse, parts of the Mt.Gox database was leaked, including trading logs, account balances and withdrawal/deposit logs. Using this data, WizSec, Japanese Bitcoin Security Specialists, conducted an informal investigation and painstaking analysis of the blockchain for transactions that spent Mt.Gox Bitcoins in an attempt to understand what had happened to the 'missing' Bitcoins. Its investigation revealed a recurring pattern: Mt.Gox Bitcoins from the hot wallet/s would suddenly get sent to new non-Mt. Gox addresses, without any withdrawal log entry. These addresses were temporary addresses and, shortly after the transaction, the Bitcoins would be collected into a larger holding address. From there, the Bitcoins would be

136 'Sentencing of OneCoin co-conspirator gets reschedule again', Maria Mikolova, FINANCEFEEDS, 25 April 2020: https://financefeeds.com/sentencing-onecoin-co-conspirator-gets-rescheduled/.

deposited onto various Bitcoin exchanges, including Mt.Gox itself, and were then sold for cash.[137]

WizSec and others continued in their investigations and, in July 2017, it was finally revealed what was thought to have happened.[138]

In September 2011, the Mt.Gox hot wallet (a cryptocurrency wallet that is connected to the internet and generally used for trading etc, as opposed to a cold wallet which is a cryptocurrency wallet that is not connected to the internet and is generally used for storage) private keys were stolen by way of a wallet.dat file being copied/lost/hacked. Cryptoassets are controlled by use of the private key – it is the private key that permits the transfer or other dealings in the cryptoasset – and so knowledge of, or access to, the private keys of hot wallets confers practical control over those cryptoassets. The theft of these hot wallet private keys gave the hacker access to a sizeable number of Bitcoins immediately, and they would also be able to spend any incoming Bitcoins deposited into any of the addresses.

Over time, the hacker emptied out whatever Bitcoins they could spend using the compromised keys, and sent them to wallets controlled by Alexander Vinnik, a Russian national. As outlined above, there were no withdrawal log entries for these 'transactions', and so there was a growing discrepancy between Mt.Gox's expected holdings and actual holdings. More on this aspect later. By mid-2013, nearly 630,000 Bitcoins had been taken from Mt.Gox in this way and there were practically no spendable Bitcoins left in Mt.Gox.

From the Vinnik-controlled wallets, 300,000 of the Bitcoins were moved to BTC-e, a cryptocurrency trading platform, whilst others were deposited into other exchanges, including Mt.Gox itself. Following the deposit into these exchanges and trading platforms, the Bitcoins were either sold or laundered further and, in relation to those sent to BTC-e, some were moved straight to internal storage rather than customer deposit addresses.

And how was Vinnik identified as being part of this money laundering? It was the deposits back into Mt.Gox. The Mt.Gox accounts used for these deposits could be linked to Vinnik's online identity of 'WME', which he had previously used in order to make a public outcry that Bitcoins had been confiscated from him.

Vinnik was indicted in 2017 by the United States ('US') Department of Justice ('DoJ') in respect of these matters, and subsequently detained in Greece, although there then followed conflicting court rulings in respect of

137 'MtGox investigation updated and preliminary release', WizSec, 14 February 2015: https://blog.wizsec.jp/2015/02/mtgox-investigation-release.html; 'The missing MtGox bitcoins', WizSec, 19 April 2015: https://blog.wizsec.jp/2015/04/the-missing-mtgox-bitcoins.html.

138 'Breaking open the MtGox case, part 1', WizSec, 27 July 2017: https://blog.wizsec.jp/2017/07/breaking-open-mtgox-1.html.

whether he should be extradited to Russia, France or the US. Despite Vinnik's identification, the actual person/s behind the theft of the wallet.dat file and who emptied the Bitcoins from the Mt.Gox hot wallets remains unknown.

There is also a fraud angle to the Mt.Gox story. First, the shared keypool of the stolen wallet.dat file led to address reuse, which confused Mt.Gox's systems into mistakenly interpreting some of the thief's spending as deposits. This, in turn, credited multiple user accounts with large sums of Bitcoins and caused Mt.Gox's numbers to go further out of balance by about 40,000 Bitcoins. The majority of these funds were withdrawn by their recipients rather than being reported as erroneous credits.

Secondly, remember the growing discrepancy between Mt.Gox's expected holdings and actual holdings as a result of the drain of Bitcoins? Unless it had major hidden fiat reserves or Bitcoin reserves, Mt.Gox was technically insolvent from 2012. How was such a discrepancy/insolvency not noticed by Mt.Gox?

WizSec's understanding is that Mt.Gox did not have continuous monitoring of its cold storage, which consisted of paper wallets generated ahead of time and stored away. These locked-up paper wallets would then gradually and automatically be filled one by one by the system, by depositing surplus Bitcoins from the hot wallet. And vice versa, whenever the hot wallet ran low, staff would manually scan a paper wallet, refilling the hot wallet with stored Bitcoins. One possibility is that, without any monitoring of the storage or comparing incoming and outgoing amounts, Mt.Gox staff may have blindly kept pouring the cold storage into the leaking hot wallet, assuming that they were just dealing with frequent swings in deposits/withdrawals and that, on average, the cold storage was being refilled at roughly the same rate that they were draining it. This is, however, just speculation.[139]

Additionally, Mark Karpelès, the CEO of Mt.Gox, was arrested in 2015 and charged (in Japan) with the creation and manipulation of private electronic records and embezzlement of customer funds or embezzlement of company funds or breach of trust. The allegations against Karpelès were that he:

(1) embezzled funds, either by sending money from Mt.Gox to his other companies or his private account, or making payments for private purposes; and

(2) manipulated the balance of his personal Mt.Gox account for the purpose of buying Bitcoins, which were then wiped from the account balance.

Karpelès' trial started in July 2017 and he maintained his innocence, claiming that Mt.Gox's financial loss was due to an external hack. In his statement at the

139 'The missing MtGox bitcoins', WizSec, 19 April 2015: https://blog.wizsec.jp/2015/04/the-missing-mtgox-bitcoins.html.

beginning of the trial, Karpelès claimed that, when he inherited Mt.Gox from Jed McCaleb in 2011, he became aware of problems that made it necessary to manage Mt.Gox's debt portfolio so that it did not fall into bankruptcy. An 'obligation exchange' was implemented, whereby Mt.Gox's Bitcoin and USD liabilities towards its customers could be exchanged at market value for the purposes of keeping Mt.Gox's debt portfolio reasonably balanced. This 'obligation exchange' was noticed by investigators following the collapse of Mt.Gox, and was termed 'Markus' and the 'Willy Bot' (to refer to manual 'obligation exchange' transactions using Karpelès' own Mt.Gox trading account and then later automated 'obligation exchange' transactions using randomly created accounts (respectively)). The premise of the 'obligation exchange' was that:

(1) the USD balance of an account would be inflated;

(2) buy orders would be issued on the exchange to purchase Bitcoins with these fake funds;

(3) real funds would be used to actually purchase the Bitcoins; and

(4) the Bitcoin balance of the account (which would be active for a while, and then become inactive, with the next account becoming active within a few hours) would then be wiped.

The result was that, by creating a fake currency and trading it on the exchange, Mt.Gox's total liabilities for that currency were increased; and, by buying Bitcoins and wiping out the balance afterwards, those Bitcoins were taken out of circulation, thus lowering MtGox's Bitcoin liabilities. Thus, one debt was traded for another.[140]

It was initially thought that 'Markus' and the 'Willy Bot' was the fraud that led to the collapse of Mt.Gox. Through the investigations, it was discovered that, although this activity resulted in a net loss for Mt.Gox, with Mt.Gox having greater liabilities than when Karpelès took it on, it was not, in fact, the cause of the collapse: the cause of the collapse was the draining of Bitcoins from Mt.Gox. However, WizSec has speculated that 'Markus' and the 'Willy Bot' may explain some of the fiat currency missing at the time of the collapse[141] as it was used to meet the increasing fund liability. It might also explain why the discrepancies between actual and expected holdings, and the draining, were not noticed sooner: Mt.Gox was too busy with 'Markus' and the 'Willy Bot' to notice what else was happening.

140 'Comments on the Mark Karpelès trial', WizSec, 12 July 2017: https://blog.wizsec.jp/2017/07/comments-on-mark-karpeles-trial.html; 'MtGox investigation updated and preliminary release', WizSec, 14 February 2015: https://blog.wizsec.jp/2015/02/mtgox-investigation-release.html.

141 'Comments on the Mark Karpelès trial', WizSec, 12 July 2017: https://blog.wizsec.jp/2017/07/comments-on-mark-karpeles-trial.html.

In March 2019, the Tokyo District Court found Karpelès guilty of the creation and manipulation of private electronic records charge. It found that, across 21 transactions between February and September 2013, Karpelès transferred roughly USD 33.5 million (from a Mt.Gox account) to a bank account operated by a Bitcoin exchange in Dallas, and that he used his personal computer and covered his tracks by falsifying company records. The court said that the issue was not that Karpelès had transferred this money, but that he had acted against the company's interests and beyond his authority when he manipulated company records to conceal the transactions. The court sentenced him to two and half years in prison, suspended for four years. He was found not guilty of the embezzlement charge, as it was not possible to determine whether or not Karpelès had embezzled funds from Mt.Gox clients, because the company did not have a proper accounting system in place for when its executives borrowed money from the company – a common arrangement in small or medium-sized firms or privately owned businesses without accounting units.[142]

Following the collapse of Mt.Gox, Bitfinex, founded in 2012, became the largest international cryptocurrency exchange. However, it is another example of cryptoassets being used to perpetrate fraud and money laundering.[143]

Case Study

In August 2016, Bitfinex lost approximately 120,000 Bitcoins, valued at more than USD 70 million, to hackers.[144] Bitfinex was insolvent as a result of this hack, meaning that they owed more Bitcoins than they actually controlled on the blockchain. To try and combat its liabilities, Bitfinex imposed a 36% loss on all its customers and gave them a 'BFX' token in return to record their dollar losses, which could be redeemed by the exchange for USD 1 per token or for shares in iFinex, its parent company.[145]

Bitfinex owns Tether, a company that builds fiat currency ledgers (USD, EUR etc) on top of a collection of cryptoasset databases (Bitcoin, Ether etc) and issues Tethers. Tethers are 'stablecoins', as Tether promises that entries in their ledger correspond to demand deposits (traditional fiat currency) held

142 'MtGox bitcoin exchange founder Mark Karpeles gets suspended term for falsifying data but is cleared of embezzlement', Magdalena Osumi and Ryusei Takahashi, The Japan Times, 15 March 2019: www.japantimes.co.jp/news/2019/03/15/national/crime-legal/mtgox/.

143 'Tether: The Story So Far', Patrick McKenzie, Kalzumeus, 29 October 2019: www.kalzumeus.com/2019/10/28/tether-and-bitfinex/.

144 'Bitfinex Announces Sizeable Token-for-Equity Exchange by Customers', Bitfinex, 13 October 2016: www.bitfinex.com/posts/155.

145 'Bitfinex exchange customers to get 36 percent haircut, debt token', Clare Baldwin, Reuters, 7 August 2016: www.reuters.com/article/us-bitfinex-hacked-hongkong/bitfinex-exchange-customers-to-get-36-percent-haircut-debt-token-idUSKCN10I06H; 'Bitfinex Announces Sizeable Token-for-Equity Exchange by Customers', Bitfinex, 13 October 2016: www.bitfinex.com/posts/155.

in reserve, such that customers can rely on one Tether being worth USD 1, EUR 1 etc and are able to surrender them for such at any time. Consequently, Tether quickly became the unit of account for most of the cryptocurrency community.

However, Tether's claim about reserves was untrue, as they did not have actual control of traditional currency reserves to the value of issued Tethers: instead, they had receivables from related parties, such as Bitfinex, and third party payment processors (a facilitator of financial transactions between parties).

Bitfinex was banking in Taiwan with Taiwanese banks, but Taiwanese banks do not have direct access to the US financial system, and so have to engage via a correspondent banking relationship. Bitfinex's Taiwanese banks corresponded through Wells Fargo, who, in March 2017, in the wake of publicity surrounding the Bitfinex hack, told Bitfinex's banks that they would no longer clear USD wires to or from Bitfinex.[146] Bitfinex sued Wells Fargo.[147]

Following the loss of the Taiwanese/US banking relationship, Tether eventually found a bank willing to bank it – Noble Bank in Puerto Rico – which had access to USD through BNY Mellon. Tether made a USD 2 million investment in Noble, and deposited hundreds of millions of dollars of its reserve into Noble. Tether warned its customers not to talk about the banking details they were exposed to when on-ramping or off-ramping USD, because they were worried about their activities coming to the attention of BNY Mellon. These activities did come to the attention of BNY Mellon, which forced Tether to find another banking partner.

Tether moved their reserves to Deltec Bank and increased their use of Crypto Capital Corp, a third party payment processor that Bitfinex had had a relationship with since January 2015. Crypto Capital Corp identified banks with poor compliance controls, opened shell entities which it claimed were engaged in real estate transactions, moved money in and out of these accounts until the bank closed the account, and then did it again.[148]

When a customer wanted to deposit money with Bitfinex, they would contact Crypto Capital Corp, who gave them the details of a shell corporation and instructions to wire the shell corporation money with a transaction description designed to not raise any red flags with the bank.[149] Bitfinex explicitly instructed customers to not reveal the wire instructions that they were given. Crypto Capital Corp would then increase Bitfinex's balance with itself and provide Bitfinex with confirmation that they had received the wire; and Bitfinex would credit the customer with a Tether-denominated receivable on their books or with actual on-chain Tethers.

146 http://media.kalzumeus.com/tether-docs/bitfinex-response-to-nyag.pdf.
147 http://media.kalzumeus.com/tether-docs/bitfinex-sues-wells.pdf.
148 http://media.kalzumeus.com/tether-docs/Crypto-Capital-Detention-Memorandum.pdf.
149 http://media.kalzumeus.com/tether-docs/Crypto-Capital-Detention-Memorandum.pdf.

When a customer wanted actual money in return for Tethers, the customer would send the Tethers to Bitfinex; Bitfinex would make a 'transfer' (accounting entry) on Crypto Capital Corp's books, using their online system, to decrease the amount that Crypto Capital Corp owed Bitfinex and increasing the amount that they owed Tether. Crypto Capital Corp would then send a wire to the customer, lying to the banks about the transaction, tell Bitfinex they had done it, and then decrease the amount that they owed to Tether.

However, as with Tether and its reserves, Crypto Capital Corp did not actually have sufficient funds to meet the Tether withdrawal requests, and was using the incoming deposits to satisfy such requests. One of the individuals behind Crypto Capital Corp, Reginald Fowler, was also taking 10% of all deposits into the system for his personal use.[150] Therefore, by August 2018, following the freezing of some of Crypto Capital Corp's shell corporation banks accounts by regulators, they could not meet the withdrawal requests from the incoming deposits, and they had exhausted their cash reserves.[151]

Rumours started that Tether was insolvent. Bitfinex attempted to meet the increasing incoming withdrawal requests by:

(1) satisfying them with alternative cryptocurrencies;

(2) satisfying them using money mules, which included using various companies owned by Bitfinex/Tether executives, as well as other 'friends' of Bitfinex, meaning human friends of Bitfinex employees who were willing to use their bank accounts to transfer money to Bitfinex clients who had requested withdrawals;[152] and

(3) satisfying Tether withdrawal requests with Bitfinex customer funds.

By May 2019, Bitfinex was running out of liquidity again, and organised a bailout by selling USD 1 billion of a 'utility token'. This seemed to work, as Bitfinex has not yet become insolvent, and remains the 'world's leading cryptocurrency trading platform'.[153]

However, Reginald Fowler and Ravid Yosef were indicted in April 2019 on charges of bank fraud and operating an unlicensed money transmitting business.[154] Fowler rejected a plea offer in January 2020, and the parties will now move to trial.[155]

150 http://media.kalzumeus.com/tether-docs/Crypto-Capital-Detention-Memorandum.pdf.

151 http://media.kalzumeus.com/tether-docs/bitfinex-response-to-nyag.pdf

152 http://media.kalzumeus.com/tether-docs/nyag-filing-against-bitfinex.pdf.

153 www.bitfinex.com/about.

154 Press Release from the US Attorney's Office, Southern District of New York, 30 April 2019: www.justice.gov/usao-sdny/pr/arizona-man-and-israeli-woman-charged-connection-providing-shadow-banking-services.

155 'Reginald Fowler Rejects Plea Deal in Crypto "Shadow Bank" Case', Wolfie Zhao, Coin Desk, 3 February 2020: www.coindesk.com/reginald-fowler-rejects-plea-deal-in-crypto-shadow-bank-case.

To combat money laundering, terrorist financing and the potential misuse of cryptoassets for criminal purposes, the European Union's ('EU') Fifth Anti-Money Laundering Directive[156] ('5AMLD') broadened the definition of 'obliged entities' to include cryptoasset exchange providers and custodian wallet providers.[157] However, the 5AMLD itself acknowledges that the inclusion of such exchange providers and custodian wallet providers will not entirely address the issues attached to virtual currency transactions, as a large part of the virtual currency environment will remain anonymous because users can transact without such providers.[158]

The Money Laundering and Terrorist Financing (Amendment) Regulations 2019 ('MLR 2019'),[159] which entered into force on 10 January 2020, transpose the 5AMLD and amend the Money Laundering, Terrorist Financing and Transfer of Funds (Information on the Payer) Regulations 2017 ('MLR 2017').[160]

The MLR 2019 provide that the 'relevant persons' to which the MLR 2017 (other than reg 7) apply now include cryptoasset exchange providers ('CEPs') and custodian wallet providers ('CWPs').[161]

'Cryptoasset' is defined as 'a cryptographically secured digital representation of value or contractual rights that uses a form of distributed ledger technology and can be transferred, stored or traded electronically'.[162]

A CEP is:

> 'a firm or sole practitioner who by way of business provides one or more of the following services, including where the firm or sole practitioner does so as creator or issuer of any of the cryptoassets involved, when providing such services–
>
> (a) exchanging, or arranging or making arrangements with a view to the exchange of, cryptoassets for money or money for cryptoassets,
>
> (b) exchanging, or arranging or making arrangements with a view to the exchange of, one cryptoasset for another, or
>
> (c) operating a machine which utilises automated processes to exchange cryptoassets for money or money for cryptoassets.'[163]

A CWP is:

> 'a firm or sole practitioner who by way of business provides services to safeguard, or to safeguard and administer–
>
> (a) cryptoassets on behalf of its customers, or

156 Directive (EU) 2018/843 of the European Parliament and of the Council of 30 May 2018 amending Directive (EU) 2015/849 on the prevention of the use of the financial system for the purposes of money laundering or terrorist financing, and amending Directives 2009/138/EC and 2013/36/EU.
157 Directive (EU) 2018/843, Art 1(c).
158 Preamble of Directive (EU) 2018/843, para 9.
159 SI 2019/1511.
160 SI 2017/692.
161 MLR 2019, reg 4(1)(b), amending reg 8(1) in the MLR 2017.
162 MLR 2019, reg 4(7), inserting reg 14A(3)(a) into the MLR 2017.
163 MLR 2019, reg 4(7), inserting reg 14A(1) into the MLR 2017.

(b) private cryptographic keys on behalf of its customers in order to hold, store and transfer cryptoassets.'[164]

Therefore, from 10 January 2020, CEPs and CWPs must comply with the existing requirements in the MLR 2017:

- Take appropriate steps to identify and assess the risks of money laundering and terrorist financing which the business is subject to.[165]
- Assess the money laundering and/or terrorist financing risks related to any new products, new business practices or new technologies prior to launch and take appropriate measures to manage and mitigate those risks.[166]
- Have in place policies, systems and controls appropriate to mitigate the risk of the business being used for the purposes of money laundering or terrorist financing. This risk-based approach should seek to mitigate the risks identified in the business's risk assessment.[167]
- Where appropriate, with regard to the size and nature of its business, appoint an individual who is a member of the board or senior management to be responsible for compliance with the MLR 2017 and the nominated officer. The nominated officer is also the person responsible for reporting suspicious activity to the National Crime Agency ('NCA') under Part 7 (money laundering) of the Proceeds of Crime Act 2002.[168]
- Where appropriate, with regard to the size and nature of its business, establish an independent internal audit function with responsibility for examining and evaluating the adequacy and effectiveness of the policies, controls and procedures, and making recommendations, as well as monitoring the controls.[169]
- Where appropriate, with regard to the size and nature of its business, undertake screening of employees.[170]
- Undertake customer due diligence ('CDD') when entering into a business relationship or occasional transactions.[171] A business relationship is a business, professional or commercial relationship entered into with a customer that is expected to have an element of duration.[172] When a business relationship is established, a CEP/CWP undertaking CDD must obtain information on the identity of the customer, the purpose of the relationship and the intended nature of the relationship.[173] Occasional transactions are transactions that are not carried out within an ongoing business relationship

164 MLR 2019, reg 4(7), inserting reg 14A(2) into the MLR 2017.
165 MLR 2017, reg 18.
166 MLR 2017, reg 19(4)(c), as amended by MLR 2019, reg 4(9)(b)(i).
167 MLR 2017, reg 19(1).
168 MLR 2017, reg 21(1)(a), (3) and (5).
169 MLR 2017, reg 21(1)(c).
170 MLR 2017, reg 21(1)(b).
171 MLR 2017, Part 3, Chapter 1.
172 MLR 2017, reg 4(1).
173 MLR 2017, reg 28(2).

subject to certain de minimis value thresholds[174] (although CEPs operating a machine which uses automated processes to exchange cryptoassets for money or money for cryptoassets – such as operators of Crypto ATMs – must apply CDD measures for all exchanges of money for cryptoassets, whatever the amount).[175]

- Undertake enhanced due diligence ('EDD') when dealing with customers who may present a higher money laundering/terrorist financing risk. This includes customers who meet the definition of a politically exposed person ('PEP'), and may include ascertaining the source of their funds.[176]
- Undertake ongoing monitoring of all customers to ensure that transactions are consistent with the business's knowledge of customer, the customer's business and risk profile.[177]
- Keep a record of all risk assessments[178] and customer due diligence measures.[179]

The Financial Conduct Authority ('FCA') has been appointed as the supervisory authority for CEPs and CWPs,[180] and so CEPs and CWPs will also be subject to the new requirements and powers vested in the FCA relating specifically to cryptoasset businesses, namely:

- From 10 January 2020, all CEPs and CWPs will need to register with the FCA,[181] with the CEP/CWP and any of its officers, managers or beneficial owners satisfying the FCA that they are 'a fit and proper person to carry on the business of a cryptoasset exchange provider or custodian wallet provider'.[182]

  The FCA will charge the following registration fees:[183]

  - £2,000 for businesses with UK cryptoasset income up to £250,000;
  - £10,000 for businesses with UK cryptoasset income greater than £250,000.

  'Income' for these purposes is defined as the gross inflow from economic benefits (that is, cash, receivables, and other assets) recognised in the UK business's accounts during the reporting year relating to the provision of relevant cryptoasset business.

- Disclosure: businesses whose cryptoasset activity does not fall within the scope of the Financial Ombudsman Service ('FOS') or the Financial Services

174 MLR 2017, reg 27(1)(b).
175 MLR 2019, reg 5(b), inserting reg 27(7D) into the MLR 2017.
176 MLR 2017, Part 3, Chapter 2.
177 MLR 2017, Part 3.
178 MLR 2017, reg 18(4).
179 MLR 2017, reg 40.
180 MLR 2019, reg 3(2)(a), amending reg 7(1)(a) of the MLR 2017.
181 MLR 2019, reg 7(9), inserting reg 54(1A) into the MLR 2017.
182 MLR 2019, reg 7(14), inserting reg 58A into the MLR 2017.
183 www.fca.org.uk/cryptoassets-aml-ctf-regime/register-fca.

Compensation Scheme ('FSCS') will be required to inform customers of this before they enter into a business relationship or transaction.[184]

- Reporting requirements: the FCA has the power to require CEPs/CWPs to provide it with such information as the FCA directs about its compliance with the MLR 2017, or as is otherwise reasonably required by the FCA.[185]
- Skilled person report: the FCA has the power to appoint a 'skilled person' to prepare a report for the FCA concerning a matter under the MLR 2017.[186]
- Power of direction: the FCA will be permitted to give a direction to a CEP/CWP before, on or after registration for the purpose of remedying a failure to comply with the MLR 2017, preventing a failure to comply, or preventing the business from being used for money laundering or terrorist financing. The power of direction allows the FCA to require or prohibit certain actions.[187]

Although these new Regulations are well intentioned and will go some way to addressing the commission of financial crime through cryptoassets, and should stop another OneCoin scenario through applying the 'fit and proper person' test, as acknowledged in the 5AMLD, these measures will not entirely address the issues, as users can transact without the need for such providers. Indeed, it is likely that those who are seeking to commit financial crime through cryptoassets – because they are still less regulated and more invisible than fiat currency and, therefore, still an ideal mechanism for financial crime – will seek to transact outside of these providers and outside of the EU. This will push these individuals and these transactions even further off-grid and, despite the growing understanding, powers and resources of investigative authorities, will make the detection and investigation of such crimes even more difficult than they already are. This is an unsurprising consequence of regulation and, although this regulation is likely to stop the lower levels of financial crime, it is unlikely to have much effect on the large-scale crimes, for those who want to commit them will find a way to do so, and cryptoassets and less-regulated countries around the world will be all too willing to oblige.

Computer games

2.38 Cryptoassets are not the only means by which technology can assist the commission of financial crime: computer games can also provide a way to launder money and finance terrorism.

184 MLR 2019, reg 7(17), inserting reg 60A into the MLR 2017.
185 MLR 2019, reg 8(4), inserting reg 74A into the MLR 2017.
186 MLR 2019, reg 8(4), inserting reg 74B into the MLR 2017.
187 MLR 2019, reg 8(4), inserting reg 74C into the MLR 2017.

Case Study

In October 2019, the gaming firm Valve halted the trading of some in-game items in its popular multiplayer shooting game, Counter-Strike: Global Offensive ('CS:GO'), after discovering that 'nearly all' of the trading was part of a money laundering scheme run by worldwide fraud networks.[188]

Players in CS:GO earn loot boxes that contain weapons and cosmetic upgrades but, in order to open the boxes, they have to purchase the keys. Valve ran an internal marketplace on Steam where it allowed players to trade the boxes and the keys for real money. Valve noticed that fraud networks were using CS:GO to liquidate their gains. Consequently, Valve released a patch to ensure that new container keys purchased in-game could no longer be sold or traded.

Valve's blog announcing the change did not go into detail of exactly how or what it had discovered, but it was speculated that the trading was used to launder income from credit card fraud and other financial crimes.[189]

Valve may have shut this particular route of money laundering down but, as one avenue closes, money launderers etc will find another route, and so this is likely to be happening in other computer games that allow in-game purchases and trading.

Although computer games and illicit activities through them are likely to be more visible than through cryptoassets, game developers are now integrating cryptocurrencies into their products. Game developers are 'tokenizing' game assets by basing them on a blockchain network and attributing value and existence to them in their own right, as opposed to them only being in-game currency. Although the token is earned and used within the game, the blockchain technology creates a cryptographic accounting system for the tokens, meaning that they can also be bought, sold and traded outside of the game.[190] This could potentially introduce invisibility into the gaming world too, thereby providing another safe haven for financial crime. The regulation of cryptoassets may have some impact, but such gaming entities are unlikely to develop cryptoassets in such a way as to fall within the MLR 2017 and be under the auspices of the FCA. Only time will tell, however, but, for the moment, gaming provides another route for financial crime.

188 https://blog.counter-strike.net/index.php/2019/10/26113/.

189 'Counter-Strike trading found to be "nearly all" money laundering', Alex Hern, The Guardian, 30 October 2019: www.theguardian.com/games/2019/oct/30/counter-strike-trading-found-to-be-nearly-all-money-laundering.

190 'How Gaming Could Drive Cryptocurrency and Blockchain Adoption', Mina Down, Hackernoon, 23 January 2019: https://hackernoon.com/how-gaming-could-drive-cryptocurrency-and-blockchain-adoption-7ab12bc88138.

Illicit items

2.39 In addition to assisting the commission of financial crimes, cryptoassets also provide a way for individuals to obtain illicit goods, such as drugs and firearms. One only has to think of the notorious Silk Road, where cryptoassets were used to buy drugs, to see how feasible it is.[191]

Cryptoassets provide a pseudonymous way of exchanging payments, and the blockchain provides a way to verify that payments have been sent; thus, the only identifying information potentially available is the address to which the illicit goods are sent, but ways can be found to anonymise that.

Although the blockchain provides an immutable record of every transaction, thereby enabling law enforcement agencies to track transactions, with wallet software able to generate a new public address for each transaction, tracking such transactions may not be as straightforward as the concept of an immutable public ledger would suggest. Cases involving the acquisition or supply of illicit items with cryptoassets are going to require technical experts to help unravel the blockchain transactions, and the cryptoasset element of cases is going to require an adjustment on how such cases are presented to juries.

Theft

2.40 In November 2019, the UK Jurisdiction Taskforce ('UKJT') delivered its Legal Statement on Cryptoassets and Smart Contracts.[192] This Legal Statement said that, in general, 'cryptoassets have all of the indicia of property' and should therefore 'be treated in principle as property'.

It should be noted, however, that the courts had already been treating cryptoassets as property before this Legal Statement was published. In *Vorotyntseva v Money-4 Ltd (t/a Nebeus.com)*[193] the High Court granted freezing orders in respect of Bitcoin and Ethereum, and in *Robertson v Persons Unknown*[194] the High Court granted an asset preservation order over Bitcoin. These authorities, and the reasoning as outlined in the UKJT's Legal Statement, were affirmed in *AA v Persons Unknown*,[195] where the High Court (Bryan J) was satisfied that cryptoassets are a form of property capable of being the subject of a proprietary injunction (see paras **9.19**, **9.21** and **9.24** for a further discussion of these cases).

191 'Silk Road: The Dark Side of Cryptocurrency', David Alder, Fordham Journal of Corporate and Financial Law, 21 February 2018: https://news.law.fordham.edu/jcfl/2018/02/21/silk-road-the-dark-side-of-cryptocurrency/#_edn3.

192 https://35z8e83m1ih83drye280o9d1-wpengine.netdna-ssl.com/wp-content/uploads/2019/11/6.6056_JO_Cryptocurrencies_Statement_FINAL_WEB_111119-1.pdf.

193 [2018] EWHC 2596 (Ch).

194 CL-2019-000444, unreported.

195 [2019] EWHC 3556 (Comm), at [59]–[61].

However, long before the courts were treating cryptoassets as property, cryptoassets were already being spoken about as though they were property and capable of being stolen. As outlined at paragraph **2.37** above, Bitcoin Security Specialists, WizSec, voluntarily conducted a non-official investigation into the collapse of Mt.Gox. Their blog posts, as early as April 2015, spoke of Bitcoins having been stolen,[196] and this was reiterated again when they released a summary of their investigation findings in July 2017.[197] Although the writers/investigators are not lawyers, and so the word 'stolen' is used in a colloquial rather than a legal sense, this shows that, before the courts engaged with questions in respect of cryptoassets, they were viewed within the online community as property: things that are definable, can be controlled, owned and transferred, and can be stolen.

Indeed, the UKJT's Legal Statement said that their conclusion that 'cryptoassets have all of the indicia of property' and should therefore 'be treated in principle as property' was likely to have important consequences for the application of a number of legal rules, for example, in cases of theft.

The Theft Act 1968 ('TA 1968') provides that a person is guilty of theft if they dishonestly appropriate property belonging to another with the intention of permanently depriving the other of it.[198]

In the case of cryptoassets, proving the 'appropriation of property belonging to another with the intention of permanently depriving the other of it' is unlikely to cause too many issues.

In light of the UKJT's Legal Statement, and the courts' willingness to treat cryptoassets as property, cryptoassets are to be treated in principle as property, and so the criminal courts are likely to find that that element of the offence is met. Although cryptoassets cannot be possessed, they can be controlled by use of the private key – it is the private key that permits the transfer or other dealings in the cryptoasset – and, as outlined in the UKJT's Legal Statement, knowledge of the private key confers practical control over the cryptoasset. Therefore, cryptoassets belong to the individuals who hold the private keys required in order to deal with the cryptoassets. Appropriation is also unlikely to be problematic to prove; this is because, where individuals gain unauthorised access to the private key required to deal with the cryptoasset, be that through physical acquisition if it is kept in hardcopy or through a hack, having the private key means that the individuals will have control over the cryptoasset and be able to deal with it (as in the Mt.Gox case – see para **2.37** above), and thus will have assumed the rights of the owner of the cryptoasset. Although it will depend on the facts of the case,

196 'The missing MtGox bitcoins', WizSec, 19 April 2015: https://blog.wizsec.jp/2015/04/the-missing-mtgox-bitcoins.html.

197 'Breaking open the MtGox case, part 1', WizSec, 27 July 2017: https://blog.wizsec.jp/2017/07/breaking-open-mtgox-1.html.

198 TA 1968, s 1(1). See ss 2 to 6 for the statutory definitions of 'dishonestly', 'appropriates', 'property', 'belonging to another' and 'with the intention of permanently depriving the other of it' (respectively).

it may be fair to assume that someone who gains unauthorised access to private keys intends to permanently deprive others of those cryptoassets.

However, the concept of 'dishonestly' may be more problematic. Whilst, instinctively, the unauthorised access to private keys is a dishonest appropriation, section 2(1)(c) of the TA 1968 provides that 'a person's appropriation of property belonging to another is not to be regarded as dishonest [...] if he appropriates the property in the belief that the person to whom the property belongs cannot be discovered by taking reasonable steps'. The case law on section 2(1)(c) is mainly in relation to abandoned property. However, the wording of the section does not appear to preclude other situations.

One of the fundamental principles underpinning cryptoassets and blockchain technology is the pseudonymity that it affords. The owners of cryptoassets are hidden and difficult to trace and, as can be seen from WizSec's investigation into Mt.Gox (see para **2.37** above), even those with significant technical capabilities find it difficult to trace and identify the owners of cryptoassets. Given this, unpalatable as it may be, is it not arguable that anyone gaining unauthorised access to private keys does so in the belief that the person to whom the cryptoasset belongs cannot be discovered by taking reasonable steps? Indeed, irrespective of the individual's technical capabilities, is it not, in fact, a reasonable belief that the person to whom the cryptoasset belongs cannot be discovered by taking reasonable steps?

In *Ivey v Genting Casinos (UK) Ltd (t/a Crockfords Club)*,[199] the Supreme Court, in a lengthy and considered *obiter dictum*, said that the subjective element of the test for dishonesty in *R v Ghosh*[200] did not correctly represent the law and directions based on it should no longer be given. Instead, the Supreme Court said that, when dishonesty is in question, the fact-finding tribunal must first ascertain (subjectively) the actual state of the individual's knowledge or belief as to the facts. Once that has been ascertained, it must then determine whether the individual's conduct was honest or dishonest by applying the (objective) standards of ordinary decent people. The court also said that there is no requirement for the individual to appreciate that what they have done is, by the objective standards of ordinary decent people, dishonest.[201] Although only *obiter dicta*, the Supreme Court's observations in *Ivey* were affirmed by the Court of Appeal in *R v Barton and Booth*[202] as the dishonesty test to be applied in criminal cases.

Applying the *Ivey* dishonesty test, it is likely that anyone gaining unauthorised access to private keys would know or believe that they were acting dishonestly, and the standards of ordinary decent people would also determine that such conduct was dishonest.

199 [2017] UKSC 67.
200 [1982] QB 1053.
201 [2017] UKSC 67, at [74].
202 [2020] EWCA Crim 575.

However, whilst the test as propounded in *Ivey* applies across both the criminal and civil spheres,[203] section 2(1) of the TA 1968 only applies to theft. The authors of Archbold 2020 state that, when considering a charge of theft, if the jury conclude that the defendant had, or may have had, one of the beliefs set out in section 2(1), then they must, as a matter of law, find that the defendant's appropriation was not, or may not have been, dishonest by the standards of ordinary decent people.[204]

Applying this in the context of cryptoassets and the *Ivey* test, if a jury concludes that a defendant believed that the person to whom the cryptoassets belong cannot be discovered by reasonable steps, then, although the defendant knew or believed that they were acting dishonestly in gaining unauthorised access to private keys, they would not, as a matter of law, be dishonest. This argument seems somewhat absurd, but one that the legislation and case law appears to permit. It also leads to a more philosophical question about cryptoassets, and one that may well form the basis of legal arguments in the future: does the pseudonymity and inability to discover the owner by reasonable steps (conducting a thorough and technical investigation of the blockchain not being a reasonable step, given its difficulty for those even of the technical persuasion) thus, in effect, equate cryptoassets with abandoned property? Whilst it is unlikely that a court will uphold such arguments, these are questions that need to be addressed.

The above arguments serve to show that, whilst current legal principles can apply, in the most part, to cryptoassets (and technology more broadly), there are very specific quirks and questions that arise where, due to their technical construction (both in terms of the technology and the legislation), the application of current legal principles produces a somewhat absurd result. Such quirks and questions will need to resolved by legislation and/or case law as, and before, these matters come before the courts.

Therefore, whilst one might colloquially talk about the theft of cryptoassets, and whilst instinctively it feels as though the unauthorised acquisition of private keys and subsequent dealing of cryptoassets should be theft, particularly given the UKJT's Legal Statement and the decisions in the High Court, there are some legal questions that require resolution before one can conclusively say that cryptoassets can be stolen.

Assuming that one can steal cryptoassets, as with the acquisition and supply of illicit items using cryptoassets, although the blockchain provides an immutable record of every transaction, the fact that wallet software can generate a new public address for each transaction means that the tracing and tracking of transactions, and thus identifying the perpetrators, may not be as straightforward as the concept of an immutable public ledger would suggest. Additionally, cases involving the theft of cryptoassets are going to require technical experts to help unravel the blockchain transactions, and the cryptoasset element of cases is going to require an adjustment on how such cases are presented to juries.

203 [2017] UKSC 67, at [63].
204 Archbold 2020, para 21-27.

Blackmail

2.41 Ransomware and ransomware-as-a-service ('RaaS') (the renting or sale of ransomware code packages, with technical support and step-by-step information on how to launch a ransomware attack, and the ransom money being divided between the service provider, coder and attacker) provide individuals with an easy way to commit blackmail, and such cases are hitting the headlines.

Case Studies

In May 2017, there was a global ransomware attack when the hacking tool 'Eternal Blue' was used to exploit a vulnerability in Microsoft and gain access to computers using Microsoft Windows. The ransomware WannaCry was deployed onto compromised computers, locking and encrypting computer files, and a Bitcoin payment was demanded in order to regain access. The most affected countries were Russia, Taiwan, Ukraine and India, although there were also telecommunications and transport targets in Spain, Portugal and Germany. In the UK, the ransomware attack hit a third of NHS hospital trusts and 8% of GP practices who, at the time of the attack, were using Windows XP, an operating system that stopped receiving security updates in April 2014. The attack caused more than 19,000 appointments to be cancelled, and cost the NHS GBP 92 million. This figure included not only the loss from the seven-day incident, but also the subsequent clean-up and upgrades to the NHS's IT systems.[205]

More recently, on New Year's Eve 2019, Travelex took all of its systems offline having discovered that it had been infected by the ransomware Sodinokibi.[206] Files were encrypted, and a ransom of USD 6 million (GBP 4.6 million) was demanded in return for unlocking the systems and deleting customer data. The incident not only affected Travelex: British banks that rely on Travelex for their online foreign currency services were also down as a result of the incident.[207] It was two weeks before Travelex began to bring its services back

205 'NHS cyber attack: Everything you need to know about "biggest ransomware" offensive in history', Chris Graham, The Telegraph, 20 May 2017: www.telegraph.co.uk/news/2017/05/13/nhs-cyber-attack-everything-need-know-biggest-ransomware-offensive/; and 'WannaCry cyber attack cost the NHS £92m as 19,000 appointments cancelled', Matthew Field, The Telegraph, 11 October 2018: www.telegraph.co.uk/technology/2018/10/11/wannacry-cyber-attack-cost-nhs-92m-19000-appointments-cancelled/.

206 Travelex Press Release, 7 January 2020: https://web.archive.org/web/20200108161750/https://www.travelex.com/.

207 'UK Banks Foiled by Travelex Ransomware Attack', Sarah Coble, Info Security Group, 9 January 2020: www.infosecurity-magazine.com/news/uk-banks-scuppered-by-travelex/; and 'Travelex customers "left high and dry" after ransomeware attack', James Cook, The Telegraph, 8 January 2020: www.telegraph.co.uk/technology/2020/01/08/travelex-customers-left-high-dry-ransomware-attack/.

online and, during that time, it resorted to offering services on a manual basis. Travelex refused to say whether the ransom had been paid.[208]

These two attacks show a trend in the targeting of infrastructure: in July 2019, City Power, the major electricity provider in Johannesburg, South Africa, was hit, affecting hundreds of thousands of people and businesses. Also in 2019, in the State of Texas, 22 Government agencies were targeted in a highly sophisticated and choreographed ransomware attack. In the State of Colorado, the attackers hit the Department of Transportation, demanding a USD 2 million ransom payment.[209]

Although the initial course of action when confronted with a ransomware blackmail demand will likely be to seek interim relief through the civil courts (see paras **9.18–9.22** and **9.23–9.25**), if the perpetrators are identified through those proceedings, and any issues relating to jurisdiction are resolved, it may be possible to initiate criminal proceedings for blackmail.

Blackmail is defined in section 21 of the TA 1968 as an unwarranted demand with menaces which is made with a view to gain or with the intent to cause loss to another.[210] 'Gain' and 'loss' are to be construed as only applying to a gain or loss in monetary or proprietary terms, but they include a temporary or permanent gain or loss; and gain includes not only keeping what one has, but also getting what one has not; whilst loss includes not getting what one might get, as well as parting with what one has.[211] Blackmail is an indictable only offence, and a person guilty of blackmail is liable on conviction to imprisonment for a term not exceeding 14 years.[212]

In the case of ransomware, a demand for payment is made; the demand is accompanied by a threat that the publication, deletion or loss etc of data will occur unless such payment is made (the menaces); the demand with menaces is (usually) unwarranted because the user of the ransomware will not (usually) have reasonable grounds for making a payment demand, and the threat is not a proper means of reinforcing the demand; and the demand is with a view to gain money or property, and/or there is an intention to cause loss. Thus, one can see how the deployment and use of ransomware can form the basis of a charge of blackmail.

Indeed, the courts are already acknowledging that the use of ransomware is akin to blackmail.

208 'Travelex refuses to say if it paid $6m ransom to hackers', James Cook, The Telegraph, 9 January 2020: www.telegraph.co.uk/technology/2020/01/09/travelex-refuses-say-paid-6m-ransom-hackers/.

209 'To Pay Or Not To Pay?', Flavia Kenyon, New Law Journal, 23 January 2020: www.newlawjournal.co.uk/content/to-pay-or-not-to-pay-.

210 TA 1968, s 21(1).

211 TA 1968, s 34(2)(a).

212 TA 1968, s 21(3).

Case Study

In *AA v Persons Unknown*[213] a Canadian insurance company was hacked and the ransomware BitPayer was installed. BitPayer encrypted all of the company's computer systems, and USD 1.2 million in Bitcoins was demanded in order to obtain the decryption tool. The ransom price was reduced to USD 950,000 in Bitcoins and, on 10 October 2019, 109.25 Bitcoins (the equivalent of USD 950,000) were transferred to the address that had been provided. The decryption tool was received the following day and deployed across the company's systems.

At paragraph 24 of his judgment in relation to interim relief, Bryan J said:

> 'There are previous authorities touching upon such matters. For example, in cases concerning blackmail – and this is certainly analogous to that, a ransom is being demanded and money is being extorted in return for the decrypting of computer systems – it is more common for the court to permit hearings to be held in private. […]'

See paragraph **9.24** for further discussion of this case.

In addition to a substantive blackmail charge, it should be noted that the hacking of a computer system in order to gain access to deploy ransomware will also be an offence under sections 1, 2 and 3 of the CMA 1990 (unauthorised access to computer material; unauthorised access with intent to commit or facilitate the commission of further offences; and unauthorised acts with intent to impair the operation of a computer, respectively); and the making, supplying or obtaining of ransomware will also be an offence under section 3A of the CMA 1990.

In the case of the WannaCry ransomware attack (see above), its deployment created a significant risk of serious damage to human welfare, as it could have caused loss to human life, human illness or injury and it disrupted health services. Although not necessarily intended, the perpetrators were reckless as to whether such damage was caused when the ransomware was deployed on NHS computer systems. As such, an offence under section 3ZA of the CMA 1990 (unauthorised computer acts causing, or creating risk of, serious damage) was likely to have been committed. A section 3ZA offence is an indictable only offence, and punishable by either imprisonment for a term not exceeding 14 years, a fine, or both,[214] or imprisonment for life, a fine, or both,[215] depending on the type of serious damage that is caused/that there is a significant risk of (see para **2.51** below for further discussion on section 3ZA of the CMA 1990).

213 [2019] EWHC 3556 (Comm).
214 CMA 1990, s 3ZA(6).
215 CMA 1990, s 3ZA(7).

Thus the effect, or potential effect, of a ransomware attack may have a significant bearing on any charges brought.

To try and protect oneself from blackmail via ransomware, security updates and patches should be downloaded in order to address any technical vulnerabilities. Additionally, to negate some of the effects of a ransomware attack, it would be advisable for corporates (and individuals) to have a secure offline backup of their sensitive and important data. That way, if a ransomware attack is deployed, rather than having to pay a ransom to have the data decrypted, following the deletion of the ransomware, the data can be restored from the backup.

These, however, are only precautionary measures, so they may not prevent a ransomware attack from being deployed. In the event of a ransomware attack, even though data may be restored from an offline backup, thus meaning that the ransom does not need to be paid, that does not mitigate the risk of the data being published etc in the event of non-payment of the ransom. In such a scenario, recourse may be needed to the courts and their interim injunctive relief, to prevent such actions being carried out or to mitigate the consequences of such actions (see paras **9.14–9.17**).

Trade sanctions and export controls

2.42

> Case Study
>
> In the WannaCry ransomware attack (see para **2.41** above), 'Eternal Blue' was used to gain access to computer systems using Microsoft Windows. 'Eternal Blue' is a 'cyber weapon' developed by the National Security Agency ('NSA'), the US military intelligence unit. It is a hacking tool that gives unprecedented access to all computers using Microsoft Windows and was developed by the NSA to gain access to computers used by terrorists and enemy states. It was stolen by Shadow Brokers and placed on an obscure public website on 14 April 2017, where it was picked up by others who committed the global WannaCry ransomware attack.[216]

'Eternal Blue' was developed by a nation's intelligence unit, but what if it had been developed by a software company – is it legal for a software company, or an individual, to develop such technology? If it is legal, are there any controls on its sale and distribution? Similarly, what about spyware that can be installed on smartphones so as to collect private data, passwords, contacts, calendar

216 'NHS cyber attack: Everything you need to know about "biggest ransomware" offensive in history', Chris Graham, The Telegraph, 20 May 2017: www.telegraph.co.uk/news/2017/05/13/nhs-cyber-attack-everything-need-know-biggest-ransomware-offensive/.

events, text messages, and live voice calls, and remotely control camera and GPS functions – is it legal to develop, sell or acquire such technology?

Computer Misuse Act 1990

2.43 The answers are found in section 3A of the CMA 1990, which provides that it is an offence to:

- make, adapt, supply or offer to supply any article intending it to be used to commit, or assist in the commission of, an offence under section 1, 3 or 3ZA of the CMA 1990;[217]
- supply or offer to supply any article believing that it is likely to be used to commit, or assist in the commission of, an offence under section 1, 3 or 3ZA of the CMA 1990;[218] or
- obtain any article intending to use it, or with a view to its being supplied for use, to commit, or assist in the commission of, an offence under section 1, 3 or 3ZA of the CMA 1990.[219]

An 'article' includes any program or data held in electronic form,[220] and section 1 of the CMA 1990 provides for the offence of unauthorised access to computer material; section 3 provides for the offence of unauthorised acts with intent to impair, or with recklessness as to impairing, the operation of a computer etc; and section 3ZA provides for the offence of unauthorised acts causing, or creating the risk of, serious damage. A person guilty of an offence under section 3A of the CMA 1990 is liable on summary conviction to a term not exceeding 12 months (six months prior to the commencement of section 154(1) of the Criminal Justice Act 2003), or a fine, or both; and, on conviction on indictment, to imprisonment for a term not exceeding two years, or a fine, or both.[221]

Any corporate or individual developing software that is out-and-out a hacking tool, spyware or ransomware may be hard pressed to argue that they did not make it intending for it to be used to commit, or to assist in the commission of, an offence under section 1, 3 or 3ZA. Some may develop such software for fun and therefore lack the requisite intent. In these circumstances, if they do nothing with the software, then no offence will have been committed. However, if it is then offered or supplied to others, given the nature of the software, it may be hard to argue that they did not intend for it to be used, or believe that it was likely to be used, to commit, or assist in the commission of, an offence under section 1, 3 or 3ZA. Therefore, offences under section 3A(1) and (2) may be made out.

217 CMA 1990, s 3A(1).
218 CMA 1990, s 3A(2).
219 CMA 1990, s 3A(3).
220 CMA 1990, s 3A(4).
221 CMA 1990, s 3A(5)(a) and (c).

What about software that, although not intended to be a hacking tool, or have spyware or ransomware capabilities, could be adapted so that they are?

Again, section 3A of the CMA 1990 may provide some assistance. Although there would likely be no offence in relation to the making of the article, if the article is supplied with the belief that it is likely to be used to commit, or to assist in the commission of an offence, then an offence would be committed under section 3A(2) of the CMA 1990.

What is the position, though, if there is no such intent or belief that the articles will be used to commit, or to assist in the commission of, an offence under section 1, 3 or 3ZA? What if, for example, the software is not for domestic supply, but for international supply? In those circumstances, the CMA 1990 may not apply, and recourse must then be had to trade sanctions and export controls legislation to ascertain whether, and in what circumstances, such software is a permitted export.

Trade sanctions

2.44 Council Regulation (EC) No 428/2009[222] ('the Dual-Use Regulation') recasts the Community regime for the control of exports, transfer, brokering and transit of dual-use items. 'Dual-use items' are defined in Article 2(1) as 'items, including software and technology, which can be used for both civil and military purposes [...]', and Article 3(1) provides that an authorisation will be required for the export of the dual-use items listed in Annex I to outside the EU. No authorisation is required in relation to exports to the EU, unless the dual-use item is listed in Annex IV. The Dual-Use Regulation entered into force on 27 August 2009 and is binding and directly applicable in the UK.

Spyware is a dual-use item under Part 1 of Category 5 of Annex I (List of Dual-Use Items) of the Dual-Use Regulation, as it is software specifically designed to provide the characteristics, functions or features of interception equipment designed for the extraction of voice or data, transmitted over the air interface.[223]

Consequently, an authorisation is required under Article 3(1) of the Dual-Use Regulation before such software can be exported outside the EU. Annexes IIa to IIf of the Dual-Use Regulation provide Union General Export Authorisations in respect of certain exports to certain non-EU countries. Where an authorisation is required under Article 3(1), but no provision is made for the authorisation in the Dual-Use Regulation, then one can either register for one of the Open General Export Licences ('OGELs') (pre-published licences granted by the Secretary of State with set terms and conditions that an exporter must adhere to) if applicable to the goods, software etc; or, if the goods, software etc are not covered by an

222 https://eur-lex.europa.eu/eli/reg/2009/428/oj. https://eur-lex.europa.eu/legal-content/EN/TXT/?uri=CELEX:02009R0428-20181215.

223 Paragraphs 5A001.f.1 and 5D001.c. of Part 1 (Telecommunications) of Category 5 of Annex I of Council Regulation (EC) 428/2009.

OGEL, apply to the Export Control Organisation for a Standard Individual Export Licence ('SIEL') or an Open Individual Export Licence ('OIEL'). There has been significant concern about the UK Government's licensed exports of spyware to jurisdictions with poor human rights records.[224]

Failure to acquire the requisite export authorisation/licence for spyware is a criminal offence under article 35 of the Export Control Order 2008 ('the ECO 2008'). The contravention of an Article 3(1) prohibition or restriction is a summary only offence, with the sentence being a fine not exceeding level 3 on the standard scale.[225] However, a person knowingly concerned in an activity prohibited or restricted by Article 3(1) with intent to evade the relevant prohibition or restriction commits an either-way offence and, if found guilty, is liable on summary conviction to a fine, imprisonment for 12 months (six months if the offence was committed before section 154(1) of the Criminal Justice Act 2003 comes into force) or both; and is liable on conviction on indictment to a fine, or imprisonment for a term not exceeding ten years, or both.[226] In addition to these offences, offences in relation to the exportation of prohibited or restricted goods may also be committed under section 68 of the Customs and Excise Management Act 1979 ('CEMA 1979').

It is also possible that certain hacking software, which has the characteristics of, or performs or simulates the function of, systems, equipment and components for defeating, weakening or bypassing information security which have been designed or modified to perform 'cryptanalytic functions', may be dual-use items under paragraphs 5A004 and 5D002.c.3 of Part 2 of Category 5 of Annex I of the Dual-Use Regulation (relating to 'Information Security') and thus also need an export authorisation under Article 3(1).

It should also be noted that 5A004 and 5D002.c.3 items are listed in Annex IV of the Dual-Use Regulation and, as such, require an export authorisation/licence to not only be exported outside of the EU, but also to be transferred within the EU.[227] A failure to obtain an export licence in respect of hacking software tools that fall within 5D002.c.3 of Annex I will carry the same penalties as outlined above in respect of spyware.

224 'Exporting repression: How Britain is supplying surveillance technology to human-rights abusing countries', Mark Curtis and Matt Kennard, Global Justice Now: www.globaljustice.org.uk/sites/default/files/files/resources/surveillance_briefing_20_sept_2019.pdf; and 'Human rights fury as UK licenses £75m of spyware exports', Jamie Doward, The Guardian, 17 March 2019: www.theguardian.com/world/2019/mar/17/uk-spyware-exports-human-rights-fury.

225 Export Control Order 2008, art 35(1). A level 3 fine has a maximum statutory limit of GBP 1,000: www.sentencingcouncil.org.uk/explanatory-material/magistrates-court/item/fines-and-financial-orders/approach-to-the-assessment-of-fines-2/9-maximum-fines/.

226 Export Control Order 2008, art 35(4)–(5).

227 Council Regulation (EC) 428/2009, Article 22(1).

Trade sanctions and Brexit

2.45 It will be apparent from the above that, at the time of writing, the main export controls in relation to spyware comes from a directly applicable EC Regulation. How, then, will such export controls/trade sanctions apply following Brexit?

The UK left the EU on 31 January 2020 ('Exit Day'), but the Withdrawal Agreement provides for an Implementation Period until 31 December 2020. During the Implementation Period, the Dual-Use Regulation (as well as most of EU law) will continue to apply in the UK as if it were a Member State.[228]

The European Union (Withdrawal) Act 2018 ('EUWA 2018') (as amended by the European Union (Withdrawal Agreement) Act 2020) provides that EU-derived domestic legislation existing before 'IP completion day' (Implementation Period Completion Day, ie 11pm on 31 December 2020)[229] continues to have effect in domestic law on and after 'IP completion day',[230] and that any direct EU legislation (including EU Regulations that are applicable to the UK by virtue of Part 4 (Transition) of the Withdrawal Agreement) operative immediately before 'IP completion day' forms part of domestic law on and after 'IP completion day'[231] ('retained EU law').

Thus, the Dual-Use Regulation will become part of the UK's domestic law following the Implementation Period ('the Retained Dual-Use Regulation').

Retained EU law, including the Retained Dual-Use Regulation, will contain deficiencies arising out of the UK's exit from the EU, either because provisions relate to reciprocal arrangements or are otherwise redundant upon exit from the EU, or because there are references to EU instruments which are no longer appropriate. Therefore, amendments will need to be made to the Retained Dual-Use Regulation in order to correct these deficiencies, to ensure that the law continues to function effectively following the Implementation Period.

Additionally, with the development of technology, Governments are becoming more aware of the dual-use nature of items and the need to subject them to export controls. For example, on 6 January 2020, the US Government amended its dual-use export controls to cover certain software used in Artificial Intelligence

228 Agreement on the Withdrawal of the United Kingdom of Great Britain and Northern Ireland from the European Union and the European Atomic Energy Community (19 October 2019), Part Four, Articles 126 and 127: https://assets.publishing.service.gov.uk/government/uploads/system/uploads/attachment_data/file/840655/Agreement_on_the_withdrawal_of_the_United_Kingdom_of_Great_Britain_and_Northern_Ireland_from_the_European_Union_and_the_European_Atomic_Energy_Community.pdf.

229 European Union (Withdrawal Agreement) Act 2020, s 39(1).

230 EUWA 2018, s 2(1) (prospective), as amended by the European Union (Withdrawal Agreement) Act 2020, s 25(1) (prospective).

231 EUWA 2018, s 3(1)–(2)(a) (prospective), as amended by the European Union (Withdrawal Agreement) Act 2020, s 25(2)(a)–(b) (prospective).

applications; specifically, licence requirements were imposed on the export and re-export of US-origin software designed to automate the analysis of geospatial imagery to all destinations, except Canada.[232] Therefore, as technology and software develop, we are likely to see more items added to the dual-use control lists for which an export licence is required and, as such, the Retained Dual-Use Regulation will require amending.

To combat these issues, on 1 April 2019, pursuant to powers conferred by section 8(1) of the EUWA 2018, the Secretary of State passed the Trade etc in Dual-Use Items and Firearms etc (Amendment) (EU Exit) Regulations 2019[233] ('the Trade in Dual-Use Items Regulations 2019') 'to address inoperabilities and deficiencies of retained EU law arising from the withdrawal of the United Kingdom from the EU and to ensure EU-derived domestic export control legislation operates effectively post-exit'.[234] (Note: amendments to correct drafting defects in the Trade in Dual-Use Items Regulations 2019 were made by the Trade etc in Dual-Use Items and Firearms etc (Amendment) (EU Exit) (No 2) Regulations 2019[235] on 4 April 2019.)

Regulation 3 of the Trade in Dual-Use Items Regulations 2019 makes amendments to the Retained Dual-Use Regulation to ensure that its rules operate as UK rules – for example, references to the supply of such goods and associated services to non-EU countries become references to the supply of such goods and associated services to all other countries; types of EU pro forma licences are adjusted to become types of UK licence; powers on the part of the European Commission, to make EU legislation to amend the Annexes to bring goods within scope of the Regulation, become powers for the Secretary of State to amend these Annexes by domestic secondary legislation; and Member State notification requirements are omitted.[236] Thus, the intention is that the legislation will operate as it did when the UK was a Member State, save that the controls on dual-use items will apply to exports from the UK, rather than exports from the EU.[237] As such, the Retained Dual-Use Regulation becomes the UK Dual-Use Regulation.

The offences for contravening a requirement for an export authorisation under Article 3(1) of the UK Dual-Use Regulation will still be contained within article 35 of the ECO 2008, and the penalties will remain the same.

Regulation 1 of the Trade in Dual-Use Items Regulations 2019 provides that they come into force on Exit Day, and regulation 5 makes transitional provisions in respect of pre-exit authorisations and licences. However, paragraph 1(1) of Part 1 of Schedule 5 to the European Union (Withdrawal Agreement) Act 2020 provides

232 www.federalregister.gov/documents/2020/01/06/2019-27649/addition-of-software-specially-designed-to-automate-the-analysis-of-geospatial-imagery-to-the-export.

233 SI 2019/771.

234 Explanatory Memorandum to the Trade in Dual-Use Items Regulations 2019, para 2.1: www.legislation.gov.uk/uksi/2019/771/pdfs/uksiem_20190771_en.pdf.

235 SI 2019/806.

236 Explanatory Memorandum to the Trade in Dual-Use Items Regulations 2019, paras 7.3 and 7.5.

237 Explanatory Memorandum to the Trade in Dual-Use Items Regulations 2019, para 2.9.

that any subordinate legislation made before Exit Day under any provision of the EUWA 2018 which uses 'Exit Day' as a point of reference for when it comes into force is to be read as using 'IP completion day' as the point of reference for when it comes into force. Paragraph 1(1) came into force immediately before Exit Day by virtue of regulation 3(b) of the European Union (Withdrawal Agreement) Act 2020 (Commencement No 1) Regulations 2020.[238]

Therefore, following Exit Day but during the Implementation Period, the Dual-Use Regulation and its export authorisation/licence requirements will continue to apply in the UK as if it were a Member State, so export authorisations/licences will be required to export spyware outside of the EU, and to export certain hacking tools both outside the EU and within the EU. Following the end of the Implementation Period, authorisations/licences will be required in respect of exporting spyware and certain hacking tools outside of the UK.

Murder and grievous bodily harm

Medical devices

2.46

> Case Study
>
> The tenth episode of the second season of 'Homeland' was called 'Broken Hearts'. In it, Carrie was taken hostage, and her captor (Abu Nazir) ordered Brody to enter Vice President Walden's home office and retrieve the serial number of Walden's pacemaker. Nazir explained that he would be able to use the serial number to manipulate the pacemaker wirelessly. Brody provided the serial number, and Nazir's associate gained access to Walden's pacemaker, accelerated his heartbeat and induced a heart attack. Walden died as a result.

The episode was derided as unrealistic when it first aired, but it was far from fiction: medical devices are susceptible to malware, unauthorised access and denial of service. Indeed, Annex I to both the Medical Devices Regulation[239] ('MDR') and In Vitro Diagnostic Regulation[240] ('IVDR') outline various cybersecurity requirements for such devices; and, in October 2013, in an interview to CBS's '60 Minutes', Dick Cheney, the former US Vice President, revealed that, when he had a device implanted to regulate his heartbeat in 2007, he had his doctors disable its wireless capabilities in order to prevent a possible assassination attempt.

Thus, medical device hacking is a real threat, and the most likely reason for an individual to gain unauthorised access to pacemakers, life support machines,

238 SI 2020/75.
239 Regulation (EU) 2017/745.
240 Regulation (EU) 2017/746.

medication administration devices etc is to cause grievous bodily harm or death: why else would someone seek unauthorised access to a device that regulates someone's breathing, heart rate, medication administration etc?

In December 2019, the Medical Device Coordination Group ('MDCG') issued new guidance[241] to help medical device manufacturers meet the cybersecurity requirements in the MDR and IVDR.

By way of background, the MDR and IVDR entered into force on 25 May 2017 and require devices placed on the EU market to be fit for the new technological challenges linked to cybersecurity risks. Specifically, the Regulations lay down essential safety requirements for all medical devices that incorporate electronic programmable systems and software that are medical devices in themselves. They require manufacturers to design, develop, manufacture and upgrade their products in accordance with state-of-the-art practices, taking into account the principles of risk management and information security. The Regulations also set out minimum requirements concerning IT security measures, including protection against unauthorised access.[242]

The MDCG guidance provides the following to assist manufacturers in fulfilling the requirements of the Regulations:

- The cybersecurity requirements to ensure safety and effectiveness of products against cybersecurity risks and threats should be considered in accordance with the nature of the device, including the device type and intended communication technologies usage.
- Manufacturers should evaluate the potential exploitation of vulnerabilities that may be the result of reasonably foreseeable misuse of the device.
- Safety, security and effectiveness are critical aspects in the design of security mechanisms for both medical devices and in vitro medical devices, and they need to be considered by manufacturers from the early stages of development and the manufacturing process, and throughout the entire lifecycle of the medical devices.
- Manufacturers are responsible for determining the minimum requirements for the operating environment as regards IT network characteristics and IT security measures that could not be implemented through the product design.
- Manufacturers have to provide clear documentation and information relating to:
  - the device's instructions for use, including IT security features/configurations (if applicable);
  - product specifications;

241 MDCG 2019-16 – Guidance on Cybersecurity for medical devices, December 2019: https://ec.europa.eu/docsroom/documents/38941.

242 Medical Device Coordination Group Guidance Document, para 1.1.

  - recommended IT security measures and IT environment configuration;
  - the risk assessment as regards the device's IT security risks;
  - specifications that the user requires in order to use the device appropriately;
  - the installation, configuration and operation of the medical device;
  - user requirements in terms of training/required skills, including IT skills required for the installation, configuration and operation of the medical device;
  - the secure configuration and application of security updates for the medical device;
  - compatibility issues as regards the operating environment; and
  - requirements regarding the operating environment, including instructions for the IT security controls related to the operating environment.

- During the support lifetime of the device, manufacturers should put in place a process to gather post-market information in respect of the security of the device. This process should take into account:
  - security incidents directly related to the medical device software;
  - security vulnerabilities that are related to the medical device hardware/software and the third party hardware/software used with the medical device; and
  - changes in the threat landscape.

  Manufacturers should evaluate the information gathered, evaluate the associated security and safety risks, and take appropriate measures to control the risk associated with such security incidents or vulnerabilities.

- At the EU level, in addition to the MDR and IVDR, the General Data Protection Regulation ('GDPR')[243] and the NIS Directive[244] are relevant to the cybersecurity of medical devices.

Such measures will go some way to mitigating the risk of medical devices being hacked and causing harm and/or death. However, as technology is always evolving, such risks will never be alleviated entirely: new vulnerabilities may be discovered and exploited, and new ways to circumvent a device's security measures may be developed.

Where harm or death results from the hacking of a medical device, proving that that was the cause of death and who was responsible will pose practical and evidential challenges for the investigative authorities.

243 Regulation (EU) 2016/679.

244 Directive (EU) 2016/1148 on measures for a high common level of security of network and information systems.

First, an individual able to circumvent the security features of a pacemaker is also likely to be able to ensure that the device shows no sign of having been tampered with, and ensure that they cannot be traced. This is a scenario that is straight out of a Hollywood movie, but it is a real possibility. Given the lack of funding in the criminal justice system, are the investigative time and resources required to undertake such an investigation beyond those which the investigative authorities can provide? It should also be noted that it would likely only be if the medical professional on the scene and/or conducting an autopsy thought that something was amiss that the case would get referred to the investigative authorities in the first place. With an underfunded health service, is an on-call doctor in A&E going to be able to determine whether someone with a pacemaker simply had a heart attack and died, or whether their pacemaker was hacked and caused them to have a heart attack? I suspect not.

Assuming, however, that the death has been correctly identified as suspicious, investigated, and the responsible individual/s identified, this then leads to the second challenge: causation. Someone using a medical device obviously has an underlying medical condition. How can it be determined whether it was the underlying medical condition or the hacking of the device that caused the harm/death? The hacking of a medical device would seek to make the underlying medical condition worse and it would be that worsening that was the ultimate cause of harm/death. However, was the hack that caused the worsening the causative factor in the death/harm? Doctors will know that patients who seem to be well and/or recovering can suddenly take a turn for the worse. Therefore, could it be said with any certainty that the hacking of the medical device was the causative factor in the harm and/or death? Would the condition have got worse on that day without the hack? Was it, in fact, the hack that caused the condition to get worse, or was the hack just a simultaneous but separate occurrence? Expert medical evidence would inevitably be required in order to address these questions of causation, as would expert technical evidence on the medical device, but would doctors and technical experts be able to determine what had happened? Might the hacking of a medical device be as close to the 'perfect murder' as one can get?

Car computer systems

2.47 Not only can medical devices be hacked in order to try and commit the 'perfect murder', but cars can be wirelessly carjacked and cause death and/or serious injury to the occupants and other road users.

> Case Studies
>
> In 2011, researchers from the University of Washington and the University of California at San Diego showed that they could wirelessly disable the locks and brakes on a sedan.[245]

245 'Comprehensive Experimental Analyses of Automotive Attack Surfaces', Stephen Checkoway, Damon McCoy, Brian Kanton, Danny Anderson, Hovav Shacham, Stefan Savage, Karl Koscher, Alexei Czeskis, Franziska Roesner and Tadayoshi Kohno: www.autosec.org/pubs/cars-usenixsec2011.pdf.

Then, in July 2015, Charlie Miller (a security researcher at Twitter) and Chris Valasek (director of Vehicle Security Research at IOActive) conducted an experiment on a Jeep Cherokee being driven by Andy Greenberg (a senior writer for WIRED, covering security, privacy, information freedom and hacker culture).[246] Mr Greenberg had agreed to take part in this experiment.

Mr Greenberg was driving at 70mph on the edge of downtown St Louis when the car's vents started blasting cold air at the maximum setting, the radio switched on and the windscreen wipers turned on. Mr Greenberg had not touched anything on the dashboard: all these features were being controlled by Miller and Valasek from Miller's home 10 miles away. Then Miller and Valasek cut the car's transmission and Mr Greenberg's accelerator stopped working.

Miller and Valasek had been conducting research for three years and had found a vulnerable element in the internet-connected computer feature that controlled Chrysler vehicles' entertainment and navigation system (Chrysler vehicles were the object of their research, specifically the Jeep Cherokee). This vulnerability allowed anyone who knew the car's IP address to gain access to its systems from anywhere in the country. Following the point of entry, Miller and Valasek's attack moved to an adjacent chip in the car's head unit – the hardware for its entertainment system – and silently rewrote the chip's firmware, planting their code. Their code enabled commands to be sent through the car's internal computer network (known as a CAN bus) to its dashboard functions, steering, brakes, engine and wheels from a laptop anywhere in the country. Thus the code not only enabled a third party to remotely control the car's radio, windscreen wipers, air-conditioning and dashboard, they could also kill the engine, engage the brakes, disable the brakes and control the steering. The code also enabled surveillance, as it could target GPS coordinates, measure speed and trace a car's route.

Although the research indicated that finding a particular person's vehicle is not easy, with sufficient scanning equipment, an individual could be found and targeted.

Miller and Valasek shared their research with Chrysler who were able to release a patch to address the vulnerability. However, as car manufacturers seek to make cars more like smartphones with increased wireless connections (Bluetooth, Wi-Fi, radios etc), and with the advent of driverless cars (which will likely use some sort of wireless connection to operate), there will be other makes and models of cars with similar security vulnerabilities. Miller's and Valasek's research suggests that practically any modern vehicle could be vulnerable to a wireless carjacking attack and, with the ability to find and target individuals, this presents another way in which individuals may be able to commit murder and grievous bodily harm.

246 'Hackers Remotely Kill a Jeep on the Highway – With Me in It', Andy Greenberg, Wired, 21 July 2015: www.wired.com/2015/07/hackers-remotely-kill-jeep-highway/.

As with medical devices, there will be evidential challenges to investigating and prosecuting murder and grievous bodily harm committed through the hacking of a car's internal computer network. Again, an individual able to gain access to a car's internal computer system is also likely to be able to ensure that the vehicle shows no sign of having been tampered with, and ensure that they cannot be traced. Although the investigative authorities will usually be involved in road traffic accidents, will they think that anything other than an accident has occurred? What circumstances will have to be present, or threshold will have to be reached, in order for investigators to entertain the possibility of the car having been hijacked and the driver attacked, as opposed to it just having been an accident? And again, will it be possible to prove that the car was hijacked and that that caused the death/harm?

As outlined above in respect of medical devices, these are scenarios that are straight out of Hollywood movies and they are hard to believe. However, they are very real, and investigators will need to start turning their minds to the possibility of offences having been committed by 'cyber' means, as opposed to just 'human' means.

WHAT ARE THE CYBER-DEPENDENT CRIMES?

2.48 The beginning of this chapter defined cyber-dependent crimes as offences that can only be committed technologically, ie by using a computer, computer networks or other forms of information communications technology, with computing being both the means and ends of a crime (for example, developing and deploying ransomware, malware etc, hacking, data destruction etc.

The preceding paragraphs have shown how ransomware, malware and spyware are digital technologies that can actually increase the scale and reach of traditional crimes. Thus, cyber-assisted crimes are quite often reliant on cyber-dependent crimes and, in fact, rather than there being a hard distinction between the two, it is more of a 'complementary' relationship. Given some of the jurisdictional and evidential issues that are likely to arise in respect of cyber-assisted crimes (some of which are discussed above, but also see **Chapters 5** and **8**), cyber-dependent crimes may be the only offences for which some individuals may be prosecuted.

Therefore, in this section, we focus on the creation and use of such software in its most simple and basic form, and the offences – the cyber-dependent crimes – that such creation and use give rise to.

Ransomware, malware, spyware etc

2.49 The offences committed by the creation and use of ransomware, malware, spyware etc are to be found in the CMA 1990.

The CMA 1990 creates five offences:

- unauthorised access to computer material (section 1);
- unauthorised access with intent to commit or facilitate the commission of further offences (section 2);
- unauthorised acts with intent to impair, or with recklessness as to impairing, the operations of a computer etc (section 3);
- unauthorised acts causing, or creating risk of, serious damage (section 3ZA); and
- making, supplying or obtaining articles for use in an offence under section 1, 3 or 3ZA (section 3A).

Section 17 – the interpretation provision – applies equally to each of the five offences, and particular note should be taken of the territorial scope of the CMA 1990. Section 4(1) provides that it is immaterial for the purposes of any offence under section 1, 3 or 3ZA whether any act or other event, proof of which is required for conviction of the offence, occurred in the home country (ie England and Wales) or whether the accused was in the home country at the time of any such act or event: all that is required is at least one significant link with the domestic jurisdiction.[247]

Section 5(2)–(3A) provides that there is a significant link with the domestic jurisdiction if:

- the individual was in the home country at the time when they did the relevant act/unauthorised act;
- the computer that was the subject of that act/unauthorised act was in the home country; or
- the unauthorised act caused or created a significant risk of serious damage of a material kind in the home country.

However, section 5(1A) provides that, where an individual was outside the UK at the time of the act constituting the offence under section 1, 3, 3ZA or 3A, there is a significant link with the domestic jurisdiction if the individual was a UK national at that time and the act constituted an offence under the law of the territory in which it occurred. Thus, the CMA 1990 has extraterritorial applicability in relation to the actions of UK nationals and it should always be borne in mind that, not only does it create broad categories of offences, but it also has a wide territorial reach.

Acquisition of ransomware, malware, spyware

2.50 Considering, then, the basic use cases of ransomware, malware and spyware: first, the acquisition of ransomware, malware or spyware, if obtained with an intent to use it to commit, or to assist in the commission of, an offence

247 CMA 1990, s 4(2).

under section 1, 3 or 3ZA, or with a view to its being supplied for use to commit, or to assist in the commission of, an offence under section 1, 3 or 3ZA, is an offence under section 3A(3) of the CMA 1990. It appears to be immaterial whether or not the substantive section 1, 3 or 3ZA offence was committed: provided that the article was obtained with the requisite intent, the offence will be made out.

The section 3A offence will also apply to the making, adapting, supplying and offering to supply ransomware, malware or spyware.

A person found guilty under section 3A will be liable on summary conviction to imprisonment for a term not exceeding 12 months (six months prior to the commencement of section 154(1) of the Criminal Justice Act 2003), or a fine, or both; and, on conviction on indictment, to imprisonment for a term not exceeding two years, or a fine, or both.[248]

Using ransomware, malware, spyware

2.51 Moving on to consider the offences committed by an individual actually using ransomware, malware or spyware, it is important to consider what each of these types of software actually does:

- Malware is software that is specifically designed to disrupt, damage or gain unauthorised access to a computer.
- Ransomware is software that is designed to block access to a computer system until a sum of money is paid.
- Spyware is software that enables a user to obtain information about another's activities by transmitting data covertly from their hard drive or phone.

Thus, malware may be the tool used to gain access to a computer or smartphone so that ransomware or spyware can be deployed (as in the case of the WannaCry ransomware attack, see para **2.41** above), or it could be the tool to cause disruption or damage.

In the case of malware simply being used as a tool to gain unauthorised access, that would constitute an offence under section 1 of the CMA 1990; and a person guilty of such an offence would be liable on summary conviction to imprisonment for a term not exceeding 12 months (six months prior to the commencement of section 154(1) of the Criminal Justice Act 2003), a fine, or both; and, on conviction on indictment, to imprisonment for a term not exceeding two years, or a fine, or both.[249]

The offence under section 1 is so broad that it also catches cases of hacking simpliciter, ie gaining access to a computer or program without the use of malware. This means that it will capture children manipulating game software

248 CMA 1990, s 3A(5)(a) and (c).
249 CMA 1990, s 1(3)(a) and (c).

in order to cheat, and it will capture individuals modifying proprietary software, such as that in smart speakers when, for example, companies decide to stop supporting software updates for its older models, and individuals seek a way to make their expensive equipment still work so that they do not have to buy newer, more expensive models.[250]

Where malware (or hacking simpliciter) is used to gain access so that ransomware can be deployed then, not only will an individual be guilty of an offence under section 1 of the CMA 1990, but they will also be guilty of an offence under section 2, as ransomware is used to commit blackmail which carries a sentence of up to 14 years.[251] Indeed, a section 2 offence will be committed where unauthorised access is gained with the intent to commit an offence, or facilitate an offence, for which a person may be sentenced to imprisonment for a term of five years[252] (for example, fraud).[253] A person guilty of an offence under section 2 would be liable on summary conviction to imprisonment for a term not exceeding 12 months (six months prior to the commencement of section 154(1) of the Criminal Justice Act 2003), a fine, or both; and, on conviction on indictment, to imprisonment for a term not exceeding five years, or a fine, or both.[254]

The use of ransomware, and the use of malware as a tool for disruption or damage, would be an offence under section 3 as their use would impair the operation of a computer (malware), prevent access to a program or data held in a computer (ransomware) and impair the operation of any such program (malware). A person guilty of such an offence would be liable on summary conviction to imprisonment for a term not exceeding 12 months (six months prior to the commencement of section 154(1) of the Criminal Justice Act 2003), a fine, or both; and, on conviction on indictment, to imprisonment for a term not exceeding ten years, or a fine, or both.[255]

Even if malware is not particularly disruptive or damaging (for example, as in the case of crypto-mining malware), a person would still likely be guilty of an offence under section 3.

Case Study

The mining of cryptocurrency is a race and so, the more resources one has, the better the chances are of mining a successful block. To increase their resources and their chances, individuals are using botnets to infect computers with malware that run mining software in the background, unbeknownst to the computer's owner; and they are also re-coding legitimate mining tools

250 'Sonos to deny software updates to owners of older equipment', Alex Hern, The Guardian, 23 January 2020: www.theguardian.com/technology/2020/jan/23/sonos-to-deny-software-updates-to-owners-of-older-equipment.

251 TA 1968, s 21(3).

252 CMA 1990, s 2(2).

253 Fraud Act 2006, s 1(3)(b).

254 CMA 1990, s 2(5)(a) and (c).

255 CMA 1990, s 3(6)(a) and (c).

used by legitimate miners and individuals so that they include such mining malware capabilities. When the proof of work algorithms on the blockchain change, the botnets etc stop working, as it is too complicated to update the software on a botnet and all the infected computers; so individuals start again and create new ones.

According to Sergio Pastrana from the Universidad Carlos III de Madrid when he presented his paper 'A First Look at the Crypto-Mining Malware Ecosystem: A Decade of Unrestricted Wealth',[256] such malware is not hugely detrimental – although there is some hard drive deterioration, there does not appear to be a spike in electricity consumption – which is why anti-virus software focuses on ransomware as opposed to this kind of malware.

Even though crypto-mining malware is not as detrimental as ransomware, the fact that it causes some deterioration of the hard drive could, arguably, be said to impair the operation of the computer. As such, the deployment of crypto-mining malware would be an offence under section 3 of the CMA 1990.

The use of ransomware, depending on its scale and effects, may also be an offence under section 3ZA if it causes, or creates a significant risk of, serious damage of a material kind and the individual using the ransomware intended to cause serious damage of a material kind or is reckless as to whether such damage is caused. Damage is of a 'material kind' if it is:[257]

- damage to human welfare in any place; an act causes damage to human welfare only if it causes:[258]
  - loss to human life;
  - human illness or injury;
  - disruption of a supply of money, food, water, energy or fuel;
  - disruption of a system of communication;
  - disruption of facilities for transport; or
  - disruption of services relating to health;
- damage to the environment of any place;
- damage to the economy of any country; or
- damage to the national security of any country.

256 Presented at the Cambridge Cybercrime Conference on 11 July 2019. The attribution to Mr Pastrana is from the author's own notes of the event rather than an official transcript. Any mistakes or omissions are entirely the fault of the author.
257 CMA 1990, s 3ZA(2).
258 CMA 1990, s 3ZA(3).

It is immaterial whether or not an act causing damage does so directly or is the only or main cause of the damage.[259] A person guilty of an offence under section 3ZA is liable on conviction on indictment to imprisonment for a term not exceeding 14 years, or a fine, or both;[260] but where the offence is committed as a result of an act causing or creating a significant risk of serious damage to human welfare in the form of loss of human life or human illness or injury, or causes or creates a significant risk of serious damage to national security, a person will be liable on conviction on indictment to imprisonment for life, or a fine, or both.[261]

Taking, then, the WannaCry ransomware attack (see para **2.41** above), which affected NHS hospital systems, causing appointments and operations to be cancelled; affected telecommunications in Spain and Portugal; and affected transport in Germany; this, arguably, caused damage of a material kind, as it caused damage to human welfare by disrupting services relating to health, a system of communication and facilities for transport. It is easy to see how, similarly, large ransomware attacks could cause the same damage and how, then, the individuals behind it would have committed a section 3ZA offence.

The above discussion has not yet addressed the use of spyware. Some spyware is also malware, in the sense that it allows an individual to gain unauthorised access, as opposed to only being deployed once access has been obtained. The use of such spyware would be an offence under section 1 of the CMA 1990. In the case of spyware that is deployed after access has been obtained, it does not appear to fall easily within any of the other offences under the CMA 1990. As such, together with a section 1 offence, recourse might need to be had to the corresponding cyber-assisted crime (for example, stalking, harassment or voyeurism).

Distributed denial-of-service

2.52 Distributed denial-of-service ('DDoS') is where more than one computer, often thousands of computers, are used to flood an internet server with so many requests that it is unable to respond quickly enough. This can cause a server to become overloaded and freeze or crash, making websites and internet services unavailable.

Consequently, DDoS is an offence under section 3 of the CMA 1990 as it is an unauthorised act done with the intention of impairing the operation of the server and/or prevent or hinder access to a program or data held. Depending on the scale of the attack and the target, an offence might also be committed under section 3ZA. Additionally, the making, supplying or obtaining of 'stresser' or 'booter' services in order to facilitate a DDoS attack will also be an offence under section 3A of the CMA 1990.

259 CMA 1990, s 3ZA(4).
260 CMA 1990, s 3ZA(6).
261 CMA 1990, s 3ZA(7).

The US is already prosecuting individuals for providing DDoS services.

> Case Study
>
> In November 2019, Sergiy Usatyuk (a 21-year-old from Illinois) was sentenced to 13 months in prison for running multiple DDoS-for-hire services that launched millions of attacks over several years. Usatyuk pleaded guilty to one count of conspiracy to cause damage to Internet-connected computers and owning, administering and supporting illegal 'booter' or 'stresser' services designed to knock websites offline, including exostress[.]in, quezstresser[.]com, betabooter[.]com, databooter[.]com, instabooter[.]com, polystress[.]com and zstress[.]net.
>
> According to the US Justice Department, in just the first 13 months of the 27-month long conspiracy, Usatyuk's booter users ordered approximately 3,829,812 DDoS attacks. As of 12 September 2017, ExoStresser advertised on its website that this one booter service had launched 1,367,610 DDoS attacks, and caused targets to suffer 109,186.4 hours of network downtime (which is roughly 4,549 days).
>
> In addition to serving the 13-month prison sentence and three years of supervised release, Usatyuk forfeited USD 542,925 in proceeds from the scheme, as well as dozens of servers and other computer equipment that powered his DDoS-for-hire businesses.[262]

In presenting his paper 'Booting the Booters: Evaluating the Effects of Police Interventions on the Market for DoS Attacks',[263] Ben Collier, from the Cambridge Cybercrime Centre, stated that DDoS-for-hire sites are the first large-scale cyberattack market for completely unskilled users. He stated that 'booters' have been kicked off 'hacker' forums and have formed their own micro-communities, and that it is not difficult for law enforcement agencies to intervene and shut down these communities. However, he said that his study suggests that:

- sentencing has had an indeterminate effect on the DDoS-for-hire services;
- wide-scale takedowns have had some short-lived deep effects in activity, but that single takedowns have no impact;
- arrests have some effect on activity, but they are of limited effect; and
- messaging seems to halt the rise in booting entirely.

262 'DDoS-for-Hire Boss Gets 13 Months Jail Time', KrebsOnSecurity, 20 November 2019: https://krebsonsecurity.com/2019/11/ddos-for-hire-boss-gets-13-months-jail-time/.

263 Presented at the Cambridge Cybercrime Conference on 11 July 2019. The attribution to Mr Collier is from the author's own notes of the event rather than an official transcript. Any mistakes or omissions are entirely the fault of the author.

Therefore, law enforcement agencies may, rather than looking to prosecute individuals, want to consider alternative methods of deterrence, such as targeted messaging of the booting micro-communities.

Cybercrime-as-a-service

2.53 As tools and technology become ubiquitous, and as there is a rising demand for malware, hacking etc, cyber criminals are selling their services: for example, DDoS, RaaS, malware, spyware, and hacking capabilities. They advertise their services on public forums, and then conduct the transactions on private encrypted communication channels that are less risky than market places which can be shut down by law enforcement.

To combat this activity, Ugur Akyazi from the Technische Universiteit Delft suggests that law enforcement agencies need to understand the criminal services business model and its development in order to plan disruption tactics.[264]

Whilst that is true in some sense, given that the advertising is visible on public forums, law enforcement agencies should be able to, at the very least, prosecute the offer to supply such services/articles under section 3A of the CMA 1990. Ascertaining the identity of the individual offering such services might then, depending on what investigatory powers are used to gain further information, lead to further charges under section 3A for the supply and acquisition of the services/articles. Depending on what was done with the services/articles, there may also be offences under sections 1, 2, 3 and 3ZA of the CMA 1990. Therefore, it seems as though there is a way for law enforcement agencies to start disrupting these activities without the need to understand the criminal services business model.

WHAT IS TECHNOLOGY DOING TO CRIMINAL INVESTIGATIONS AND THE CRIMINAL JUSTICE SYSTEM?

2.54 'Cyber' and technology not only have an impact on the types of crimes that can be committed and the ways in which crimes can be committed, they also have an impact on the way in which investigations and disclosure are conducted, and they may even have a role to play (in the future) in deciding cases and determining sentences.

264 'Advertise publicly, trade privately? Analysing the Cybercrime-as-a-Service Offerings and Their Links to Private Communication Channels in Underground Forums' – Ugur Akyazi, Technische Universiteit Delft, presented at the Cambridge Cybercrime Conference on 11 July 2019. The attribution to Mr Akyazi is from the author's own notes of the event rather than an official transcript. Any mistakes or omissions are entirely the fault of the author.

This section focuses on the technological and cyber news and developments that have been seen in criminal investigations and case resolutions/hearings, and provides some commentary on those developments.

Investigations

Encryption

2.55 Encrypted information is especially challenging for law enforcement agencies conducting investigations, and so ways are sought to defeat encryption and view the protected information.

Disclosure notices

2.56 Part III (sections 49–56) of the Regulation of Investigatory Powers Act 2000 ('RIPA 2000') deals with the investigation of data protected by encryption.

Section 49 sets out the powers of law enforcement agencies when protected information is obtained or otherwise seized or intercepted. Where it is not otherwise reasonably practicable to obtain possession of the protected information in an intelligible form, a notice requesting disclosure of the key to the protected information may be served on someone reasonably suspected to be in possession of the key, provided that the imposition of the disclosure requirement is:[265]

- necessary:
  - in the interests of national security;
  - for the purpose of preventing or detecting crime;
  - in the interests of the economic well-being of the UK; or
  - for the purpose of securing the effective exercise or proper performance by any public authority of any statutory power or statutory duty; and
- proportionate to what is sought to be achieved.

Section 50 sets out the effect of a notice imposing a disclosure requirement, and a knowing failure to comply with a section 49 notice is a criminal offence under section 53. Section 54 creates an offence of tipping-off, which may be committed where the section 49 notice contains a provision requiring the person to whom the notice is given, and every other person who becomes aware of it or of its contents, to keep secret the giving of the notice, its contents and things done in pursuance of it.

Thus, section 49 affords a wide power to enable the decryption of protected material. However, a section 49 disclosure notice can only be sought in relation to protected material that has come into the possession of a relevant person by

265 RIPA 2000, s 49(2)–(3).

means of the exercise of a statutory power to seize, detain, inspect, search or otherwise interfere with documents or other property.[266] Therefore, it will not be appropriate in all circumstances.

'Cyber kiosks'

2.57

Case Study

From 20 January 2020, Police Scotland began using 'cyber kiosks', also known as a Digital Triage Device ('DTD'), which allow officers to bypass encryption and read personal data from certain digital devices without using a password.[267]

The cyber kiosks (41 cyber kiosks) were bought almost two years ago, the intention being to deploy them at police stations across Scotland from Autumn 2018. However, their introduction was postponed due to concerns about the legal basis for their use. The Scottish Police Authority faced criticism from the Scottish Parliament's Justice Sub-Committee on Policing for lack of effective scrutiny, while MSPs warned that Police Scotland had not followed best practice before trialling the devices. The Sub-Committee said that, during the trials, police in Edinburgh and Stirling searched the mobile phones of suspects, witnesses and victims without undertaking the required governance, scrutiny and impact assessments. Indeed, it emerged that members of the public who had had their phones seized and searched were not made aware that they were taking part in the trial.[268]

The Crown Office and independent senior counsel, Murdo MacLeod QC, have since confirmed the legal basis for use of this technology.[269]

A Data Protection Impact Assessment ('DPIA'), as required by Article 35 of the GDPR and section 64 of the Data Protection Act 2018, has also been completed and states the following:[270]

- The only devices that may be the subject of triage using a DTD are a mobile phone or tablet. Although a DTD has the capability to examine

266 RIPA 2000, s 49(1).

267 'Scottish police get green light to use encryption-busting "cyber kiosks"', Liam Kirkaldy, PublicTechnology.net, 16 January 2020: www.publictechnology.net/articles/news/scottish-police-get-green-light-use-encryption-busting-'cyber-kiosks'.

268 'New police equipment to search mobile devices', BBC News, 14 January 2020: www.bbc.co.uk/news/uk-scotland-51110586.

269 Legal Basis for the Seizure and Examination of Digital Devices: www.scotland.police.uk/spa-media/pqup21kj/digital-device-seizure-examination-legal-basis.pdf.

270 Data Protection Impact Assessment – Cyber Kiosks: www.scotland.police.uk/spa-media/z4kkk1ab/cyber-kiosk-dpia.pdf.

other items such as USBs or SD cards, the facility to examine anything other than a mobile phone or tablet has been disabled.

- A DTD can be used to triage lawfully seized or voluntarily submitted devices.
- A DTD will only be used in cases where the evidential relevance of the device is unknown. If it is known that the device contains potential evidence, that device will be submitted, without triage, within existing processes.
- The purpose of the triage is to identify if the device contains any evidential data. If the triage process shows that the device does not contain anything of evidential relevance, it will be returned to the owner.
- The areas of the device that will be examined during the process will be guided by the device owner and the investigation.
- The search for evidential material can be filtered, directing the triage to specific areas such as text messages, call data, chat (WhatsApp/Snap Chat), multimedia (audio, video, photographs), internet history, email etc. This also includes the ability to limit the search using a date range or keyword search criteria.
- Contemporaneous notes may be taken by officers.
- Although the equipment has the capacity to copy data, this facility has been disabled and cannot be enabled by standard operators. No data will be held or extracted – this is a triage tool – thus, the DTD is only to provide a viewing facility and will not record any data from the device.
- A DTD is password protected for use, and only trained authorised officers will undertake the triage via a DTD. These officers will be subject to audit and compliance checks to ensure adherence with prescribed guidelines.
- Personal details to identify the police officer or member of police staff conducting the triage will be recorded by the DTD.
- Prior to carrying out the assessment, a record of what is to be done is recorded by the DTD software and, for each device that is to be assessed, the operator must fill in a field to define the category of data subject.
- DTDs will only be located within police offices. Their location has been determined and selected so as to ensure privacy during any triage process.
- DTDs are stand-alone systems that are not connected to any network, and data cannot be egressed from them due to restrictions placed on the controlling software.
- The use of the system will be audited.

- When a DTD is to be used, an individual will be informed of this intention and will be provided with information products, which will also be publicly available via the Police Scotland website.[271] Individuals will be provided with a public information document/leaflet, the Digital Device Journey Flow Process,[272] an FAQs sheet[273] and a Digital Device Examination and Consent FAQ.[274]

Question 6 of the FAQs outlines how a 'Cyber Kiosk' works, and says the following:

> '1. Digital device is connected to the Cyber Kiosk.
>
> 2. Trained operator specifies the information type(s) and time period(s) which the investigating officer has identified as being of relevance to their investigation.
>
> 3. The Cyber Kiosk thereafter searches the device and displays any matching information on screen.
>
> 4. Information is then reviewed by the operator and the investigating officer to establish if there is evidence present and further examination is required by a Digital Forensic Hub.
>
> 5. All device **information is deleted** from the Cyber Kiosk when the examination is completed.'

Interestingly, the final stage in the process 'all device information is deleted […] when the examination is completed' suggests that, contrary to the DPIA, the copying capability of the DTDs has not, in fact, been disabled: the equipment copies the data from the device, but it is deleted at the end of the process.

Indeed, the Digital Device Examination and Consent FAQs seem to explicitly contradict the DPIA, saying that the DTDs copy all available information from the device, and they outline what happens if evidential material is found:

> **'Q13. What information will the police take from my device?**
>
> The technology used will **copy all available information from your device**, but police will **only look** at what is necessary, justified, proportionate, and relevant to the investigation. (emphasis added)
>
> […]
>
> **Q16. Do the police keep the copied information, and if so how long it is held?**
>
> If no evidence is found, no information will be kept.
>
> If evidence is found on the device we are required by law to keep the copied information as follows:

271 www.scotland.police.uk/about-us/police-scotland/specialist-crime-division/cybercrime-investigations-and-digital-forensics/cyber-kiosks.

272 www.scotland.police.uk/spa-media/wpbpy43s/digital-device-journey-flow-process.pdf.

273 www.scotland.police.uk/spa-media/zqxibu3s/cyber-kiosk-faqs.pdf.

274 www.scotland.police.uk/spa-media/3qriietk/digital-examination-consent-faqs.pdf.

Nature of Case	How Long Stored
Serious, unresolved, cases	Until the case is resolved
Standard, unresolved, cases	Current year + 2 years'
All resolved cases and death investigations	Until disposal instructed by Procurator Fiscal (COPFS)

There may be technical nuances and differences between the definitions of 'copy, held and extracted' in the DPIA and the Digital Device Examination and Consent FAQs. However, to a lay person (indeed, to a lawyer), these documents seem contradictory.

Also interestingly, neither the DPIA nor the FAQs make any mention of a DTD being able to bypass the encryption on devices.

The Digital Device Examination and Consent FAQs do, however, make explicit reference to the possibility of bypassing encryption:

> **'Q12. Can the police bypass PIN codes and passwords?**
>
> Sometimes. The ability to bypass security measures such as PIN codes varies depending on the make and model of the device, the version of the operating system being used, and any security measures enforced by the manufacturer. A specific answer regarding this can only be given on a case-by-case basis. PIN codes or passwords will only be bypassed where absolutely necessary to progress the investigation.'

Despite the limited references to it in the documentation, bypassing encryption is a key element of the DTDs. The DTDs are built by Cellebrite,[275] an Israeli vendor that specialises in providing law enforcement agencies with tools to bypass passcode locks on handsets. Basic Cellebrite tools plug into smartphones via USB and attempt to forcibly unlock the handsets, thus allowing the encrypted contents to be decrypted and examined.

Cellebrite openly boasts about its ability to bypass lock screens on iPhone and Android handsets, and the technology works in various ways, depending on the hardware and operating system combination. For some models, its equipment copies a custom bootloader (a program that loads an operating system when a computer is turned on) to the device's RAM and runs that to bypass security mechanisms. In other cases, such as with Android devices, it tries to temporarily root the handset (ie obtain root access to the operating system code), giving the user privileges to modify the software code or install other software not normally permitted by the manufacturer. The equipment can also attempt to exploit vulnerabilities in the phone firmware (permanent software programmed into a read-only memory), including iOS, to ultimately extract data.[276]

275 www.cellebrite.com/en/law-enforcement/investigation/.

276 'Unlocking news: We decrypt those cryptic headlines about Scottish cops bypassing smartphone encryption. New perspective on FBI, Interpol demands for backdoors', Shaun Nichols, The Register, 17 January 2020: www.theregister.co.uk/2020/01/17/scottish_cops_cellebrite_kiosks/.

The Scottish 'cyber-kiosks' are not the only instance of law enforcement agencies using decryption software. Forbes reported that, in 2019, the FBI tried to use a GrayShift product (GrayKey) to read the contents of a locked and encrypted iPhone 11 Pro Max.[277] As the article points out, the use of such software raises the question as to why the US DoJ is making demands that Apple create law enforcement backdoors to devices.

The use of the Scottish 'cyber-kiosks' also raises other, more practical, questions in terms of investigations. One of the benefits of the triaging 'cyber-kiosk' process is said to be that it is less inconvenient for suspects, witnesses and victims, as they are able to get their devices back more quickly than if they were subjected to full digital forensic processing. What happens, though, as the investigation progresses, new issues arise and what is evidentially relevant changes/develops? Can devices be re-examined/re-triaged multiple times throughout the investigation?

As a DTD will only be used in cases where the evidential relevance of a device is unknown, it is arguable that, by considering the re-examination of a device, a determination may implicitly be being made that the device contains potential evidence. On that basis, rather than being re-examined/re-triaged, it should be submitted for full forensic processing.

However, as no copy of the data is kept following the initial triage, and contemporaneous notes may not have been made in relation to the now evidentially relevant information (because it was not relevant at the time of the initial triage), then all that would be being relied upon to say that the device contains evidentially relevant material is an officer's memory of something that they viewed. Is that enough to say that the device 'is known' to contain potential evidence and should be subjected to full forensic processing? If that is enough, should that be enough?

On the other hand, what if the initial triage search terms, date range etc did not relate to these new issues and, as such, it is not known whether the device contains potential evidence? In those circumstances, a device should, arguably, be re-examined rather than be sent for full forensic processing.

If an officer's memory is not enough, or the terms of the initial triage did not include these new issues, there is a risk that a device could be re-examined several times during the course of an investigation. Does that, in fact, make the process more inconvenient? Would it not be more convenient for individuals to just hand the device over and get another one, rather than having to lose access to it on multiple occasions?

277 'The FBI Got Data From A Locked iPhone 11 Pro Max – So Why Is It Demanding Apple Unlock Older Phones?', Thomas Brewster, Forbes, 15 January 2020: www.forbes.com/sites/thomasbrewster/2020/01/15/the-fbi-got-data-from-a-locked-iphone-11-pro-max—so-why-is-it-demanding-apple-unlock-older-phones/.

Additionally, whether the device is re-examined or subject to full forensic processing, is there not a risk that the now evidentially relevant information will have been lost between returning the device to the owner and the re-examination? Information may have been deleted on the basis that it was not evidentially relevant to the police. This could be done innocently, in which case it may be possible to retrieve it; or it could be done nefariously (which will only be apparent in the new context of the investigation); or as a result of a sensible data destruction policy/process, in which case additional steps may have been taken to ensure that the information has been securely deleted (for example, by using a program such as shred).[278] Unless there are contemporaneous notes of what was viewed, how could the police tell whether something had been deleted? If something is securely deleted, could someone be prosecuted for perverting the course of justice by destroying evidence? Arguably not, because, irrespective of the status of the information at a later stage in the investigation, the device was returned as the information was not thought to be evidentially relevant.

Given the risk of losing evidentially relevant information, should the return of a device following a DTD triage be accompanied by an undertaking/court order or injunction that nothing will be deleted from the device until the investigation has been concluded, supported by a perverting the course of justice charge if information is then deleted? If so, does this then not mean that the operator of the DTD undertaking the triage will need to take contemporaneous notes of everything that they view, so as to ensure that, in the event of re-examination or full processing, nothing has been deleted? If that is the natural conclusion, does the taking of full contemporaneous notes not undermine the concept of a copy of the information viewed via the DTD not being held? Also, what rights may be infringed by requiring such an undertaking/complying with a court order/injunction, when the reason the device is being returned is that it has been determined that it does not contain evidentially relevant material?

In light of the above considerations, it is questionable whether 'cyber kiosks' will, as per the reasoning in the DPIA, actually save resources and reduce strain. However, these are new devices, only just being implemented, and so only time will tell.

International data requests

2.58 The traditional route for international electronic data requests in criminal investigations is through a Mutual Legal Assistance Treaty ('MLAT') and Letters of Request ('LoRs') under section 7 of the Crime (International Co-operation) Act 2003. The MLAT process, however, requires LoRs from law enforcement agencies to be submitted and approved by central governments,[279] and can often take months, if not years, to be processed and answered.

278 https://linux.die.net/man/1/shred.

279 See Crime (International Co-operation) Act 2003, s 8.

In March 2018, the US passed the Clarifying Lawful Overseas Use of Data Act ('the CLOUD Act'),[280] which allows the US to enter into executive agreements with foreign governments in order to facilitate law enforcement access to electronic data. These executive agreements will remove MLATs from the data request equation, so that signatory countries can directly request data and records from US-based providers.

On 3 October 2019, the US and the UK signed the first CLOUD Act Executive Agreement: the US-UK Bilateral Data Access Agreement ('the US-UK Agreement').[281] The intention is that the US-UK Agreement will allow law enforcement agencies in either country to 'demand electronic data regarding serious crime, including terrorism, child sexual abuse, and cybercrime, directly from tech companies based in the other country, without legal barriers',[282] whilst also ensuring that privacy, civil liberties and 'open Internet' are protected and that the obtaining of material is consistent with the laws of both parties.[283]

'Serious Crime' is defined in Article 1(14) of the US-UK Agreement as an offence that is punishable by a maximum term of imprisonment of at least three years, and Article 1(7) provides that a 'Covered Provider' to whom a data request can be made means:

> 'any private entity to the extent that it: (i) provides to the public the ability to communicate, or to process or store computer data, by means of a Computer System or a telecommunications system; or (ii) processes or stores Covered Data on behalf of an entity defined in subsection (i).'

'Computer System' means any device or a group of interconnected or related devices, one or more of which, pursuant to a program, performs automatic processing of data;[284] and 'Covered Data' means content of an electronic or wire communication; computer data stored or processed for a user; traffic data or metadata pertaining to an electronic or wire communication or the storage or processing of computer data for a user; and Subscriber Information when sought pursuant to an Order that also seeks any of the other types of data referenced in the definition of 'Covered Data'.[285] 'Subscriber Information' means information that identifies a subscriber or customer of a Covered Provider, including name, address, length and type of service, subscriber number or identity (including assigned network address and device identifiers), telephone connection records, records of session times and durations, and means of payment.[286]

280 www.justice.gov/dag/page/file/1152896/download.

281 https://assets.publishing.service.gov.uk/government/uploads/system/uploads/attachment_data/file/836969/CS_USA_6.2019_Agreement_between_the_United_Kingdom_and_the_USA_on_Access_to_Electronic_Data_for_the_Purpose_of_Countering_Serious_Crime.pdf.

282 Press Release from the Department of Justice, Office of Public Affairs, 3 October 2019: www.justice.gov/opa/pr/us-and-uk-sign-landmark-cross-border-data-access-agreement-combat-criminals-and-terrorists.

283 US-UK Agreement, Article 2(1).

284 US-UK Agreement, Article 1(2).

285 US-UK Agreement, Article 1(3).

286 US-UK Agreement, Article 1(15).

Thus, the US-UK Agreement applies to a wide range of entities, including Apple, Facebook and WhatsApp, and allows a wide range of information to be sought. The US-UK Agreement only came into force on 8 July 2020 although, at the time of writing, it is not actually in use, as it remains subject to law enforcement authorities putting data minimisation processes in place.[287] However, when it is finally in use, the value of the information that can be sought under it to a financial crime or terrorism investigation will be immense, and the ability to approach the Covered Providers directly means that investigation timelines should be significantly reduced.

UK law enforcement authorities will have two routes to seek electronic data under the US-UK Agreement.

In so far as they are consistent with the Agreement, for intelligence gathering purposes, certain UK law enforcement agencies will be able to issue targeted interception warrants, authorised notices and retention notices to overseas telecommunications operators under the IPA 2016 in order to intercept communications, obtain communications data and require the retention of communications data[288] (see paras **8.11–8.15** for a full discussion of law enforcement powers under the IPA 2016).

Alternatively, where UK law enforcement authorities are seeking to gather evidence for criminal proceedings, they can apply to the court for an overseas production order under the Crime (Overseas Production Orders) Act 2019 ('COPOA 2019'). An application will only be granted if the conditions of section 4 are met; specifically, that there are reasonable grounds for believing that:[289]

- all or part of the electronic data specified in the application is likely to be of substantial value to the proceedings or investigation;
- all or part of the electronic data specified in the application is likely to be relevant evidence in respect of the offence alleged; and
- it is in the public interest for the electronic data to be produced.

If an overseas production order is made, or an IPA 2016 warrant or notice issued, the relevant UK 'designated authority' (the Home Office) will have to review the order/warrant/notice, certify that it is lawful and complies with the US-UK Agreement, and then issue it to the relevant US Covered Provider.[290] In the case of an overseas production order, the US Covered Provider has seven days

287 'Law enforcement without borders: The US-UK Data Access Agreement', Simmons & Simmons LLP, 2 October 2020: www.simmons-simmons.com/en/publications/ckfsgi94zp7vy0900pq4yxeyb/law-enforcement-without-borders-the-us-uk-data-access-agreement; and US-UK Agreement, Article 7. It is anticipated that requests under the IPA 2016 may begin in November 2020, with requests under COPOA 2019 to follow.

288 IPA 2016, Part 1, Chapter 1, Part 3 and Part 4; and 'UK-US Bilateral Data Sharing Agreement: What Companies Need to Know', Michael Drury and Julian Hayes, BCL Solicitors LLP.

289 COPOA 2019, s 4(5)–(7).

290 US-UK Agreement, Article 5(5)–(7).

(beginning on the day on which the order is served) to produce, or provide access to, the electronic data.[291]

If a US Covered Provider wishes to challenge the order/warrant/notice, any objections should, in the first instance, be raised with the UK's 'designated authority'. If the objections cannot be resolved, the US Covered Provider can raise their objections with its own designated authority, whereupon both the UK and US designated authorities may confer in an effort to resolve the objections.[292] If they agree that the order/warrant/notice is valid, the US Covered Provider will need to comply with the order/warrant/notice; if, however, there is disagreement between the UK and US designated authorities over the validity of the order/warrant/notice, the US-UK Agreement will not apply to the order/warrant/notice,[293] and the UK law enforcement authority will need to resort to the traditional MLAT and LoR procedure, or the extraterritorial provisions of the IPA 2016.

In addition to raising objections with the designated authority, section 7 of COPOA 2019 provides that any person affected by the overseas production order may make an application to vary or revoke the order. Therefore, it appears that a US Covered Provider would be able to apply to a UK court to revoke an overseas production order.

The production of information by Covered Providers is addressed in Article 6 of the US-UK Agreement. It provides that the information should be provided directly to the 'designated authority', but it is completely silent on the method and form of transmission and production, allowing the designated authority to make arrangements and stipulate requirements with the Covered Providers. One such requirement that designated authorities may seek to insist upon is that the production produce electronic data in an unencrypted format, so as to save time and resources in decrypting the data.

The US-UK Agreement revolutionises the way in which UK law enforcement agencies will seek electronic data from the US. Whilst the US-UK Agreement anticipates a two-way flow of demands, it is likely that most requests will be from the UK to the US as a result of where the Covered Providers are located and where they hold data. However, UK law enforcement agencies should be aware that orders/warrants/notices subject to the US-UK Agreement may not intentionally target a Receiving Party Person, ie a US Government entity (at any level), a US citizen or national, a person lawfully in the US admitted for permanent residence, a corporation that is incorporated in the US, a person located in the US or an unincorporated association with a substantial number of members who are US citizens, nationals or are lawfully there.[294] Therefore, the scope of what can be obtained under the US-UK Agreement is not as broad

291 COPOA 2019, s 5(4)(b) and (5).
292 US-UK Agreement, Article 5(11).
293 US-UK Agreement, Article 5(12).
294 US-UK Agreement, Articles 4(3) and 1(12).

as it may at first appear. Further, although the law of the demanding state is the operative law,[295] the response to the order/warrant/notice must also comply with domestic law (for example, US First Amendment Freedom of Speech rights),[296] so responses to UK law enforcement requests under the US-UK Agreement will be subject to US law.

Covered Providers in the US also need to be aware that, although they will receive notice of applications for overseas production orders under COPOA 2019 and can make representations, there is no notice or participation in the warrant or notice processes under the IPA 2016, so the first opportunity for consideration will be on receipt of the warrant or notice from the UK's 'designated authority'.[297]

Despite the anticipated direction of the flow of requests under the US-UK Agreement, UK companies should be aware that they might now find themselves the direct recipient of requests from US law enforcement agencies. Given that the response to such requests must comply with domestic law (for example, the GDPR and the forthcoming UK GDPR), they may need to seek advice and guidance on how to comply and/or challenge these requests.

In light of Brexit, the UK may seek to pass its own legislation so that it will be able to make similar agreements with other countries and bypass the cumbersome MLAT process.

Evidence

2.59 In jury trials, having visual evidence can dramatically assist or ruin your case, and photographs, CCTV, text messages and copies of documents can bring a case to life for a jury.

What happens, though, if practitioners (and therefore, juries) can no longer trust, or rely on, what they see?

Sender spoofing

2.60 Sender spoofing is the process of faking the apparent sender of a message in order to mislead the recipient or others – much like signing a letter with someone else's name. Can you be sure that text messages or emails really came from the person that they say they are from?

At its simplest, text message sender spoofing can be done by using a third party service to construct raw short message service ('SMS') messages (ie an individual sets the sender details, the content of the message, and the recipient

295 US-UK Agreement, Article 5(1).
296 US-UK Agreement, Article 4(2).
297 'UK-US Bilateral Data Sharing Agreement: What Companies Need to Know', Michael Drury and Julian Hayes, BCL Solicitors LLP.

details). Thus it can be used to impersonate people and, by extension, it could be used to fabricate evidence. For example, that SMS asking for drugs may not be real. That SMS sending thanks for a bribe payment may not be real. That SMS arranging a meeting or date at the time of the offence might not be real. And that SMS saying that, after years of saying that you were not keen on the idea, you have finally decided that you would, in fact, like to get a puppy, and that you want to go and visit rescue centres this coming weekend, might not be real.[298]

As indicated above, it is not just text messages that are susceptible to sender spoofing: emails are too.

Does the fact of sender spoofing mean that law enforcement agencies need to (or should) verify the source of any text messages or emails that they are seeking to rely on, or does such an exercise only need to be carried out if/when raised by a suspect/defendant? Arguably, it is only proportionate to do so once veracity has been raised as an issue. However, law enforcement agencies will need to be aware of the possibility of such an argument so that they are prepared to undertake any forensic technical investigations required.

On the other side, does the fact of sender spoofing mean that defence counsel should, in all cases where a suspect/defendant says that they did not do it, or that they have been set up, and the main evidence is text messages or emails, raise the issue of veracity? Arguably so, because, unless the issue is one of pure construction and meaning, if they did not do it, the messages or emails showing or suggesting that they did are wrong/false. However, counsel would also be wise to advise their clients that, if a forensic technical investigation into the veracity of text messages or emails does not show exculpatory evidence, the result is likely to strengthen the case against them.

Deepfakes

2.61 Deepfakes are another way in which evidence can be falsified. Deepfakes are fake videos created by artificially intelligent systems, predominantly trained using machine learning methods, which generate or manipulate human bodies, faces and voices to fabricate footage of people and things. They are distinguishable from 'cheap fakes', which rely on accessible software, or no software at all, and use conventional editing techniques such as changing the speed of footage, re-staging, photoshopping, re-dubbing sounds, or re-contextualising by deleting or cutting together footage, changing narration, captions or video titles.

According to a report published in September 2019 by the research institute Data & Society,[299] the first widely known example of amateur, artificial intelligence

298 The author actually received this text message seemingly from her husband when he was at a tech conference in Heidelberg and he was demonstrating this technology.

299 'Deepfakes and Cheap Fakes – The Manipulation of Audio and Visual Evidence', Britt Paris and Joan Donovan, Data & Society, 18 September 2019: https://datasociety.net/output/deepfakes-and-cheap-fakes/; and https://datasociety.net/wp-content/uploads/2019/09/DS_Deepfakes_Cheap_FakesFinal-1.pdf.

('AI') manipulated face-swap videos was in November 2017, when a Reddit user with the username 'deepfakes' uploaded a series of videos with the faces of famous female actors grafted onto other actors' bodies in pornography.

Deepfake technology only really became something of general public awareness, though, in early 2018.

> Case Studies
>
> In early 2018, former US President, Barack Obama, spoke out about the growing dangers of false news and videos. However, it was not actually Obama making the video appearance: the video was a deepfake, created by Jordan Peele (an American actor, comedian, writer, director and producer) in conjunction with BuzzFeed. The goal was to help educate the public about the potential dangers of deepfakes.[300]
>
> Then, in 2019, a fake video of Mark Zuckerberg talking about amassing power and control through a nefarious organisation called Spectre was posted to Instagram.[301] The video was created using a proprietary video dialogue replacement ('VDR') model made by Canny, an Israeli advertising company, which uses a suite of machine learning and AI techniques that enables the sophisticated manipulation of visual data, specifically the movement of bodies.[302]

There are other examples of deepfakes and, with almost ubiquitous social media, there are thousands of images, videos etc of people on which deepfake technology can be trained and then fabricate videos. With increasingly sophisticated machine learning, combined with inexpensive, easy-to-use video editing software and open source projects for deepfake creation being hosted in public repositories, deepfake technology allowing face-mapped performance videos and artificial lip-syncing is becoming accessible to more and more people.[303] The deepfake videos, once created, can then be used to blackmail people, commit fraud or in cases of revenge pornography.

The advances in AI technology (and the availability of programs) is allowing the creation of fake audio-visual materials that are almost indistinguishable from authentic content, especially to ordinary human senses. Although a trained eye may be able to spot irregularities in deepfake videos, even among experts human detection is not totally effective. Consequently, researchers are developing

300 'Will Deepfakes Do Deep Damage?', Samuel Greengard, Communications of the ACM, 01/2020, Vol 63, No 1.

301 www.instagram.com/p/ByaVigGFP2U/.

302 'Deepfakes and Cheap Fakes – The Manipulation of Audio and Visual Evidence', Britt Paris and Joan Donovan, Data & Society, 18 September 2019.

303 'Will Deepfakes Do Deep Damage?', Samuel Greengard, Communications of the ACM, 01/2020, Vol 63, No 1; and 'Deepfakes and Cheap Fakes – The Manipulation of Audio and Visual Evidence', Britt Paris and Joan Donovan, Data & Society, 18 September 2019.

machine detection and forensics (detection algorithms), as well as ways to authenticate videos, to detect deepfakes. Some of the detection approaches focus on basic reality (for example, considering whether the lighting is consistent, whether shadows are correct, and whether the weather and lighting match the supposed date of capture). Others will look at smoothness in areas and unusual pixel formations.[304]

The existence of deepfakes means that trust in real videos is diminished. That, however, is based on the assumption that video and photography were previously objective and accurate evidence, and CCTV evidence has been manipulated in the past.

Case Study

In the US in 1991, four Los Angeles police officers were on trial for the beating of Rodney King. The trial focused on a central piece of video evidence – captured by an onlooker – that showed King being brutally beaten by the group of officers.

During the defence, the officers' lawyers played the video slowed to a fraction of its normal speed. As they did, they asked the officers, 'Was he complying here with your order to stay down?'. At this slowed-down speed, the video made King's involuntary physical reactions to blows appear as though he were attempting to get up.

The jurors decided that the police officers were not guilty of using excessive force on King and said that the slowed video in the courtroom 'made all the difference'. The slowed video captured the events, but its manipulation allowed a new interpretation.[305]

This shows that evidence does not always speak for itself: it is open to manipulation and interpretation. However, deepfakes are a different construct. Although, as with any evidence, what they depict is open to interpretation, the more fundamental feature of deepfakes is questioning the very veracity of what they are depicting. Deepfakes technology allows CCTV to be fabricated, which may place people at crime scenes or even depict them committing crimes.

The effect of deepfakes in relation to law enforcement and criminal cases was seen in September 2019, around the time of the publication of the Data & Society's report, when the BBC aired a new drama called 'The Capture'.

304 'Will Deepfakes Do Deep Damage?', Samuel Greengard, Communications of the ACM, 01/2020, Vol 63, No 1.

305 'Deepfakes and Cheap Fakes – The Manipulation of Audio and Visual Evidence', Britt Paris and Joan Donovan, Data & Society, 18 September 2019.

> Case Study
>
> The basic plot of 'The Capture' was that, after being acquitted of a war crime in Afghanistan, former UK Special Forces Lance Corporal Shaun Emery is accused of the kidnapping and murder of his barrister. The case against him is supported by damning CCTV evidence.
>
> As Emery works to clear his name, Detective Inspector Rachel Carey, who is assigned to investigate the case, uncovers a complex conspiracy surrounding Emery which calls into question the validity of the CCTV footage. It is revealed that the covert intelligence practice of 'correction', where video evidence is manipulated to convict suspects, has been used in relation to the CCTV, to make it look like Emery committed the kidnap and murder; and that the intention was that, after Emery's trial for murder, the 'victim' would be revealed as alive and well, uncovering the practice of 'correction' and exposing real miscarriages of justice.

And it is not just CCTV evidence that can be 'deepfaked': photographs, dashcams, amateur footage etc, all of which can play a role in criminal cases, can be fabricated. If the existence of deepfakes means that audio-visual evidence can no longer be trusted as proof of what they show, does this not mean that, unless it can be proved that the evidence is genuine (potentially no easy feat for the CPS and other law enforcement agencies, given the technical work involved in this), it is arguable that any such evidence is unreliable and, as such, should be excluded under section 78 of the Police and Criminal Evidence Act 1984, as it would have an adverse effect on the fairness of the proceedings? That would likely be a bold step for a court to take, so it may not be minded to do so. Therefore, if such evidence is not excluded, surely a closing speech point, in a case where the defendant says that they did not do it but CCTV has them at the crime scene committing the offence, and the CPS has offered no technical evidence as to the veracity of the footage, is that the very existence of deepfakes means that the jury cannot be sure that the CCTV is reliable and, as such, cannot be sure that the defendant did commit the crime, despite what the CCTV shows, and so they cannot find them guilty? That may be a somewhat convoluted argument, but it is one that could be made, and one that would resonate with juries: it could just as easily be them or one of their family members depicted in seemingly incriminating footage and on trial.

Perhaps this argument ultimately leads to the more fundamental issue of funding in the criminal justice system. Unless and until the criminal justice system is properly funded, law enforcement agencies are going to struggle to dispute arguments based on technological advances because they do not have the time, resources or funds to undertake the necessary, and proper, investigations that would enable them to do so. Indeed, 'public service' salaries are also unlikely to attract people of the necessary calibre to conduct the requisite forensics on potential deepfake material. Will law enforcement agencies contract out such work? Given private practice fees, they are unlikely to be able to do so without more funding. Likewise, would legal aid funding allow the instruction of a deepfakes digital forensic expert?

There is a limited amount of US legislation dealing with deepfakes. For example, the Malicious Deep Fake Prohibition Act of 2018[306] introduces penalties for those who create, with intent to distribute, fake videos that facilitate criminal or tortious conduct, and Texas and California have passed laws prohibiting various deepfake video activity in respect of elections.[307] There is no UK legislation that specifically deals with deepfakes. Should the creation of deepfakes, when it is deemed to produce harmful effects, be criminalised? Or should reliance just be placed on being able to prosecute individuals for the harmful effects (for example, harassment or perverting the course of justice)? Either scenario requires the creator to be identified, so the first step may be to require the mandatory registration of content creators before items can be posted. This would not, however, assist in the deepfake CCTV, photographs, dashcams or amateur footage in criminal proceedings scenarios, where the material is unlikely to be posted, but the creator in these scenarios should be more easily discoverable. Therefore, it may be that a prosecution for perverting the course of justice may be the most appropriate recourse.

Nevertheless, the very existence of deepfakes means that everyone within the criminal justice system is going to be more wary about relying on what they see, which, unless and until these issues are dealt with by the courts, could have a significant impact on cases.

Decision making

2.62 The definition of what constitutes AI will depend on who you ask. In the 1950s, it was described as 'any task performed by a programme or a machine that, if a human carried out the same activity, we would say the human had to apply intelligence to accomplish the task'. That is a broad definition, so it may be more helpful to think of AI systems as those which typically demonstrate at least some of the following behaviours associated with human intelligence: planning, learning, reasoning, problem solving, knowledge representation, perception, motion, manipulation and, to a lesser extent, social intelligence and creativity.[308]

To a lay person, the term 'AI' can conjure up Hollywood images of robots taking over the world. This type of AI, with adaptable intelligence capable of learning how to carry out vastly different tasks or reason about a wide variety of topics

306 Section 3805.

307 'Will Deepfakes Do Deep Damage?', Samuel Greengard, Communications of the ACM, 01/2020, Vol 63, No 1.

308 'What is AI? Everything you need to know about Artificial Intelligence', Nick Heath, ZDNet, 12 February 2018: www.zdnet.com/article/what-is-ai-everything-you-need-to-know-about-artificial-intelligence/.

based on accumulated experience, is what is sometimes termed 'general AI'. It is currently theoretical and only found in the realms of Hollywood.[309]

Real-world AI, sometimes referred to as 'narrow AI', involves systems that have been taught or have learnt how to carry out specific tasks without being explicitly programmed how to do so. It is seen in Siri, Alexa and recommendation engines that suggest products you might like based on what you bought in the past etc. Other potential applications include flagging inappropriate content online and assisting radiologists to detect potential tumours in X-rays.[310]

The process through which an AI is 'taught' is usually termed 'machine learning'. The system is fed a large amount of data which it then uses to learn how to carry out a specific task, such as understanding speech, captioning a photograph or identifying objects. Neural networks are key to the process of machine learning. They are brain-inspired networks of interconnected layers of algorithms, called neurons, that feed data into each other, and which can be trained to carry out specific tasks by modifying the importance attributed to the input data as it passes between the layers. During the training of these neural networks, the weight attached to different inputs will continue to be varied (by the system itself) until the output from the neural network is very close to what is desired, at which point the network will have 'learnt' how to carry out a particular task. Machine learning can take the form of supervised learning, unsupervised learning or reinforcement learning:

- Supervised learning is where the system is fed a huge amount of data which has been annotated to highlight the features of interest. Once trained, the system can apply the labels to new data (for example, whether a photograph that has just been uploaded contains a dog).
- Unsupervised learning is where the algorithms try to identify patterns in data, looking for similarities that can be used to categorise that data.
- In reinforcement learning, the system attempts to maximise a reward based on its input data, and basically goes through a process of trial and error until it arrives at the best possible result.[311]

AI is already beginning to be implemented in the legal sector. For example, narrow AI can be used in relation to document analysis. AI can be used to recognise patterns in language (for example, in contracts) and compare them against industry and/or client standards in order to find any anomalies or deviations. Thus, deviations from standard practice can be highlighted to a lawyer in order

309 'How Far Are We From Achieving Artificial General Intelligence?', Naveen Joshi, Forbes, 10 June 2019: www.forbes.com/sites/cognitiveworld/2019/06/10/how-far-are-we-from-achieving-artificial-general-intelligence/.

310 'What is AI? Everything you need to know about Artificial Intelligence', Nick Heath, ZDNet, 12 February 2018: www.zdnet.com/article/what-is-ai-everything-you-need-to-know-about-artificial-intelligence/.

311 'What is AI? Everything you need to know about Artificial Intelligence', Nick Heath, ZDNet, 12 February 2018: www.zdnet.com/article/what-is-ai-everything-you-need-to-know-about-artificial-intelligence/.

for them to review and analyse. In this context, the machine learning assists, but does not replace, the lawyer: it allows the lawyer to review much greater quantities of information much faster, but it is still the lawyer who is doing the work, conducting the analysis etc. However, it must be remembered that it cannot be assumed that the information labelled in the training data is going to apply to the specific situation that is being analysed.[312] Therefore, several AI platforms may be required for different standards, different clients etc.

Additionally, in transactional drafting and due diligence, AI can assist parties to craft dispute provisions which are fit for purpose and tailored to the parties' needs. Machine learning tools collate all the relevant factors, and can aggregate drafting and drafting analysis from vast quantities of similar contracts, as well as the advice given around them when they were being negotiated.

There have also been some negative media stories about AI being used in the legal sector.

Case Studies

The Home Office has been using an AI algorithm to 'allocate' UK visa applications to caseworkers, using data to indicate whether an application might require more or less scrutiny. The Home Office insists that the final decision on an application remains in the hands of human caseworkers, not the algorithm. Although the Home Office claims that the algorithm fully complies with the Equality Act 2010 and does not discriminate on the basis of race and nationality, the Joint Council for the Welfare of Immigrants ('JCWI') has brought a case against the Home Office to try and force it to explain on what basis the algorithm streams visa applications and determines the level of scrutiny required.[313]

In June 2019, a report titled 'Algorithms in the Criminal Justice System' was published by The Law Society Commission on the Use of Algorithms in the Justice System and The Law Society of England and Wales.[314] This found that AI algorithms (mostly in pilot or experimental stages) were being used by police in predictive hot-spotting, facial recognition, risk assessments of individuals, digital forensics and mobile device extraction. At the most basic level, the Commission found a lack of explicit standards, best practice and

312 'The Changing Legal Sector – Automating Legal Services, Utilising AI and the Regulatory Framework', Emily Foges, Westminster Legal Policy Forum Keynote Seminar: Legal Technology in the UK, 2 December 2019. The attribution to Ms Foges is from the author's own notes of the event, and the transcript of the event, which speakers do not have an opportunity to review. Therefore, any mistakes, omissions or misinterpretations are entirely the fault of the author.

313 'AI system for granting UK visas is biased, rights groups claim', Henry McDonald, The Guardian, 29 October 2019: www.theguardian.com/uk-news/2019/oct/29/ai-system-for-granting-uk-visas-is-biased-rights-groups-claim.

314 www.lawsociety.org.uk/support-services/research-trends/algorithm-use-in-the-criminal-justice-system-report/.

transparency around the use of these algorithmic systems. It also said that the use of some of the algorithms may lack a clear and explicit lawful basis, and made a list of recommendations.

It is clear from the June 2019 report that AI is making its way into the criminal justice system. The question is, then, can, or should, AI platforms be created to aggregate data from past cases and judgments so that they can be used to make decisions (such as charge, disclosure, legal professional privilege ('LPP'), verdicts and sentences) in criminal cases?

Case Studies

In terms of the position in other jurisdictions, in Estonia, the Ministry of Justice has commissioned a 'robot judge' to adjudicate small claims disputes of less than EUR 7,000. The hope is that the system will clear a backlog of cases for judges and court clerks. The concept is that the parties will upload documents and other relevant information, and the AI will issue a decision that can be appealed to a human judge.[315]

Looking then to the practice in the US, in some states in the US, algorithms help recommend criminal sentences.[316]

And, in terms of research in this area, in 2016, academic researchers developed AI that, after considering the legal evidence and other data from the judgments of 584 cases relating to torture and degrading treatment, the right to a fair trial and the right to privacy, was able to correctly predict the result reached by the European Court of Human Rights ('ECtHR') in 79% of cases.[317]

Despite the above indications that case decisions being made by AI could become a reality, AI is very unlikely to be used in the criminal justice system in England and Wales to render charging decisions, verdicts and sentencing decisions.

Part 3 of the Data Protection Act 2018 ('DPA 2018') relates to law enforcement processing, and section 49 provides that a controller may not take a significant decision based solely on automated processing unless that decision is required

315 'Can AI Be a Fair Judge in Court? Estonia Thinks So', Eric Niiler, Wired, 25 March 2019: www.wired.com/story/can-ai-be-fair-judge-court-estonia-thinks-so/.

316 'Should We Be Afraid of AI in the Criminal-Justice System?', Derek Thompson, The Atlantic, 20 June 2019: www.theatlantic.com/ideas/archive/2019/06/should-we-be-afraid-of-ai-in-the-criminal-justice-system/592084/.

317 'Predicting judicial decisions of the European Court of Human Rights: a Natural Language Processing perspective', Nikolaos Aletras, Dimitrios Tsarapatsanis, Daniel Preotiuc-Pietro and Vasileios Lampos, PeerJ Computer Science, 24 October 2016: https://peerj.com/articles/cs-93/.

or authorised by law.[318] A decision is a 'significant decision' if, in relation to a data subject, it produces an adverse legal effect concerning the data subject, or significantly affects the data subject.[319]

A charging decision, verdict or sentencing decision will significantly affect a data subject and/or produce an adverse legal effect concerning a data subject. As such, they are 'significant decisions'. These significant decisions are, arguably, required by law and/or authorised by law. Consequently, they are 'qualifying significant decisions' under section 50, and section 50(2) applies, which provides that, in relation to a qualifying significant decision based solely on automated processing, the data subject may request that the controller reconsiders the decision or takes a new decision that is not based solely on automated processing.[320]

'Taking a new decision that is not based solely on automated processing' means that the data controller needs to take a new decision on the basis of human intervention.[321] The Information Commissioner's Office ('ICO') website provides that:[322]

> 'To qualify as human intervention, you must ensure that you carefully analyse the decision and consider all the available input and output data, rather than just a token review. This should be carried out by someone who has the authority and competence to change the decision.'

Therefore, if a charging decision, verdict or sentencing decision was rendered solely by AI, an individual would effectively be able to obtain a reconsideration of the decision by a prosecutor or judge. Given that these decisions are of such gravity, with significant consequences for an individual, it is likely that, in every case where there was a positive charging decision, conviction or custodial sentence, human intervention would be requested. Thus, any efficiencies from using this AI would be defeated by the frequency of appeals to 'human judges' which, in the case of a conviction, would end up effectively being re-trials. Additionally, given the statutory one-month time limit for the reconsideration of the decision,[323] it would be very challenging for all the re-trials requested to be heard as well as usual court listings.

In considering the practical implications of rendering such decisions by AI, it seems unlikely that AI systems will be introduced to make such decisions. This is supported by the Explanatory Notes to the DPA 2018, which state that 'In practice, currently automated decision-making that leads to an adverse

318 DPA 2018, s 49(1).
319 DPA 2018, s 49(2).
320 DPA 2018, s 50(2)(b).
321 Explanatory Notes to the DPA 2018, para 204: www.legislation.gov.uk/ukpga/2018/12/pdfs/ukpgaen_20180012_en.pdf.
322 https://ico.org.uk/for-organisations/guide-to-data-protection/guide-to-law-enforcement-processing/individual-rights/right-not-to-be-subject-to-automated-decision-making/.
323 DPA 2018, s 50(3).

outcome is rarely used in the law enforcement context and is unlikely to have any operational implications'.[324]

However, were these decisions to become automated, there is an important difference between the 'robot judge' in Estonia, the ECtHR research and AI determining a verdict in England and Wales: the machine learning in the ECtHR research was based upon published judgments of the ECtHR; Estonia's 'robot judge's' learning will, presumably, be based on civil cases where reasons are given for judgments; but, in England and Wales, no reasons are given for jury verdicts. The inviolability of jury deliberations means that there is currently no rationale or reasoning data on which machine learning could be conducted. The only data available would consist of court transcripts as to witness evidence, legal arguments and summing up; documentary evidence; and the resultant verdict. The whole decision-making process would be missing from the learning process. Additionally, an AI system deciding the verdict in criminal cases would, presumably, have to be based on evidence submitted in document form as opposed to live evidence, thus radically changing the adversarial nature of the criminal justice system.

Thus, whilst it is possible to see how charging and sentencing decisions could be automated, as there is data upon which machine learning could be conducted, the same cannot be said for verdicts in criminal cases.

In addition to the DPA 2018 considerations in respect of AI decisions in the criminal justice system, the limitations of AI mean that it is not suited to making decisions in the criminal justice system. AI and algorithms are not good at dealing with ambiguity and grey areas; they do not understand context or nuance; and they are not good at making judgement calls or critical thinking.[325]

Case Study

Although AI is making strides in the detection of cancer, there is a rumour on the medical grapevine that, in the early days, rather than being taught to detect whether a patient had a potentially cancerous tumour, the AI had been taught to detect rulers.

The data that was the subject of the machine learning contained images of cancerous tumours which had been measured next to rulers (size being used as a potential indicator of cancer), whereas non-cancerous tumours were not imaged next to rulers. Thus the AI had been taught that cancerous tumours were always measured next to rulers, so if there was no ruler, there was no cancerous tumour. The AI did not understand the context of what it was

324 At para 206.

325 'AI and jobs: Where humans are better than algorithms, & vice versa', Jason Hiner, ZDNet, 3 December 2017: www.zdnet.com/article/ai-and-jobs-where-humans-are-better-than-algorithms-and-vise-versa/.

supposed to be doing, ie looking at patient data to determine whether, due to the size of a mass, they had a potentially cancerous tumour. Therefore, although a patient might have had a cancerous tumour, because it was not measured next to a ruler, the AI did not recognise it as such.

In the context of decisions in criminal cases, AI will similarly lack the context necessary to make final determinations in LPP and disclosure reviews. Although AI can recognise communications between a lawyer and client, the nuances as to the relationship and whether the content of the communication is legal advice or protected by litigation privilege, or whether the document contains anything that could undermine or assist, are more problematic for AI.

Although LPP and disclosure have established principles, their application is nuanced and calls for judgement, critical thinking, experience and context. Indeed, different lawyers may give different answers on LPP and disclosure in respect of the same document/s. If a data set being used for machine learning contains different answers as to what constitutes LPP and what is disclosable, it would seem that a narrow AI system could not be taught to properly recognise and determine what is LPP or disclosable material. Therefore, instead of using AI to make these decisions, a better system would be (similar to the case of document analysis outlined above) for AI to be used to highlight all communications between a lawyer and client so that counsel could make the ultimate LPP determinations. This does not, however, necessarily work in the case of determining disclosable documents, as what may undermine or assist requires a level of critical thinking and judgement which may be beyond what narrow AI can do.

Ignoring, for a moment, the practical and legal considerations of decisions in the criminal justice system being rendered by AI, were such decisions to be rendered by AI there would be inherent biases within the algorithms. Despite perceptions to the contrary, AI is almost always biased because of the inherent biases within the data sets provided for the machine learning: where the data has come from humans, their biases, whether conscious or subconscious, will be incorporated into the algorithms. In the legal sector, which is one of the most human sectors in society, past charging decisions, disclosure, verdicts and sentencing etc will all have been made by humans and, as such, the data set used for the machine learning will contain these biases, and the AI will display and replicate them when rendering decisions. Therefore, the AI decisions may end up being discriminatory because of the nature of the data set used.

In the Westminster Legal Policy Forum Keynote Seminar on Legal Technology in the UK,[326] Emily Loges, the Chief Executive Officer of Luminance, a leading

326 'The Changing Legal Sector – Automating Legal Services, Utilising AI and the Regulatory Framework', Emily Foges, Westminster Legal Policy Forum Keynote Seminar: Legal Technology in the UK, 2 December 2019. The attribution to Ms Foges is from the author's own notes of the event, and the transcript of the event, which speakers do not have an opportunity to review. Therefore, any mistakes, omissions or misinterpretations are entirely the fault of the author.

artificial intelligence platform for the legal profession, said that law 'is all about the human being able to analyse the information themselves based on their experience and their understanding of the world; a machine can't replace that, so don't try and make the machine replace that'. The author feels that this is a very apt description of how AI should be used within the criminal justice system; indeed, within the legal sector: it should be a tool for assistance and augmentation, not replacement.

Chapter 3

Cyber Litigation and Civil Law

In this chapter, we consider the following areas:

- cybersecurity and the legal redress available in the cases of breach of security;
- the developing regulation of online content, including online harms;
- automated vehicle development and testing;
- the protection of artificial intelligence applications and databases;
- regulation in the field of financial technology; and
- cryptoassets and smart contracts.

CYBERSECURITY

3.1 Cyberattacks leave the victims open to claims on a variety of potential bases.

This section focuses on the civil causes of action that may arise. We deal here with cybersecurity issues in a broad sense – whether they involve a failure of internal controls leading to data loss (whether personal or otherwise) or an external malefactor hacking into a system.

The personal data field, involving situations where the security breach results in the loss or misuse of personal data, is covered elsewhere in this work.[1]

Contract and tort

3.2 In many cases, there is likely to be some form of contractual arrangement between the entity which has been attacked and the person who has had their data unlawfully accessed.

In the business-to-business context, there may be specific terms governing data security. In the consumer context, there are likely to be terms of service. In either case, there may be scope for the implication of terms on the basis of a recognised need to protect sensitive data.

1 See **Chapter 4**, in particular para **4.44**.

The more interesting developments in the common law have been around causes of action in tort.

In *Google Inc v Vidal-Hall*[2] the Court of Appeal confirmed that a cause of action for misuse of private information is a tort. The case concerned the collection and usage of cookie data from private computer users by Google. The reason why the classification as a tort was important (as opposed to an equitable claim for breach of confidence) was so that permission to serve proceedings on Google out of the jurisdiction could be obtained under CPR 6.36 and Practice Direction 6B.

Although *Vidal-Hall* is not a cybersecurity case as such, its significance in that context arises from the decision that a cause of action in tort exists in addition to whatever contractual rights there may be in the hands of the individual whose private information has been unlawfully accessed. That may occur as a result of a security breach by cyberattack or where the holder of information uses it wrongfully. In such cases, there is no need to rely on an equitable obligation of confidence to establish a breach of confidence claim. Neither are the causes of action restricted to a General Data Protection Regulation ('GDPR') claim (also in tort) relating to the loss of personal data, although in many cases a personal data claim may also be available, as indeed it was in *Vidal-Hall* to those claimants.

The Supreme Court considered the issue of vicarious liability in *Wm Morrison Supermarkets Ltd v various claimants*.[3] One Mr Skelton, having developed a grudge against his employer, posted details of the entire workforce's payroll data on the internet, having only been asked to send them to an auditor. He was convicted of offences under the Computer Misuse Act 1990 and section 55 of the Data Protection Act 1998. Morrisons faced claims from the employees for breach of confidence, misuse of private information and breach of statutory duty under section 4(4) of the 1998 Act.

Overturning the High Court and the Court of Appeal, the Supreme Court set out the vicarious liability test as being whether the wrongful conduct was so closely connected with acts that the employee was authorised to do that, for the purposes of the liability of the employer to third parties, it might fairly and properly be regarded as done by the employee while acting in the ordinary course of their employment.

An unbroken chain of causation, from his being given the data and his posting it on the internet, was insufficient to establish liability on the part of the employer for Skelton's actions. The posting did not form part of his 'field of activities' and his motive for the wrongdoing was not irrelevant, because it was important to know whether he was acting on his employer's business or for personal reasons. He was pursuing a personal vendetta and so he could not fairly and properly be regarded as acting in the ordinary course of his employment.

2 [2015] EWCA Civ 311.
3 [2020] UKSC 12.

However, and importantly for the non-GDPR and non-DPA 2018 causes of action in relation to cybersecurity, the Supreme Court rejected Morrisons' argument that the Data Protection Act 1998 excluded vicarious liability for the breaches claimed – and not just for the claim under that Act. It is not inconsistent with a statutory obligation on a data controller that vicarious liability is imposed (which may involve no fault) on the employer. As a result, there is no bar in principle, in an appropriate case, to vicarious liability for a cybersecurity breach being established in accordance with the law as clarified by the Supreme Court.

Other sources of cybersecurity law

Communications Act 2003

3.3 The Communications Act 2003 imposes requirements on providers of public electronic communications networks and public electronic communications services to take technical and organisational measures to manage risk to security of those networks and services.[4]

The measures required include:

- preventing or minimising the impact of security incidents on end-users; and
- preventing or minimising the impact of security incidents on the interconnection of networks.

In the case of a breach of security having a significant impact on the operation of a network, or a reduction in the availability of a network with a significant impact, a provider must notify Ofcom.

Ofcom has published guidance, updated in 2017, on the measures that providers must take.[5]

Section 105D(2) creates a statutory duty to comply with sections 105A to 105C which is owed 'to every person who may be affected by a contravention of a requirement'.

In addition, Ofcom has enforcement powers as follows:

- to notify regulated providers of contraventions;
- to gather information from regulated providers;
- to Issue directions suspending the entitlement to provide networks or services; and
- to impose fines up to £2,000,000.

4 Communications Act 2003, ss 105A–105D.

5 'Ofcom guidance on the security requirements in sections 105A to D of the Communications Act 2003', 2017 version.

Privacy and Electronic Communications (EC Directive) Regulations 2003

3.4 The Privacy and Electronic Communications (EC Directive) Regulations 2003 ('PECR', as amended) implement the E-Privacy Directive[6] into UK law. The ICO is responsible for enforcing and overseeing the PECR.

The E-Privacy Directive is set to be replaced by an EU e-Privacy Regulation, currently in draft and not finalised in time for the implementation of the GDPR on 25 May 2018.

The PECR require communications service providers to take appropriate technical and organisational measures to safeguard the security of their services in order:

- to ensure that personal data can be accessed only by authorised personnel for legally authorised purposes;
- to protect personal data stored or transmitted against:
  - accidental or unlawful destruction;
  - accidental loss or alteration; or
  - unauthorised or unlawful storage, processing, access or disclosure; and
- to ensure the implementation of a security policy regarding the processing of personal data.[7]

If a personal data breach occurs, the service provider has certain obligations aimed at safeguarding the personal data.

It must notify the ICO of the breach,[8] except in a case where the provider has demonstrated to the ICO's satisfaction that it has implemented appropriate technological protection measures which render the data unintelligible to any person who is not authorised to access it, and that those measures were applied to the data concerned in that breach.[9] The ICO has issued detailed guidance on how to respond to a security breach and how to report it. The provider is also required to maintain a log of personal data breaches to enable the ICO to verify compliance with the PECR.[10]

The service provider must notify the individuals concerned of the breach without undue delay after its detection, if the breach is likely to adversely affect the personal data or privacy of a subscriber or user.[11]

6 Directive 2002/58/EC.
7 PECR, reg 5(1) and (1A).
8 PECR, reg 5A(2), (4) and (5).
9 PECR, reg 5A(6).
10 PECR, reg 5A(8).
11 PECR, reg 5A(3).

The ICO has powers to enforce the PECR which mirror those set out under the Data Protection Act 1998.[12] These include the power of audit of providers, of enforcement notices, information notices and monetary penalty notices of up to £500,000, the power to prosecute for failure to comply with a notice, and the power to conduct 'dawn raid' search and seizure investigations with a warrant.

A failure to comply with the requirement to notify a breach is limited to a fixed monetary penalty notice of a maximum of £1,000.[13]

An individual who suffers damage as a result of a breach of the PECR is given a right of action against the service provider for a claim for compensation.[14]

Network and Information Systems Regulations 2018

3.5 The Network and Information Systems Regulations 2018 ('NIS Regulations') transpose the EU's Network and Information Security Directive of 2016[15] ('Cybersecurity Directive') into UK law. They apply to two types of operator: relevant digital service providers ('RDSPs'); and operators of essential services ('OESs').

RDSPs and OESs are operators and services which play a vital economic role. The aim of the NIS Regulations is therefore to achieve a minimum level of security standards for the protection of the network and information systems.

OESs are within the key sectors of energy, transport, health, drinking water supply and distribution and digital infrastructure. Schedule 2 to the NIS Regulations specifies the requirements in these sectors.

Banking and financial market infrastructure is not within the scope of the NIS Regulations as essential services (although they are within the scope of the Cybersecurity Directive), on the grounds that the standards set by the Bank of England and the FCA are analogous and sufficient.

The ICO regulates RDSPs. These are entities satisfying all of the following conditions:

- providing one or more of the following in the UK:
  - an online marketplace;
  - an online search engine; and
  - a cloud computing service;

12 PECR, reg 31.
13 PECR, reg 5C.
14 PECR, reg 30.
15 Directive (EU) 2016/1148.

- employing more than 50 persons with an annual turnover and/or balance sheet total exceeding EUR 10 million; and
- having either a head office in the UK or a nominated representative established in the UK.

RDSPs must also self-identify and were obliged to register with the ICO by 1 November 2018, or within three months of meeting the criteria if after that date.[16]

The obligations of OESs and RDSPs differ somewhat under the NIS Regulations, but they have two major goals:

- to have technical and organisational measures in place, having regard to the available technology (the 'state of the art'), to manage the risks to the security of their network and minimise the impact of incidents with a view to ensuring continuity;[17] and
- to notify the competent authority without delay and no later than 72 hours after an incident which has a significant impact on the service.[18]

In relation to OESs, the NIS Regulations set out sector-specific regulation.[19] As stated above, the ICO is the competent authority for all RDSPs. It has issued guidance which is available on its website and which it states 'may also be useful for OES'.

EU member states set their own financial penalty rules under the Cybersecurity Directive. In the UK, these do not follow the formula of a percentage of global annual turnover, unlike the GDPR. The tiers of fine are set out in the NIS Regulations[20] and operate as upper limits based on the type of contravention.

The maximum fine of £17 million is for a material contravention which the relevant enforcement authority determines has caused, or could cause, an incident resulting in an immediate threat to life or significant adverse impact on the UK economy.

There is nothing to prevent penalties being imposed under the NIS Regulations and other provisions (for example, GDPR) in relation to the same event.

The financial services sector

3.6 As noted above, the financial services sector was excluded from the scope of the NIS Regulations because those entities that are regulated by the FCA have

16 NIS Regulations, reg 14.
17 NIS Regulations, reg 10 for OES, reg 12 for RDSP.
18 NIS Regulations, reg 11 for OES, reg 12 for RDSP.
19 See NIS Regulations, reg 3(1) and Sch 1.
20 NIS Regulations, reg 18.

standards put in place within the FCA Handbook which directly or indirectly cover cybersecurity. The measures are for management, governance, systems and controls and are aimed at security, risk management, financial crime reduction and client confidentiality. The third Principle for Business in the FCA Handbook (PRIN 2.1.1) requires a firm to 'take reasonable care to organise and control its affairs responsibly and effectively, with adequate risk management systems'.

The Senior Management Arrangements, Systems and Controls ('SYSC') are more detailed, and of particular relevance in this context are:

- SYSC 3 Systems and controls;
- SYSC 4 General organisational requirements;
- SYSC 6.1 Compliance;
- SYSC 7 Risk control; and
- SYSC 8 Outsourcing.

The FCA is responsible for enforcement of its Handbook. Large fines have arisen in the past for failures to implement systems or controls resulting in loss of customer data – for example, against Zurich Insurance plc in 2010 for loss by an inadequately supervised subcontractor of an unencrypted back-up tape with the data of 46,000 customers (a fine of almost £2.3 million).

THE REGULATION OF ONLINE CONTENT

3.7 The prevention of harm has become the focus of developing content regulation in the online space.

This section draws on three sources to describe the likely shape of future litigation:[21]

- the ICO's Age Appropriate Design Code;
- the Government's Online Harms White Paper; and
- the Department for Digital, Media, Culture and Sport's Report on Immersive and Addictive Technologies

Age Appropriate Design Code

3.8 The Information Commissioner's Office issued a draft code of practice for consultation on 15 April 2019 under the obligation contained in section 123

21 Readers should also bear in mind the EU's current consultation on a new Digital Services Act to replace the existing E-Commerce Directive 2000/31/EC. This is promised to contain illegal content rules for online platforms. We have not sought to deal with it here, due to the uncertainty of Brexit and the fact that consultation is at a very early stage.

of the Data Protection Act 2018 to prepare such a code on standards of age-appropriate design. The goal is the regulation of online material that is likely to be accessed by children.

The resulting Age Appropriate Design Code ('AADC') was laid before Parliament on 12 August 2020 and came into force on 2 September 2020. There will be a transition period of 12 months, after which the Commissioner must take the code into account in considering whether obligations under the GDPR and the PECR have been met.

'Information society service' is a phrase derived from EU jurisprudence and means 'any service normally provided for remuneration, at a distance, by electronic means and at the individual request of a recipient of services'.[22] The AADC makes it clear that the remuneration need not come directly from the end user but could be funded by other means, such as advertising. The vast majority of online content and modes of access will be covered, whether on websites, gaming apps or social media.

The AADC applies to 'relevant information society services', which means organisations processing personal data to which the GDPR applies and which are not 'preventive or counselling services'.[23]

The AADC interprets the statutory phrase 'likely to be accessed by children' (defined as under-18s) as meaning that the possibility of access by children is 'more probable than not'. The focus is said to be on services which children use in reality. The guidance thus goes well beyond services aimed solely at children.

The Code itself is contained in 15 Standards for online services. The first Standard is that 'the best interests of the child should be a primary consideration' in developing and designing relevant online services. We believe that it is likely to be difficult to give this phrase any real meaning in litigation. The 'primary consideration' is not restricted to the prevention of harm and requires designers to imagine the 'best interests' of some child devoid of any particular characteristics. This Standard is only likely to be meaningful in cases of obvious harm or failure of best practice, which are capable of being defined otherwise both within and outside the Code. As such, the 'primary consideration' and 'best interests' phrasing are unlikely to take any argument in litigation any further.

Many of the other Standards are much more helpful – for example, those on geolocation (which begins 'Switch geolocation options off by default …') and default settings ('Settings must be "high privacy" by default …'). The ICO's remit of data protection gives rise to three linked issues that the AADC attempts to balance:

22 Article 1(1)(b) of EU Directive 2015/1535 laying down a procedure for the provision of information in the field of technical regulations and of rules on Information Society services; referred to in GDPR, Article 4(25).

23 DPA 2018, s 123.

(1) The privacy rights of children are capable of competing with the protection and support potentially available from parents. Standard 11 'Parental controls' is for the provision of age appropriate information to the child about the existence of such controls and an obvious sign to the child if and when they are being monitored.

(2) The sharing of data gathered for the (minimised) purposes of the online access is a standard GDPR issue which is covered by Standard 9 'Data sharing'. But this does not cover the sharing of personal data in an unguarded way in chatrooms and forums within games, and the onward usage to which such personal data might be put by other players or other actors.

(3) Standards 8 'Data minimisation' and 12 'Profiling' restrict privacy risks arising from the collection of children's personal data. The Profiling Standard asserts that, 'Data protection law … does make you responsible for the content you serve to children who use your service, based on your use of their personal data'. On the other hand, the same Standard recognises 'the rights of children to access information from the media'.

These are tensions which, as we suggest in respect of the AADC in general, are likely to create significant work not just for the gaming industry but for most content providers, and which could well result in litigation around the meaning and effect of the Standards.

Online Harms White Paper

3.9 In April 2019 the Government[24] presented its Online Harms White Paper to Parliament. At the time of writing, the potential legislation has reached the stage of an initial response to the ensuing public consultation.[25] There has been criticism of the pace of progress, but the following paragraphs set out the direction of travel.

The harms identified in the White Paper encompassed content and activity, including child sexual abuse material, terrorist content, hate crimes, harassment and cyberbullying, and misinformation and disinformation.

The central plan for regulation was to impose a statutory duty of care and to appoint a regulator to oversee it. The intention remains to appoint Ofcom as the online harms regulator in reliance on its experience with the sector. Although there are no specifics on the sanctioning powers that might be made available, the various options mentioned include fines, the imposition of personal liability on senior managers, the obligatory improvement of systems, and ISP blocking.

24 Jointly in the person of the Home Secretary and the Secretary of State for Digital, Culture, Media and Sport.
25 Published on 21 February 2020.

The new duty of care would apply to any online service that facilitates the hosting, sharing or discovery of user-generated content or facilitates online interactions between users. Business-to-business services would fall outside the scope.

The duty would be to ensure that companies can react to harmful content by having appropriate systems and processes in place. The intention is for a different approach to illegal content and activity (eg criminal sexual content and hate crimes) from the approach to harmful but legal content, such as cyberbullying. While illegal content would have to be removed expeditiously, the duty in respect of legal content would merely be to state publicly what is unacceptable on the service, and to enforce this. This could be set out in the terms of service. Freedom of expression would be protected to the extent that providers define what is acceptable, and keep to those rules.

The intention is to provide a higher standard of protection for children from inappropriate content by requiring age verification technologies. This goes hand-in-hand with transparency requirements on providers enforced by way of annual reports on the types of harmful content and the effectiveness of the enforcement processes.

The House of Lords Select Committee on Democracy and Digital Technologies has separately produced its own report which engages with many of these issues and which criticises the Government's approach in many instances.[26]

In particular, it is said that the Government's proposals do not go far enough in making platforms directly responsible for the content they host, and that legal content such as misinformation and disinformation should still be regulated. Inaccurate political advertising should be controlled and powers created to ban and remove it. These measures are seen as important safeguards for democracy.

Select Committee Report on Immersive and Addictive Technologies

3.10 On 12 September 2019 the Digital, Culture, Media and Sport Select Committee of the House of Commons published its report 'Immersive and Addictive Technologies'[27] and the Government published its Response in June 2020.

The Report offers the following definition of immersive technology:

> 'Immersive technologies integrate virtual content with the physical environment, thus "immersing" the user in a simulated experience. The term often refers to technologies such as virtual and augmented reality, which offer varying levels of immersion in digital worlds.'

26 'Digital Technology and the Resurrection of Trust', 29 June 2020.

27 Fifteenth Report of Session 2017–19.

The concept of 'addiction' in the Report does not have an exclusively clinical meaning and it is not co-extensive with an identifiable harm. The Report asserts that there is a 'newly established concept of online harms'.[28] In our view, certainly as far as mental health issues are concerned, such an assertion may not be of much use to litigators without some form of regulatory backing. Before that arrives, they will have to rely on traditional legal concepts of harm, financial or physical, and transpose them into the online context.

Particular types of online harm

3.11 The remainder of this section deals with the position on various specific forms of online harm, as informed by the sources set out above.

Excessive screen time

3.12 According to the sources mentioned in this section, the problem of excessive screen time is wider in scope than the addictive properties of games, and is not restricted to children – no comfort for parents of teenagers everywhere who are growing up with their eyes fixed on a screen of one sort or another.

The AADC suggests that service providers should 'consider nudging children in ways that support their health and wellbeing'.[29] The detail refers to features which promote taking breaks and pausing and saving – aspects with most relevance to gaming. These kinds of suggestions arguably go beyond the ICO's remit of personal data. They do not sit easily with the rewards provided by many games for continuous play, ultimately leading the player to make purchases. For many online games, such suggestions come into conflict with the business model.

The DCMS Select Committee's view is that the AADC does not fully deal with the problem of disordered technology use, because it is aimed at protecting children and not adults.[30] As has been argued above, it is not wholly clear what kind of online harm is actually being targeted, and on what basis. There is clearly concern around 'nudged' detrimental behaviour in gaming or social media use, without a clear picture of what counts as detrimental in this context.

The current state of play appears to be to place a great deal of hope in the kind of regulation envisaged by the White Paper and the imposition of an overarching duty of care.

28 At para 14.

29 Standard 13 'Nudge techniques'.

30 Select Committee Report, para 156.

Problem gaming

3.13 The World Health Organisation ('WHO') formally designated 'gaming disorder' in 2018 and describes it as follows:

> 'Gaming disorder is defined in the 11th Revision of the International Classification of Diseases (ICD-11) as a pattern of gaming behaviour ("digital-gaming" or "video-gaming") characterized by impaired control over gaming, increasing priority given to gaming over other activities to the extent that gaming takes precedence over other interests and daily activities, and continuation or escalation of gaming despite the occurrence of negative consequences.
>
> For gaming disorder to be diagnosed, the behaviour pattern must be of sufficient severity to result in significant impairment in personal, family, social, educational, occupational or other important areas of functioning and would normally have been evident for at least 12 months.'[31]

The designation is not without controversy by reason, as has been argued, of an unfavourable comparison with the more substantial evidential basis for other forms of addiction, including their prevalence and symptoms.[32] The WHO has not backed up its classification with any published report – the e-sports industry has been particularly critical of 'singling out' gaming in this way.[33] The commercial interests are powerful: in 2016 the games sector directly employed 20,340 people and contributed £1.25bn in gross value added to the economy.[34]

With that background, and perhaps unsurprisingly, the DCMS Select Committee Report notes that games companies are unwilling and purportedly unable to tackle problematic gaming. In its recommendations, the Report goes no further than summarising the evidence from various experts and calling for further study and debate, but with a call for mandatory data sharing and financial contributions by the industry to such studies. The Government makes no such commitments in its Response.

In respect of gaming, potential litigators are therefore left with a situation analogous to the earliest days of concerns about the tobacco industry: an uncertain evidential basis for causation, an unwillingness by the industry to accept a duty of care, powerful commercial interests, and the absence of any clear path to establishing the nature and extent of any harm caused.

31 www.who.int: 'What is Gaming Disorder?'.

32 See eg Hans-Jürgen Rumpf, et al., 'Including gaming disorder in the ICD-11: The need to do so from a clinical and public health perspective, Commentary on: A weak scientific basis for gaming disorder: Let us err on the side of caution (van Rooij et al., 2018),' Journal of Behavioral Addictions, vol 7.3 (16 July 2018).

33 See www.ukie.org.uk (website of the Association for UK Interactive Entertainment) statement on 'the inclusion of gaming disorder in the WHO's ICD-11', published 20 May 2019.

34 Source: BFI, 'Screen Business: How tax incentives help power economic growth across the UK', October 2018.

Online age ratings

3.14 The physical distribution of games is regulated under the Video Recordings Act 1984 (as amended), which creates a classification system and provides for criminal offences in the event of breach by physical discs being sold to gamers below the ages of 12, 16 or 18, as the case may be.[35] It applies to devices capable of storing media.[36] The Act has thus been outmoded by changing technology, so that games published and played online (with or without a purchase) do not fall within its regime.

One option for regulation, therefore, is to extend the 1984 Act regime to cover online games. The Government's Response has been to state that a majority of video games platforms already use the Pan European Game Information ('PEGI') and International Age Rating Coalition ('IARC') ratings and best practice guidelines, in the same way that physical discs use them. There has been no commitment to legislate in the area before further assessment of voluntary compliance takes place.

The impact of the AADC in this area, we suggest, is not likely to be limited to games with a rating below 18. The AADC does indeed state that it 'should not lead to the perverse outcome of providers of restricted services having to make their services child-friendly'.

The difficulty is as to what enforceable regime there is to restrict usage and whether that prevents the real-world situation (which the AADC is keen to bear in mind) of older children accessing 18-rated games. It may be that these requirements will end up in more use of AI to detect the age of the player (or wider user of online content) as part of more sophisticated age verification techniques.

'Loot boxes' and in-game purchases

3.15 Any link between gambling-type plays within games and the wider effects on health, particularly that of children, is not currently well understood. The lament of the DCMS Select Committee is that this is because the data which might assist academics in conducting such research is held by gaming companies.[37]

An example of such plays is 'loot boxes'. These are 'items in video games that may be bought for real-world money, but which provide players with a randomised reward of uncertain value' for use within the game.[38] They are a major source of

35 Video Recordings Act 1984, ss 9–15.
36 As defined in VRA 1984, s 1.
37 Select Committee Report, paras 71–72.
38 David Zendle, Rachel Meyer, Stuart Waters, Paul Cairns, 'The prevalence of loot boxes in mobile and desktop games', Society for the Study of Addiction (14 January 2020): https://doi.org/10.1111/add.14973.

revenue for gaming companies, the model for monetisation being that the game is free to download and play but offers in-game purchases for faster or more entertaining progress.

It is important to be clear that the issue of loot boxes within games is separate from that of gambling websites and online platforms where the predominant purpose is the placing of a bet or the playing of a game of chance or mixed skill and chance. The distinction argued for, in the online games context, is that the option is given to the player to make purchases which, although in terms of their decision-making character are arguably akin to gambling, often look and feel somewhat different, and are merely incidental to the gameplay.

There are essentially two types of legal approach to the issue. The first tries to capture the true nature of the transaction and proceed from there. This approach argues that loot boxes are no different to a slot machine or a 'one-armed bandit'. There is said to be an addictive thrill to the sensation of a near miss from the hoped-for reward.

The difficulty is that this kind of characterisation, especially in the absence of good scientific data, is open to a high margin of interpretation fuelled by metaphor. The Association for UK Interactive Entertainment (ukie), which represents the e-sports industry, submitted evidence to the Select Committee, stating that 'there is a clear distinction between our industry and the gambling industry which we will continue to work actively with the regulatory authorities to maintain'.[39] Other evidence characterised loot boxes as 'surprise mechanics'[40] – they are fun, like a Kinder egg or an unopened physical pack of football trading cards, and harmless.

An alternative argument is that the slot machine analogy is simply false. Unlike the slot machine user starting with a handful of coins and ending up empty-handed, the loot box purchaser always receives a reward – it is just that the precise nature of the reward is unknown at the point of purchase.

Nonetheless, a focus on the essential character of the loot box has resulted in legislation in some jurisdictions. The Dutch Betting and Gambling Authority has concluded that loot box rewards do not meet the legal definition of a gambling 'prize' under the relevant legislation, on the grounds that they cannot be traded outside the game – this in a jurisdiction where, historically, online gambling websites have not been able to obtain licences.[41] Belgian legislation circumvents the issue entirely by applying a subjective test of value to the notion of a gambling prize, which, by the industry's own lights, would be met in the gaming context. Subjectively, the gamer would surely attach at least a 'fun' value.

39 Available at data.parliament.uk at IMM0023, para 3(c).

40 Select Committee Report, para 78.

41 Although the position has now moved on with the Dutch Remote Gaming Act of 2019.

In the UK, the first approach involves identifying whether, as a matter of law, the purchase of loot boxes is caught by section 6 of the Gambling Act 2005. There is a risk of terminological confusion in the context of the present discussion, in that one of the activities regulated by the Act is 'gaming', which is defined as 'playing a game of chance for a prize', where 'prize' means 'money or money's worth'.[42] On this basis, a website devoted to betting and gaming of the obviously 'roulette wheel' type is licensable and is regulated by the 2005 Act.

The view of the Gambling Commission is that the purchase of loot boxes is not licensable gambling because they have no real-world value outside the game, and therefore do not count as 'money or money's worth'.

One criticism of this view is that items acquired in this way have a real value to players of the game. In a game of sufficient scope in terms of co-participants, there seems to be no reason why players could not trade game items for real currency. Indeed, evidence given to the Select Committee is to the effect that gaming companies employ staff and ban players in an effort to prevent real-world trading of game artefacts.[43] The phenomenon of 'skin betting' is one where items acquired in-game are used as payment for an unlicensed bet outside the game. There may also be parallels with cryptocurrency, in that genuine objective real-world value can ultimately be ascertained through the operation of market forces.

The second approach is to focus on the harm resulting from the game methodology. This is more sophisticated than a reliance on the disputed or poorly evidenced psychological effects. It also involves what is alleged to be a kind of unfairness through deception of an enticing-looking object – judging a book by its cover, perhaps.

A class action was launched in the US at the end of February 2019 against the popular online game Fortnite, based upon the allegation that its loot boxes, held out by llamas displaying thought bubbles containing a prime reward, in reality had 'undisclosed, abysmal odds' of the gamer receiving that reward.[44] Fortnite apparently made its makers, Epic Games, US$2.4 billion in 2018.[45]

The class action is based on California's Consumer Legal Remedies Act, False Advertising Law and Unfair Competition Law, and is a claim in unjust enrichment for injunctive and monetary relief, including compensatory and punitive damages. It alleges that the minor plaintiffs became hooked on spending via the unfair practice of coding aimed at predatory monetisation.

42 Gambling Act 2005, s 6(1) and (5).

43 Select Committee Report, para 90.

44 *RA, a minor v Epic Games Inc* US District Court, Central District of California, Case 2:19-cv-01488-GW-E.

45 Epic Games also faces US copyright lawsuits over its alleged appropriation of famous dance moves 'Milly Rock' and 'flossing': respectively *Redd v Epic Games Inc*; *Ribeiro v Epic Games Inc*.

Readers planning similar schemes may wonder whether a thinking llama is guaranteed to extract money from online dupes, or whether another high-functioning ungulate would be more deceptive.

This suggests some challenges waiting to be made by sufficiently determined litigators.

First, there is the challenge under the existing law, despite the view of the Gambling Commission, that loot boxes amount to money's worth and therefore give rise to licensing obligations under the existing UK regime.

Secondly, the question arises of whether gaming companies have enforced their own terms of service adequately. The fact, as noted above, that companies deploy measurable resources in doing so already could point towards various enforceable obligations as between the gamer and the company.

These obligations may not necessarily be founded solely on a breach of contract in the form of the terms of service. The AADC requires providers to uphold their own 'published terms, policies and community standards (including but not limited to privacy policies, age restriction, behaviour rules and content policies' (Standard 6 'Policies and Community Standards').

This line can be seen as an offshoot of the second approach to regulation, in that it seeks to deploy law which uncontroversially applies to the relationship between the gamer and the publisher – here, the law of contract, or the applicable regulatory Standards – and marshals the facts to build a case, for example, for breach of contract, misuse of private information or breach of the DPA 2018.

If the current UK licensing regime were extended to games involving loot boxes, it would impose obligations around transparency, duty of care and age restrictions on gaming companies which they do not currently have, backed up by the threat, as in Belgium, of criminal sanctions. There may be political difficulties with extending the regime in this way, given the commercial interests at stake, and it may be that a different form of regulation is ultimately settled upon.

Any form of regulation risks disturbing the business model of games which are free to play but rely on in-game purchases for revenue. There remains the possibility that gaming companies may reduce or cease altogether their reliance on this form of monetisation. On the other hand, one suggestion for compromise is to make the contents of loot boxes, or at least their odds, fully transparent.[46] In Japan, there is a system of self-regulation and standard setting by codes of practice, rather than hard legal regulation.

46 This is understood to be the position in China.

In the meantime, the UK Government has committed to reviewing the Gambling Act 2005, and has called for evidence on its extension to the loot box phenomenon.[47]

E-sports

3.16 E-sports is a growing industry and one in which, combined with games software development, the UK has historically been in a strong position. There is a mix of voluntary codes of conduct.

As yet, the prospect of further regulation of this arena is aspirational. The language of the Select Committee report and the Government's response is, again, that of the duty of care model adopted by other sports, focused on preventing exploitation and ensuring integrity of competition and player well-being.

DEVELOPMENT OF AUTOMATED VEHICLES

3.17 The common label of 'driverless cars' does not completely capture the developing technology in automated driving. The extent to which modern cars are already cyber-enabled is striking. Common features include built-in satellite navigation, parking sensors, tyre-pressure warnings and cruise control. The quantum leap, of course, is to fully automated vehicles in which a driver is not necessary at all.

The policy context

3.18 Contrary to what might be imagined, one factor in favour of automated driving is the belief that it will increase road safety. This is on the basis, according to the European Commission, for example, that human error is involved in more than 90% of all traffic accidents.[48] Intelligent transport systems (or 'road telematics') are also seen as an important feature of a 'smart city' capable of addressing public issues through ICT-based solutions.[49]

In the UK, the relevant agencies are the Department for Transport ('DfT') and the Centre for Connected and Autonomous Vehicles (a joint policy unit of the DfT and the Department for Business, Energy and Industrial Strategy). In February 2015, the DfT published 'The Pathway to Driverless Cars', setting out a strategy to update UK laws and regulations to allow automated vehicles to be sold to the

47 In the Queen's Speech of 19 December 2019 and in its Response to the DCMS Select Committee Report.

48 www.europa.eu: 'Intelligent Transport Systems'.

49 European Parliament Directorate-General for Internal Policies, 'Mapping Smart Cities in the EU', published January 2014.

public, but also to encourage the relevant industries to base themselves in the UK for the development and manufacture of the technologies involved.

This was before the Brexit vote.

The main action points were as follows:

- to develop a code of practice for testing automated vehicles; and
- to review and amend domestic legislation in order to:
  - clarify liabilities in the event of a collision;
  - amend regulation on the use of vehicles, such as MOT requirements and the Highway Code; and
  - consider whether higher standards of safety are required, in particular to deal with possible cyber threats.

The Law Commission of England and Wales and the Scottish Law Commission have issued two joint consultations as part of a three-year review.

In the November 2018 exercise, the focus was on safety by design in the following ways:

- issues relating to the vehicles themselves, training for users (ie beyond the current driving test), accident investigation and the proper regulator for these;
- the rules of the road and protocols for the expected reactions built into the driverless car's AI (for example, when an emergency vehicle passes); and
- criminal and civil liability, including civil liability under the Automated and Electric Vehicles Act 2018.

For present purposes, the most important of the results, which came in June 2019, were that the Government could start work on safety assurance whereby unauthorised systems could be made unlawful and the implementation of the Automated and Electric Vehicles Act 2018 could be supported. The 2018 Act received Royal Assent on 19 July 2018 but most of its sections are yet to come into force.

The second exercise, commencing in October 2019, dealt with:

- public transport and other passenger services, suggesting a new regulatory regime for Highly Automated Road Passenger Services ('HARPS') – although responses concerning freight were also invited;
- responsibility for insurance, maintenance and supervision in the case of personal vehicles where passengers are involved; and
- questions of safety by operation (as opposed to by design), in the sense of the ability of remote HARPS operators to ensure proper supervision.

The questions brought forward by these consultations are a useful introduction to the legal issues that arise in this field. Perhaps the most interesting possibility is the suggestion that an automated driving system would be proposed for regulatory authorisation by an entity – for example, the vehicle manufacturer or the software developer, or a combination of such interests – to be known as the Automated Driving System Entity ('ADSE'). The Law Commissions do not rule out the possibility that the ADSE could be the HARPS operator.

On that basis, the defendant in some road traffic claims, the likes of which are seen daily in county courts up and down the country, would not be a private or public mass transport company, but could be the ADSE.

The responses to the second consultation were published on 20 May 2020.[50] The Commissions intend to publish a third consultation in 2020 before gathering all the results for final presentation in 2021.

Testing of automated vehicles

3.19 The DfT's view in 2015[51] was that testing of an automated vehicle on public roads in the UK is lawful, as long as there is a test driver present to be responsible for its safe operation. The further assumption is that the vehicle is capable of being used compatibly with road traffic law. There is no limitation on the location of testing. The test driver has to have a licence and the testing company must be insured in the normal way.

This relaxed approach, and the fact that the set-up is capable of being analysed in accordance with existing law, puts the UK at odds with many other countries. In some US states, there is a requirement for a surety bond. In some countries, driverless technology is prohibited on the basis of their existing law and the Vienna Convention on Road Traffic. This states that 'every moving vehicle or combination of vehicles shall have a driver' and that 'every driver shall at all times, be able to control his vehicle'. The UK signed but did not ratify this Convention.

The Japanese approach has been to issue special licence plates to allow testing on public roads since 2013. In the US, a car without a human driver was not considered roadworthy until, in February 2016, the US National Highway Traffic Safety Administration stated that it would consider non-human AI to be a 'driver' under the Federal Motor Vehicle Safety Standards.

In keeping with that light touch approach, in July 2015 the UK Government published a non-binding 'Code of practice for testing of automated vehicle technologies', which emphasises the importance of safety. It states that testing on public roads should only follow extensive testing on the test track. It reminds the

50 www.lawcom.gov.uk: 'Automated Vehicles Consultation'.

51 Department for Transport: 'The Pathway to Driverless Cars', 2015.

reader that automated vehicles must still comply with the current law governing road traffic, the licensing of drivers and the roadworthiness of vehicles,

On 6 February 2019 an updated version of the Code, 'Code of Practice: Automated vehicle trialling', was published. This is still under consultation.

As with many such non-binding codes, there is potential evidential value in a litigation context of the best-practice style standards and expectations set out. A failure to comply in testing is relevant, we suggest, to establishing liability where there is scope for a factual assessment. We outline some of these areas below.

The legal issues

Vehicle approval, standards and maintenance

3.20 Although the EU has issued various Directives, harmonisation at a European level in this field remains some way off, and of course it is unclear how the UK will adapt after Brexit. The overarching position in the EU, for vehicle approval in general, is set out in the Framework Directive 2007/46/EC. The Intelligent Transport Systems Directive (2010/40/EU) provides the Commission with powers for the adoption of technical and organisational specifications for intelligent transport systems in the EU.

The general approach in the UK has been that existing law is sufficient to encompass automated vehicles. Such vehicles remain subject to the Road Vehicles (Construction and Use) Regulations 1986. The various policy sources detailed above envisage that the MOT test and the Highway Code can simply be reviewed and adapted.[52]

Design features

3.21 The Code of Practice deals with two specific design features which are likely to be highly relevant to future litigation.

Where a vehicle is not fully automated, there will be a transition at some point between modes so that the driver can take manual control, particularly in an emergency situation. The Code sets out requirements for the transition system around its being easy and clear to understand, giving the driver sufficient warning of which mode is operational and when a switch is needed, and allowing a quick transition to manual operation when necessary.

The Code also deals with what should happen in the event of systems failures. There should be an audible warning for the driver. The vehicle should be designed

52 See, in particular, the DfT's 2015 review.

so that, if there is a failure in the system for automated braking or steering, it can achieve a 'minimal risk condition' by acting in a way which brings itself out of danger, such as an emergency stop or avoidance manoeuvre.

Cybersecurity

3.22 Driverless cars will rely on data and communications networks and will therefore be at risk from cyberattacks.

In August 2017 the Government published its principles for vehicle cybersecurity:[53]

- organisation security is owned, governed and promoted at board level;
- security risks are assessed and managed appropriately and proportionately, including those specific to the supply chain;
- organisations need product aftercare and incident response, to ensure that systems are secure over their lifetime;
- all organisations, including sub-contractors, suppliers and potential third parties, work together to enhance the security of the system;
- systems are designed using a defence-in-depth approach;
- security of all software is managed throughout its lifetime;
- storage and transmission of data is secure and can be controlled; and
- systems are designed to be resilient to attacks and respond appropriately when their defences or sensors fail.

The British Standards Institute has also published a new dedicated cybersecurity standard, which has been endorsed by the DfT.[54]

Liability and insurance

3.23 The Automated and Electric Vehicles Act 2018 defines 'automated vehicles' as those 'designed or adapted to be capable, at least in some circumstances or situations, of safely driving themselves', and such vehicles are kept on a list by the Secretary of State identifying them by type, by reference to a registration document, or in some other way.[55] The existence of a list should make it straightforward to establish whether the legal provisions applicable to such vehicles are in play.

The Act provides for liability in the event of an accident causing damage by a vehicle when 'driving itself': the insurer is liable if the vehicle is insured, and

53 'The key principles of vehicle cyber security for connected and automated vehicles', 6 August 2017.

54 PAS 1885:2018: 'The fundamental principles of automotive cyber security. Specification'.

55 Automated and Electric Vehicles Act 2018, s 1.

the owner is liable if not. Liability cannot be excluded by a policy,[56] with caveats enabling a policy to limit liability and for the insurer to recover from the insured person if safety-critical software updates were not made, or if software alterations which were prohibited under the policy were made.[57] The law of contributory negligence is preserved, with a clarification that the owner or insurer is not liable to the person in charge of the automated vehicle if the accident was 'wholly due' to the latter allowing the vehicle to begin driving itself 'when it was not appropriate to do so'.[58]

On the basis of the 2018 Act's outline, the remaining areas of doubt seem to us to be:

- When will an automated vehicle be 'driving itself'? Presumably, this will be either defined in regulations or left to a factual assessment.
- When will an automated vehicle be deemed to have caused an accident?
- How will the obligations to update software be interpreted? Will there be any margin for error by the owner?

More broadly, what is noticeable by its absence is any specific reference in this Act to the software or vehicle manufacturer. Our view is that the Act simply leaves in place any potential argument for a contribution against the manufacturers that might have existed in relation to vehicles which are not automated.

Data protection and privacy

3.24 The Information Commissioner's Office stated, relatively early on, that collision data, telematics, geolocation data and driver settings are likely to be personal data.[59] The various considerations under the GDPR and Data Protection Act 2018 are likely to be relevant to any transmission or storage of such data.[60]

This presents a real practical issue, given that the infrastructure for automated vehicles will require roadside communication points and even, potentially, communications capability between vehicles.

ARTIFICIAL INTELLIGENCE AND DATABASES

3.25 We consider the topic of artificial intelligence from the perspective of the developing law of the protection of valuable data. This has to be distinguished from the separate legal regime of the GDPR – although, of course, AI can and

56 2018 Act, s 2.
57 2018 Act, s 4.
58 2018 Act, ss 3 and 5.
59 'ICO's response to the government's consultation on the testing infrastructure', 9 September 2016.
60 See paras **4.19** to **4.31**.

does engage with information which counts as personal data under the GDPR and the DPA 2018.

It is also necessary to distinguish:

- the computer code or algorithm which enables the AI operations to be performed;
- the dataset used to train and test the AI system;
- the data subsequently used to produce outputs for analysis or use; and
- the results of that analysis, which may or may not themselves be produced by the AI.

To take one example, various products exist to measure 'trust' in organisations. They do so by examining the natural language used on specific social media platforms such as Twitter and Instagram. The public content is not valuable in itself. The AI is capable of picking up instances where the target organisation is mentioned, and analysing the natural language in order to determine the trust rating afforded by the writer when mentioning it. The AI is valuable intellectual property, as are the results it produces, which enable the organisation to adapt and monitor itself as it sees fit. In order to arrive at those outputs, training data is required so that the AI can analyse the social media inputs effectively, and this too is a valuable and important part of the exercise.

The value of the AI, and of the datasets involved in its use, depends on the fact that the information or algorithms involved are not publicly known. The confidentiality of information can be protected by equitable rules of confidence. In *Coco v AN Clark (Engineers) Ltd*,[61] Megarry J set out the requirements as follows:

> 'In my judgment, three elements are normally required if, apart from contract, a case of breach of confidence is to succeed. First, the information itself… must "have the necessary quality of confidence about it". Secondly, that information must have been imparted in circumstances importing an obligation of confidence. Thirdly, there must be an unauthorised use of that information to the detriment of the party communicating it.'

The information must be shown to be both confidential and acquired under a duty of confidence.

In practical terms, litigation seeking to preserve confidentiality over information has often been played out in cases of misuse by departing employees. In *Faccenda Chicken v Fowler*[62] the courts identified three categories of information: that which is not confidential; that which is acquired during the normal course of employment and becomes part of the employee's skills and experience; and that which has the character of specific trade secrets. During employment, the

61 [1969] RPC 41; approved in *A-G v Guardian Newspapers and Ors (No 2)* [1990] 1 AC 109.
62 [1985] FSR 105 (in the High Court) and [1987] Ch 117 (on appeal to the Court of Appeal).

implied contractual obligation of good faith and fidelity prevents the misuse or unauthorised disclosure of any information belonging to the employer. The extra protection afforded to the third category is that the obligation not to use or disclose the information concerned derives from an implied contractual term which survives the termination of the employment.

Although other information may be protectable by express restrictive covenants which are reasonable in scope, the significance for present purposes is what counts as a trade secret at common law. In *Faccenda Chicken v Fowler* the Court of Appeal's judgment[63] was that this is likely to depend on four factors by which it can be recognised:

(i) the nature of the employment; if confidential material is regularly handled, this may impose a higher obligation, as the employee should realise the sensitive nature of the material;

(ii) the nature of the information; a secret process may be an obvious example, and the fact that the information is limited to certain individuals may throw light on the status of the information and degree of confidentiality;

(iii) whether the employer impressed on the employee the confidentiality of the information; and

(iv) whether the relevant information can be easily isolated from other information.

In the AI context, it may be more or less clear that the computer code itself is analogous to a 'secret process'. However, other information contained in the various datasets, such as the training data, the raw data from social media and the valuable outputs from the analysis, may be argued to have varying degrees of confidentiality.

The concept of a trade secret now has a statutory footing as a result of the EU Trade Secrets Directive.[64] Article 2(1)(a) of the Directive defines a trade secret as:

> 'information which …
>
> (a) is secret in the sense that it is not as a body or in the precise configuration and assembly of its components generally known among or readily accessible to persons within the circles that normally deal with the kind of information in question;
>
> (b) has commercial value because it is secret; and
>
> (c) has been subject to reasonable steps under the circumstances, by the person lawfully in control of the information, to keep it secret.'

The Directive was transposed into law in the UK on 9 June 2018 by the Trade Secrets (Enforcement etc) Regulations 2018. The Explanatory Notes state that:

63 Per Neill LJ at 137–138.
64 Directive (EU) 2016/943.

> 'the issue of whether the acquisition, use or disclosure of a trade secret is unlawful is determined by reference to the principles of the law of confidence
>
> ...
>
> ... where the measures, procedures and remedies available in an action for breach of confidence offer wider protection to a trade secret holder than that offered under the [Regulations], the trade secret holder may apply for, and a court may grant, them provided they comply with [safeguards set out in Article 1 of the Directive].'

In other words, the intention was to preserve the full force and effect of UK law, insofar as the law of confidence gives wider rights to protection of information.

The High Court considered the overlap between the law of confidence and the statutory provisions on trade secrets in *Trailfinders Limited v Travel Counsellors Limited & Ors*.[65] The travel agency Trailfinders claimed that their customer database had been accessed and their customer list wrongfully exploited by four former employees who had joined competitor TCL.

In the view of the court, such information fell into the second category in *Faccenda Chicken v Fowler* – ie it was not a trade secret under the pre-existing common law. It did, however, meet the definition of a trade secret under the Directive and its use was unlawful because it had been obtained by copying for the purposes of use after the end of employment.

The judgment in *Trailfinders* is particularly useful for understanding from two perspectives. First, it confirms that the Directive and Regulations will now inform questions of what amounts to a trade secret and what information is protectable.

Secondly, there was a finding against TCL which was not based on vicarious liability for the actions of the individuals involved. TCL operated on a franchise model but, in any event, there was separate liability arising from the equitable obligation of confidence. TCL encouraged potential franchisees to bring existing client details with them. It knew or ought to have known that the information was confidential and that it was too extensive to have been carried in the heads of the franchisees as part of their own skill and knowledge.

FINANCIAL TECHNOLOGY

3.26 The term 'financial technology', or 'FinTech', refers to the application of technology to financial services. It can be observed in a variety of guises:

- increased use of technology by large traditional institutions in commercial and retail banking;
- infrastructure and financial services facilitation, including payment services such as Apple Pay; and

65 [2020] EWHC 591 (IPEC).

- disruptive FinTech deployed by smaller companies seeking to disrupt existing markets (for example, peer-to-peer lending platforms).

Financial services in the UK are regulated by the Financial Conduct Authority ('FCA') and the Prudential Regulation Authority ('PRA'). There is no separate structure or single source of regulation for FinTech firms or products.

We set out below two forms of FinTech, in algorithmic trading and crowdfunding, which have attracted specific regulation. We deal with cryptoassets and smart contracts in a separate section (see para **3.29** onwards).

Algorithmic trading

3.27 Algorithmic trading, also known as high frequency trading, is the use of a computer algorithm, with limited or no human intervention, to determine whether to initiate a trade in a financial instrument, or its conditions such as timing and price. The risk identified by regulators is that the increased speed and complexity of which automation is capable could turn manageable limited errors into major events.

This risk is addressed in legal terms by the creation of a regulatory environment which sets standards around the management of such trading. The legislative backdrop is the Markets in Financial Instruments Directive (2014/65/EU) and the Markets in Financial Instruments Regulation (Regulation (EU) 600/2014), which together are referred to as MiFID II.[66] This has been implemented in the UK in various ways and the expectation is that, at the end of the Brexit transition period (on 31 December 2020), the UK will remain compliant with European standards.

Accordingly, the UK regulatory bodies' focus is on governance and oversight, testing, risk management and business continuity.

The FCA's rules are in chapter 5 of the Market Conduct sourcebook. For example, MAR 5.3A ('Systems and controls for algorithmic trading') states that:

> 'A firm must ensure that the systems and controls, including procedures and arrangements, used in the performance of its activities are adequate, effective and appropriate for the scale and nature of its business.'[67]

The PRA has set out its expectations in Supervisory Statement 5/18.[68]

66 They, in turn, replaced the Markets in Financial Instruments Directive (2004/39/EC).

67 See also MAR 5A.5 and MAR 7A, and the FCA's February 2017 report, 'Algorithmic trading compliance in wholesale markets'.

68 See also Commission Delegated Regulation (EU) 2017/589; PRA Policy Statement: Algorithmic Trading, June 2018.

Crowdfunding

3.28 Crowdfunding enables money to be raised from a large pool of remote funders via an online platform.

The platform will host the pitch for funding and will facilitate the funding process.

In order to identify the legal relationships and potential regulatory regime, it is important to recognise the various types of crowdfunding:

- Donation-based crowdfunding has been used by charities and other not-for-profit organisations with significant success. JustGiving is a well-known example. Captain Tom Moore is reported to have raised over £32 million in 2020 for the NHS through the platform.[69]
- Reward crowdfunding is giving money to receive a reward, product or service worth less than the money given (at least in the recipient's hands) but nonetheless valuable. Frequently, the business seeking funding gives away samples of its product.

Neither donation-based nor rewards-based crowdfunding is currently regulated in the UK.

The regulated activities are:

- loan-based crowdfunding, also known as peer-to-peer ('P2P') lending; and
- investment-based crowdfunding – also called equity crowdfunding.

In relation to loan-based crowdfunding, an amendment was made to the Financial Services and Markets Act 2000 (Regulated Activities) Order 2001[70] ('RAO'), to come into force on 1 April 2014, in recognition of the increasing importance of P2P lending. Under article 36H of the RAO, loan-based crowdfunding was then regulated as the 'activity of operating an electronic system in relation to lending'.

Article 36H does not catch business-to-business lending. But, where there is an 'article 36H agreement', which in essence catches lending and borrowing between consumers or between consumers and businesses, the RAO provides that there is a regulated activity where an electronic system is a platform for the investment without being a participant.

If it is carrying on a regulated activity and no exemptions apply,[71] the platform will require FCA authorisation. In addition, such a loan may also amount to a

69 www.justgiving.com/fundraising-v2/tomswalkforthenhs.

70 SI 2001/544.

71 Charities (by Financial Services and Markets Act 2000 (Exemption) Order 2001, SI 2001/1201, Sch, para 44(A1)) and appointed representatives acting on behalf of a firm directly authorised by the FCA or PRA (by FSMA 2000 (Appointed Representatives) Regulations 2001, SI 2001/1217, reg 2(1)(abd)) are exempt.

regulated credit agreement under the Consumer Credit Act 1974, and the rules in the FCA's consumer credit sourcebook ('CONC') will apply. If the lender is lending in the course of a business, the agreement will be subject to the rules in CONC introduced specifically for firms operating P2P platforms:

- provision of adequate pre-contract explanations of the credit agreement, including risks for the borrower (CONC 4.3);
- undertaking an assessment of the borrower's creditworthiness (CONC 5.5A);
- complying with the rules in CONC relating to default, arrears and recovery (CONC 7.17–7.19); and
- providing a 14-day cooling-off period for the borrower, allowing them to withdraw (CONC 11.2).

Any promotion of P2P agreements must be fair, clear and not misleading (CONC 3.7A).

Investment-based crowdfunding is likely to involve unlisted shares or debt securities which, in the FCA's view, carry significant risks. Existing rules relating to arranging deals in investments and making arrangements with a view to participating in deals for investments, under article 25 of the RAO, are likely to apply. The online platforms are likely to require FCA authorisation, on the basis that they are carrying on a regulated activity.

CRYPTOASSETS AND SMART CONTRACTS

3.29 A concerted effort is being made in the UK to explore the risks and benefits of cryptoassets and the underlying technology, including smart contracts. The FCA, Bank of England and HM Treasury are part of a Cryptoassets Taskforce, which first met in 2018 and has produced various guidance referred to below.

Definitions and characteristics

3.30 The term 'cryptoassets' is deliberately broad. It captures the digital representation of value which is cryptographically secured by some form of distributed ledger technology ('DLT').

DLT allows information to be recorded on a database – a ledger – which is decentralised and distributed rather than being held in one 'master' version. The various locations are synchronised and available to those accessing the network. Blockchain is one type of DLT, and DLT has various other applications outside cryptoassets.

Cryptocurrencies, such as Bitcoin, Litecoin and Ethereum, are one type of cryptoasset. The term 'cryptocurrency' is itself somewhat controversial, since it cannot be used as a currency in the same way that traditional money can be used. 'Fiat money' or 'fiat currency' are the terms used to identify money that a government has issued and declared to be legal tender without having intrinsic value derived from a physical commodity. In the UK, bank notes represent fiat money but gold coins do not.

By contrast, cryptocurrency is a type of digital or virtual currency which is issued and controlled by developers and can function as a currency not in the real world, but only between members of a virtual community. It may or may not count as electronic money under the Electronic Money Regulations 2011.

Cryptoasset regulation

3.31 The overall picture, after the final Cryptoassets Taskforce report[72] and FCA guidance issued in July 2019,[73] is that not all cryptoasset activity is believed by the FCA to fall within its 'regulatory perimeter'. Cryptoassets are categorised into four types of 'tokens'.

E-money tokens are those which satisfy the definition of e-money under regulation 2(1) of the Electronic Money Regulations 2011.

Security tokens are cryptoassets which give the holder rights akin to a 'specified investment' as set out in the RAO. Examples of a specified investment are a debt instrument, such as a debenture, and a share in a company.

Those two types of tokens are believed by the FCA to be regulated, as matters stand. The particular legislation governing them may be the secondary legislation already referred to, in addition to the MiFID II legislation as financial instrument or the Payment Services Regulations 2017.[74]

The other two types of tokens are deemed to be unregulated, on the basis that they fall short of granting the rights which would cause them to meet the statutory definitions such as for specified investments: these are exchange tokens, which are intended to function as a means of exchange but which are not e-money; and utility tokens, which give access to a product or service (whether now or in the future).

In July 2020, HM Treasury published a consultation aimed at bringing the promotion of certain currently unregulated cryptoassets within the scope of regulations on the communication of invitations or inducements to invest.[75]

72 Cryptoassets Taskforce: Final report, October 2018.
73 FCA Policy statement guidance on cryptoassets; Feedback and final guidance to CP19/3.
74 SI 2017/752.
75 Under Financial Services and Markets Act 2000, s 21.

Legal characteristics of cryptoassets

3.32 Whether or not cryptoassets are regulated by the FCA, the UK Jurisdiction Taskforce ('UKJT') has taken a position on their legal character. The UKJT is part of the LawTech Delivery Panel, whose six taskforces have the overall objective of showing that English law and the jurisdiction of England and Wales 'together provide a state-of-the-art foundation for the development of DLT, smart contracts and associated technologies'.[76] This was the first jurisdiction to take a position on how the law should regard cryptoassets.

In its 'Legal statement on cryptoassets and smart contracts' (November 2019), the UKJT reached the view that cryptoassets have all the legal characteristics of property and are, in principle, to be treated as property under English law. It did so without seeking to arrive at a legal definition of what a cryptoasset is, but rather by identifying the 'principal novel or characteristic features of cryptoassets', which are said to be:[77]

- intangibility;
- cryptographic authentication;
- use of distributed transaction ledger;
- decentralisation; and
- rule by consensus.

The feature which is key to the deeper analysis is that a cryptoasset typically contains a pair of data parameters, one public and one private.[78] The public parameter is visible to all participants or the world at large. It contains information such as ownership of the asset, value and transaction history. The private parameter (or private key) 'permits transfers or other dealings in the cryptoasset to be cryptographically authenticated by digital signature'. Practical control and ownership of the asset is with the person who has knowledge of the private key.[79]

The UKJT went on to reach the view that several important features of 'property' are to be found:

- they are definable and certain, because the public parameter is sufficient to define the asset;
- they are controllable by the holder of the private key, to the exclusion of all others;
- they are capable of being owned – by the holder of the private key – and, in principle, capable of being transferred or assigned, albeit in possibly novel and difficult ways; and

76 It is chaired by Sir Geoffrey Vos, Chancellor of the High Court.
77 Legal statement, para 31.
78 Legal statement, para 28.
79 Legal statement, para 43.

- they appear to be as permanent or stable as other financial assets which may exist until they are cancelled, redeemed, repaid or exercised.

The UKJT made an important distinction from mere information, which the courts have historically been reluctant to treat as property. Although undoubtedly the public and private parameters constitute information, that is not where the commercial value of the asset lies. The data merely allows transactions to be authenticated.

Equally, they cannot be physically possessed, because they are virtual assets. They are therefore not 'goods' for the purposes of the Sale of Goods Act 1979; they cannot be the object of a bailment; pledges and liens cannot be created over them; they are not 'instruments' under the Bills of Exchange Act 1882, since the Act requires physical possession; and they are not documents of title or negotiable instruments.

The UKJT faced up to the difficulty that English law is sometimes seen to allow for only two types of personal property: things in possession and things in action.[80] Cryptoassets cannot be things in possession, because they are not tangible objects. The question of whether they can be things in action is more complex. The term generally means a right of action which can be enforced in court, such as a debt or contractual right. A cryptoasset does not normally confer such a right in itself. The participants in the DLT do not normally take on legal obligations to each other.

Nevertheless, in the view of the UKJT, there are a number of examples from statute and case law in which novel kinds of intangible assets were treated as property. To take a couple of examples: section 30 of the Patents Act 1977 provides that a patent or application for a patent 'is personal property (without being a thing in action)'; and in *Armstrong DLW GmbH v Winnington Networks Ltd*,[81] the court held that an EU carbon emissions allowance could be a form of 'other intangible property', even though it was neither a thing in possession nor a thing in action, for the purposes of a tracing action.

Taking such examples into account, 'the fact that a cryptoasset might not be a thing in action on the narrower definition of that term does not in itself mean that it cannot be treated as property'.[82]

The UKJT's analysis has now been approved by the Commercial Court, which, in *AA v Persons Unknown*,[83] held that a Bitcoin holding was capable of being the subject of a proprietary injunction.

80 Legal statement, paras 66–84; and see *Colonial Bank v Whinney* (1885) 30 Ch D 261 (CA), 285.
81 [2012] EWHC 10 (Ch).
82 Legal statement, para 84.
83 *AA v Persons Unknown Who Demanded Bitcoin on 10th and 11th October 2019, Persons Unknown Who Own/Control Specified Bitcoin, iFINEX trading as Bitfinex, BFXWW Inc trading as Bitfinex* [2019] EWHC 3556 (Comm), released for publication 17 January 2020.

The action in *AA v Persons Unknown* was brought by an insurer in respect of ransom money which had been demanded from its customer and paid in Bitcoin. A cyberattack had disabled the customer's computer systems. The hackers provided a relatively simple decryption key following payment of the ransom worth US$950,000. The decryption process took five days for servers and ten days for 1,000 desktop computers.

The ransom demand was made by the first defendant; the Bitcoin account was controlled by the second defendant; and they were linked to a Bitcoin exchange operated by the third and fourth defendants which were apparently based outside the jurisdiction.

The causes of action were not in their final form at the hearing, which was ex parte on notice and held in private. The judge recorded them as being 'proprietary claims in restitution and/or constructive trustees or for the tort of intimidation and/or fraud and/or conversion'.[84] The proprietary remedy sought at the hearing was for an interim injunction over the Bitcoins held by the third and fourth defendants, traced through as the proceeds of the US$950,000 paid over by the claimant insurer.

Citing *Colonial Bank v Whinney*,[85] the judge (Bryan J) referred to the traditional binary classification of things in possession and things in action, and noted that, if judged solely on that basis, Bitcoin could not be a form of property. He went on to rely on the UKJT's reasoning to find that, while a cryptoasset might not be a thing in action on a narrow definition of that term, that did not mean it could not be treated as property. There was a serious issue to be tried against each defendant in relation to the ransom demand and the consequent Bitcoin holding. The balance of convenience lay firmly in favour of granting relief, and damages would not be an adequate remedy since the Bitcoin could be dissipated and the insurer had a strong claim to it.

Similar conclusions had previously been reached to grant relief, albeit not based on the detailed UKJT analysis, in the High Court[86] and in the Singapore International Commercial Court.[87]

Smart contracts

3.33 A smart contract is not necessarily a contract in the traditional sense of offer, acceptance and consideration; it is a part of a DLT application which executes certain pre-defined functions in response to an agreed input.

84 [2019] EWHC 3556 (Comm) at para 51.

85 *Colonial Bank v Whinney* (1885) 30 Ch D 261 (CA), 285.

86 See eg *Vorotyntseva v Money-4 Ltd (t/a Nebeus.com)* [2018] EWHC 2596 (Ch) (28 September 2018) – worldwide freezing order granted over a quantity of Bitcoin and Ethereum; *Liam David Robertson v Persons Unknown*, CL-2019-000444 (19 July 2019) – asset preservation order over cryptocurrencies.

87 *B2C2 Limited v Quoine PTC Limited* [2019] SGHC (I) 03 [142].

For example, at a very simple level, if A pays £X in fiat money to B's bank account, the smart contract issues a set amount of cryptoasset tokens to A. There is no need of further human intervention – the computer code does the work.

This kind of technology has applications well beyond cryptoassets. For example, smart contracts are being used by the Danish shipper Maersk for the insurance market to rate and price insurance and re-insurance products for its vessels.[88] In July 2018 a trade finance blockchain platform 'we.trade' was launched by a consortium of banks (including HSBC, Santander and Deutsche Bank), enabling companies to conclude transactions where smart contracts automate the final payment based upon the fulfilment of specified conditions.

The UKJT's 'Legal statement on cryptoassets and smart contracts' (November 2019), referred to at paragraph **3.32** above, contains, in our view, an extremely useful discussion of many of the issues likely to come into play in litigation where a smart contract is involved.

Legal characteristics of smart contracts

3.34 As it did with cryptoassets, the UKJT avoided attempting a legal definition in favour of describing the defining feature of smart contracts. This is automaticity, in that human intervention is not needed because the contract is performed, at least in part, automatically. As part of that automaticity, the terms of the contract are recoded in computer-readable form, ie in computer code.

This automaticity, in the UKJT's view, is no reason to dispense with the conventional requirements of contract law, namely whether there is offer and acceptance, an intention to be legally bound and consideration for the promise. An analysis of the facts will reveal the objective reality of the parties' words and conduct. Equally, the place of the smart contract within those intentions will depend on what the overall agreement is found to be. We suggest that, usually, the parties will have agreed to be bound by what the code does, but that does not capture the whole of their agreement.

The UKJT's view is that the normal rules of contractual interpretation would apply to a smart contract. In extreme cases, the complete contract could exist in code, and there would be no room for interpretation of its effects. We suggest that the more usual scenario will be that the code governs some but not all aspects of the contract. For example, there will usually be some evidence about the transaction the performance of which is governed by the smart contract. Questions of interpretation are likely to arise at least at that stage. There may also be areas of doubt around the behaviour of the code in different circumstances. This could be a matter on which expert evidence is required.

88 This is via a bespoke platform called Insurwave.

In terms of formal requirements, in the view of the UKJT a private key is highly likely to be capable of meeting a statutory signature requirement. This is because an electronic signature intended to authenticate a document will generally satisfy such a requirement. Note that the Law Commission has twice come to the same conclusion.[89]

The UKJT suggests that even a statutory 'in writing' requirement would be met by code capable of being displayed or printed out. It may be that, in fact, the terms of the real agreement between the parties can easily be reduced to writing and that the place of the smart contract is only to govern the execution. Such an analysis would circumvent most difficulties that can be envisaged.

89 'Electronic Commerce: Formal Requirements in Commercial Transactions: Advice' (2001); Law Commission, 'Electronic execution of documents' (Law Com No 386, 2019).

Chapter 4

Causes of Action in Data Protection Law

In this chapter, we consider:

- the scope and boundaries of data protection law under the General Data Protection Regulation and the Data Protection Act 2018;
- the concept of personal data, and related terminology and definitions;
- the data protection principles, including lawful processing and consent;
- accountability and liability of controllers and processors;
- data subject rights; and
- data security and personal data breaches.

INTRODUCTORY

4.1 The commercial value of personal data and information is now well established. Businesses lay claim to it and seek to protect it. Consumers and employees are given rights connected to its use and management. Governments seek to referee between competing interests by regulation, but also to deploy personal data where it is expedient or in the public interest to do so. This chapter examines the legal and regulatory framework surrounding personal data as the subject matter of actual or potential litigation.

The phrase 'data protection' connotes a kind of shielding of data from misuse. It is true that the law recognises the rights of individuals in respect of information which, in some sense, is about them and therefore belongs to them. There are nonetheless important ways in which the framework seeks to recognise legitimate and lawful uses of personal data by others. The positive view of data protection obligations is that they are facilitative in nature, in that they create a level playing field within which compliant organisations are free to operate.

General Data Protection Regulation

4.2 The personal data territory is now dominated by the General Data Protection ('GDPR').[1] The GDPR became directly applicable in the UK and all

1 Regulation (EU) 2016/679.

EU member states on 25 May 2018. On the same date, the main provisions of the Data Protection Act 2018 ('DPA 2018') came into force, repealing and replacing the 1998 Act of the same name, and modifying to some extent the provisions of the GDPR. UK regulations provide for the continued applicability of the GDPR after Brexit.[2]

The predecessor Data Protection Directive[3] dated from 1995 and was repealed by the GDPR, but many of the principles and much of the case law remains relevant. A detailed analysis of the differences is beyond the scope of this work but, where appropriate, this chapter will refer to case law which sheds light on causes of action available under the GDPR regime.

The GDPR thinks of personal data as a commodity. Article 1 speaks of the 'free movement of personal data' and frames the 'protection of personal data' as one of the 'fundamental rights and freedoms of natural persons'.

While avoiding EU-style statements of principle, DPA 2018 adopts the same structure, with modifications and a certain amount of 'gold-plating'. The application of the correct law, and its citation where appropriate in pleadings, will of course be crucial in a litigation context.

Since this is a book about litigation, we will focus on rights and corresponding obligations, but it is first necessary to understand the principles of the GDPR from the UK perspective.

Supervisory authorities

4.3 Given the easy movement of personal data across borders, a complaint about a single act of data processing might potentially be justiciable in more than one jurisdiction. A business may process personal data in one member state of data subjects located in a second member state.

This is dealt with in Articles 55 and 56 of the GDPR, which make it clear that a 'supervisory authority' ('SA') of a member state is competent to handle complaints relating to an establishment within it, or which substantially affects data subjects within it.[4] Entities running establishments in more than one member state are able to designate a 'lead supervisory authority' of the 'main establishment'. These provisions are aimed partly at ensuring consistency and co-operation on enforcement and regulatory questions, and partly at streamlining the recourse for potential EU-based complainants, who will usually, if not always, have recourse to the supervisory authority in their own country.[5]

2 Data Protection, Privacy and Electronic Communications (Amendments etc) (EU Exit) Regulations 2019, SI 2019/419.

3 Directive 95/46/EC

4 GDPR, Articles 55(1) and 56(2); see also Recitals 117–123 and, for definitions, Article 4(21) and (22)

5 GDPR, Article 56(1) and Recitals 124–138.

The SA for the UK is the Information Commissioner's Office ('ICO'). It publishes guidance on general and specific aspects of the GDPR and DPA 2018, and texts of its regulatory decisions.[6]

At the European level, the European Data Protection Board ('EDPB') is a creature of the GDPR and exists to monitor, ensure and advise upon its correct application.[7] Its precursor was the Article 29 Working Party (WP29),[8] which ceased to exist on 25 May 2018.

SCOPE AND BOUNDARIES OF DATA PROTECTION LAW

Territorial scope

4.4 As an EU Regulation, the GDPR is directly applicable in EU member states, but it is subject to permitted derogations.[9] Brexit notwithstanding, DPA 2018 is the UK's particular example of legislation which frames the GDPR for national purposes while leaving the essential GDPR picture undisturbed.

The GDPR applies to the processing of personal data in the context of the activities of an establishment of a controller or processor in the EU, whether or not the processing takes place in the EU.[10] The concept of establishment is one which 'implies the effective and real exercise of activity through stable arrangements'.[11] The legal form of such arrangements is not the determining factor.

The use of the word 'implies', in the English text of Recital 22, seems capable of various shades of meaning. The French text uses the verb 'supposer' in its place, which in this context is consistent with a usage of 'to imply' meaning 'to indicate' rather than some weaker sense of suggestion.

ECJ case law under the previous Directive has grappled with the concept of an establishment in the EU. This was found to be the case in both the following examples:

- a property-dealing website is written in the member state's language, is directed at properties in that state and has a bank account and postbox located in it;[12] and

6 See www.ico.org.uk.
7 GDPR, Articles 68–76.
8 Named for Article 29 of the 1995 Directive, under which provision it was set up.
9 See, in particular, GDPR, Article 23.
10 GDPR, Article 3(1).
11 GDPR, Recital 22.
12 *Weltimmo s.r.o. v Nemzeti Adatvédelmi* és *Információszabadság Hatóság*, Case C-230/14, 1 October 2015.

- the Spanish subsidiary of Google directs its advertising sales and orientates its activity towards Spanish users, capturing their personal data in the process.[13]

Note that, although these examples relate to operations within a member state, there is no GDPR requirement for that to be the case. If the Google Spain situation were reversed and an EU-based search engine set up a branch in the US, the GDPR would apply to the Spanish entity in respect of its US operations, and in respect of the personal data of natural persons in the USA.

Where there is no EU establishment, the issue is where the data subjects are located. The GDPR envisages two broad categories:

- goods and services being offered to data subjects in the EU, irrespective of whether payment is required;[14] and
- the monitoring of the behaviour in the EU of data subjects.[15]

This is plainly wide enough to capture most, if not all, commercial activity in relation to data subjects passing through the EU, together with online activity involving tracking cookies or usage information.

In a non-establishment case of this type, the controller or processor is required to designate in writing a representative in the EU who is established there.[16]

Finally, the GDPR will apply if an establishment is in a place where member state law applies by virtue of public international law.[17]

The EDPB has adopted useful 'Guidelines on the Territorial Scope of the GDPR',[18] with specific discussion of previous case law and the concepts set out above.

The application of the GDPR

4.5 The GDPR applies to the processing of personal data:

- wholly or partly by automated means; and
- other than by automated means if the data forms part, or is intended to form part, of a filing system.[19]

13 *Google Spain SL and Google Inc v Agencia Española de Protección de Datos (AEPD) and Mario Costeja González*, Case C-131/12, 13 May 2014.
14 GDPR, Article 3(2)(a) and Recital 23.
15 GDPR, Article 3(2) and Recital 24.
16 GDPR, Article 27.
17 GDPR, Article 3(3) and Recital 25.
18 Guidelines 3/2018 on the territorial scope of the GDPR (Article 3), Version 2.0, 12 November 2019.
19 GDPR, Article 2(1) and Recital 15.

We will deal below with the issue of what counts as a 'filing system', since the DPA 2018 provides further detail.

Certain types of processing of personal data are outside the scope of the GDPR altogether, ie those undertaken:

- in the course of an activity which is outside the scope of EU law;[20]
- by member states carrying out an activity falling within Chapter 2 of Title V of the Treaty on European Union, ie common foreign and security policy;[21]
- by a natural person carrying out a purely personal or household activity;[22]
- by competent authorities for the purposes of the prevention, investigation, detection or prosecution of criminal offences or the execution of criminal penalties, including the safeguarding against and the prevention of threats to public security – these will instead be regulated by the Law Enforcement Directive (EU) 2016/680;[23]
- by EU institutions, bodies, offices and agencies[24] – this is regulated by Regulation (EC) 45/2001 on the processing of personal data by the Community institutions and bodies, although the GDPR requires compliance with that Regulation; and
- in relation to deceased persons, although member states may legislate around the processing of their personal data.[25]

The ambit of a 'purely personal or household activity' is likely to be quite narrow. The activity should have 'no connection to a professional or commercial activity' and the operators providing the means of processing would count as controllers or processors in such a context – these points are made in Recital 18.

Plainly the owners or providers of social networking apps or cloud storage facilities are caught as controllers or processors. The ECJ has reached further, under the previous Data Protection Directive, and ruled that quite anodyne and minor postings by a parochial church worker on a social networking website were not within the exemption for 'exclusively personal or domestic' activities (in the words of the previous Directive). What took them outside the exemption was the very fact that they were published on the internet.[26]

Similarly, in 2009, WP29 produced an opinion on social networking which concluded that not all activities of a social networking user are necessarily covered by the personal or domestic exemption, although most will be.

20 GDPR, Article 2(2)(a) and Recital 16.
21 GDPR, Article 2(2)(b) and Recital 17.
22 GDPR, Article 2(2)(c) and Recital 18.
23 GDPR, Article 2(2)(d), Article 10 and Recitals 19–20.
24 GDPR, Article 2(3), Article 98 and Recital 17.
25 GDPR, Recital 27.
26 *Lindqvist* (Case C-101/01) [2003] ECR I-12971, especially paras 46–47.

The role of the DPA 2018

4.6 The DPA 2018 bolts on to the GDPR its own regime to cover some processing in the UK which would otherwise fall outside scope by reason of Article 2(2) of the GDPR. This is the concept of the 'applied GDPR'.[27]

The bolt-on engineered by Chapter 3 of DPA 2018 relates to automated or structured processing done in the course of an activity:

- falling outside the scope of EU law; or
- within the common foreign and security policy framework.[28]

It also includes unstructured manual processing by a public authority which is subject to the Freedom of Information Act 2000.[29]

In addition, and further to Chapter 3, processing by law enforcement and intelligence services is covered by Parts 3 and 4 of the DPA 2018.

The applied GDPR therefore captures large areas of processing within the public sector, including paper records. These areas should nonetheless be approached with care: a number of exemptions apply in relation to manual unstructured data and national security in particular.[30]

TERMINOLOGY AND DEFINITIONS

4.7 Litigation in the data protection space requires an understanding of a set of somewhat technical concepts. Article 4 sets out 26 separate legal definitions. We need not deal with all of them here, but some of the concepts are crucial. Where it is important or helpful, we refer to variations between the GDPR and DPA 2018 definitions, and to guidance from the ICO.

Personal data

4.8 Personal data is any recorded information relating to an identified or identifiable natural person (the 'data subject').[31] The DPA 2018 variant is to replace 'natural person' with 'living individual', which amounts to the same thing, given that Recital 27 of the GDPR rules out 'deceased persons'.[32]

27 DPA 2018, Chapter 3 and Sch 6.
28 DPA 2018, s 21(1).
29 DPA 2018, s 21(2).
30 DPA 2018, ss 24–28.
31 GDPR, Article 4(1).
32 DPA 2018, s 3(2), (3) and (5).

'Identified or identifiable'

4.9 An identifiable individual is one who can be identified, directly or indirectly, in particular by reference to:

- an identifier such as a name, an identification number, location data, or an online identifier; or
- one or more factors specific to the physical, physiological, genetic, mental, economic, cultural or social identity of the individual.

Note that the information does not have to be unique to the individual. While an online identifier such as an IP address may be wholly unique to an individual's laptop, even their name may well not be so – there will be plenty of others in the world sharing the same given and family names. The name is nonetheless plainly sufficient identification for these purposes. The inclusion of 'an identifier such as a name' within the concept of identifiability seems to mean that, in reality, the distinction between a person who is straightforwardly identified, and one who merely 'can be' identified, is likely to be of little practical significance.

There are two more complex points to consider.

First, online identifiers will include IP addresses, cookie identifiers and radio frequency tags.[33] This is consistent with previous rulings of the ECJ applying the concept of personal data to include online user activity.[34] It reinforces the point that the issue of identifiability is far from a simple exercise in asking whether a person could connect the identifier to a living individual in the course of ordinary human interaction.

Secondly, as the ICO's guidance makes clear, the identifiability criterion is satisfied if a combination of identifiers – 'one or more factors' – can be applied so as to distinguish the individual from a group. In a case of direct identification, according to the ICO, this can be done by the use of a description, for example:

> 'The oldest male resident of The Retirement Castle in Springfield.'
>
> 'The last person shown on CCTV entering Moe's Bar on the night of 4 July.'

These are both sufficient in themselves to single out an individual without more, and therefore directly identify that individual.

The concept of indirect identification, by contrast, is that of identifying from a combination of the information in question and other information available. Such information might be publicly available or might simply be held separately from that with which it needs to be combined.

33 GDPR, Recital 30.

34 See *Scarlet Extended SA v Société belge des auteurs compositeurs et* éditeurs *SCRL* (Case C-70/10) EU:C:2011:771 [2011] ECR I-11959; *Patrick Breyer v Bundesrepublik Deutschland* (Case C-582/14) EU:C:2016:779.

Examples

A list of vehicle registration numbers parked in private parking spaces outside an office block, combined with a list of names of the owners signing in on a particular day.

A list of identification numbers issued to exam candidates and held by the examination centre, combined with a restricted file held by the exam board containing the list of names and the corresponding candidate number.

In that context, regard need not be had to every conceivable theoretical possibility for combining the information under scrutiny and other sources. The GDPR's formulation is to take into account 'all the means reasonably likely to be used', taking account of all objective factors, such as cost and amount of time, and available technology.[35]

The ICO's guidance is to consider all the means likely to be available to a determined searcher with a particular reason to want to identify the individual – an 'interested and sufficiently determined person'.[36]

'Relating to'

4.10 Identifiability alone is not a sufficient criterion for the information to amount to personal data – an extra ingredient of 'relating to' the living individual is required. The ICO's guidance offers four main ways in which this might arise, all of which assume that, at some point, identification can be made:[37]

(1) Data which is 'obviously about' an individual or their activities – eg medical history, criminal record, work performance, bank statements.

(2) Data which becomes personal data when linked to an individual. Generic salary details are not personal data when placed in a job advertisement, but become personal data in the hands of the employer once the post is filled.

(3) Data which becomes personal data once it is processed for the purpose of making decisions about an individual. Logs of telephone activity at work may well not be personal data in themselves, but will become so if used to judge the productivity of employees.

(4) Data which, although not processed with an intention or primary purpose of having an impact on an individual, could be used in a way which has an impact. This has to be distinguished from the scenario in which data is actually processed in a way that affects an individual – for example, the work telephone logs. At that point, it will obviously be personal data

35 GDPR, Recital 26.
36 ICO: 'Guide to the General Data Protection Regulation: What is personal data?'.
37 ICO: 'Guide to the General Data Protection Regulation: What is the meaning of "relates to"?'.

in accordance with scenario (3) above. However, the ICO's guidance is wider, in that, if the data *could* be processed in a way which influences or determines how the individual is treated, even if not collected or further processed for that purpose, then it is likely to be personal data.

Given these categories, it is important to mention two types of issue that could come into focus in a litigation context.

First, inaccurate information could still be personal data, assuming the necessary identification conditions. The fact that the information is inaccurate does not take it outside the ambit of relatedness. The GDPR is, after all, designed in part to protect individuals from the misuse of information about them – an example of which is the dissemination of inaccurate information. It follows that inaccurate information must be included within the concept of personal data.

On the other hand, if the information is so inaccurate that no individual can be identified, it will fail the test for personal data on identification grounds.

Secondly, an opinion about an individual could amount to personal data.

Examples

An assessment of the likelihood of a particular customer buying more of a particular product would be that customer's personal data.

An opinion expressed in an employee appraisal about their performance would count as personal data.

The opinion or assessment is still personal data even if it is wrong – and the customer never buys another thing – or it is biased, perhaps because the manager has a concealed personal dislike of the employee.

Processing

4.11 Processing is:

> 'any operation or set of operations which is performed on personal data or on sets of personal data, whether or not by automated means, such as collection, recording, organisation, structuring, storage, adaptation or alteration, retrieval, consultation, use, disclosure by transmission, dissemination or otherwise making available, alignment or combination, restriction, erasure or destruction'.[38]

Rather than adding to the thesaurus of words within the legislation, it suffices to point out that the definition is plainly intended to be comprehensive, and

38 GDPR, Article 4(2); DPA 2018, s 3(4).

that it conceivably encompasses any form of use of personal data, including, importantly for litigation purposes, its disclosure and the mere fact that it is collected and held – its storage.

Controller

4.12 A controller is an entity which determines 'the purposes and means of the processing of personal data'.[39] This can be a natural or legal person, public authority, agency or other body. A controller can be a joint controller with others.

The European Court of Justice decided, under the previous Data Protection Directive, that an internet search engine is a controller because of its role in indexing and categorising, for the purposes of search, the personal data it gathers. This was in the well-known 'Google Spain'[40] case which also established the 'right to be forgotten' and which is dealt with below.

DPA 2018 adds that, when personal data is processed only for the purpose and by the means for which it is required to be processed by legislation, the person who has the legislative obligation is the controller.[41]

Processor

4.13 A processor is 'a natural or legal person, public authority, agency or other body which processes personal data on behalf of the controller'.[42] The ICO states that, 'Processors act on behalf of, and only on the instructions of, the relevant controller'.[43] The reference here to the controller's instructions has to be unpacked to be properly understood. Accordingly, we deal with the difference in the potential liabilities of controller and processor more fully at paragraph **4.33** below.

Consent

4.14 The consent of the data subject is defined as any 'freely given, specific, informed and unambiguous indication of the data subject's wishes by which he or she, by a statement or by a clear affirmative action, signifies agreement to the processing of personal data relating to him or her'.[44] The consent rules under the GDPR require further explanation and are dealt with more fully at paragraph **4.22** below.

39 GDPR, Article 4(7); DPA 2018, ss 3(6) and 6(1).

40 *Google Spain SL and Google Inc v Agencia Española de Protección de Datos (AEPD) and Mario Costeja González* C-131/12 (decided on 13 May 2014).

41 DPA 2018, s 6(2).

42 GDPR, Article 4(8).

43 ICO: 'Guide to the General Data Protection Regulation, Controllers and Processors'.

44 GDPR, Article 4(11).

Special categories of personal data

4.15 This was known under the previous legislation as 'sensitive personal data', although there is some updating under the GDPR. The categories relate to the characteristics of a data subject and are:[45]

- racial or ethnic origin;
- political opinions;
- religious or philosophical beliefs;
- trade union membership;
- genetic data;
- biometric data processed for the purpose of uniquely identifying a natural person;
- data concerning health; and
- data concerning a natural person's sex life or sexual orientation.

The main effect of these categories is to restrict the permitted types of processing in ways which we deal with at paragraph **4.25** below.

Profiling

4.16 Profiling is defined as any form of automated processing of personal data used to evaluate certain personal aspects relating to a natural person, in particular to analyse or predict the following:

- performance at work;
- economic situation;
- health;
- personal preferences;
- interests;
- reliability;
- behaviour;
- location; and
- movements.[46]

45 GDPR, Article 9.
46 GDPR, Article 4(4).

Profiling has a number of applications, but one which has especially interested the ICO recently is advertising technology through the use of website cookies. This is dealt with at paragraph **4.43** below.

Filing system

4.17 This definition goes to the scope of the GDPR itself. Article 2 provides that the GDPR applies to processing 'wholly or partly by automated means and to the processing other than by automated means of personal data which form part of a filing system or are intended to form part of a filing system'.

The GDPR definition of 'filing system' is 'any structured set of personal data which are accessible according to specific criteria, whether centralised, decentralised or dispersed on a functional or geographical basis'.[47] In the material respects, the definition under the previous Directive was the same.[48]

In *Durant v Financial Services Authority* [2003] EWCA Civ 1746 the Court of Appeal was asked to determine whether a 'relevant filing system', which was the phrase used under the Data Protection Act 1998, included a manual set of records. The Court concluded that it was limited to a system:

- 'in which the files forming part of it are structured or referenced in such a way as clearly to indicate at the outset of the search whether specific information capable of amounting to personal data of an individual requesting it under section 7 is held within the system and, if so, in which file or files it is held; and
- which has, as part of its own structure or referencing mechanism, a sufficiently sophisticated and detailed means of readily indicating whether and where in an individual file or files specific criteria or information about the applicant can be readily located.'[49]

On the facts, the FSA's filing systems did not satisfy these requirements.

The DPA 2018 adds the words 'whether held by automated means or manually' to the GDPR definition.[50] This clarification does not alter the position reached in *Durant* that the applicability of the data protection regime to records held only manually is circumscribed.

Having said this, the fact that neither the GDPR nor the DPA 2018 applies to manual records that are not filing systems is obviously neither here nor there in relation to obligations outside the data protection regime. A bundle of papers accidentally left on a train is still likely to result in regulatory difficulty for the hapless professional who does so, even if not with the ICO. Obligations

47 GDPR, Article 4(6).
48 Directive 95/46/EC, Article 2(c).
49 Per Auld LJ at para 50.
50 DPA 2018, s 3(7).

of confidence, and contractual and other obligations arising from commercial sensitivity, for example, will exist whether or not the data protection regime applies. Such issues are, however, outside the scope of this chapter.

Secondly, the act of producing the manual records in the first place, assuming that they are the result of printing out documents held electronically, will itself amount to automated processing and will be within the scope of the GDPR insofar as personal data is concerned.

Pseudonymisation

4.18 The concept of pseudonymisation did not appear in the previous Directive. This is the processing of personal data in such a way that the personal data can no longer be attributed to a data subject, without additional information. The additional information must be kept separately and is subject to technical and organisational security measures to ensure that the personal data is not attributed to an identified or identifiable natural person.[51] It remains personal data on the basis that a natural person is identifiable by combining the information, but pseudonymisation is a security measure which helps controllers and processors to meet their obligations.[52]

DATA PROTECTION PRINCIPLES

4.19 We can now turn to the substantive obligations on controllers and processors under the GDPR.

Article 5(1) of the GDPR prescribes that personal data 'shall be' processed in accordance with the following six principles:

(a) lawfulness, fairness and transparency;

(b) purpose limitation;

(c) data minimisation;

(d) accuracy;

(e) storage limitation; and

(f) integrity and confidentiality.

There is a seventh principle of 'accountability', which is the responsibility placed on controllers for the six other principles, and for being able to demonstrate compliance with them.[53] In a litigation context, it is important to understand that

51 GDPR, Article 4(5).
52 GDPR, Recitals 26 and 28.
53 GDPR, Article 5(2).

the obligation to comply with these principles, if not met, gives rise to a right of action under the GDPR.

We examine the issues of enforcement and remedies in **Chapter 9**, but we engage with the principles themselves in this section.

(a) 'Personal data shall be processed fairly and lawfully and in a transparent manner'[54]

Fairness and transparency – the privacy notice

4.20 This principle requires controllers to provide the data subject with a prescribed set of information about the processing. The GDPR requires all information to be given in writing and in a 'concise, transparent, intelligible and easily accessible form using clear and plain language, in particular for any information addressed specifically to a child'.[55] In practice, information is often given in a single privacy notice accessible by clicking through from a web page or appended to a contract.

Where the controller collects personal data from the data subject directly, Article 13 sets out a list of the information to be provided, free of charge, at the time of collection. The list includes:

- the intended purposes and legal basis of the processing;
- any legitimate interests relied upon by the controller or a third party (see below);
- the recipients or categories or recipients of the personal data;
- if applicable, certain details concerning the fact that the controller intends to transfer personal data outside the European Economic Area or to an international organisation; and
- the existence of various rights of the data subject in relation to their personal data, including the right to withdraw consent (if processing is based on consent).

If the controller subsequently wishes to process the personal data for a different purpose, the data subject must be given further information on it before that processing takes place.[56]

Where the personal data is collected from someone other than the data subject, the list of information to be provided to the data subject is similar but also includes information about the categories of personal data so collected and the sources of

54 GDPR, Article 5(1)(a).
55 GDPR, Article 12(1).
56 GDPR, Article 13(2).

it.[57] In those cases of personal data being collected from sources other than the data subject, the GDPR envisages the information being given to the data subject other than at the time of its collection or before, as follows:

- within a reasonable period up to one month, having regard to the specific purposes in which the personal data is processed;
- if it is to be used for communication with the data subject, at the time of that communication at the latest; or
- if disclosure to another recipient is envisaged, at the time of first disclosure at the latest.[58]

Articles 13 and 14 both contain permitted derogations about the notice requirements in cases where the data subject already has the information. In the third-party collection case, Article 14 extends the derogations to cases where providing the information proves impossible or would involve disproportionate effort, where obtaining or disclosure is expressly 'laid down' by EU or member state law which protects the data subject's legitimate interests, or where the personal data must remain confidential under an obligation of professional secrecy regulated by EU or member state law.[59]

Lawful processing conditions

4.21 The GDPR requires one of six conditions to be met in order for processing to be lawful. These are necessary but not sufficient conditions – the processing must also comply with the general law, for example, where applicable, under the law of confidence. The GDPR's lawful bases are set out in Article 6 and are as follows:

(a) the data subject has consented to the processing for one or more specific purposes;

(b) the processing is necessary to perform a contract with the individual or for taking steps to comply with a request made by the individual with a view to entering into a contract;[60]

(c) the processing is necessary to comply with the controller's legal obligations;[61]

(d) the processing is necessary to protect the vital interests of the data subject or another natural person;

(e) the processing is necessary for the performance of a task carried out in the public interest or in the exercise of official authority vested in the controller; or

57 GDPR, Article 14.
58 GDPR, Article 14(3).
59 GDPR, Article 14(5).
60 See also 'Guidelines on the processing of personal data under Article 6(1)(b) in the context of online services', European Data Protection Board, 8 October 2019.
61 See also GDPR, Recital 46.

(f) processing is necessary for the legitimate interests of the controller or a third party – but this potential basis is disapplied in relation to public authorities.

The ICO publishes an interactive tool to assist with the decision-making about which lawful basis to rely upon.

Article 6(2) affords limited rights to member states to make more specific provision concerning the lawful bases. In the UK the DPA 2018 provides a non-exhaustive list of the public interest tasks, or those exercising official authority,[62] and provides for exemptions and adaptations of various other requirements of the GDPR. Litigators therefore still need to scrutinise local GDPR implementation in cases where personal data is transferred between member states.

Consent

4.22 Obtaining the consent of the data subject might be seen as the simplest route to showing a lawful basis of processing. However, the stringency of the GDPR's requirements make it harder to demonstrate in practice. The task of doing so is not made any easier by the fact that wording about consent is dotted around the GDPR itself: for example, there are lines about it in Articles 4(11), 6(1)(a), 7, 8 and 9(2)(a), and Recitals 32, 38, 40, 41, 42–43, 51 and 171.

The main themes are as follows.

The controller must be able to demonstrate that consent was given. If this was done in a written document which also concerns other matters, such as a contract of employment, or terms of service for consumers, then the request for consent has to be distinguishable from the rest of the document and presented as such in clear and plain language.[63]

The individual must be given the right to withdraw consent at any time and must be informed of that right, and it must be as easy to withdraw it as it was to give consent in the first place.[64]

The consent must be freely given. Article 7(4) provides for the law to take 'utmost account' of contractual situations where performance is made conditional on consent being given, but consent is not necessary for that performance. This scenario will be familiar to anyone who has been asked for personal details at the point of sale which are irrelevant to the purchase being made. In such cases, there is a presumption that consent is not freely given.[65]

Recitals 42 and 43 pick out situations for a presumption against freely given consent where:

62 DPA 2018, s 8.
63 GDPR, Article 7(2).
64 GDPR, Article 7(3).
65 GDPR, Recital 43.

- there is a clear imbalance between the data subject and the controller, particular where the controller is a public authority; or
- there is no facility for separately consenting to different processing operations, if that would be appropriate.

The detail in Recital 32 again points towards a requirement for consent to be specifically given for each different type of processing. There is a need for a clear affirmative act by a written (including electronic) or oral statement. Ticking a box would be sufficient, but reliance on a pre-ticked box or silence would not be. The ICO and WP29 have both issued guidance around consent which reinforces these points.[66]

On 4 March 2020, Advocate General Szpunar delivered an opinion on valid consent conditions in a case concerning the telecommunications service provider Orange retaining copies of identity documents for Romanian customers annexed to paper-based contracts.[67] According to the Advocate General, the appropriate consent requirement is for an indication of the data subject's wishes in terms of active behaviour, requiring a high degree of autonomy for the individual. There must not be any room for doubt as to whether the data subject was sufficiently informed, including as to the identity of the data controller, the specific purposes and the manner of processing, and the consequences of it, as well as whether entering into the contract depends on the data processing. At the time of writing, the CJEU's decision is awaited.

The GDPR makes special provision for safeguarding children. Article 8 relates to the offer of 'information society services', which are defined as 'any service normally provided for remuneration, at a distance, by electronic means and at the individual request of a recipient of services',[68] and which will obviously capture most online services including gaming websites and content services hosting music and video. In a case where consent is relied upon as a lawful basis of processing, if services are offered directly to a child below the age of 16, the consent of a person with parental responsibility is required for the processing to be lawful. Controllers are obliged to make 'reasonable efforts' to verify the appropriate parental consent, taking available technology into account. Member states may lower the relevant age of consent to a minimum of 13 years – that is the age at which the DPA 2018 sets it.[69]

66 WP29 'Guidelines on consent under Regulation 2016/679' adopted on 10 April 2018.

67 *Orange România SA v Autoritatea Națională de Supraveghere a Prelucrării Datelor cu Caracter Personal* (Case C-61/19) EU:C2020:158; see also *Planet49 GmbH v Bundesverband der Verbraucherzentralen und Verbraucherverbande – Verbraucherzentrale Bundesverband eV* (C-673/17) EU:C:2019:246 (21 March 2019).

68 GDPR, Article 4 (definitions); and Technical Standards and Regulations Directive (EU) 2015/1535.

69 DPA 2018, s 9.

The ICO has issued its own guidance on the overall position of children within the GDPR.[70] In January 2020 it issued a code of practice on age appropriate online service design, coming into force on 2 September 2020.[71]

Vital interests of the data subject

4.23 Recital 46 makes clear that this basis should be relied upon only where another basis for processing cannot be relied upon. It is designed to meet cases where processing is essential to protect the life of the data subject or another natural person. This may include necessary processing for humanitarian purposes such as monitoring epidemics, and other natural and man-made disaster emergencies.

Legitimate interests of the controller

4.24 Article 6(f) refers to the legitimate interests of the controller or a third party. Recital 47 gives three examples of what might count as a legitimate interest in processing:

- where there is a relevant and appropriate relationship between the data subject and the controller in situations such as where the data subject is a client or in the service of the controller;
- strict necessity for the purposes of preventing fraud; or
- for direct marketing purposes.

All three examples appear to relate to essentially economic interests on the part of the controller or the third party. On the face of it, this condition is therefore the most likely to be suitable for use by businesses able to justify processing as part of a 'relevant and appropriate relationship'. The ICO and the WP29 have published guidance.

As Recital 47 also makes clear, this basis is not for public authorities exercising their functions in accordance with the legal framework laid down for them. They will be governed by the national legal framework and will process personal data on the lawful basis given by Article 6(1)(e).[72]

The DPA 2018 further clarifies and defines the entities which count as public authorities and public bodies for UK purposes, and deals with a possible lacuna hinted at in Recital 47 by specifying that such entities only fall within the definitions for GDPR purposes when they are carrying out a task in the public

70 ICO: 'Guide to Data Protection: Children and the GDPR'.

71 ICO: 'Age Appropriate Design: A Code of Practice for online services' (see para **3.8** onwards).

72 See also *Valsts policijas Rigas regiona parvaldes Kartibas policijas parvalde v Rigas satiksme* (Case C-13/16) EU:C:2017:336, a decision under the previous Data Protection Directive.

interest or in the exercise of official authority.[73] They will therefore potentially be able to rely on the legitimate interests lawful basis for processing when not carrying out such functions. For that reason, lawful bases at Article 6(1)(e) and (f) are not mutually exclusive.

In all cases, however, there is a need to balance the legitimate interests of the controller against the fundamental rights and freedoms of the data subject. Recital 47 straightforwardly states that the individual data subject's rights override those of the controller in circumstances of processing which fall outside the reasonable expectation of the data subject.

In that manner, the legitimate interest basis for processing is intimately linked to the fairness and transparency principle. If the processing has been fairly and transparently notified to the individual, it will weigh favourably in the balance for the controller in deciding whether or not a legitimate interest has been engaged.

Special category data

4.25 We set out above the list of special category data in Article 9. Further assistance with the meaning of 'genetic data', 'biometric data' and 'data concerning health' is given in Article 4(13) to (15), and section 205 of the DPA 2018. The latter includes patient data, ie information about healthcare services which reveals information about the data subject's health.

The starting point for special category data is a prohibition on processing. There is, however, a 10-point list of exceptions given in Article 9(2) allowing for it. The list need only be summarised here as follows:

(a) explicit consent given by the data subject;

(b) specific purposes in the field of employment and social security and social protection law;

(c) necessary processing to protect the vital interests of the data subject or another natural person, where the data subject is incapable (physically or legally) of giving consent;

(d) processing by a foundation, association or not-for-profit body with a political, philosophical, religious or trade union aim;

(e) personal data manifestly made public by the data subject;

(f) the establishment, exercise or defence of legal claims, or courts acting in their judicial capacity;

(g) necessary and proportionate processing for the purposes of substantial public interest;

73 DPA 2018, s 7; the Freedom of Information Act 2000 definitions (and the equivalent Scottish definitions) apply.

(h) preventative or occupational medicine;

(i) necessary processing in the public interest in the area of public health; or

(j) necessary processing for archiving purposes in the public interest, scientific or historical research purposes.[74]

Sections 10 and 11 of, and Schedule 1 to, the DPA 2018 add detail about these exceptions, including as to the employment, health and research purposes (b), (h), (i) and (j) and the substantial public interest involved in (g). The ICO's detailed guidance sets out the circumstances in which organisations must have an 'appropriate policy document' in place in order to rely on these exceptions.

The ICO's guidance also explains that personal data is not special category data if sensitive details can only be guessed at from information held. In the ICO's view, the threshold is one of reasonable certainty. For example, ethnicity might be guessable from names, but the ICO regards it as a step too far to say that names are therefore necessarily special category data. On the other hand, if a database of names is analysed in order to target individuals on the basis of ethnicity by inference from those same names, there would be processing of special category data. In that case, the inferred information about the special category of ethnicity is being used to drive the processing.

The ICO's guidance illustrates a common theme in the GDPR, namely that the purpose of processing can convert what might appear to be a factual question into a more fluid concept: in this example, the conversion of a list of names from 'ordinary' personal data into something for which a special category exception has to be found if the processing is to be lawful.

Criminal convictions and offences

4.26 The GDPR does not classify data relating to criminal convictions and offences as special category data in the way that they were classified as 'sensitive personal data' under the previous data protection regime. Under the GDPR, there must be a lawful basis under Article 6 together with legal or official authority for the processing under Article 10.

The DPA 2018's treatment is more similar to special category data and is set out in sections 10, 11(2) and Parts 1 to 3 of Schedule 1. The conditions for lawful processing must be determined before the processing occurs and should be documented. A register can only be kept on a comprehensive basis if it is under the control of an official authority. Until 28 February 2020 the ICO was conducting a survey to identify gaps in the understanding of controllers about their Article 10 obligations as transposed into UK law.

74 See also GDPR, Article 89(1) and Recital 156.

(b) 'Personal data shall be collected for specified, explicit and legitimate purposes and not further processed in a manner that is incompatible with those purposes …'[75]

4.27 The *purpose limitation principle* is reflected in much of the discussion above about the lawful basis of processing. As well as being collected for legitimate purposes that are made explicitly clear in the privacy notice, personal data should not then be processed for incompatible other purposes. As we have seen, such ulterior purposes could even be argued to make information, which was not special category data at the point of collection, special category data by dint of subsequent processing with purposes directed towards a special category under Article 9(2).

This is not the same thing as processing data in a way which was unanticipated at the point of collection but which remains compatible with the original purposes. This is implicit in the Article 5(1)(b) formulation set out above, and is made explicitly clear in Recital 50. Accordingly, no new legal basis need be identified if the further processing is compatible with the original purposes.

There are three exceptions to the purpose limitation principle:

- consent given by the data subject to the further processing – valid consent is only likely to follow notification by the controller to the data subject of the new purpose;[76]
- processing based on member state or EU law as a necessary and proportionate means in a democratic society to safeguard objectives such as national or public security or defence;[77] and
- processing for archiving purposes in the public interest, scientific or historical research or statistical purposes, which are deemed not to be incompatible with the original purpose.[78]

In relation to the last category of 'not incompatible' further processing, the GDPR expressly indicates the matters to be taken into account by a controller in determining the compatibility or otherwise with the original purpose:[79]

- any link between the original purposes and the further purposes;
- the context of the data collection, in particular the relationship between the controller and the data subjects;
- the nature of the personal data and whether it is special category data or data relating to criminality;
- the possible consequences for data subjects of further processing; and

75 GDPR, Article 5(1)(b).
76 GDPR, Article 6(4) and Recital 50.
77 GDPR, Articles 6(4) and 23(1).
78 GDPR, Articles 5(1)(b) and 89(1) and Recital 50.
79 GDPR, Article 6(4).

- the existence of appropriate safeguards, including encryption or pseudonymisation.

(c) 'Personal data shall be adequate, relevant and limited to what is necessary in relation to the purposes for which it is processed'[80]

4.28 The *data minimisation principle* may be one which features more and more in the coming years, with the increasing reach and commercial value of 'big data'. On the one hand, the principle allows for 'adequacy' of data by reference to the purposes of processing but, on the other, the limitation by reference to necessity calls into question some standard approaches to data gathering. It is common, for example, for online registration for access, membership or booking purposes to request wholly unnecessary information, such as telephone numbers where no telephone contact is envisaged, or the user's position in an organisation where no particular authority on behalf of the organisation need be sought. The likelihood is that such details are being requested for marketing purposes rather than for access to the service. If the provider's privacy notice, or better yet the online form itself, makes that clear and explicit, it may be good evidence of meeting the purpose limitation and data minimisation principles. If not, the provider risks falling foul of them.

Sometimes, fields requesting these details may be marked as optional rather than mandatory. We suggest that this, by itself, would be no answer to the criticism that the data minimisation principle is infringed. In the absence of explicit reference to the marketing purpose, or subsequent express consent of the data subject, the fact that the extraneous personal data was volunteered would not suffice to satisfy the principle of data minimisation.

(d) 'Personal data shall be accurate and, where necessary kept up to date. Every reasonable step must be taken to ensure that personal data that is inaccurate, having regard to the purposes for which it is processed, is erased or rectified without delay'[81]

4.29 The *accuracy principle* would seem to flow logically from the data minimisation principle, but it adds directives to perform further processing so as to erase or rectify for the purposes of compliance. In the example of the subscription or access services referred to above, it is hard to see how an organisation could rectify data if the end user does not inform it of updated contact details. For example, it is common to use an email address as a user login. The user might well be able to change the email used for receiving notifications from the service without changing the old defunct email address used as the login. Would the accuracy principle require the defunct username to be rectified by the provider to

80 GDPR, Article 5(1)(c).
81 GDPR, Article 5(1)(d).

match the new email address, or could the provider legitimately rely on the user to do so?

(e) 'Personal data shall be kept in a form which permits identification of the data subjects for no longer than is necessary for the purposes for which it is processed …'[82]

4.30 The *storage limitation principle* is expressed so as to make the form in which the data is kept a function of the need to keep it no longer than necessary. In practice, this may cover a range of ways in which the data can be kept, between a simple ability to delete information manually to the automated expiry of records. There are exceptions in place for archiving in the public interest, scientific or historical research and statistical purposes.

(f) 'Personal data shall be processed in a manner that ensures appropriate security of the personal data …'[83]

4.31 The *integrity and confidentiality principle* is expressed to 'include' protection against unauthorised or unlawful processing and accidental loss, destruction or damage, and is therefore not restricted to these risks. It is suggested that this amounts to an obligation to take security measures which will bite independently of any breach.

The requirement is to use 'appropriate technical or organisational measures'. This points towards organisational policies and procedures governing human interaction as well as appropriate security of IT arrangements.

Cases involving data breach are obviously highly likely to involve a breach of this principle, even if no other principle is engaged.

The ICO's January 2020 decision to fine DSG Retail £500,000 is a case in point, albeit one issued under the Data Protection Act 1998.[84] Malware infected 5,390 point of sale tills at various retail stores over the period July 2017 to April 2018, allowing unauthorised access to details of 5.6 million payment cards and 14 million people. The decision did not proceed from any identified monetary loss or particular detriment to an individual data subject, although there had been 158 complaints to the ICO and 3,300 complaints to the retailer by the time the decision was reported.

Instead, the decision is based upon a detailed analysis of the technological and software standards for point of sale terminals, DSG's knowledge of the vulnerabilities in the system, both actual and presumed, and the extent and nature

82 GDPR, Article 5(1)(e).

83 GDPR, Article 5(1)(f).

84 Monetary Penalty Notice dated 7 January 2020, issued under DPA 1998, s 55A.

of the breaches of personal data. The decision expressly states that it was 'not certain whether the compromised personal data was used for successful identity theft or fraud',[85] but as a mitigating factor only, with the focus being firmly on the adequacy of the systems from a security standpoint.

The GDPR and DPA 2018 regime has resulted in two substantial fines from the ICO in October 2020. The decision notices in the cases of British Airways (£20 million)[86] and Marriott International (£18.4 million)[87] repay close reading for their rigorous analysis of the technical and organisational measures expected, particularly in the case of large corporates. In our opinion, they give an early and compelling illustration that the security-based approach of the ICO to enforcement will continue under the GDPR and the GDPR-based regime that the UK is likely to operate in the future.

ACCOUNTABILITY

4.32 In addition to the six data protection principles, controllers are required to process data in such a manner as to be able to demonstrate compliance and to be responsible for it. Again, the focus is on the system for processing set up so as to comply with this requirement. A number of aspects of accountability are worth mentioning for their potential for litigation. As we have seen, the GDPR imposes liability in relation to any breach of the obligations set out within it.

Controller to processor contracts

4.33 Many controllers outsource personal data processing as a matter of course. Payroll services are an obvious everyday example. Article 28 of the GDPR mandates a written contract between the controller and processor to govern the processing, and does so at what might be said to be a fairly detailed level. The effect is to impose minimum standards for private contracts insofar as personal data processing is envisaged. Amongst the requirements are conditions on the engagement of sub-processors and the presence of technological and organisational measures to assist the controller in complying with its own GDPR obligations.

Perhaps the clearest requirement is to process the personal data only on documented instructions from the controller, including where transfer of personal data to a third country or an international organisation is in prospect, save for a legal requirement to act otherwise.[88]

There are two significant overall effects of these provisions. First, controller to processor contracts need to be drafted with sufficient precision at the outset to allow for all the activity intended to be handled by the processor. Subsequent instructions to process would need to fall within the terms of that overarching

85 Notice, para 32(2).
86 Monetary Penalty Notice dated 16 October 2020, issued under DPA 1988, s 155.
87 Monetary Penalty Notice dated 30 October 2020, issued under DPA 1988, s 155.
88 GDPR, Article 28(3)(a).

contract. In default of adequate contractual provision, the risk lies in a claim by the data subject of a breach of one of the data protection principles. This could be the case even if the type of processing is exactly that which was envisaged and understood by the data subject.

Example

A contract between an employer and an outsourced payroll provider fails to put in place proper confidentiality obligations with respect to the personal data in the hands of the processor. It also fails to provide for adequate control by the employer of the processor's technological measures used for processing. It is therefore not compliant with Article 28.

The personal data is at risk of unauthorised disclosure and, it emerges, at risk of total loss in the event of a technical incident at the processor's offices. No loss or misuse has, in fact, occurred.

A data subject argues that there is a breach of the sixth data protection principle: integrity and confidentiality.

The data subject argues further that there is a breach of the first principle: lawfulness of processing. Although the controller and processor both have a legitimate interest in the processing by reference to Article 6 of the GDPR, this is not sufficient in itself to provide a lawful basis. The failure to comply with Article 28 makes the processing unlawful.

Secondly, a cause of action based upon a breach of the controller to processor contract might accrue in situations where the processor has gone 'beyond its brief' and processed personal data in a way which is not provided for under the contract or by documented instruction.

Example

A sports club provides a bespoke fitness app for its members. Amongst other things, the app is capable of tracking fitness data so that members can monitor their progress.

The software and data management for the app is outsourced to a company which provides the same service for many other clubs. The company packages the data and starts to publish leaderboards with named individuals such as 'Best 5k of the week' for all members to see.

Some members object and complain to the club of a breach of the purpose limitation principle. They cancel their membership.

The club seeks damages from the software company.

If a claim by a controller or processor arises in contract, it is distinctly possible that terms as to appropriate data protection safeguards might be implied as a necessary incident of the parties contemplating the processing of personal data.

As for the data subjects' rights in such a situation, Article 82 of the GDPR provides for enforcement action to be taken directly against processors and for joint and several liability to be established in an appropriate case.

Notification and registration requirements

4.34 The Data Protection (Charges and Information) Regulations 2018[89] came into force on 25 May 2018 and continue the regime of fees for notification and registration for controllers with the ICO, subject to various exemptions. This followed consultation on the exemptions, the result of which was only to introduce a new exemption in respect of standing for or fulfilling the duties of the office of all elected representatives and members of the House of Lords.[90]

The ICO has keenly enforced in this area.

In *Roy and Partners v The Information Commissioner* EA/2019/0096, 8 October 2019, the Tribunal dismissed an appeal against a £400 penalty for failure to pay a £40 annual registration fee. The appellant argued that its cancellation of the direct debit, which had previously been used to pay the fee, had been an error. The Tribunal accepted this but, applying a test of 'reasonable excuse' read across from other jurisdictions of the First Tier Tribunal, found that a reasonable data controller would have systems in place to prevent such an eventuality. The door was left open to an argument that there was 'some particular difficulty or misfortune' excusing departure from the standard, but on the facts in that case there was none.

Other accountability measures

4.35 There is a suite of measures contained in Chapter 4 of the GDPR which are designed to secure and embed compliance.

Article 24 makes reference to technical and organisational measures and their upkeep and audit, data protection policies and codes of conduct and certification. The latter are explained further in Articles 40–43. Essentially, member states are encouraged to draw up codes of conduct relating to particular sectors, and provide for certification of compliance by accredited certification bodies.

The ICO has issued detailed guidance on codes of conduct, which it describes as being a tool to be drawn up by trade associations and other representative bodes

89 SI 2018/480.

90 See DPA 2018, Sch 1, para 23(3) for the details.

to identify and address data protection issues that are important to their members. Such a code would be subject to criteria set by the ICO.[91]

The ICO has now finalised its submission process for the certification regime but, at the time of writing, there are no approved or accredited certification bodies under the ICO's jurisdiction. It has published detailed guidance on the process and envisages that, once approved, a certification body would be able to issue certification for a maximum of three years.[92]

For the litigation context, it is important to note that it is not envisaged that certification, or purported adherence to a code of conduct, would absolve a controller or processor of responsibility for a GDPR breach. It can be anticipated, however, that tranches of case law established in other fields might come into play.

One area where this might be the case is in an attempt to fix a certification body with responsibility for a personal data breach at common law, on the basis that the certification should never have been given. The most obvious legal route for such an allegation is in negligence. However, it would have to overcome the principles of tortious liability which have been developed so as to exclude, in many instances, tortious liability to third parties. This is so even if it is foreseeable that a negligent lack of care would lead to loss and damage. A claimant would first have to establish a duty of care by reference to the well-established tests of whether there is a sufficiently proximate relationship between the tortfeasor and the claimant and, if so, whether it is fair, just and reasonable to impose the duty. It is suggested that this is unlikely to be the case, at least as between the data subject and the certification body.[93]

The position could well be different in disputes arising between the certification body and the entity seeking certification. In that kind of scenario, assuming no contract would exist, various possibilities immediately suggest themselves for a legal model of the relevant relationship. Principles similar to those in public law could apply to the decision-making of the certification body. Alternatively, the legal relationship could be similar to that of a regulatory authority in the sporting, financial or similar arena. If the latter turns out to be the correct model, principles of restraint of trade might come into play if an entity's commercial prospects were to hinge on continuing certification or licensing as a controller of personal data.

As far as codes of conduct are concerned, the force of such codes in English law often depends on whether and to what extent they have a statutory foundation.

91 See also GDPR, Recitals 77, 98, 99 and 168 and EDPB's 'Guidelines 1/2019 on Codes of Conduct and Monitoring Bodies under Regulation 2016/679'.

92 EDPB 'Guidelines 1/2018 on certification and identifying certification criteria in accordance with Articles 42 and 43 of the Regulation', 4 June 2019; and 'Guidelines on the accreditation of certification bodies under Article 43 of the GDPR (2016/679)', 4 June 2019.

93 See, for example, *Marc Rich & Co v Bishop Rock Marine Co Ltd* [1996] AC 211 (HL).

The point can readily be seen in the employment field. In the law of unfair dismissal, a test of reasonableness is applied in order to determine whether a dismissal was fair, and an employer facing a discrimination or whistleblowing claim might seek to deploy the statutory defence that it did all it could to prevent the discrimination from occurring. Such a test, which is inevitably fact-sensitive, will almost always engage with the employer's policies and those relevant Codes of Practice issued by ACAS as part of the overall assessment of reasonableness, or in weighing up the statutory defence.

By way of contrast, in assessing compensation for many types of breach of employment rights, a tribunal is entitled to take into account the specific provisions of relevant statutory Codes of Practice issued by ACAS and to adjust compensation by a percentage according to whether or not they have been followed.

The particular way in which codes of conduct might have direct or background relevance to causes of action in data protection law is yet to be determined. But one can see possibilities for the law to incorporate either or both of these models into actions between a data subject and a controller or processor.

DATA SUBJECT RIGHTS

4.36 In addition to the requirements imposed by the data protection principles, the GDPR directly awards rights to individual data subjects. These appear in Chapter 3 of the GDPR and are explored below.

Rights of transparency and information

4.37 Articles 12 to 14 of the GDPR require certain information to be given by controllers to the data subject in a 'concise, transparent, intelligible and easily accessible form'.[94] We have explained above the need for information notices to be given to the data subject as an incident of the first data protection principle of fairness, lawfulness and transparency.

Article 12(5) provides that the information provided in answer to the various data subject rights must be provided free of charge. There is an exception, however, in cases where 'requests from the data subject are manifestly unfounded or excessive, in particular because of their repetitive character'. If that is the case, the controller may either charge a reasonable fee, taking into account the administrative costs, or refuse to act on the request altogether. The controller bears the burden of showing that the request is manifestly unfounded or excessive.

The ICO's guidance on these exceptions suggests that 'manifestly unfounded' could mean that there is:

94 GDPR, Article 12(1).

- no genuine intention to exercise the right for the purposes for which it is intended – for example, if the data subject offers to withdraw it in exchange for a benefit; or
- it is malicious in intent and being used to harass and disrupt – for example, by making unsubstantiated allegations or as part of a systematic campaign;

but also suggests that the unfounded nature should be of an obvious or clear quality, with an emphasis on the genuineness of the desire to exercise the right.

It suggests that 'excessive' could mean that there are repeat requests in substance, or that overlap with previous requests, but asks the controller to look at all the circumstances, including whether overlapping previous requests have been properly complied with or relate to a separate set of information.

Subject access requests

4.38 The subject access request is a familiar concept which is now contained in Article 15 of the GDPR. It is sometimes quite wrongly interpreted as an obligation on a controller to send to the data subject a minimal level of heavily redacted copies of documents, and to do no more. Respondents to requests have been known to withhold personal data on the ground that documents within which it is contained are 'confidential'.

The use of a subject access request is part of the armoury of a potential litigant in obtaining a measure of disclosure for use in the decision-making process about whether to start litigation and on what basis. A requirement to comply with the data protection regime is not yet enshrined formally within the Civil Procedure Rules in England and Wales, but that may come.

For these sorts of reasons, as well as the fact that the subject access right is directly enforceable under the GDPR and DPA 2018, it should be properly understood on both sides in actual and potential litigation.

The right of rectification

4.39 This right appears to flow directly from the accuracy principle and the obligation it imposes to rectify 'without delay' personal data which is inaccurate.[95] Interestingly enough, the time requirement within Article 16, which is where the corresponding right is set out, is stated to be 'without undue delay'. This may turn out to be a distinction without a difference, but it is suggested that the actual time allowed for enforcement purposes, in accordance with a common theme emerging from ICO decisions, is likely to be a function of the state of available technology and systems, and best practice guidelines. Little sympathy is likely

95 GDPR, Article 5(1)(d).

to be given for delay which is due to the particular difficulties of the controller if proper systems are not in place to respond to such requests.

The other interesting feature of this right is that the data subject has a right to have incomplete personal data completed, 'including by means of a supplementary statement', but this is expressed to be by 'taking into account the purposes of the processing'. Although the drafting of this provision leaves something to be desired, we believe it means that the standard by which the personal data is judged to be incomplete, and the corresponding data judged as being required to complete it, is determined by reference to the purposes of the processing.

Example

A record of the ages of a set of people could be kept by an insurer for the purposes of deciding whether or not they qualify for a particular healthcare benefit which is age-related. The insurer also provides benefits which are not age-related but subject to other tests.

If a birthday was wrongly recorded, a data subject would have a GDPR right (as well as potentially a contractual right) to have it corrected so as to benefit at the appropriate age threshold. However, they would not have the right to require the insurer to include any statement to the effect that, because of their true age, they are likely to qualify for other benefits which do not depend on the age threshold.

There is also the prospect, which has been raised in the EU jurisprudence, that a right very similar to the right of rectification could apply to search engines. *GC and others v Commission Nationale de l'Informatique et des Libertés*[96] in the CJEU principally concerns the right to be forgotten (see below for further detail on that topic). One issue was the fact that personal data concerning criminal offences or investigations might be accurate when published, but become inaccurate when an investigation proceeded over time such that the published data might no longer accurately reflect the legal position of the individual. It was stated that, if a search engine were to conclude, on balance, that 'de-listing' or 'de-referencing' of the problematic search results against a named individual is not required, the search engine as data controller is:

> 'in any event required, at the latest on the occasion of the right for de-referencing, to adjust the list of results in such a way that the overall picture it gives the internet user reflects the [individual's] current legal position, which means in particular that links to web pages containing information on that point must appear in first place on the list.'[97]

Although the reasoning of the court on this point is not made explicitly clear, it seems to us that it must flow from the same source as the right to rectification –

96 Case C-136/17, 24 September 2019.
97 At para 78.

that is, as identified above, the accuracy principle. It seems unlikely that it is an incident of the right to rectification itself, because the controller would not be rectifying the personal data in any obvious sense, but instead providing context for the personal data which gives an accurate overall picture to the internet user.

The right of erasure and the right to be forgotten

4.40 The right of erasure also follows from the accuracy principle, but more particularly from the storage limitation principle. Yet it does not solely respond to the obsolescence or inaccuracy of the data. A request to erase personal data must be complied with by the controller without undue delay[98] where one of the following applies:[99]

- the personal data is no longer necessary for the purposes – note that this is not expressed in terms of the *processing* no longer being necessary;
- the data subject withdraws consent or objects, where there is no other lawful basis of processing;
- the processing is unlawful;
- the personal data has to be erased for compliance with an EU or national legal obligation; or
- the personal data has been collected in relation to the offer of information society services directly to a child.

The right to be forgotten involves an extra layer of responsibility on a controller where one of the tests set out above is met. Where, in addition, the controller has made the personal data public, it is obliged to take reasonable steps to inform other controllers processing the data of the data subject's request. The controller may take into account available technology and the cost of implementation, but the reasonable steps required include technical measures.[100]

In our view, there are significant problems with the drafting of these provisions. The right to request erasure in Article 17(1) is confusingly drafted as if it exists independently of an obligation on the controller to erase the data, whether or not a request is made, if one of the tests set out therein is met. In respect of the right to be forgotten, it appears that, once a valid request (ie one falling within the Article 17(1) cases) has been made to one controller, and that controller has made the personal data public, the request is effectively treated as a request to all controllers to erase 'any links to, or copy or replication of' the personal data, which request the first controller has the obligation to pass on.

98 See para **4.39** above for the suggested meaning of this.
99 GDPR, Article 17.
100 GDPR, Article 17(2).

The Article 17(1) and (2) rights do not apply to the extent that the processing is necessary:[101]

- for exercising the right of freedom of expression;
- for compliance with a legal obligation or the performance of a task carried out in the public interest or in the exercise of official authority;
- for reasons of public interest in the area of public health;
- for archiving purposes in the public interest, scientific or historical research purposes or statistical purposes, which would make their aims impossible to achieve or seriously impair them; or
- for the establishment, exercise or defence of legal claims.

The EDPB has published 'Guidelines 5/2019 on the Criteria of the Right to be Forgotten in the search engine cases under the GDPR (part 1)' (11 December 2019). There was a public consultation on these which closed on 5 February 2020. The responses can be viewed on the EDPB website but, at the time of writing, there is no formal response.[102]

Before the GDPR came into force, the ECJ had already taken the view that the old Directive included a general right to be forgotten in the 'Google Spain' case.[103] One of the outcomes in that case was the requirement to balance the legitimate interests of the search engine with the data subject's rights. Another issue was that the right to be forgotten is to be judged at the time the request is made, and not by reference to whether the information was true or lawfully published at the time. This leads into the controversial issue of individuals using the right to be forgotten for the purposes of reputation management. Although the court did consider and address the public interest in maintaining access to information, the huge size of data controllers such as Google might lead to a blanket approach to requests for erasure which operates in favour of individual privacy rights and against the public interest.

The Google Spain ruling was developed further in the *GC and others v CNIL*[104] case which has already been referred to above. The data subjects in that case complained of search results turning up web pages, mainly referring to press publications, containing satirical images and text, including references to the criminal investigation and conviction of political figures and others in the public eye. This is special category data under the GDPR. It was confirmed that the rights of the data subject override, in principle, the economic interest of the search engine operator and the public interest in maintaining access.

101 GDPR, Article 17(3).

102 https://edpb.europa.eu/our-work-tools/public-consultations-art-704_en.

103 *Google Spain SL and Google Inc v Agencia Española de Protección de Datos (AEPD) and Mario Costeja González*, Case C-131/12 (decided on 13 May 2014).

104 *Google LLC v Commission Nationale de l'Informatique et des Libertés*, Case C-136/17.

However, the right is not absolute. The Court went on to hold that, in GDPR terms, it has to be balanced against Article 17(3)(a) (freedom of expression).[105] The compromise with the data subject's rights brings the accuracy principle into play, even if the right to be forgotten is defeated by considerations of public interest.[106]

The language of Article 17(3) is not obviously that of a balancing of competing rights – it reads more like a cancellation of the data subject's rights if the controller can fit within one of the exceptions. Nonetheless, the effect is to require search engines to put in place a case-by-case assessment of the Article 17 factors.

As we have seen, the Court also stated that there is a requirement for a search engine operator to adjust the list of results if it concludes that de-listing or de-referencing is not appropriate, so that the list puts the true up-to-date situation in first place.[107] Leaving aside questions of practicality, it is interesting that this is framed as an obligation which arises 'at the latest on the occasion of the request for de-referencing'. It must therefore be the case that the obligation could arise prior to, and independently of, the request.

We believe that this is further support for our view that the obligation on search engines to set results in their proper context is an incident of the accuracy principle and does not arise from the exercise of the right to erasure or to be forgotten as they are articulated in Article 17. Within the terms of Article 17 as it is set out, the Court's comments in *GC and others v CNIL* may also point towards an interpretation, as we have referred to above, that the obligation to erase in fact arises independently of a request to do so.

On the same day as the *GC* decision, the Court also decided *Google LLC v CNIL*[108] to the effect that, where the search engine does decide to accede to a request for de-referencing, it need only do so 'on versions of that search engine corresponding to all the Member States',[109] ie those available to internet users conducting a search from one of the Member States.

Right to restriction of processing

4.41 The right to restrict processing can be exercised by the data subject in the following situations:[110]

- where the accuracy is contested by the data subject, for a period allowing the controller to verify it;

105 At paras 56 and 59.
106 At paras 76 to 78.
107 At para 78.
108 Case C-507/17, 24 September 2019.
109 At para 64.
110 GDPR, Article 18.

- where the processing is unlawful but the data subject desires restriction rather than erasure;
- where the controller no longer requires the personal data but the data subject requires it for the purposes of a legal claim; or
- where the data subject exercises the right to object pending the resolution of any exception to that right (see below in relation to the Article 21 right to object).

The restriction means that the data can only be processed with the data subject's consent, subject to processing by way of storage, for the purposes of legal claims, for the protection of the rights of another person, or for reasons of important public interest.

There is, in effect, a holding pattern adopted so that disputes and potential disputes are not traversed by the controller carrying on in a way which is objectionable to the data subject. It may also be noted that, in some situations, the controller will be obliged to retain and store data that it would otherwise erase. Potential litigants may therefore wish to exercise this right so as to place a burden on a controller and obtain a tactical advantage.

Data portability

4.42 The data portability right is the right for data subjects to have a copy of their personal data provided free of charge to them or to another controller in a 'structured, commonly used and machine-readable format'.[111]

The right is restricted by Article 20 to situations where all of the following apply:

- the data subject has provided the data to the controller;
- the processing is based on consent or the performance of a contract; and
- the processing is carried out by automated means.

One potential application of this right is in the transfer of data between commercial service providers such as banks or insurance companies. In some cases, the personal data will be regarded as a business asset. Article 20(4) states that the right 'shall not adversely affect the rights and freedoms of others'. It remains to be seen how the law might be able to deal with an argument that commercial interests are adversely affected by the data portability right. In the meantime, WP29 has published guidelines on data portability.[112]

111 GDPR, Article 20.
112 WP29 'Guidelines on the right to data portability', 5 April 2017.

Right to object, and automated decision-making

4.43 The right to object applies where processing is taking place on the basis of either the legitimate interests of the controller or a task purportedly carried out in the public interest or the exercise of official authority.[113] In those cases, if the data subject objects, the controller must cease the processing unless it can demonstrate 'compelling legitimate grounds for the processing which override the interests, rights and freedoms of the data subject or for the establishment, exercise or defence of legal claims'.

There is no such opportunity, even based on reversing the burden of proof, if the data subject objects to processing for direct marketing purposes.

As far as automated decision-making is concerned (including profiling), the data subject ought to have been informed from the outset that automated decision-making was taking place, and the significance of it, in accordance with Article 13(2)(f).

The right given by Article 22 is the right not to be subject to a decision based solely on automated processing producing legal or similarly significant effects on them. This is subject to the processing being necessary for entering into or performing a contract between the parties, authorised by EU or Member State law or based on the data subject's explicit consent. If those exceptions apply, the controller must nonetheless implement measures to safeguard the data subject's interests, including at least allowing the data subject to contest the decision by way of human intervention.

Where the processing is based on special category personal data, the exceptions are further restricted by their application only where processing is based on the data subject's explicit consent or the processing is necessary for reasons of substantial public interest.

The ICO has published detailed guidance on automated decision-making and profiling, as has WP29.

The use of cookies is the almost ubiquitous methodology for carrying out profiling in the online space. As online identifiers, cookies and similar technologies are specifically brought within the concept of personal data.

During the second half of 2019 the ICO was subjecting the advertising technology (adtech) industry to heavy scrutiny around its use of cookies, particularly in respect of their use in real-time bidding applications. The ICO announced a temporary suspension of work in May 2020 but the ambition to secure reform and compliance remains.

113 GDPR, Article 21.

DATA SECURITY AND PERSONAL DATA BREACHES

4.44 Articles 32 to 34 of the GDPR[114] contain obligations on the controller and processor to have appropriate data security provisions in place, and on the controller to report a personal data breach to the SA and to the data subject.

The sorts of security measures that the GDPR envisages are referred to in Article 32:

- pseudonymisation and encryption;
- ensuring the ongoing confidentiality, integrity, availability and resilience of processing systems and services;
- the ability to restore the availability and access to personal data in a timely manner in the event of a physical or technical incident; and
- a process for regularly testing, assessing and evaluating the effectiveness of technical and organisational measures for ensuring the security of the processing.

The focus is on the measures which are appropriate having regard to the risks. Detailed analysis of the security measures is a common feature of the ICO's decisions in data breach cases.

The time period for notification to the SA is without undue delay and, where feasible, within 72 hours of becoming aware of it.[115] There is a threshold of seriousness for the need to report, but it is low: it is not necessary to report a breach if it is 'unlikely to result in a risk to the rights and freedoms of natural persons'.

Controllers and processors are separately required to notify the SA of any breaches under Article 33. The controller is also required to document any breach, including any remedial action, to enable the SA to verify compliance with the notification requirement. The requirement itself includes a description of the likely consequences and the measures taken to address it and mitigate its effects.

The obligation to notify data subjects under Article 34 arises where the breach is 'likely to result in a high risk to the rights and freedoms of natural persons'. Note that the risk giving rise to the need to report is not restricted to the rights and freedoms of the data subject, but that the reporting requirement is so restricted.

Again, there is an obligation to describe the measures being taken to address the breach. However, the controller does not have to notify the data subject if any of the following apply:

114 See also GDPR, Recitals 85, 87 and 88.
115 GDPR, Article 33.

- appropriate protection measures have been applied, meaning making the data unintelligible by a method such as encryption;
- measures have been taken to eliminate the high risk to the rights and freedoms of individuals; or
- notification would involve a disproportionate effort, as might be the case in a large-scale breach of consumer data, in which case a controller can use some form of public communication instead which will be equally effective in informing individuals.

The SA can overrule controllers and order specific notification following its own assessment of the high risk resulting from the breach.

In practical terms, these notification requirements are powerful evidential tools available to data subjects in the event of a breach.

WP29 issued 'Guidelines on personal data breach notification under Regulation 2018/679' in February 2018.

We consider the implications of data security breaches in **Chapter 9** on remedies and enforcement.

Part III

Litigation and Evidence

Chapter 5

Jurisdiction

This chapter examines:

- the general rules on jurisdiction in cyber litigation;
- how these general rules can be amended;
- particular areas of cyber litigation – cryptoassets and smart contracts – that have specific jurisdictional considerations;
- the Court List and Pre-Action Protocol for Data Claims; and
- the impact of Brexit on the rules on jurisdiction.

INTRODUCTION

5.1 Generally speaking, with the possible exception of claiming jurisdiction by territorial link (see para **5.8** below), no special jurisdictional rules apply at present to cyber litigation, despite the potential territorial complexities of cyber cases.

For example, an individual conducting a Distributed-Denial-of-Service or deploying ransomware in the United Kingdom ('UK') may be located outside England and Wales. In the civil sphere, a celebrity gossip magazine headquartered in Germany may publish defamatory remarks about a member of the Danish Royal Family on its French-market website, which is hosted on an American server.

Where an individual's or corporate's actions and their consequences straddle different countries and jurisdictions, who has jurisdiction to hear cyber claims and/or cyber criminal cases against them?

What are the general rules on jurisdiction in cyber litigation?

5.2 At present, the rules on jurisdiction vary depending on whether or not a defendant is within the European Union ('EU').

Natural and legal persons within the European Union

5.3 Article 4(1) of the Recast Brussels Regulation[1] provides that, subject to certain exceptions outlined in sections 2 to 7 of Chapter II, for civil or commercial

1 Regulation (EU) 1215/2012 of the European Parliament and of the Council on jurisdiction and the recognition and enforcement of judgments in civil and commercial matters.

proceedings commenced on or after 10 January 2015, persons (both natural and legal) should be sued in the courts of the Member State where they are domiciled. Therefore, if a natural or legal person is domiciled in England or Wales, they will be subject to the jurisdiction of the English and Welsh courts.

A natural person is domiciled in a jurisdiction if they are:

- resident in the jurisdiction; and
- the nature and circumstances of their residence indicate a substantial connection with the jurisdiction.

A natural person can be resident in a number of Member State jurisdictions. Therefore, the test is whether, in all the circumstances, there is sufficient permanency for them to be settled in a particular jurisdiction so that it is their usual place of abode. Courts will compare the ties to the various jurisdictions and time spent there in order to determine a person's residency.

A legal person, ie a corporate body, is domiciled at the place where it has its:[2]

- statutory seat;
- central administration; or
- principal place of business.

Article 7 provides some of the exceptions to the general Article 4(1) rule. The most relevant to cyber litigation are:

- 'in matters relating to a contract, [a person may be sued] in the courts for the place of performance of the obligation in question';[3]
- 'in matters relating to tort, delict or quasi-delict, [a person may be sued] in the courts for the place where the harmful event occurred or may occur';[4] and
- 'as regards a civil claim for damages or restitution which is based on an act giving rise to criminal proceedings, [a person may be sued] in the court seised of those proceedings, to the extent that that court has jurisdiction under its own law to entertain civil proceedings'.[5]

It should be noted that, in matters relating to tort etc, the 'place where the harmful event occurred' is 'intended to cover both the place where the damage occurred and the place of the event giving rise to it'.[6]

2 Regulation (EU) 1215/2012, Article 63(1).
3 Regulation (EU) 1215/2012, Article 7(1).
4 Regulation (EU) 1215/2012, Article 7(2).
5 Regulation (EU) 1215/2012, Article 7(3).
6 *eDate Advertising GmbH v X* (Joined Cases C-509/09 and C-161/10) [2011] ECR I-10269, at [41].

Consequently, for example, where England and Wales is the place where the damage occurred or the place of the event giving rise to the damage, the natural or legal person may be sued in England and Wales regardless of where they are domiciled.

However, in cyber cases, it is not necessarily straightforward to determine where particular events happened, so it may not be straightforward to determine where proceedings should be brought.

Case Study

Wintersteiger AG v Products 4U Sondermaschinenbau GmbH[7] was a case under the predecessor to the Recast Brussels Regulation – Council Regulation (EC) No 44/2001 of 22 December 2000 on jurisdiction and the recognition and enforcement of judgments in civil and commercial matters ('Regulation 44/2001').

The claimant ('W') was an Austrian-based company that manufactured and distributed ski and snowboard servicing tools and accessories. W was the proprietor of an Austrian trade mark, 'WINTERSTEIGER', which was protected in other Member States, including Germany. The defendant ('P') was a German company that sold W's accessories, although W did not supply them nor authorise P's sale of them.

P registered the AdWord 'Wintersteiger' on Google's search service, but limited the registration to searches carried out via the top-level domain for Germany, which could be accessed in Austria. Each time the word was entered into Google's search engine for that top-level domain, an advertising link appeared on the side of the page in addition to a link to W's website. The advertising link directed the user to the section of P's website selling W's accessories.

W sought an injunction in the Austrian courts, to require P to desist from using the trade mark as an AdWord on the Google search engine for the top-level domain for Germany.

The Austrian Supreme Court asked the European Court of Justice for a preliminary ruling on the interpretation of Article 5(3) of Regulation 44/2001: a person domiciled in a Member State may, in another Member State, in matters relating to tort, delict or quasi-delict, be sued in the courts for the place where the harmful event occurred or may occur. The issue referred was what criteria were to be used to determine jurisdiction to hear an action relating to an alleged infringement of a trade mark registered in a Member State through the use, by an advertiser, of a keyword identical to that trade mark on the website of an internet search engine operating under a top-level

7 (C-523/10) [2013] Bus LR 150.

domain different from that of the Member State where the trade mark was registered.

The First Chamber reiterated that, as outlined in *eDate Advertising GmbH v X* (Joined Cases C-509/09 and C-161/10), the rule of special jurisdiction laid down in Article 5(3), by way of derogation from the principle of jurisdiction of the courts of the place of domicile of the defendant, was based on the existence of a particularly close connecting factor between the dispute and the courts of the place where the harmful event occurred, which justified the attribution of jurisdiction to those courts for reasons relating to the sound administration of justice and the efficacious conduct of the proceedings. The expression 'place where the harmful event occurred or may occur' in Article 5(3) covered both the place where the damage occurred and the place of the event giving rise to it. The defendant, therefore, might be sued in the courts of either of those places, since both could constitute a significant connecting factor from the point of view of jurisdiction.[8]

In terms of jurisdiction to hear a claim of infringement of a national mark, the court held that the objectives of foreseeability and the sound administration of justice militated in favour of conferring jurisdiction, in respect of the damage sustained, on the courts of the Member State in which the trade mark at issue was registered, since those courts were best able to assess whether a situation actually infringed the protected national mark.[9]

In relation to the place where the event giving rise to the damage occurred, it was the activation by the advertiser of the technical process displaying the advertisement which constituted the event. Although the process was activated, ultimately, on a server belonging to the search engine used by the operator, the court held that, in view of the objective of foreseeability, which the rules of jurisdiction must pursue, the place of establishment of the server could not, by reason of its uncertain location, be considered to be the place where the event giving rise to the damage occurred. Therefore the court held that, since it was a definite and identifiable place, and therefore likely to facilitate the taking of evidence and the conduct of the proceedings, the event took place at the establishment of the advertiser, that being the place where the activation of the display process was decided.[10]

Accordingly, the action could be brought in either the courts of the Member State in which the trade mark was registered or the courts of the Member State of the advertiser's place of establishment.[11]

8 [2013] Bus LR 150, at [18]–[20].
9 [2013] Bus LR 150, at [25]–[29].
10 [2013] Bus LR 150, at [32]–[38].
11 [2013] Bus LR 150, at [39].

Thus a close analysis of the elements of the tort alleged, and the technology employed, might be necessary in order to establish where the place of any harmful event occurred. It should be noted, however, that the place where the 'harmful event' occurred should not include the place where a person claims to have suffered financial loss consequential on initial damage arising and being suffered by them in another Member State.[12] Neither should it include, without other connecting factors, the place where solely financial damage is suffered as a result of an unlawful act committed in another Member State.[13]

Article 8 provides a further exception to the general Article 4(1) jurisdiction by domicile rule. A person domiciled in a Member State may also be sued, where they are one of a number of defendants, in the courts of the place where any one of them is domiciled, provided that the claims are so closely connected that it is expedient to hear and determine them together to avoid the risk of irreconcilable judgments resulting from separate proceedings.[14]

Natural or legal persons outside the European Union

5.4 In terms of the European Free Trade Association ('EFTA') countries, ie Switzerland, Norway, Iceland and Liechtenstein, similar rules to those in the Recast Brussels Regulation apply under the 2007 Lugano Convention. This regulates the jurisdiction and enforcement of legal matters as between those countries and EU Member States.

Where a party is both outside the EU and the EFTA, jurisdiction becomes a question of private international law and the common law rules apply.

The courts of England and Wales will have jurisdiction over a defendant domiciled outside the EU if they can be served with a claim form in England and Wales. This includes not only a defendant having consented to the service of proceedings in England and Wales by, for example, having solicitors within England and Wales who have instructions to accept service, but also serving papers on an individual whilst they are only visiting England and Wales.[15] In these circumstances, the defendant may argue that the English and Welsh courts should not exercise their jurisdiction if there is a more appropriate forum by applying the doctrine of forum non conveniens.

If service cannot be effected on a defendant within England and Wales, a claimant will need the court's permission under Part 6 of the Civil Procedure Rules ('CPR') to serve the claim form on them out of the jurisdiction.[16]

12 *Marinari v Lloyds Bank plc* (C-364/93) [1995] ECR I-02719.
13 *Universal Music International Holding BV v Schilling* (C-12/15) [2016] ECR I-00000.
14 Regulation (EU) 1215/2012, Article 8(1).
15 *Maharanee of Baroda v Wildenstein* [1972] 2 QB 283.
16 CPR, r 6.36.

In order to serve a claim form out of the jurisdiction, a claimant will need to establish that:

- the claim falls within one or more of the jurisdictional gateways set out in paragraph 3.1 of Practice Direction 6B of the CPR;[17]
- the claim has a reasonable prospect of success;[18] and
- England and Wales is the proper place in which to bring the claim.[19]

Case Study

In *AA v Persons Unknown*[20] a Canadian insurance company, which was itself insured with an English insurance company, was hacked and the ransomware BitPayer was installed. BitPayer encrypted all of the company's computer systems, and USD 1.2 million in Bitcoins was demanded in order to obtain the decryption tool. The ransom price was reduced to USD 950,000 in Bitcoins and, on 10 October 2019, 109.25 Bitcoins were transferred to the address that had been provided. The decryption tool was received the following day and deployed across the company's systems.

The claimant contacted a specialist company that provides software to track payments of cryptocurrency: Chainalysis. It was discovered that some of the Bitcoins were transferred into fiat currency and that 96 Bitcoins were transferred to an address that was linked to the Bitfinex cryptoasset exchange. Bitfinex's parent company, iFINEX, and trading company for non-US persons, BFXWW, are BVI companies.

The claimant applied to the High Court for:

- a Bankers Trust order and/or a Norwich Pharmacal order requiring Bitfinex to provide specified information in relation to the cryptocurrency account holding the 96 Bitcoins; and/or
- a proprietary injunction in respect of the Bitcoin held in the account; and/or
- a freezing injunction in respect of the Bitcoin held at the specified account; and
- consequential orders to serve the same, including alternate service and service outside the jurisdiction.

During the course of the hearing, the applications for the Bankers Trust/ Norwich Pharmacal order and freezing injunction were adjourned.[21]

17 CPR, r 6.36.
18 CPR, r 6.37(1)(b).
19 CPR, r 6.37(3).
20 [2019] EWHC 3556 (Comm).
21 See paras 44 to 49 of the judgment for the reasoning behind this.

In respect of the application to serve the remaining proprietary injunction outside the jurisdiction, a number of the gateways under Practice Direction 6B were relied on:[22]

- a claim is made for an injunction ordering the defendant to do or refrain from doing an act within the jurisdiction;[23]
- a claim is made against a person upon whom the claim form has been served or will be served otherwise than in reliance on this paragraph, and:
  - there is between the claimant and that person a real issue which it is reasonable for the court to try; and
  - the claimant wishes to serve the claim form on another person who is a necessary or proper party to that claim;[24]
- a claim is made for an interim remedy under section 25(1) of the Civil Jurisdiction and Judgments Act 1982;[25] and
- a claim is made in tort where damage was sustained or will be sustained within the jurisdiction, or damage which has been or will be sustained results from an act committed or likely to have been committed within the jurisdiction.[26]

The court was satisfied that the proprietary injunction sought fell within paragraph 3.1(5) (a claim for an interim remedy under section 25(1) of the Civil Jurisdiction and Judgments Act 1982) and paragraph 3.1(9) (a claim in tort, where damage was sustained within the jurisdiction). The insurer was an English insurance company who paid the ransom money from an English bank account and was registered in England and Wales. It had suffered loss in the form of the money which was used to buy the Bitcoins which ended up with, and were traced through to, Bitfinex.[27]

The court also considered that the paragraph 3.1(3) gateway was potentially applicable because of the application of the other gateways identified. This provided that any of the defendants could fall within those other gateways, and there would be other defendants that would fall within the provisions of the paragraph 3.1(3) gateway, giving rise to a prospect of a trial involving all of the defendants.[28]

Therefore the court was satisfied that it was appropriate to serve the claim form out of the jurisdiction and granted permission to do so.[29]

22 [2019] EWHC 3556 (Comm), at [67].
23 CPR, PD 6B, para 3.1(2).
24 CPR, PD 6B, para 3.1(3).
25 CPR, PD 6B, para 3.1(5).
26 CPR, PD 6B, para 3.1(9).
27 [2019] EWHC 3556 (Comm), at [68].
28 [2019] EWHC 3556 (Comm), at [70].
29 [2019] EWHC 3556 (Comm), at [71].

See also paragraph **5.16** below, and **Chapters 2** and **9** for further discussion of various aspects of this case.

A further example of the court granting permission to serve out of the jurisdiction is *PML v Persons Unknown*.[30]

Case Study

The claimant was a UK company that had been hacked and had a large quantity of data stolen. The defendant emailed the claimant, threatening to publish the information unless the claimant paid GBP 300,000.

The claimant reported the matter to the police and obtained a without notice interim non-disclosure order which restrained the threatened breach of confidence and ordered delivery-up and/or destruction of the stolen data. The defendant's identity was unknown and the injunction order had been served on it using the email account by which it had been corresponding with the claimant.

The defendant responded by removing the password protection on the website that hosted the stolen data, although the company which hosted the website had blocked access to the website in compliance with a further order obtained by the claimant. The claimant subsequently identified further websites hosting the stolen documents and took steps to ensure that the hosting companies prevented access to the documents by serving the injunction on them.

The defendant continued to threaten publication of the data, and the claimant applied for the continuation of the interim non-disclosure order.

The court granted the application to continue the injunction. Little had changed since the without notice injunction had been granted and the defendant had continued to threaten to publish the stolen data unless it was paid a substantial sum of money. Indeed, it appeared that it had tried to publish some of the data. The claimant was likely to demonstrate at trial that the circumstances in which the defendant came to be in possession of the relevant documents and information imposed an obligation of confidence on the defendant. The defendant had not suggested that there was any public interest that could justify the publication of the data. The claimant was likely to establish at trial that publication of the stolen data should not be allowed, and the defendant's failure to deliver up or delete the stolen data was a further prima facie breach of the injunction order which justified the continuation of the order.[31]

30 [2018] EWHC 838 (QB).
31 [2018] EWHC 838 (QB), at [13].

> The court noted that there was the potential that the defendant was resident in a country which would require the court's permission to serve the claim form outside the court's jurisdiction. The court stated that the claim was for breach of confidence, the detriment would be suffered within the jurisdiction if the threatened publication were to take place, and the defendant was threatening to do an act (ie publication) that would take place within the jurisdiction. The court was also satisfied that England and Wales was the proper place in which to bring the claim. Consequently, it granted permission, pursuant to CPR rule 6.37 and paragraph 3.1(21) of CPR PD 6B (a claim is made for breach of confidence or misuse of private information where detriment was suffered or will be suffered within the jurisdiction, or detriment which has been or will be suffered results from an act committed or likely to be committed within the jurisdiction), to serve the claim form and other documents outside the jurisdiction if that proved necessary.[32]

CPR rule 6.37(1) and (2) outlines what an application for permission to serve a claim form out of the jurisdiction must include.

Alternatively, rather than jurisdiction based on service, the courts of England and Wales may have jurisdiction over a defendant who has submitted to the jurisdiction of the English and Welsh courts. In order to ascertain this, the question is whether the defendant has taken a step in the proceedings which can be seen as an unequivocal submission to the jurisdiction, or whether their conduct is in any other way inconsistent with a challenge to the jurisdiction.[33]

Under Part 11 of the CPR, a defendant submits to the jurisdiction of the courts of England and Wales by:

- acknowledging service and not indicating that they intend to dispute the court's jurisdiction; or
- taking a step inconsistent with a jurisdiction challenge.

How can the general rules on jurisdiction be amended?

5.5 The two main ways in which the general rules on jurisdiction can be amended are jurisdiction clauses and legislative provisions providing for extraterritoriality.

32 [2018] EWHC 838 (QB), at [18].

33 *SMAY Investments Ltd v Sachdev* [2003] EWHC 474 (Ch); *Global Multimedia International Ltd v ARA Media Services* [2006] EWHC 3612 (Ch).

Jurisdiction clauses

5.6 Parties to a contract can insert a clause whereby they agree to submit to the exclusive jurisdiction of a particular country: jurisdiction clauses.[34]

Once the parties have chosen a jurisdiction, the courts in England and Wales will generally be slow to interfere.

However, jurisdiction clauses will not always be determinative if a party can show strong reasons for bringing a claim in a non-contractual forum.

> Case Study
>
> In *Donohue v Armco Inc*,[35] prosecution proceedings were commenced in the United States ('US') for alleged fraudulent activity by the claimant and others. The basis of the fraud was alleged to relate to a management buy-out, which was governed by a sale and purchase agreement and two transfer agreements. Each of the agreements contained a clause giving exclusive jurisdiction to the courts of England and Wales.
>
> Following the commencement of proceedings in the US, the claimant sought to invoke the jurisdiction clauses and applied under section 37(1) of the Supreme Court Act 1981 (renamed 'Senior Courts Act 1981') for an anti-suit injunction to restrain the prosecution proceedings in the US. The anti-suit injunction was refused at first instance,[36] but allowed on appeal.[37]
>
> The defendants, a group of companies incorporated in the US and Singapore, appealed against the anti-suit injunction.
>
> In its judgment, the House of Lords stated, first, where contractual parties agree to give a particular court exclusive jurisdiction to rule on claims between those parties, and a claim falling within the scope of the agreement is made in proceedings in a forum other than that which the parties have agreed, the English court will ordinarily exercise its discretion (whether by granting a stay of proceedings in England, or by restraining the prosecution of proceedings in the non-contractual forum abroad, or by such other procedural order as is appropriate in the circumstances). Second, in order to secure compliance with the contractual bargain, the party suing in the non-contractual forum (the burden being on them) needs to show strong reasons for suing in that forum. Thus the general rule is clear that, where parties have bound themselves by an exclusive jurisdiction clause, effect should ordinarily be given to that obligation in the absence of strong reasons for departing from it. Whether a party can show strong reasons, sufficient to displace the

34 See Regulation (EU) 1215/2012, Article 25, and CPR, PD 6B, para 3.1(6)(d).

35 [2001] UKHL 64.

36 [2000] 1 All ER (Comm) 425.

37 [2000] 1 All ER (Comm) 641.

> other party's prima facie entitlement to enforce the contractual bargain, will depend on all the facts and circumstances of the particular case.[38]
>
> In the present case, the House of Lords allowed the appeal, holding that the Court of Appeal had erred in the exercise of its discretion. On the facts, the defendants had shown a sufficiently strong reason to displace the claimant's right to rely upon the exclusive jurisdiction clause: namely, that, if the injunction was granted, it was very likely that litigation would proceed in both England and the US. This was undesirable, particularly in a conspiracy case, and so it was best that the matter was dealt with by a single tribunal. This could only be achieved if the US proceedings continued.[39]

Despite the potential non-determinative effect of jurisdiction clauses, parties seeking some semblance of certainty in a world where data, actions and consequences can transcend many jurisdictions may wish to insert an exclusive jurisdiction clause into their contracts in order to resolve disputes.

Extraterritorial legislative provisions

5.7 The criminal courts of England and Wales tend to only have jurisdiction over criminal offences committed within the territory of England and Wales. However, various legislative provisions extend the territorial scope of some criminal offences, specifically:

- money laundering, terrorist financing, and bribery (which are all capable of being cyber-assisted crimes); and
- cyber-dependent crimes.

See further **Chapter 2**.

Computer Misuse Act 1990

5.8 Section 43 of the Serious Crime Act 2015 amended sections 4 and 5 of the Computer Misuse Act 1990 ('CMA 1990') and extended the territorial scope of the CMA 1990.

Section 4(1) of the CMA 1990 provides that it is immaterial, for the purposes of any offence under section 1, 3 or 3ZA (unauthorised access to computer material; unauthorised acts with intent to impair, or with recklessness as to impairing, the operation of a computer; and unauthorised acts causing, or creating risk of, serious damage), whether any act or other event, proof of which is required for conviction of the offence, occurred in the home country or whether the accused

38 [2001] UKHL 64, at [24].
39 [2001] UKHL 64, at [34]–[39].

was in the home country at the time of the act or event. All that is required is at least one significant link with the domestic jurisdiction.[40]

Section 4(4A) also provides that it is immaterial, for the purposes of an offence under section 3A (making, supplying or obtaining articles for use in an offence under section 1, 3 or 3ZA), whether the accused was in the home country concerned at the time of any act or other event, proof of which is required for conviction of the offence, if there is a significant link with the domestic jurisdiction in relation to the offence.

In terms of what constitutes a significant link with the domestic jurisdiction where an individual is outside the UK at the time of the act constituting the offence under section 1, 3, 3ZA or 3A, section 5(1A) provides that there is a significant link with the domestic jurisdiction if the individual was a UK national at the time of the act and the act constituted an offence under the law of the territory in which it occurred.

Thus, the CMA 1990 has extraterritorial applicability in relation to the actions of UK nationals and it should always be borne in mind that, not only does it create broad categories of offences (see **Chapter 2**), but it also has a wide territorial reach.

Proceeds of Crime Act 2002

5.9 The Court of Appeal in *R v Rogers*[41] held that money laundering offences in the Proceeds of Crime Act 2002 ('POCA 2002') have extraterritorial effect.

> Case Study
>
> The appellant, R, who held a UK passport and was living and working in Spain, was accused of participating in frauds which involved convincing UK citizens to pay advance fees on the basis of false promises of debt elimination or escort services. The profits were transferred from UK bank accounts to bank accounts in Spain, one of which was held by R.
>
> R was charged with two counts of conspiracy to defraud and one count of money laundering. He resisted the charges on the basis that he had had no criminal involvement. The particulars of the money laundering offence alleged that R had removed GBP 715,000 from the jurisdiction, which was criminal property obtained by the fraud, by arranging for that sum to be transferred and delivered into his Spanish bank account.
>
> At the end of the Crown's case, the judge accepted R's submission of no case to answer in relation to the money laundering charge, on the basis that the evidence did not show that R was involved in the removal of the money.

40 Computer Misuse Act 1990, s 4(2).
41 [2014] EWCA Crim 1680.

However, the judge permitted an amendment to the indictment which took the form of a new count. The new count alleged that R had converted the GBP 715,000, contrary to section 327(1)(c) of POCA 2002, by permitting its receipt into his Spanish bank account and then allowing its subsequent withdrawal.

R was acquitted of the conspiracy to defraud charges but convicted of converting criminal property.

R appealed against his conviction, submitting that the judge had erred in, amongst other things, ruling that the Crown Court had jurisdiction to deal with the amended count when all of the alleged activities were undertaken in Spain by a non-resident of the UK in relation to a Spanish bank account.

The Court of Appeal dismissed the appeal and held that POCA 2002 provided extraterritorial jurisdiction in relation to money laundering offences.[42]

The court noted that the following indicated that extraterritorial reach was intended by Parliament:[43]

- Section 327(1)(e) of POCA 2002 stipulates that criminal property must be removed from England, Wales, Scotland or Northern Ireland, but no such geographical limitation is placed on the other methods of committing the offence, including the conversion of criminal property under section 327(1)(c).
- Section 327(2A) provides a defence to a person who knows or believes that relevant criminal conduct occurred outside the UK in circumstances where such conduct was not unlawful in that country at the time it took place. Section 340(2)(b) provides that criminal conduct is conduct which would constitute an offence in any part of the UK if it occurred there. The court stated that these provisions, taken together, give a strong indication that a defendant's money laundering activity abroad is potentially within the jurisdiction of the English courts.
- The definition of criminal property in section 340(3), together with the provision in section 340(9) that 'property is all property wherever situated [...]' is a further indication of the extraterritorial reach intended by Parliament.
- The specific provision in section 340(11)(d), that money laundering is an act which would constitute an offence (including one under section 327) if done in the UK, appears to admit no other construction than that Parliament intended extraterritorial effect to this legislation.
- The offence of money laundering is par excellence an offence which has no respect of national boundaries, and so it would be surprising indeed if Parliament had not intended POCA 2002 to have extraterritorial effect.

42 [2014] EWCA Crim 1680, at [52].
43 [2014] EWCA Crim 1680, at [43]–[47] and [52].

> The court held that sections 327(2A) and 340(2) and (11) clearly relate to the conduct element of the offence rather than the criminal property element, and it concluded that, based on the provisions referred to and, in particular, section 340(11)(d), there was jurisdiction to try the appellant.[44] While the monies obtained by the fraud in the UK became criminal property once they reached a bank account in the UK controlled by the conspirators, those proceeds did not cease to be criminal property when they arrived in the appellant's bank account in Spain. By permitting the use of that bank account for receipt and then withdrawal of those monies, the appellant was converting them. The actions of the appellant continued the harmful consequences of the fraud to be experienced by those victims in the UK by providing a haven further beyond the reach of UK consumers for the criminally obtained monies.[45]

Therefore, UK nationals based overseas could face criminal liability for cyber-assisted money laundering committed wholly overseas.

Money Laundering, Terrorist Financing and Transfer of Funds (Information on the Payer) Regulations 2017

5.10 The Money Laundering, Terrorist Financing and Transfer of Funds (Information on the Payer) Regulations 2017 ('MLR 2017') provide for a number of criminal offences.[46] These are given extraterritorial effect by regulation 90, which enables courts to treat offences 'committed wholly or partly outside the United Kingdom' as 'having been committed within the jurisdiction of the court' for all incidental purposes.[47]

Bribery Act 2010

5.11 The offences under sections 1, 2 and 6 of the Bribery Act 2010 ('BA 2010') (bribing another person, being bribed, and bribery of a foreign public official) also have extraterritorial effect. Thus, individuals outside the UK may be prosecuted in the UK for these offences, even where no act or omission forming part of the offence took place in the UK, provided that:[48]

- the person's acts or omissions outside the UK would form part of such an offence if they had occurred in the UK; and
- the person has a 'close connection with the UK'.

What constitutes 'a close connection with the UK' is defined in section 12(4) of the BA 2010 and includes being a UK citizen or a UK company.[49]

44 [2014] EWCA Crim 1680, at [48] and [49].
45 [2014] EWCA Crim 1680, at [49] and [50].
46 MLR 2017, regs 86–88.
47 MLR 2017, reg 90(3).
48 Bribery Act 2010, s 12(2)-(3).
49 Bribery Act 2010, s 12(4)(a) and (h).

The corporate offence under section 7 of the BA 2010 also has extraterritorial effect. The section 7 offence is committed by a 'relevant commercial organisation' if a person associated with the organisation (an associated person)[50] bribes another person intending to obtain or retain business or an advantage in the conduct of business for the organisation.[51] The organisation's only defence to the strict liability offence is to show that it had 'adequate procedures' in place designed to prevent associated persons from undertaking such conduct.[52]

A 'relevant commercial organisation' includes not only companies and partnerships incorporated in the UK and which carry on business in the UK or elsewhere, but also a company or partnership (wherever incorporated) that carries on any part of its business in the UK.[53] The Ministry of Justice's guidance on the BA 2010[54] recommends a 'common sense approach' when considering whether a relevant commercial organisation carries on any part of its business in the UK, and notes that a 'demonstrable business presence' is required. The guidance states that neither the mere fact of having the company's shares listed on the London Stock Exchange nor having a UK subsidiary necessarily means that a foreign company is carrying on business in the UK for the purposes of section 7 of the Act.[55]

What are the particular areas of cyber litigation that have specific jurisdictional considerations?

5.12 Due to the inherent features of cryptoassets and smart contracts, cases involving these have specific jurisdictional considerations.

Cryptoassets

5.13 Cryptoassets present an interesting conundrum in the question of jurisdiction. The UK Jurisdiction Taskforce's ('UKJT') Legal Statement on Cryptoassets and Smart Contracts,[56] issued in November 2019, stated that, in general, 'cryptoassets have all of the indicia of property' and should therefore 'be treated in principle as property'. The courts have also held that cryptoassets constitute property[57] (see **Chapters 2** and **9**). However, being decentralised

50 Bribery Act 2010, s 8.
51 Bribery Act 2010, s 7(1).
52 Bribery Act 2010, s 7(1).
53 Bribery Act 2010, s 7(5).
54 www.justice.gov.uk/downloads/legislation/bribery-act-2010-guidance.pdf.
55 Ministry of Justice Guidance on the Bribery Act 2010, para 36: www.justice.gov.uk/downloads/legislation/bribery-act-2010-guidance.pdf.
56 https://35z8e83m1ih83drye280o9d1-wpengine.netdna-ssl.com/wp-content/uploads/2019/11/6.6056_JO_Cryptocurrencies_Statement_FINAL_WEB_111119-1.pdf.
57 *Vorotyntseva v Money-4 Ltd (t/a Nebeus.com)* [2018] EWHC 2596 (Ch); *Robertson v Persons Unknown* CL-2019-000444, unreported; and *AA v Persons Unknown* [2019] EWHC 3556 (Comm).

and intangible, cryptoassets do not have situs. How does this reconcile with jurisdiction based on the location of property?

Additionally, being pseudonymous, how does the inability to determine the owner of cryptoassets reconcile with the principles of jurisdiction and a claimant's ability to serve a claim form?

Situs

5.14 Her Majesty's Revenue and Customs ('HMRC') guidance on cryptoasset taxation for individuals[58] states that:

> 'Using the residency of the beneficial owner of the exchange tokens to determine the location [of the exchange token] gives a clear, logical, predictable and objective rule which can be easily applied.'

HMRC does not say what is meant by 'residency', nor whether this is tax residency under the statutory tax residence test or residency based on the principles of residence for the purposes of jurisdiction, .. an individual's usual place of abode.

We have seen at paragraph **5.4** above how the courts have considered the question of jurisdiction in relation to a claim concerning cryptoassets. However, where such principles or arguments do not or cannot apply, the courts may look to HMRC's guidance, and use the residency of the beneficial owner of cryptoassets to determine the location of the cryptoassets and, therefore, who has jurisdiction. It is likely that, in such circumstances, the courts would use the jurisdiction residency test, ie an individual's usual place of abode to determine the residency of the beneficial owner and, thus, jurisdiction.

This will, however, be conditional on the beneficial owners of cryptoassets being identified.

Unknown parties

Service of claim forms and orders against unknown parties

5.15 Orders against, and serving claim forms on, 'persons unknown' are not unknown concepts, provided that the defendants are clearly identified.[59]

However, where defendants are not identifiable (as opposed to just unnamed) the courts may not permit the service of a claim form nor make orders against them.

58 www.gov.uk/government/publications/tax-on-cryptoassets/cryptoassets-for-individuals#other-considerations.

59 *Bloomsbury Publishing Group Plc v News Group Newspaper Ltd (Continuation of Injunction)* [2003] EWHC 1205 (Ch) and *CMOC v Persons Unknown* [2017] EWHC 3599 (Comm).

Case Study

In *Cameron v Liverpool Victoria Insurance Co Ltd*[60] the claimant was injured in a hit-and-run collision in which the car and its registered keeper were identified, but the driver was not. The insurance policy covered one named individual, who was not the registered keeper, to drive the car.

The claimant issued proceedings against the keeper, erroneously believing him to be the driver. When it became clear that he was not, the insurer was added as a defendant, and the claimant sought a declaration under section 151 of the Road Traffic Act 1988 that it was obliged to satisfy any unsatisfied judgment against the keeper. The insurer denied liability, claiming that the policy did not cover the keeper and that the driver had not been identified.

The claimant applied for permission to amend the claim form and particulars of claim to remove the keeper as the first defendant and substitute 'the person unknown driving vehicle [registration number] who collided with vehicle [registration number] on [date of accident]'.

The District Judge dismissed the application and granted summary judgment in favour of the insurer. The Court of Appeal reversed the decision, holding that the court had discretion to permit an unknown person to be sued when the driver could not be identified, because otherwise it would not be possible to obtain a judgment which the car's insurer would be bound to satisfy.

The insurer appealed to the Supreme Court. The court identified that the critical question was what, as a matter of law, was the basis of the court's jurisdiction over parties, and in what (if any) circumstances jurisdiction could be exercised against persons who could not be named.[61]

The court considered the distinction between unnamed and unidentified defendants, noting that the first category comprised anonymous defendants who were identifiable but whose names were unknown, such as squatters occupying a property who are identifiable by their location but not by their names; while the second category comprised defendants who were not only anonymous but also could not be identified. The key distinction, the court said, is that, in the first category, the defendant was described in a way that made it possible to locate or communicate with them and to know without further inquiry whether they were the same as the person described in the claim form, such that they could be served with claim forms or other originating process, if necessary by alternative service under CPR rule 6.15. This would not be the case in the second category.[62]

60 [2019] UKSC 6.
61 [2019] UKSC 6, at [12].
62 [2019] UKSC 6, at [13] and [15].

The court held that an unknown person could not be identified simply by referring to something that they had done in the past, as that does not enable one to know whether any particular person is the one referred to. The impossibility of service in such cases is due to not just the fact that the defendant cannot be found, but also the fact that it is not known who the defendant is. The problem, the court held, is conceptual, not just practical.[63] It is a fundamental principle that a person cannot be made subject to the court's jurisdiction without having such notice of the proceedings as would enable them to be heard, and it is an essential requirement for any form of alternative service that the mode of service should be such as can reasonably be expected to bring the proceedings to the attention of the defendant.[64]

The legitimacy of issuing or amending a claim form so as to sue an unnamed defendant can properly be tested by asking whether it is conceptually (not just practically) possible to serve it,[65] and a person, who is not just anonymous but cannot be identified with any particular person, cannot be sued under a pseudonym or description, unless the circumstances are such that the service of the claim form can be effected or properly dispensed with.[66]

Thus the Supreme Court held that the description proposed did not identify anyone, and service on the driver would be impossible, thus breaching the fundamental principle that a person could not be made subject to the court's jurisdiction without having such notice of the proceedings as would enable them to be heard.

In light of the above, the pseudonymous nature of cryptoassets might mean that, in cases where individuals cannot be identified – for example, where there has been no previous correspondence or a wallet is not associated with a cryptoasset exchange provider that could provide wallet holder details[67] – claimants may not be able to serve claim forms and so the courts of England and Wales may not be able to establish jurisdiction. Such cases might be unlikely, but it is worth noting this potential inability. It highlights the importance of specialist cryptoasset tracing in cryptoasset cases to try and ascertain an identifiable individual in order for jurisdiction to be established.

Bankers Trust and Norwich Pharmacal Orders

5.16 As outlined at paragraph **5.4** above, in the case of *AA v Persons Unknown*, the application for the Bankers Trust/Norwich Pharmacal order was adjourned.

63 [2019] UKSC 6, at [16].
64 [2019] UKSC 6, at [16], [17] and [21].
65 [2019] UKSC 6, at [14].
66 [2019] UKSC 6, at [26].
67 See *AA v Persons Unknown* [2019] EWHC 3556 (Comm) at para 75 where the court outlined the terms of the alternative service sought on the unknown first and second defendants, which included an email address by which they had already corresponded or details provided by the third and fourth cryptoasset exchange provider defendants. See also *PML v Persons Unknown* [2018] EWHC 838 (QB) where an injunction order was served on the defendant using the email account by which it had been corresponding with the claimant.

This was because there was a question as to whether the court had jurisdiction to require an institution outside the jurisdiction to provide information pursuant to a court order of the English court, and to serve such an order out of the jurisdiction.[68]

Case Study

In *AA v Persons Unknown*[69] the claimant applied to the High Court for, amongst other things, a Bankers Trust order and/or a Norwich Pharmacal order requiring Bitfinex to provide specified information in relation to the cryptocurrency account holding the 96 Bitcoins.[70]

The court identified that there was a question as to whether the court had jurisdiction to require an institution outside the jurisdiction to provide information pursuant to a court order of the English court, and to serve such an order out of the jurisdiction, as the authorities had not definitively determined the issue.[71]

The court referred to the decision of Waksman J in *CMOC v Persons Unknown*,[72] in which an application was sought for worldwide freezing relief against persons unknown and an order relating to Bankers Trust type relief. In that case, Waksman J assumed that it would be possible to make a Bankers Trust order and serve it out of the jurisdiction on a foreign entity, relying upon the necessary and proper party gateway in paragraph 3.1(3) of CPR Practice Direction 6B.[73]

The court also referred to another decision, that of Teare J in *AB Bank Ltd v Abu Dhabi Commercial Bank PJSC*,[74] which it did not appear that Waksman J had been referred to. In the case of *AB Bank Ltd v Abu Dhabi Commercial Bank PJSC*, Teare J considered an application to serve a claim form out of the jurisdiction where there was a foreign bank innocently mixed up in a fraud, the question being whether Bankers Trust/Norwich Pharmacal type relief was a claim for an interim remedy for the purposes of the jurisdictional gateway in paragraph 3.1(5) of CPR Practice Direction 6B. Teare J concluded that such relief was not an interim remedy under section 25(1) of the Civil Jurisdiction Judgments Act 1982 but was indeed a final remedy. He also concluded that it was not an injunction ordering an act within the jurisdiction on the facts of that case. The necessary and proper party gateway (para 3.1(3)) was also not met, as the claim against the defendant was quite different from that against the perpetrator of the fraud; the claim against the defendant would be

68 [2019] EWHC 3556 (Comm), at [44].
69 [2019] EWHC 3556 (Comm).
70 For more information on Norwich Pharmacal orders, see Simon Bushell and Gary Milner-Moore, *Disclosure of Information: Norwich Pharmacal and Related Principles* (2nd edition), Bloomsbury Professional, 2019.
71 [2019] EWHC 3556 (Comm), at [44] and [45].
72 [2017] EWHC 3599 (Comm).
73 [2017] EWHC 3599 (Comm), at [10]; and [2019] EWHC 3556 (Comm), at [45] and [46].
74 [2016] EWHC 2082 (Comm).

established long before the fraud claim was established and the two claims would never be tried together. Consequently, Teare J held that there was no gateway through which the claim for Norwich Pharmacal relief could pass, and so he set aside the order for service out of the jurisdiction.[75]

Due to the potential difficulties that could arise, the claimants in *AA* adjourned the Bankers Trust/Norwich Pharmacal orders.[76] However, the proprietary injunction included an application that information as to the identity and address of the wallet holders be provided. The court was satisfied that that information was necessary to police the proprietary injunction, and that the information would be appropriate for provision by way of pre-action disclosure in the action which the claimant was undertaking to commence forthwith against all defendants.[77]

Given that the issue has not yet been definitively determined, where claimants are seeking a proprietary injunction in respect of cryptoassets (see para **9.23–9.25** for further details in relation to this), rather than seeking Norwich Pharmacal relief against any cryptoasset exchange providers that are innocently mixed up in the action, they may wish to have terms included within the injunction that require the provision of the identity and address (and/or any other information) of cryptoasset wallet holders.

Indeed, the courts have shown their willingness, in other forms of cyber litigation, to require unknown defendants to identify themselves and provide their details.

Case Study

In *PML v Persons Unknown*[78] (see para **5.4** above) the court noted that, where a defendant in a case of threatened unlawful publication hides behind anonymity, the court has the power to include within the injunction order a requirement that the defendant identify itself and provide an address for service ('a self-identification order'). Once a claimant has satisfied the court that they are likely to demonstrate that publication should not be allowed, that may well justify the making of a self-identification order, and such an order is necessary if, in the event of success in the claim, the remedies to which the claimant would be entitled are to be effective. A defendant might disobey such an order, but it could not be assumed that all defendants would do so, and few defendants could remain confident that they would ultimately manage to evade identification. If they failed, punishment for contempt of court would loom large.[79]

75 [2016] EWHC 2082 (Comm), at [6]–[21]; and [2019] EWHC 3556 (Comm), at [46]–[48].
76 [2019] EWHC 3556 (Comm), at [49].
77 [2019] EWHC 3556 (Comm), at [81].
78 [2018] EWHC 838 (QB).
79 [2018] EWHC 838 (QB), at [17].

Smart contracts

5.17 As outlined in the UKJT's Legal Statement on Cryptoassets and Smart Contracts, the characteristic feature of a smart contract is automaticity: a smart contract is performed, at least in part, automatically and without the need for, and in some cases without the possibility of, human intervention. That requires the terms of the contract to be recorded in computer-readable form (ie in code), and many smart contracts are embedded in a networked system that executes and enforces performance using techniques such as cryptographic authentication, distributed ledgers, decentralisation and consensus.[80]

These features, particularly the automaticity of smart contracts, mean that it is imperative for smart contracts to include dispute resolution and jurisdiction clauses. Indeed, at the Westminster Legal Policy Forum Keynote Seminar – Legal Technology in the UK – on 2 December 2019, Sir Geoffrey Vos (Chair of the UKJT) said that there was 'one further piece in the jigsaw' of smart contracts and 'that is to crack the way in which disputes about them will be resolved'. Sir Geoffrey's view was that English law and UK jurisdiction dispute resolution clauses, which would either allow for arbitration or a streamlined online dispute resolution mechanism, should now be created so that programmers can include them in the code of smart financial services contracts.

Therefore, if parties are using smart contracts, they will need to ensure that appropriate dispute resolution and jurisdiction clauses are included, either within the source code or within any complementary natural language contract/s. The former will require liaising with the technical community to ensure that code-based jurisdiction clauses do, in fact, represent the intentions and agreement of the parties, and operate as expected.

New Court List and Pre-Action Protocol for Data Claims

5.18 In 2019, the process for pursuing data litigation was refined. The Civil Procedure (Amendment No 3) Rules 2019[81] substituted Part 53 of the CPR to provide that, from 1 October 2019, High Court data litigation claims (claims that are or include a claim for misuse of private information or a claim in data protection law) should be issued in the specialist Media and Communications List of the High Court.[82] Practice Direction 53B applies to such claims.

A new Media and Communications Pre-Action Protocol[83] was also developed, introducing specific requirements for raising data claims in correspondence. The new Pre-Action Protocol applies to claims involving:

- misuse of private information;

80 UKJT Legal Statement on Cryptoassets and Smart Contracts, para 135.
81 SI 2019/1118.
82 CPR, r 53.1(3).
83 www.justice.gov.uk/courts/procedure-rules/civil/protocol/prot_def.

- breach of confidence;
- defamation;
- slander;
- malicious falsehood; and
- harassment by publication.

Therefore, where the High Court has jurisdiction over such cyber litigation, this new Pre-Action Protocol and the new CPR provisions should be followed.

Privacy Shield

5.19 In the United Kingdom, the General Data Protection Regulation ('GDPR') is implemented by the Data Protection Act 2018.

The UK government has *also* incorporated the GDPR into the UK's domestic law under section 3 of the European Union (Withdrawal) Act 2018. This means that data protection law in the UK will remain aligned with the GDPR, even after the transitional period of the UK's withdrawal from the EU ends.

Transfer of personal data to a country outside the EU or the EEA for processing – so called 'third countries' – is only lawful if the GDPR's conditions for transfers are met.

The GDPR's conditions for transfers to third countries are set out in Chapter 5 of the Regulation. Broadly speaking, for personal data transfers to a third country to be lawful, they must be based on one of three options.

The first option is an adequacy decision of the European Commission. These are decisions by the Commission which confirm that there is an adequate level of protection of personal data within the country or organisation that the data is to be exported to. The Commission has recognised that several countries, including Canada, Japan and New Zealand, provide adequate protection, and it has therefore adopted adequacy decisions in respect of them. The effect of an adequacy decision is that personal data can flow from the EU to the specified third country without any further safeguard being needed.

Another way in which personal data transfers to third countries can be lawful is where the data controller or processor provides appropriate safeguards. Those safeguards will need to ensure that enforceable rights and effective legal remedies are available for people whose data is transferred. A number of safeguards are specified in the GDPR, and these include legally binding and enforceable instruments between public authorities or bodies as well as standard contractual clauses. The latter are standard sets of contractual terms and conditions adopted by the Commission which the sender and the receiver of personal data both sign up to.

The third option for transfer is by means of a derogation. The derogations set out in the GDPR include where a person has freely given their explicit, specific, informed and unambiguous consent to the transfer – *but* they must first have been informed of the possible risks of the transfer. Derogation is also possible, for example, where a data transfer is necessary for important reasons of public interest.

The bar is high for data transfers to third countries by way of a derogation. So it should be no surprise that the first two of the options available – adequacy decisions and appropriate safeguards – are frequently used instead. And, given their ready-made nature, adequacy decisions adopted by the Commission are often the easiest choice for businesses involved in third country data transfers.

The EU-US Privacy Shield was one-such ready-made solution, until the recent ECJ ruling. It enabled thousands of participating organisations to self-certify their adherence to principles governing their use of EU citizens' personal data. Among those organisations was Facebook Inc, the US parent company of Facebook Ireland Limited. And Facebook Ireland is the company of interest in the ECJ's decision regarding the Privacy Shield.

The court's decision followed a complaint by Mr Maximillian Schrems concerning the transfer of his personal data by Facebook Ireland to Facebook Inc in the United States.

The matter began some years back when Mr Schrems asked the Data Protection Commissioner in Ireland to prohibit Facebook from transferring his data from Ireland to the US. He did so on the basis that the law and practice in the US did not ensure the adequate protection of his personal data. This was because of the surveillance activities that public authorities in the US were engaged in.

The court recognised that the reach of US data surveillance programs, such as PRISM and UPSTREAM which rely on mass-surveillance, went beyond targeted measures limited to what was strictly necessary. In this way, they were not proportionate. Proportionality is a key principle of EU law generally and it is a key principle specifically in respect of any limitations on the rights and freedoms that are enshrined in the EU Charter of Fundamental Rights.

The ECJ decision recognised that the primacy of US national security, public interest and law enforcement requirements amounted to an interference with the fundamental rights of EU citizens whose data is transferred to the US under the Privacy Shield. Therefore, the Privacy Shield could not ensure a level of protection essentially equivalent to that guaranteed by EU law, and the ECJ concluded accordingly that an earlier Commission decision validating the Privacy Shield was invalid.

In Mr Schrems' case, the ECJ upheld an earlier Commission decision that standard contractual clauses could be used by businesses as an alternative means of transferring personal data outside the EU. However, it observed that these clauses should include effective mechanisms that allow compliance with EU law to be ensured. Yet, given the stated primacy of US national security and law enforcement requirements, one wonders how any standard contractual clauses could prove effective in practice in that jurisdiction.

At the time of writing, this potentially leaves those businesses using standard contractual clauses at risk of their agreements being invalidated too.

The GDPR gives individuals a right to claim compensation if they suffer damage as a result of an organisation breaking data protection law, so these are very important issues and, as matters currently stand, the Privacy Shield is not a lawful means of transferring personal data from the EU to the US, and standard contractual clauses may be at risk as well.

At this point in time, the UK Information Commissioner's Office (ICO) has advised UK organisations already using the Privacy Shield to continue to do so until new guidance is available, although it cautions organisations against using it if they do not already do so. Given the impact of the ECJ's ruling, however, the changes that may ultimately be needed to EU-US data transfer arrangements and agreements could prove extensive. At the time of writing, both US and UK Governments have expressed a desire to seek alternative means of lawfully transferring personal data between the two countries.

How will the rules on jurisdiction be impacted by Brexit?

5.20 The Civil Jurisdiction and Judgments (Amendment) (EU Exit) Regulations 2019[84] will, from the end of the transition period, revoke the Recast Brussels Regulation.

The UK is seeking to accede to (and continue its participation in) the 2007 Lugano Convention, which regulates the jurisdiction and enforcement of legal matters as between EFTA countries and EU Member States. However, the UK Government has recognised that some of the provisions of the 2007 Lugano Convention have been overtaken and that it is limited in scope. Consequently, it is exploring a new bilateral agreement with the EU which would create a 'coherent package of rules' on jurisdiction, applicable law, and recognition and enforcement of judgments in civil, commercial, insolvency and family matters.[85]

Unless the UK accedes to the 2007 Lugano Convention and/or there is a bilateral agreement between the EU and the UK on the regime that will apply after

84 SI 2019/479.

85 White Paper on The Future Relationship Between the United Kingdom and the European Union, para 128(g): https://assets.publishing.service.gov.uk/government/uploads/system/uploads/attachment_data/file/786626/The_Future_Relationship_between_the_United_Kingdom_and_the_European_Union_120319.pdf.

31 December 2020, jurisdiction will be determined under the common law rules and, where it applies, the Hague Convention on Choice of Court Agreements 2005.

Thus, jurisdiction will be governed by:

- the rules on the service of process (either within or outside the jurisdiction) (see para **5.4** above, although note that the Civil Procedure Rules 1998 (Amendment) (EU Exit) Regulations 2019[86] and the 107th Update – Practice Direction Amendments will make changes to CPR Part 6 and Practice Directions 6A and 6B);
- the defendant submitting to the jurisdiction; or
- if it applies to the subject matter of the case, the Hague Convention, which gives effect to exclusive choice of court agreements in favour of contracting states.

The definition of 'domicile' of a company 'or other legal person or association of natural or legal persons' contained in Article 63 of the Recast Brussels Regulation (see para **5.3** above) has been retained and restated by regulation 42 of the Civil Jurisdiction and Judgments (Amendment) (EU Exit) Regulations 2019 and will apply[87] in determining when a corporation or association is domiciled in the UK for the purposes of jurisdiction under consumer and employment cases[88] and other civil proceedings.[89]

With the Recast Brussels Regulation ceasing to apply, the common law discretion to grant a stay in the case of parallel proceedings (as opposed to the 'first come first served' approach of the lis pendens rules that apply under the Recast Brussels Regulation) creates an increased risk of parallel proceedings, which could increase the number and complexity of disputes before the courts and the cost of litigation for parties.[90] However, where the courts of England and Wales take jurisdiction in an international case, they may use anti-suit injunctions (which are not permitted under the Recast Brussels Regulation) to try and limit the ability of a party to pursue competing proceedings in another country.[91]

As with all things post-Brexit, there is a degree of uncertainty over the precise terms of the future relationship between the UK and EU after the end of the transition period. Therefore, parties will just have to wait and see what the future is going to bring in terms of the rules on jurisdiction.

86 SI 2019/521.

87 Civil Jurisdiction and Judgments Act 1982, s 42A.

88 See Civil Jurisdiction and Judgments Act 1982, ss 15A–15E.

89 See Civil Jurisdiction and Judgments Act 1982, s 16(1)(b).

90 Explanatory Memorandum to the Civil Jurisdiction and Judgments (Amendment) (EU Exit) Regulations 2019, paras 7.5 and 7.21.

91 Explanatory Memorandum to the Civil Jurisdiction and Judgments (Amendment) (EU Exit) Regulations 2019, para 7.5.

Chapter 6

Group Actions

This chapter examines:

- the various options for bringing Group Actions in England and Wales under the Civil Procedure Rules ('CPR');[1]
- recent 'cyber' cases where Group Actions have been brought; and
- the future of Group Actions in cyber litigation in light of these cases.

INTRODUCTION

6.1 The term 'class action' evokes images straight out of Hollywood movies: huge American lawsuits, an enormous number of claimants and eye-watering amounts awarded in compensation. However, at its most basic, 'class action' simply refers to the procedural mechanism by which claims can be brought (or defended) by a large number of claimants (or defendants).

There is no 'class action' per se in England and Wales: the concept of a class action is an American construct. However, there are a number of procedures by which collective or representative actions ('Group Actions') can be brought in the courts of England and Wales.

Class actions generally can be broadly divided into 'opt-in' and 'opt-out' regimes:

- 'Opt-in' regime: a class action can only be brought on behalf of claimants who are identified in the proceedings and who authorise the claim to be brought on their behalf. Thus, unless a claimant specifically opts in, they will not be included.
- 'Opt-out' regime: a class action is brought on behalf of a defined class and, as such, it is not necessary to identify all the claimants, nor to obtain their authorisation. Thus, unless a claimant specifically opts out, they will automatically be included, and so many claimants will only become involved in, or aware of, the proceedings when it comes to claiming their share of any damages.

The American class action is an 'opt-out' regime, whereby a court awards permission to an individual or individuals to bring the claims of other similarly

1 This chapter will not examine the specific collective redress procedure for competition claims in the Competition Appeal Tribunal.

situated individuals (the class members) in a single case,[2] with all claimants included in the action being bound by the outcome unless they specifically 'opt-out'.

GROUP ACTIONS IN ENGLAND AND WALES

Consolidation of claims and multiparty litigation

6.2 By virtue of its discretionary and general case management powers under Part 3 of the CPR, the courts can consolidate claims by multiple claimants.[3] Thus, the courts have the discretion to manage multiple individual claims together so that they become part of a de facto collective action.

The CPR also allows for multiparty litigation, as CPR rule 7.3 provides that a claimant may use a single claim form to start all claims which can be conveniently disposed of in the same proceedings, and CPR rule 19.1 provides that any number of claimants or defendants may be joined as parties to a claim.

Whether claims should be consolidated or whether individuals can be joined as a party tends to be a question of effective case management, and the court will have regard to the overriding objective of the CPR, which requires that cases be dealt with justly and at proportionate cost.

Representative parties

6.3 Under Section II of Part 19 of the CPR, where more than one person has the same interest in a claim, a representative may bring or defend an action on behalf of the others who have the same interest in the claim.[4]

In order to have the 'same interest', the parties must have:

- the same interest in the proceedings; and
- a common grievance; and

the relief sought must be beneficial to all.

It must be possible to say at all stages of the proceedings, and not just at the date of judgment, whether a particular person qualifies for membership of the represented group by virtue of having the 'same interest'. This does not mean, however, that the membership of the represented group must remain constant and

2 See Rule 23 of the Federal Rules of Civil Procedure for the prerequisites of a US class action: www.federalrulesofcivilprocedure.org/frcp/title-iv-parties/rule-23-class-actions/.

3 CPR, r 3.1(2)(g).

4 CPR, r 19.6(1)(a).

closed throughout.[5] Historically, the 'same interest' test has been strictly applied, and generally been a bar to representative party actions. However, the Court of Appeal's decision in *Richard Lloyd v Google LLC*[6] ('the *Google* case') may have relaxed the test, thereby opening the door to the increased use of representative party actions in the future (see para **6.10–6.12** below for further discussion of the *Google* case).

When a party wishes to act as a representative for others who have the same interest in a claim, it should indicate this in its claim form. It is not necessary for those represented to be named as parties to the proceedings, nor is it necessary for the person intending to act as a representative to have the authority of those it represents: all that is required is that the 'same interest' test is met. Thus, representative party actions operate on an opt-out basis, similar to the American class action.

However, unlike the American class action, the permission of the court is not required for a claim to be pursued by a representative party action. That said, it is the court that determines whether or not the individuals have the 'same interest', and it can determine that a person cannot act as a representative.[7] The court can also order that existing claims continue under a representative party action,[8] or refuse to allow them to continue as a representative party action.[9]

There is no limit to the number of individuals who may be represented in a representative party action (although it must be at least two), all types of claim can be filed under a representative party action and, in theory, there is no limit to the types of relief available, and so both damages and declaratory relief can be sought. However, where relief relies on the particular circumstances of each individual claimant, the 'same interest' test is unlikely to be met and a representative party action will be unable to proceed.[10]

The representative party undertakes the day-to-day management and decisions on the running of the proceedings, and a person who is represented but not named in the claim is able to take no active part in the litigation. Thus, they are only subject to the disclosure obligations or litigation cost consequences of non-parties.[11] However, unless the court directs otherwise, any judgment or order given to a representative party is binding on all persons represented in the claim and, although it may only be enforced against a person who is not a party to the claim with the permission of the court,[12] the High Court has held that the

5 *Independiente Ltd and others v Music Trading On-Line (HK) Ltd and others* [2003] EWHC 470 (Ch) and *Emerald Supplies Ltd v British Airways plc* [2010] EWCA Civ 1284.

6 [2019] EWCA Civ 1599.

7 CPR, r 19.6(2).

8 CPR, r 19.6(1)(b).

9 *Richard Lloyd v Google LLC* [2018] EWHC 2599 (QB).

10 *Richard Lloyd v Google LLC* [2018] EWHC 2599 (QB) and [2019] EWCA Civ 1599.

11 *Howells and another v Dominion Insurance Company Ltd* [2005] EWHC 552 (QB).

12 CPR, r 19.6(4).

court's permission to enforce orders should only be withheld where there are exceptional circumstances.[13]

Group Litigation Orders

6.4 Section III of Part 19 of the CPR provides for Group Litigation Orders ('GLO').

A GLO is an order made under CPR rule 19.11 that provides for the case management of claims which give rise to common or related issues of fact or law.[14] Thus, the purpose of a GLO is to collectively manage individual claims linked by common issues, although each claim within the GLO remains an individual claim. The issues within each individual claim cannot vary from the global issues claimed – a GLO must relate to a unanimous global issue[15] – and a GLO works on an 'opt-in' basis, so that a party must issue their individual claim before they can be part of a GLO.[16] Consequently, before applying for a GLO, the solicitor acting for the proposed applicant should consult the Law Society's Multi Party Action Information Service in order to obtain information about other cases giving rise to the proposed GLO issues.[17]

A court may make a GLO on its own initiative or following an application by a party. The procedure for applying for a GLO is outlined in CPR Practice Direction 19B. An application for a GLO must be made in accordance with CPR Part 23, may be made at any time before or after any relevant claims have been issued, and may be made either by a claimant or by a defendant.[18] The Practice Direction recommends that the claimants' solicitors form a Solicitors' Group and choose one of their number to take the lead in applying for the GLO and in litigating the GLO issues.[19] The application for the GLO should include a summary of the nature of the litigation, the number and nature of the claims already issued, the number of parties likely to be involved, the common issues of fact or law that are likely to arise ('the GLO issues'), and whether there are any matters that distinguish smaller groups of claims within the wider group.[20] Where there are, or are likely to be, a number of claims giving rise to the GLO issues, the court has the discretion to make a GLO.[21]

13 *Chandra v Mayor and others* [2016] EWHC 2636 (Ch).
14 CPR, r 19.10.
15 *Tew and Others v BoS (Shared Appreciation Mortgages) No 1 plc and others* [2010] EWHC 203 (Ch) and *Various v Barking, Havering & Redbridge University Hospitals NHS Trust* [2014] 5 WLUK 715.
16 CPR, PD 19B – Group Litigation, para 6.1A.
17 CPR, PD 19B – Group Litigation, para 2.1.
18 CPR, PD 19B – Group Litigation, para 3.1.
19 CPR, PD 19B – Group Litigation, para 2.2.
20 CPR, PD 19B – Group Litigation, para 3.2.
21 CPR, r 19.11(1).

As with a claim in a representative party action, all types of claim can be filed under a GLO and, in theory, there is no limit to the types of relief available, and so both damages and declaratory relief can be sought.

If a GLO is made or granted, it will specify the GLO issues so as to identify the existing claims to be managed under the GLO, as well as any future claims to be managed under the GLO.[22] The GLO will contain directions about the establishment of a group register, which will list the claims to be managed under the GLO,[23] and will usually provide that any new claims issued after the GLO is made which raise the GLO issues should be included on the register of claims.[24] There is no maximum number of claimants that can be added to the group register although, if the court is not satisfied that a case can be conveniently case managed with the other cases on the group register, or its entry would adversely affect the case management of the other cases, the court may refuse to allow the details of the case to be entered on the group register, despite the fact that the case gives rise to one or more of the GLO issues.[25] Additionally, the management court may specify a date ('the cut-off date') after which no further claims may be added to the group register unless the court gives permission.[26]

The court may order that one or more claims on the group register proceed as test claims,[27] in order to address a specific issue of fact or law, with the outcome then being applied to the remaining cases.

Where a judgment or order is given or made in a claim on the group register in relation to one or more GLO issues, unless the court directs otherwise, the judgment or order is binding on the parties to all other claims that are on the group register at the time the judgment is given or the order is made.[28] The court may also give directions as to the extent to which that judgment or order is binding on the parties to any claim which is subsequently entered on the group register.[29]

GLOs are advantageous for litigants as they:

- split the costs between the group litigants;
- increase the availability of similar evidence; and
- provide for the sharing of knowledge and litigation risk.

It is these very features, though, that mean they are not well-suited to claims that are not economically viable in their own right, as litigants will each be liable for:

- the costs of their own claim;

22 CPR, r 19.11(2)(b).
23 CPR, r 19.11(2)(a).
24 CPR, r 19.11(3)(a) and (b).
25 CPR, PD 19B – Group Litigation, para 6.4.
26 CPR, PD 19B – Group Litigation, para 13.
27 CPR, r 19.13(b).
28 CPR, r 19.12(1)(a).
29 CPR, r 19.12(1)(b).

- a share of the common costs of the litigation; and
- adverse costs if the claim or defence is unsuccessful.

Consequently, parties should seriously consider the use of industry-specific mediation schemes in appropriate cases, along with ways in which they can maximise savings through overlapping work, and the application of success fees which reflect a realistic analysis of risk.[30] Litigation funding is also something that should be considered when there is a potential GLO.

GROUP ACTIONS IN CYBER CASES

6.5 Recent years have seen a wave of Group Actions being brought in England and Wales by data subjects in respect of breaches of data protection legislation, thus highlighting the additional liabilities that corporates and organisations may face in addition to any regulatory fines imposed.

GLOs have tended to be the main route for these Group 'Cyber' Actions due to the fact that, although there must be common or related issues of fact or law, the underlying individual claims can vary from individual to individual. This is in contrast to representative party actions, where the representative must prove to the court that the affected individuals have the 'same interest' in the proceedings, ie that there is a common interest, a common grievance and remedy that is beneficial to all. Consequently, representative party actions have tended to be a less-used tool for Group Actions. However, given the nature of data breaches and the recent cyber cases, the courts may begin to see an increase in their use.

GLOs

6.6 These are becoming increasingly common and are likely to form much more of the landscape, particularly in the data and cyber world.

The Morrisons *case*

6.7 In November 2015, in *Various claimants v Wm Morrisons Supermarkets plc*[31] ('the *Morrisons* case'), the High Court granted a GLO in respect of Morrisons employees whose data was disclosed by the actions of a rogue employee, Mr Skelton, in January and March 2014. For full details of the case, see paras **7.5–7.15**.

30 *Briggs and others v First Choice Holidays and Flights Ltd* [2016] 9 WLUK 445 (Senior Courts Costs Office).

31 [2017] EWHC 3113 (QB).

Mr Skelton was convicted of offences under the Computer Misuse Act 1990 ('CMA 1990') and section 55 of the Data Protection Act 1998 ('DPA 1998') and sentenced to eight years' imprisonment.

The GLO granted was in respect of a claim for compensation for breach of statutory duty under section 4(4) of the DPA 1998 ('to comply with the data protection principles in relation to all personal data with respect to which he is the data controller'), misuse of private information and breach of confidence. The claim was put on the basis that Morrisons had both primary liability for their own acts or omissions, and were also vicariously liable for the actions of one of their employees harming his fellow workers.

A cut-off date of 8 April 2016 was set for entry to the group register, and 5,518 Morrisons employees issued claims and opted in to the GLO.

The court at first instance found that Morrisons were not directly liable for the acts of Mr Skelton, but they were vicariously liable. Morrisons appealed this decision to the Court of Appeal, which upheld the decision of the High Court. Morrisons further appealed to the Supreme Court, with the hearing held in November 2019. (See **Chapter 7** for the full reasoning of the High Court and Court of Appeal in the *Morrisons* case.)

In *Wm Morrisons Supermarkets plc v Various claimants* [2020] UKSC 12, the Supreme Court overturned the Court of Appeal's decision to find that Morrisons were *not* vicariously liable for the actions of a rogue employee in deliberately disclosing the personal data of almost 100,000 employees.

In doing so, the Supreme Court reaffirmed the fundamental tenets of vicarious liability as established by key cases, including *Lister v Hesley Hall Ltd* [2001] UKHL 22, [2002] 1 AC 215; *Dubai Aluminium Co Ltd v Salaam* [2002] UKHL 48, [2003] 2 AC 366; and *Mohamud v Wm Morrisons Supermarkets plc* [2016] UKSC 11, [2016] AC 677.

However, although the judgment released Morrisons from any liability, it emphasised the importance of the obligation on employers to supervise and ensure compliance of employees and their conduct during the course of their employment.

In assessing the Supreme Court's reasoning, it is important to restate that, both at first instance and in the Court of Appeal, Morrisons were found to have adequate safeguards to protect relevant data.

The issues

6.8 The issues decided by the Supreme Court (see paras **7.5–7.15**) were:

> '1. Whether Morrisons is vicariously liable for Skelton's conduct.
>
> 2. If the answer to (1) is in the affirmative:

a. Whether the DPA 1998 excludes the imposition of vicarious liability for statutory torts committed by an employee data controller under the DPA 1998.

b. Whether the DPA 1998 excludes the imposition of vicarious liability for misuse of private information and breach of confidence.'

The British Airways *case*

6.9 Following the GLO in the *Morrisons* case, on 4 October 2019, the High Court granted a GLO for claims brought against British Airways PLC ('BA') in respect of its data breach in 2018.[32]

In June 2018, users of BA's website were diverted to a fraudulent website which collected the personal details of approximately 500,000 people. The Information Commissioner's Office ('ICO') conducted an investigation and found that the information was compromised by BA's poor security arrangements. The ICO issued a notice of intention to fine BA GBP 183.39 million in July 2019.[33]

BA made an application for a GLO pursuant to CPR Part 19, and the High Court granted a GLO on 4 October 2019[34] in respect of claims which gave rise to some or all of the following GLO issues:

1. Whether BA is liable to the Claimants, or any of them, for potential damages under the English law of contract and/or pursuant to the DPA 1998 and/or the General Data Protection Regulation[35] ('GDPR') as supplemented by the DPA 2018 and/or misuse of private information and/or breach of confidence in English law arising from the Data Event (the breaches of BA's systems, including systems containing Personal Data, which were notified by BA to potentially affected customers in September and October 2018), or any of them;

2. If so, which Claimants are entitled to damages and on what basis?

The GLO provides that the cut-off date for entry onto the group register is 17 January 2021; thus, any developments in this case are not likely to happen in the near future.

32 *Weaver and others v British Airways plc* (unreported) 4 October 2019 (QBD), Claim No BL-2019-001146.

33 https://ico.org.uk/about-the-ico/news-and-events/news-and-blogs/2019/07/ico-announces-intention-to-fine-british-airways/.

34 www.judiciary.uk/wp-content/uploads/2019/10/Weaver-ors-v-British-Airways-PLC-sealed-order.pdf.

35 Regulation (EU) 2016/679.

Representative actions

The Google *case*

The facts

6.10 In May 2017, Mr Lloyd lodged a representative party action against Google LLC on behalf of more than 4.4 million iPhone users in England and Wales, claiming compensation under section 13 of the DPA 1998 for breach of section 4(4) of the DPA 1998 arising out of non-compliance with the first, second and seventh data protection principles. In November 2017, Mr Lloyd applied to the High Court for permission to serve the proceedings on Google out of the jurisdiction (in California).

The claim related to a 'Safari Workaround' by which Google was able to bypass a restriction on Apple's Safari browser, which blocked third party ad-tracking cookies (cookies which are placed on a user's device by a domain other than the main website which the user is visiting and which track use and then send them tailored advertisements), and set its own DoubleClick Ad cookie on a user's device. Between August 2011 and February 2012, this cookie enabled Google to obtain information about users' internet activity, through browser generated information ('BGI'), including sensitive personal data, without their knowledge or consent. Google sold the information to advertisers and then, through the cookie, tailored internet-based ads were delivered and displayed to the users.

No financial loss or distress was alleged in Mr Lloyd's representative party action. Instead, the claim was for an equal, standard, 'tariff' award for each class member, to reflect the infringement of their data protection rights, the commission of the wrong and their loss of control over their personal data. The figure of GBP 750 was advanced in the letter of claim as the amount of compensation per claimant, meaning that Google's potential liability is GBP 3 billion. In the alternative, there was a claim for damages reflecting the value of the use to which the data was wrongfully put by Google, ie damages based on the hypothetical fee that class members could have charged for allowing the use of their data.[36]

There was no dispute that Google's alleged role in the collection, collation and use of the data obtained via the 'Safari Workaround' was wrongful and a breach of duty. Google paid a civil penalty of USD 22.5 million to settle charges brought against it by the United States ('US') Federal Trade Commission ('FTC') in relation to its misrepresentations to users of the Safari browser that it would not place tracking cookies or serve targeted advertisements on those users.[37] In November 2013 it agreed to pay USD 17 million to settle US state consumer-based actions brought against it by attorneys general representing 37 US states and the District of Columbia. Google was required to give a number of

36 *Richard Lloyd v Google LLC* [2018] EWHC 2599 (QB), at [3]–[4] and [24].

37 www.ftc.gov/news-events/press-releases/2012/08/google-will-pay-225-million-settle-ftc-charges-it-misrepresented and [2018] EWHC 2599 (QB), at [13].

undertakings governing its future conduct in its dealings with users in the USA. Google settled the case brought against it in the English courts by Judith Vidal-Hall and two others.[38] Therefore, the main issues before the High Court were whether the pleaded facts disclosed any basis for claiming compensation under the DPA 1998 and, if so, whether the court should, or would, permit the claim to continue as a representative action.[39]

The decision at first instance

6.11 The High Court[40] found against the claimant on both matters and consequently refused permission to serve out of the jurisdiction. It decided that the claimant had failed to establish that the claim was one that arguably fell within the jurisdictional gateway of paragraph 3.1(9) of Practice Direction 6B – namely, that it was a claim in tort where damage was sustained within the jurisdiction or damage was sustained from an act committed within the jurisdiction, and that it had a real prospect of success.

First, the court found that a claim for compensation under section 13 of the DPA 1998 required proof of damage. The court held that, based on statutory construction, the right to compensation was defined as a right to compensation 'for that damage' and, as such, the statute presented the infringement and the damage as two separate events, connected by a causal link. Thus, it was not apt to characterise a contravention, in and of itself, as amounting to damage.[41] Additionally, the court held that it could not make an award of 'vindicatory' damages merely to mark the commission of a wrong.[42] In the instant, the court observed that the bare facts pleaded did not assert any case of harm to the value of any claimant's right of autonomy that amounted to 'damage' within the meaning of section 13 of the DPA 1998. It found that the claimant had failed to identify any damage caused as a result of the alleged breach. The claimant only claimed compensation for the fact of the infringement, the commission of the wrong and associated loss of control over the personal data. The court held that bringing a class action on that basis was based on an artificial notion of 'damage'.[43] The court also rejected the alternative claim for user damages, saying that it was barred by authority and that, in any event, it was wholly artificial to envisage a bargaining process involving the claimants in this case, where the only realistic option open to them was to refuse consent.[44]

Secondly, the court held that it would not, in any event, exercise its discretion to allow the continuation of the representative proceedings, because the claimant should not be permitted to consume substantial resources in the pursuit of officious litigation on behalf of others who had little to gain from it, had not

38 [2018] EWHC 2599 (QB), at [13]–[15].
39 [2018] EWHC 2599 (QB), at [5].
40 [2018] EWHC 2599 (QB).
41 [2018] EWHC 2599 (QB), at [54]–[56].
42 [2018] EWHC 2599 (QB), at [68].
43 [2018] EWHC 2599 (QB), at [58], [60], [74]–[75] and [106].
44 [2018] EWHC 2599 (QB), at [76]–[80].

authorised the pursuit of the claim, nor indicated any concern about the matters to be litigated.[45] Additionally, CPR rule 19.6 provides that a claim may be begun or continued by or against one or more persons as representatives of any others who have the 'same interest' in the claim. The court found that, in the present case, the 'same interest' requirement was not met.[46] In the court's view, a representative action could not be brought unless every member of the class had suffered the same damage, or their share of a readily ascertainable amount was clear; nor could such an action be brought where different potential defences were available in respect of claims by different members of the class. Here, even if the judge was wrong about what amounted to damage for the purposes of section 13(1) of the DPA 1998, the amount of compensation would still depend on the facts of each individual's case, as neither the breach of duty nor the impact of it would be uniform across the entire class membership. Thus the court found that these principles applied to the facts of the case so as to disqualify the claim from being a representative action.[47] Furthermore, even if the class could be appropriately defined, there were insuperable practical difficulties in ascertaining whether any given individual was a member of the class, such that it was impossible to reliably ascertain and verify the members of the class.[48]

The decision of the Court of Appeal

6.12 Mr Lloyd appealed the decision to the Court of Appeal.[49] The appeal raised the following points:

(1) whether proof of pecuniary loss or distress is required in order to claim compensation under section 13 of the DPA 1998;

(2) whether the members of the class have the 'same interest' and are identifiable; and

(3) whether the judge's exercise of discretion not permitting the representative action to proceed could be vitiated.

In relation to the first point, the court held that proof of pecuniary loss or distress was not required in order to claim compensation under section 13 of the DPA 1998.

In its consideration of the matter, the court stated that it did not agree with Warby J that it was circular to plead that the alleged infringement of the class members' data protection rights caused a loss of control over their personal data. Indeed, in the court's view, 'the key to these claims is the characterisation of the class members' loss as the loss of control or loss of autonomy over their personal data'.[50]

45 [2018] EWHC 2599 (QB), at [82] and [99]–[105].
46 [2018] EWHC 2599 (QB), at [82].
47 [2018] EWHC 2599 (QB), at [86] and [89]–[92].
48 [2018] EWHC 2599 (QB), at [82], [94]–[98] and [106].
49 [2019] EWCA Civ 1599.
50 [2019] EWCA Civ 1599, at [45].

The court stated that:[51]

> '46. The first question that arises is whether control over data is an asset that has value. That question should, in this context, be answered as a matter of EU law. […] Even if data is not technically regarded as property in English law, its protection under EU law is clear. It is also clear that a person's BGI has economic value: for example, it can be sold. It is commonplace for EU citizens to obtain free wi-fi at an airport in exchange for providing their personal data. If they decline to do so, they have to pay for their wifi usage. The underlying reality of this case is that Google was able to sell BGI collected from numerous individuals to advertisers who wished to target them with their advertising. That confirms that such data, and consent to its use, has an economic value.
>
> 47. Accordingly, in my judgment, a person's control over data or over their BGI does have a value, so that the loss of that control must also have a value […]'

The court approved the decision and reasoning in *Gulati v MGN Ltd*,[52] a phone-hacking case where damages were awarded for misuse of private information without proof of material loss or distress. It found that it was particularly relevant, albeit not binding, and applicable by analogy, because the underlying rights on which misuse of private information and infringements of the DPA 1998 are based are themselves founded on the same principle: namely, that privacy be protected. Accordingly, since the torts of misuse of private information and breach of the DPA 1998 are similar domestic actions derived from the same core right to privacy, it would be prima facie inappropriate for the court to apply differing approaches to the meaning of damage. Thus, since the loss of control over telephone data was held to be damage for which compensation could be awarded in *Gulati*, it would be wrong in principle if the represented claimants' loss of control over BGI data could not, likewise, for the purposes of the DPA 1998, also be compensated. Additionally, the EU law principles of equivalence and effectiveness point to the same approach being adopted to the legal definition of damage in the two torts which both derive from a common European right to privacy.[53]

The court considered further authorities which it said supported the proposition that privacy breaches leading to loss of control over data ought to be compensated without proof of distress or pecuniary loss.[54]

The court accepted Warby J's reasoning that a domestic statutory construction would require proof of both a contravention and consequent damage. However, it held that section 13 of the DPA 1998 should be construed on the basis that it was giving effect to the right of privacy under Article 8 of the European Convention of Humans Rights ('ECHR') and the right to protection of personal data under Article 23 of the Charter of Fundamental Rights of the European Union.[55] In

51 [2019] EWCA Civ 1599, at [46]–[47].
52 [2015] EWHC 1482 (Ch) and [2015] EWCA Civ 1291.
53 [2019] EWCA Civ 1599, at [52]–[53] and [57].
54 [2019] EWCA Civ 1599, at [58]–[61].
55 [2019] EWCA Civ 1599, at [42] and [45].

this vein, acknowledging that it did not govern the DPA 1998 but that it was nonetheless helpful to consider, the court considered the GDPR, specifically Recital 85, which gives 'loss of control over their personal data' as an example of 'physical, material or non-material damage' that might be caused to natural persons as a result of a data breach.[56]

Therefore, the court concluded that damages are, in principle, capable of being awarded for loss of control of data under section 13 of the DPA 1998, even if there is no pecuniary loss and no distress. The wording of section 13 justified such an interpretation when read in light of EU legislation and having regard to the decision in *Gulati.* The court held that only by construing the legislation in this way could individuals be provided with an effective remedy for the infringement of such rights.[57]

In relation to the second point and whether the members of the class had the 'same interest', the court held that Warby J had applied the 'same interest' test too stringently, partly because of his determination as to the meaning of 'damage'. The court said:[58]

> 'Once it is understood that the claimants that Mr Lloyd seeks to represent will all have had their BGI – something of value – taken by Google without their consent in the same circumstances during the same period, and are not seeking to rely on any personal circumstances affecting any individual claimant (whether distress or volume of data abstracted), the matter looks more straightforward. The represented class are all victims of the same alleged wrong, and have all sustained the same loss, namely loss of control over their BGI. [...] once the claim is understood in the way I have described, it is impossible to imagine that Google could raise any defence to one represented claimant that did not apply to all the others. The wrong is the same, and the loss claimed is the same. The represented parties do, therefore, in the relevant sense have the same interest. Put in the more old-fashioned language of Lord Macnaghten in *The Duke of Bedford* at [8], the represented claimants have a "common interest and a common grievance" and "the relief sought [is] in its nature beneficial to all".'

The court noted, however, that, by not relying on any facts affecting any individuals, damages would be reduced to the lowest common denominator.[59]

In terms of whether the members of the class were identifiable, the court held that:[60]

> '[...] the only applicable test is that "it must be possible to say of any particular person whether or not they qualify for membership of the represented class of persons by virtue of having" the same interest as Mr Lloyd "[a]t all stages of the proceedings, and not just at the date of judgement".'

56 [2019] EWCA Civ 1599, at [64]–[65].
57 [2019] EWCA Civ 1599, at [70].
58 [2019] EWCA Civ 1599, at [75].
59 [2019] EWCA Civ 1599, at [75] and [77].
60 [2019] EWCA Civ 1599, at [80].

Consequently, the court could not see why the test was not satisfied in this case. Every affected person would, in theory, know whether they satisfied the conditions specified. Also, the data in the possession of Google would be able to identify who was, and who was not, in the class. Both exercises could be undertaken at the same time and, whilst it is true that some persons' memories may be at fault and there could, in theory, be abuse, the court concluded that those factors are practical ones, and not ones that affect the formal ability to identify the class.[61]

Therefore, the members of the represented class had the same interest under CPR rule 19.6(1) and were identifiable.[62]

In relation to the third point, the court found that, as Warby J had taken two matters into account which were irrelevant to his discretion, it was open to the court to exercise its discretion afresh.[63] Consequently, the court held that the representative action should be allowed to proceed as a matter of discretion, as:[64]

> '[…] this representative action is in practice the only way in which these claims can be pursued. I do not accept the judge's characterisation of this claim as "officious litigation". To the contrary, this case, quite properly if the allegations are proved, seeks to call Google to account for its allegedly wholesale and deliberate misuse of personal data without consent, undertaken with a view to commercial profit. It is not disproportionate to pursue such litigation in circumstances where, as was common ground, there will, if the judge were upheld, be no other remedy. The case may be costly and may use valuable court resources, but it will ensure that there is a civil compensatory remedy for what appear, at first sight, to be clear, repeated and widespread breaches Google's data processing obligations and violations of the Convention and the Charter.'

Thus the Court of Appeal allowed the appeal and made an order granting Mr Lloyd permission to serve the claim on Google out of the jurisdiction.

Google is reportedly set to appeal the Court of Appeal's decision to the Supreme Court.

The Equifax *case*

6.13 In May 2017, Equifax Inc, Equifax Ltd's US parent company, was the victim of a cyberattack. The FTC stated that Equifax had been warned in March 2017 that one of its databases, the Equifax Automated Consumer Interview System, suffered from a critical vulnerability. The FTC alleged that Equifax Inc's security team ordered that the vulnerable systems be patched within 48 hours of being informed of the discovery. However, Equifax Inc failed to check whether this had been carried out, which meant that hackers could exploit the flaw and steal consumers' personal details over several months. The FTC alleged that,

61 [2019] EWCA Civ 1599, at [80].
62 [2019] EWCA Civ 1599, at [81].
63 [2019] EWCA Civ 1599, at [83]–[85].
64 [2019] EWCA Civ 1599, at [86].

among the stolen information, the hackers copied around 147 million names and dates of birth, 145.5 million social security numbers and 209,000 payment card numbers and expiration dates.[65]

Although Equifax Ltd was not breached, the attack compromised the personal information of UK consumers. A file containing 15.2 million UK records, dating from between 2011 and 2016, and which contained data relating to actual consumers, was attacked during the incident. Equifax Ltd contacted 693,665 consumers, those deemed to be in the highest risk category as a result of the data compromised, by post, offering them Equifax and third party risk mitigation products (identity protection products), with instructions on how to get started. In relation to the remaining 14.5 million consumers affected, Equifax Ltd apologised for the compromise of their data, but stated that the data potentially compromised (name and date of birth) did not introduce any significant risk to these individuals.[66]

In September 2018, the ICO issued Equifax Ltd with a fine of GBP 500,000, the maximum permissible under the DPA 1998, for failing to protect the personal information of up to 15 million UK citizens during the cyberattack in 2017. The ICO investigation found that, although the information systems in the US were compromised, Equifax Ltd was responsible for the personal information of its UK customers. The UK arm of the company failed to take appropriate steps to ensure that its US parent, which was processing the data on its behalf, was protecting the information.[67]

In July 2019, it was reported that Equifax Inc had agreed to pay up to USD 700 million as part of a settlement with the FTC.[68] A global settlement of up to USD 425 million was approved on 13 January 2020,[69] although this is being appealed.[70]

Following the Court of Appeal's decision in the *Google* case, a representative party action was brought in the High Court in October 2019 by Richard Atkinson on behalf of the approximately 15 million allegedly affected individuals. Mr Atkinson's case is that:

- data held on individuals in the UK was controlled by Equifax Ltd and was processed by Equifax Inc in its capacity as a data processor;[71]
- the company intruded on his privacy; and
- it failed to comply with the DPA 1998.

65 www.stewartslaw.com/news/equifax-fights-uk-opt-out-data-privacy-class-action/.
66 www.equifax.co.uk/about-equifax/press-releases/en_gb/-/blog/equifax-ltd-uk-update-regarding-the-ongoing-investigation-into-us-cyber-security-incident.
67 https://ico.org.uk/action-weve-taken/enforcement/equifax-ltd/.
68 www.bbc.co.uk/news/technology-49070596.
69 www.ftc.gov/enforcement/cases-proceedings/refunds/equifax-data-breach-settlement.
70 www.equifaxbreachsettlement.com/.
71 www.stewartslaw.com/news/equifax-fights-uk-opt-out-data-privacy-class-action/.

The claim is seeking damages for infringement of his and the class's data protection rights, misuse of private information and loss of control of their personal data.[72]

The claim is currently ongoing and, on 10 February 2020, the US Department of Justice issued a statement concerning the indictment of individuals in connection with the 2017 theft of consumer data held by Equifax.[73]

THE FUTURE OF GROUP ACTIONS IN CYBER LITIGATION

A new attitude from the courts?

6.14 The above cases show the courts entertaining a more claimant-friendly approach to Group Actions although, in the case of GLOs, this does not appear to be anything more than the courts applying the CPR. The same cannot, however, be said in respect of representative party actions.

By holding that the loss of control over personal data is damage for which compensation may be claimed, the Court of Appeal's decision in the *Google* case will potentially allow representative party actions to be brought in cases where they were not previously permitted. The law has historically been slow to realise new areas of damage/harm for which compensation can be claimed. It is only relatively recently (in terms of the history of the legal system) that compensation for emotional distress became recoverable, and it still tends to be for nominal amounts. Indeed, the Data Protection Act 2018 ('DPA 2018') recognises that emotional distress is not automatically considered to be a form of damage for which compensation may be claimed – section 168 of the DPA 2018 specifically provides that non-material damage includes distress. Thus, for the Court of Appeal to hold that a person's control over their personal data has value, and the loss of such control is capable of being compensated, irrespective of whether or not there is pecuniary loss or distress, is a monumental decision.

Additionally, by holding that the 'same interest' test only requires individuals to have been the victim of the same wrong and to have suffered the same loss, this potentially broadens not only the types of class that may be represented under a representative party action, but also the individuals who may fall within such classes. This apparent relaxation of the 'same interest' test might also allow representative party actions which were not previously permitted, which could encourage more representative party actions to be brought.

In addition to the above, representative party actions overcome the difficulty associated with GLOs of finding others who may have claims which give rise

72 www.stewartslaw.com/wp-content/uploads/2020/01/GDR-Equifax-fights-UK-opt-out-class-action.pdf.

73 www.justice.gov/opa/pr/chinese-military-personnel-charged-computer-fraud-economic-espionage-and-wire-fraud-hacking.

to common or related issues of fact or law. They also mean that the litigation is conducted by one party, as opposed to a consortium, and the individuals affected do not have to become involved unless or until the case is decided or settled, and the 'opt-out' process means that it is easier to get financially viable claims off the ground. Thus, representative party actions are, arguably, the easier of the two Group Action options.

With this mind, and given the Court of Appeal's decision in the *Google* case, it is easy to see how the floodgates of representative party actions in respect of data breaches may open, as such actions may become the favoured approach to cyber litigation in the aftermath of data breaches.

The Court of Appeal's reasoning indicates that damages may be awarded for an infringement of individuals' data protection rights, even if there is no damage whatsoever to a data subject. The court found that there is an inherent value in data. Therefore, it is not only in the case of data breaches and loss of control over data where representative party actions may be brought: such an action may be brought in respect of any infringement of data subjects' rights, as there has been an infringement of a right that has value. The floodgates of representative party actions may be opened further if, as indicated at paragraph 46 of the Court of Appeal's judgment, the courts are willing to hold that data, or a database, is property capable of possession. If the courts were to take this step, data would, arguably, be subject to all the rights and remedies of property law, thus further increasing the scope for Group Actions in respect of infringements to data and/or data rights, and 'data claims' in general.

Loss of control extended?

6.15 However, even though the 'same interest' test was satisfied in the *Google* case on the basis of the 'same wrong and same loss', the 'same interest' test is unlikely to be met in claims, including claims relating to data breaches in respect of personal data, where there is a degree of variation between the circumstances of the represented individuals. Indeed, by noting that damages would be reduced to the lowest common denominator by not relying on any facts affecting any individuals, the decision of the Court of Appeal implied that a representative party action would not be appropriate if damages for financial loss or distress are sought in respect of a data breach, as these will vary depending on personal circumstances. Therefore, the relaxation of the 'same interest' test is fact- (or rather, claim-) specific, and only appears likely to apply in the 'lowest common denominator' cases, as alleging anything more than the bare minimum is likely to involve varying personal circumstances, harm etc, which would not necessarily satisfy the 'same interest' test. If the Court of Appeal's argument were to be extended to any infringement of data subjects' rights due to the inherent value in data, this 'variation of circumstances' limitation on representative party actions would also seem to be a bar for anything other than the bare minimum of infringement.

A further potential limiting factor on representative party actions is the question as to whether the Court of Appeal's reasoning applies to cases, such as the *Morrisons* case, where individuals had, arguably, already parted with the control of their personal data? It was data provided to Morrisons by the individuals, held by Morrisons as the data controller, for Morrisons to choose how to process it. As such, although the individuals would have had an expectation of privacy and confidentiality, the individuals lost control of their personal data per se as soon as they provided it to Morrisons: they provided it to someone who could decide what they were going to do with it. Thus, does the Court of Appeal's reasoning and decision only apply to data breaches and/or infringements directly against individuals, such as in the *Google* case?

On the other hand, the data was provided to Morrisons on the understanding that it was going to be used/processed in a particular way, and kept safe; so had the individuals really lost control of the data, or did they retain control of it because they had consented to the terms on which Morrisons was going to hold it?

Taking the *Equifax* case, one of the arguments advanced in Equifax's defence is that there can be no meaningful loss of control over data when it has been gathered from sources other than the subjects themselves. Whilst technically true that the individuals had lost control of the data by way of having provided it to other sources prior to it being provided to Equifax, presumably the provision of that data was on the understanding of how it would be used, how it would be stored, who it would be provided to etc, and so the individuals had control over it in that sense.

If this is the correct interpretation, loss of control over personal data does not only occur when the data is 'taken' from a data subject. It is submitted that, as long as there is a chain of consent, understanding etc from a data subject's first provision of the data through to an organisation that is subsequently compromised, a data subject will only lose control of any personal data as a result of the data breach. The entire chain of processing constitutes the individual's control over their personal data, and the breach is the only loss of that control. Such an interpretation is likely to have a massive impact on organisations, as it means that any organisation could face a representative party action in respect of any data breach and, based on the *Morrisons* case (see para **6.7** above and **Chapter 7** for a fuller discussion of this case), could face liability even though they are not at fault and have appropriate technical and organisational measures in place. Therefore, arguably, the Equifax case and its consideration of what constitutes a loss of control over personal data is even more important than the Court of Appeal's decision in the *Google* case. The decision in the Equifax case is likely to determine whether the Financial Conduct Authority might find itself the target of a representative party action for the 'loss of control over personal data' resulting from its accidental publication of personal information on its website in November 2019 in response to a Freedom of Information Act request.[74]

74 www.fca.org.uk/news/statements/fca-data-breach.

It should be noted that the Court of Appeal's judgment in the *Google* case was heavily reliant on an interpretation of the DPA 1998 that was consistent with protections provided by EU law and EU principles. Whilst Brexit should not affect decisions made in respect of claims under the DPA 1998, as any such decisions should be rendered in light of the EU principles and protections in place at the time of the infringement, the same cannot be said in respect of infringements going forward post-Brexit. Although the GDPR is, in theory, to be domesticated and become the UK GDPR,[75] it will be interesting to see the data and privacy protections that the UK Government will provide in a post-Brexit world and, consequently, the approach that the courts will take to the question of the value of data and the loss of control over data.

Thus the decision in the Equifax case, and any appeal in the *Google* case, are eagerly awaited, and the floodgates may temporarily close until these decisions are rendered. Indeed, depending on the UK Government's approach to data protection and privacy post-Brexit, they may remain closed in a post-Brexit world.

A growth in Group Actions?

6.16 It should be borne in mind that regulatory decisions may prompt Group Actions and are often relied on in order to demonstrate breaches of data protection legislation. Therefore, on the basis that the Court of Appeal's decision in the *Google* case may stand and may be followed in the Equifax case, in order to mitigate the risk of any potential Group Actions (and the risk of regulatory fines) organisations should seek to ensure that they have comprehensive data protection policies, practices and agreements in place, and revisit their GDPR and e-privacy compliance, specifically focusing on data security and breach response. It would also be advisable to ensure that staff who handle personal data are appropriately trained and managed, and organisations may wish to seek insurance to cover any potential Group Actions. However, if the damages to be awarded in Group Actions are anything like the figure suggested in the *Google* case, bearing in mind that this is a figure in respect of the 'lowest common denominator' cases, insurers may not be willing to provide such insurance. The willingness or otherwise to provide insurance may be determined by what happens in the cases referred to above, but it will be a little while yet before these cases reach the quantum of damages stages of litigation, if they do so at all. Therefore, in the meantime, there is likely to be a level of uncertainty for organisations and insurers alike.

On the other side of the table, there are also risks for the 'classes' in bringing Group Actions, and so any individuals considering embarking on a Group Action might want to consider obtaining litigation funding and/or after-the-event ('ATE') insurance. Therefore, if there is going to be an increase in Group Actions, these markets may flourish.

75 European Union (Withdrawal) Act 2018, s 3 (prospective) and the Data Protection, Privacy and Electronic Communications (Amendments etc) (EU Exit) Regulations 2019, SI 2019/419.

Although the above has focused on the future of cyber litigation in respect of data breaches and breaches of data protection legislation, with the advent of new technologies it is possible that an increase in Group Actions might also be seen in other areas of cyber litigation. For example, with the introduction of driverless cars, Group Actions might be brought against the manufacturers; and Group Actions might be brought against organisations in the Adtech industry for past infringements in respect of personal data etc.

Thus, GLOs and representative party actions are likely to, subject to any appeal to the Supreme Court in the *Google* case and the decision in the *Equifax* case, become more commonplace in the world of cyber litigation, particularly in relation to infringements of data protection legislation.

Chapter 7

Vicarious Liability

This chapter:

- provides a high-level overview of the law in relation to vicarious liability;
- examines the decisions in *Mohamud v Wm Morrison Supermarkets plc*[1] ('the *Mohamud* case') and *Wm Morrison Supermarkets plc v various claimants*[2] ('the *Morrisons* case');
- examines what these decisions mean in respect of cyber litigation; and
- seeks to provide some advice to organisations in respect of protecting themselves from the actions of their employees and claims of vicarious liability.

INTRODUCTION

7.1 Organisations have always known that they are vulnerable to attacks from unknown outside third parties. Large companies and organisations are targets for hacking, malware and ransomware aimed at causing data breaches or otherwise misusing data. The individuals responsible for these attacks, if identified and subject to the jurisdiction of the courts of England and Wales, may be prosecuted for the criminality of their actions or have civil claims brought against them; and, if such attacks are successful due to the company's own poor technical and organisational measures, the organisation itself may also be held directly liable for any harm or loss caused by its failures.

VICARIOUS LIABILITY

7.2 Vicarious liability is a common law principle of strict, non-fault liability for wrongs committed by another person. As Lord Sumption JSC said in *Bilta (UK) Ltd v Nazir (No 2)*:[3]

> '[...] Vicarious liability does not involve any attribution of wrongdoing to the principal. It is merely a rule of law under which a principal may be held strictly liable for the wrongdoing of someone else. This is one reason why the law has been able to impose it as broadly as it has. It extends far more widely than

1 [2016] UKSC 11.
2 [2018] EWCA Civ 2339.
3 [2015] UKSC 23, at [70].

responsibility under the law of agency: to all acts done within the course of the agent's employment, however humble and remote he may be from the decision-making process, and even if his acts are unknown to the principal, unauthorised by him and adverse to his interest or contrary to his express instructions (*Lloyd v Grace Smith & Co* [1912] AC 716), indeed even if they are criminal (*Lister v Hesley Hall Ltd* [2002] 1 AC 215) […]'

Thus, vicarious liability is a form of secondary liability, and it is first necessary to identify the primary wrong that has been committed and the claim against the primary wrongdoer.

There is then a two-stage test for determining whether vicarious liability arises:[4]

1. Is there a relationship between the primary wrongdoer and the person alleged to be liable which is capable of giving rise to vicarious liability? If so;

2. Is there a connection between (a) the relationship between the primary wrongdoer and the person alleged to be liable, and (b) the wrongful act or default of the primary wrongdoer, such as to make it just and reasonable to hold the person legally responsible to the claimant for the consequences of the wrongdoer's conduct?

In terms of the first stage, there are several established categories of relationship that can give rise to vicarious liability (for example, employment, partnership and limited liability partnership). Where an established category of relationship does not exist, the test is whether the relationship between the person alleged to be liable and the primary wrongdoer is sufficiently akin to employment for it to be just and reasonable to impose vicarious liability. The relevant considerations in addressing this question are:[5]

- *Integration*: does the primary wrongdoer, for whose conduct the defendant may be vicariously liable, carry on activities assigned to them by the defendant as an integral part of the defendant's operation and for its benefit?

- *Risk*: has the defendant, by assigning those activities to the primary wrongdoer, created the risk of them committing the wrong?

- *Control*: is the defendant able to direct what the primary wrongdoer does?

- *Fair, just and reasonable*: having applied the above criteria, is the imposition of vicarious liability fair, just and reasonable in all the circumstances?

For the 'connection' stage, the question is whether the wrongful act is so closely connected with the employment or relationship that it would be fair and just

4 *Mohamud v Wm Morrison Supermarkets plc* [2016] UKSC 11, at [1].

5 *E v English Province of our Lady of Charity* [2012] EWCA Civ 938; *Various Claimants v Catholic Child Welfare Society and Others* [2012] UKSC 56; and *Cox v Ministry of Justice* [2016] UKSC 10.

to hold the employer/defendant vicariously liable.[6] This requires the court to consider two matters:[7]

- First, addressing the question broadly, what functions or 'field of activities' have been entrusted by the employer to the employee (or other person for whom vicarious liability is alleged), ie what is the nature of the job?
- Secondly, is there a sufficiently close connection between the position in which the employee was employed (or the position of the person for whom vicarious liability is alleged) and the wrongful conduct so as to make it just and reasonable for there to be vicarious liability? To determine this question, it will be important to identify the various elements which link the wrongdoing to the employment/position, including:
  - the nature of the duties and responsibilities, and the connection with the wrongdoing;
  - the closeness to the employment/position, and what was authorised or expected in terms of the nature of the work;
  - proximity in time to work-related matters;
  - whether the incident occurred at or close to work;
  - causation and whether the incident was caused by something work related;
  - whether the employment/position entailed a responsibility of the safekeeping of someone or something, and whether the wrongdoing entailed a failing in that responsibility;
  - whether the wrongdoer was seeking to pursue the employer's/defendant's ends, or whether their actions were for personal reasons or other reasons unrelated to work;
  - whether the wrongdoing involved the exercise of authority derived from the employment/position;
  - whether the wrongful act involved the use of any indicia of employment/position or equipment derived from the employment/position;
  - whether the use of reasonable force or the existence of friction is inherent in the nature of the employment/position; and
  - applying the principle of social justice, that those who carry on a business should bear the loss caused by the risks associated with that business materialising, whether the employment/position materially increased the risk of harm.

Vicarious liability most often occurs in employment relationships, and the cases in which a 'sufficiently close connection' has been found and deemed to be a

6 *Lister v Hesley Hall Ltd* [2001] UKHL 22 and *Mohamud v Wm Morrison Supermarkets plc* [2016] UKSC 11.

7 *Mohamud v Wm Morrison Supermarkets plc* [2016] UKSC 11, at [44] and [45].

just and reasonable basis for vicarious liability have been those cases in which an employee has used or misused the position entrusted to them in a way that injured a third party.[8] Therefore, it is just and reasonable for vicarious liability to attach to those who carry on a business and where the risk of an employee misusing their position materialises.

The rationale behind imposing vicarious liability is policy driven, seeking to ensure not only that those responsible for economic activities and enterprises are held liable for the harm arising from wrongs committed in the conduct of those activities and enterprises, but also that the liability is borne by a defendant with the means to compensate those who have been caused harm.[9] More recent decisions have, however, focused on the policy consideration of holding an entity responsible for the risks associated with their activities or enterprises materialising, including the risk of an employee misusing their position,[10] because the risk of an employee misusing their position is 'one of life's unavoidable facts'.[11]

The Mohamud case

The facts

7.3 A customer attended a petrol station kiosk run by Morrisons and approached one of the staff members, Mr Khan, with an enquiry about printing some documents from a USB stick. Mr Khan, whose job was to serve customers and see that the petrol pumps and kiosk were kept in good running order, responded with foul and racist abuse and ordered the customer to leave. The customer did so and got into his car. Mr Khan followed the customer onto the forecourt, opened the passenger door of the customer's car, told the customer to keep away and then subjected him to a violent and unprovoked assault.

The customer brought proceedings against Morrisons, claiming that it was vicariously liable for the assault. The trial judge held that Morrisons was not liable because there was no sufficiently close connection between the assault and what Mr Khan was employed to do: although Mr Khan's job involved some interaction with customers and members of the public who attended the kiosk, it involved nothing more than serving and helping them. The Court of Appeal upheld the decision, finding that, whilst Mr Khan's employment involved interaction with customers, that was insufficient to fix Morrisons with vicarious liability for Mr Khan's violence, as his duties did not involve him being placed in situations where there was a clear possibility of confrontation.

8 *Mohamud v Wm Morrison Supermarkets plc* [2016] UKSC 11, at [40].

9 *Majrowski v Guy's and St Thomas NHS Trust* [2006] UKHL 34, at [9]; and *Various Claimants v Catholic Child Welfare Society and Others* [2012] UKSC 56, at [34] and [35].

10 *Mohamud v Wm Morrison Supermarkets plc* [2016] UKSC 11; and *Various Claimants v Wm Morrison Supermarkets plc* [2017] EWHC 3113 (QB).

11 *Mohamud v Wm Morrison Supermarkets plc* [2016] UKSC 11, at [40].

The customer appealed against the Court of Appeal's decision to the Supreme Court, the issue being whether there was sufficient connection between Mr Khan's employment and his conduct towards the customer to make Morrisons legally responsible.

The decision of the Supreme Court

7.4 The Supreme Court unanimously allowed the appeal.

The court examined the origins and development of the doctrine of vicarious liability, including the public policy justification for imposing vicarious liability:

> '[...] for seeing somebody must be a loser by this deceit, it is more reason that he that employs and puts a trust and confidence in a deceiver should be a loser, than a stranger.'[12]

and

> 'The employer puts in the community an enterprise which carries with it certain risks. When those risks materialise and cause injury to a member of the public despite the employer's reasonable efforts, it is fair that the person or organisation that creates the enterprise and hence the risk should bear the loss.'[13]

In light of the above, Lord Toulson quoted Immanuel Kant – 'Out of the crooked timber of humanity, no straight thing was ever made' – and concluded that the risk of an employee misusing his position is one of life's unavoidable facts.[14]

The court then outlined the present law relating to vicarious liability:[15]

> '44. In the simplest terms, the court has to consider two matters. The first question is what functions or "field of activities" have been entrusted by the employer to the employee, or, in everyday language, what was the nature of his job. As has been emphasised in several cases, this question must be addressed broadly [...]
>
> 45. Secondly, the court must decide whether there was sufficient connection between the position in which he was employed and his wrongful conduct to make it right for the employer to be held liable under the principle of social justice which goes back to Holt. To try to measure the closeness of connection, as it were, on a scale of 1 to 10, would be a forlorn exercise and, what is more, it would miss the point. The cases in which the necessary connection has been found for Holt's principle to be applied are cases in which the employee used or misused the position entrusted to him in a way which injured the third party. *Lloyd v Grace, Smith & Co*, *Peterson* and *Lister* were all cases in which the employee misused his position in a way which injured the claimant, and that is the reason why it was just that the employer who selected him and put him in that position should be held responsible. By contrast, in *Warren v Henlys Ltd*

12 Holt CJ in *Hern v Nichols* (1708) 1 Salk 289.

13 McLachlin J in *Bazley v Curry* (1999) 174 DLR (4th) 45 at [31].

14 *Mohamud v Wm Morrison Supermarkets plc* [2016] UKSC 11, at [40].

15 [2016] UKSC 11, at [44] and [45].

> any misbehaviour by the petrol pump attendant, qua petrol pump attendant, was past history by the time that he assaulted the claimant. The claimant had in the meantime left the scene, and the context in which the assault occurred was that he had returned with the police officer to pursue a complaint against the attendant.'

The court acknowledged,[16] as per the House of Lords decision in *Dubai Aluminium Co Ltd v Salaam*,[17] that this test affords no guidance on the type or degree of connection which will normally be regarded as sufficiently close to give rise to vicarious liability. The lack of precision is inevitable, given the infinite range of circumstances where the issue arises, and so the court must make an evaluative judgement in each case, having regard to all the circumstances and, importantly, having regard to the assistance provided by previous court decisions.[18]

Applying this approach to the facts, the court found that it was Mr Khan's job to attend to customers and to respond to their enquiries. His conduct in answering the customer's request in a foul-mouthed way and ordering him to leave was inexcusable but within the 'field of activities' assigned to him. The court found that what happened thereafter was an unbroken sequence of events and that there did not cease to be any significant connection between Mr Khan's employment and his behaviour towards the customer when he came out from behind the counter and followed the customer onto the forecourt.

- First, the court did not consider that it was right to regard Mr Khan as having metaphorically 'taken off his uniform' the moment that he stepped from behind the counter. He was following up on what he had said to the customer and it was a seamless episode.
- Secondly, when Mr Khan followed the customer back to his car and opened the front passenger door, he again told the customer, in threatening words, that he was never to come back to the petrol station.

The court found that this was not something personal between them; it was an order to keep away from his employer's premises, which he reinforced by violence, and that, in giving such an order, he was purporting to act about his employer's business. The court found that Mr Khan's actions were a gross abuse of his position, but it was in connection with the business in which he was employed to serve customers. His employers entrusted him with that position and, therefore, it was just that, as between them and the customer, they should be held responsible for their employee's abuse of that position.[19]

The court also stated that Mr Khan's motive was irrelevant: it was obvious that he was motivated by personal racism rather than a desire to benefit his employer's business, but the court held that that was neither here nor there.[20]

16 [2016] UKSC 11, at [41].
17 [2002] UKHL 48.
18 [2002] UKHL 48, at [25] and [26].
19 [2016] UKSC 11, at [47].
20 [2016] UKSC 11, at [48].

The Morrisons case

The facts

7.5 During an audit in 2012, KPMG requested a copy of Morrisons' payroll data, which was held on secure PeopleSoft software. Only 'super users' had unfettered access to the data held on the PeopleSoft system. A senior IT internal auditor, Andrew Skelton, was recruited by Morrisons' internal audit team to assist with the exercise, but he was not a super user and did not have direct access to the PeopleSoft system.

During 2013, Mr Skelton was disciplined for an incident involving his unauthorised use of Morrisons' postal facilities for his private purposes ('the white powder incident') and was given a formal verbal warning on 18 July 2013. Aggrieved following the disciplinary process, on 9 October 2013, Mr Skelton searched for 'TOR' on his work computer, which is software capable of disguising the individual identity of a computer that has accessed the internet.

On 1 November 2013, KPMG requested a number of categories of data from Morrisons in order to undertake the annual audit. The task of arranging the transmission of payroll and other data to KPMG was delegated to Mr Skelton. The requisite data was obtained from PeopleSoft by Michael Leighton, a super user, on 14 November 2013. Mr Leighton attempted to email the data internally to Mr Skelton. However, the internal email system was unable to cope with the transfer of a data file of that size, and so, despite documentation suggesting that the transfer was effective, the email bounced. The following day, Mr Leighton copied the data from his computer onto a USB stick, which he then took to Mr Skelton. Mr Skelton downloaded the data from the USB stick to his computer, returning the USB stick to Mr Leighton. Mr Skelton then downloaded the data to an encrypted USB stick provided to him by KPMG and provided KPMG with that USB stick.

However, on 18 November 2013, Mr Skelton also downloaded the data to his personal USB stick. On 16 December 2013, Mr Skelton attempted to access the TOR website from his work laptop.

On 12 January 2014, from his home computer, Mr Skelton posted a file containing the personal details of 99,998 Morrisons employees on a file sharing website. The data consisted of the names, addresses, gender, dates of birth, phone numbers (home or mobile), national insurance numbers, bank sort codes, bank account numbers and the salary each employee was being paid. Mr Skelton used the initials and date of birth of another Morrisons employee in a deliberate attempt to frame him. Shortly thereafter, links to the site were then posted elsewhere.

On 13 March 2014, Mr Skelton, acting anonymously, sent a CD-ROM containing a copy of the information to three newspapers, one of which notified Morrisons of the incident. Morrisons immediately took steps to remove the data and links to the website, and alerted the police. Morrisons were, however, about to announce its annual financial reports, and the revelation of the data leak had serious implications for the share value.

Mr Skelton was convicted of offences under the Computer Misuse Act 1990 ('CMA 1990') and section 55 of the Data Protection Act 1998 ('DPA 1998') and sentenced to eight years' imprisonment. In a class action, 5,518 employees claimed compensation from Morrisons for breach of statutory duty under section 4(4) of the DPA 1998, breach of confidence and misuse of private information. The issue was whether Morrisons was liable, directly or vicariously, for Mr Skelton's criminal actions.

The decision of the High Court[21]

7.6 The High Court (Langstaff J) held: that the DPA 1998 did not impose primary liability on Morrisons; that Morrisons were not proved to be at fault by breaking any of the data protection principles, save in one respect which was not causative of any loss; and that neither primary liability for misuse of private information nor breach of confidentiality could be established. However, the court found that vicarious liability could be established under the DPA 1998, and that the terms of the Act were such that vicarious liability was not excluded in respect of actions for misuse of private information or breach of confidentiality, and that, applying the principles from the *Mohamud* case, vicarious liability was established.[22]

Direct liability

7.7 In terms of direct liability, the court found that Mr Skelton was a data controller in respect of the data that he downloaded and disclosed on the internet, as he put himself in the position of determining how and why the personal data was processed. Morrisons were not the data controller at the time of any breach of the DPA 1998 data protection principles in respect of the information disclosed on the internet and, since they were not the data controller in relation to it, Morrisons owed no duty to the claimants in respect of which they were in breach. The acts said to breach the data protection principles were those of a third party, not their own, and, consequently, Morrisons were not liable directly under section 4(4) of the DPA 1998.[23]

On this reasoning, the court also found that the assertion of direct liability in respect of breach of confidence or misuse of private information failed: it was not Morrisons nor an agent that disclosed the information; and Morrisons did not directly misuse any information, nor did they authorise its misuse, nor permit it

21 *Various Claimants v Wm Morrison Supermarkets plc* [2017] EWHC 3113 (QB). Note the paragraph numbers in the Weekly Law Reports differ from those on BAILII because the latter has two paragraphs numbered 35. This chapter uses the numbers in the Reports.

22 [2017] EWHC 3113 (QB), at [197] to [198].

23 [2017] EWHC 3113 (QB), at [45] to [51] and [65].

by carelessness on its part: it was Mr Skelton, acting criminally, without authority or facilitation.[24]

In relation to whether Morrisons had breached the seventh data protection principle under the DPA 1998 – requiring appropriate technical and organisational measures to be taken against unauthorised or unlawful processing of personal data and against accidental loss or destruction of, or damage to, personal data – Langstaff J said that:[25]

> '[...] in any system which permits human access to data there are inevitably risks that that data might be mis-processed, mishandled, or even disclosed without authority. The evidence is that Morrisons took precautions to prevent that so far as they could by limiting access to a few trusted employees only. I am satisfied that the data was protected by restriction on access, and there were sufficient internal checks available to see which of the few authorised super users had access to the data any more generally than to inquire about their own particulars.'

Langstaff J accepted the evidence that storing data temporarily on an employee's encrypted laptop was no less secure than holding the data in the PeopleSoft software, and that storing the data on a collator's individual computer, whilst all the data from the various sources was collated, was a sensible system and necessary for an effective audit. The data had to remain on the work laptop for a sufficient period to enable any requests from KPMG to be dealt with. Therefore the court held that, seen in broad overview, and save for two matters – namely the identity of Mr Skelton himself as the recipient of the information and the question of whether, in Mr Skelton's case, deletion from his computer should have been more carefully checked – there was no failure of Morrisons to provide adequate and appropriate controls.[26]

'The white powder incident'

7.8 In respect of the two specific matters mentioned, the court went on to hold that the question as to permitting Mr Skelton access to the data came down to whether it was inappropriate to trust him. The court found that the only reason not to do so was 'the white powder incident' – sending non-controlled drugs through the Morrisons post room as part of a business additional to his employment – taken together with the exhibits of disenchantment with work which followed. The court viewed the white powder incident as thoughtless rather than an attempt to defraud or prejudice colleagues, and that to restrict Mr Skelton's handling of confidential data as a result of it would have been an action for which there was no obvious logical basis. Consequently, the incident itself did not suggest that Mr Skelton was not to be trusted, and a lack of motivation does not equate to a positive criminal desire to harm the employer. Thus the court

24 [2017] EWHC 3113 (QB), at [66] and [124] to [125].
25 [2017] EWHC 3113 (QB), at [80].
26 [2017] EWHC 3113 (QB), at [81] to [83].

found that, taking the two together, permitting Mr Skelton to have the data was not a breach of the seventh data protection principle.[27]

Seventh data protection principle

7.9 In terms of the deletion of the data by Mr Skelton, the court found that Morrisons could not be criticised for not asking Mr Skelton before mid-December 2013 whether the data had been deleted, or checking that it had, because it would have been appreciated that there was a need to keep a copy of the information on Mr Skelton's work laptop in case of audit queries. Indeed, the court found that, as the data was copied to Mr Skelton's personal USB stick on 18 November 2013, it was probable that he deleted the data a short while after transferring it to KPMG, and did so at the conclusion of what would have been a reasonable period of time in which to anticipate requests for further information generated by the audit process, as not only had the data been copied by that time with a view to the later commission of the crime, but also to have given the appearance to anyone who looked that it had been removed. Therefore, the court found that, if there was a failure to ask or check whether the data had been deleted prior to mid-December 2013, there was no breach of the seventh data protection principle; accordingly, since the data had by then already been copied, the request for evidence of deletion, whether made at that time or after, would have been ineffective to prevent Mr Skelton's subsequent criminal misuse of the data.[28]

However, the court found that it could not be satisfied that a request or check in respect of the deletion of the data had occurred prior to March 2014, when enquiries were being made as to the source of the data leak. Therefore, there was no organised system for the deletion of data, such as the payroll data stored for a brief while on Mr Skelton's computer, and that there was no failsafe in respect of it. Consequently, Morrisons fell short of the requirements of the seventh data protection principle; namely, where data is held outside of the usual secure repository used for it (in the case of the payroll data, within the PeopleSoft system), there is an unnecessary risk of proliferation and of inadvertent disclosure revealing some of that data. Morrisons took this risk, not needing to do so, and organisational measures which would have been neither too difficult nor too onerous to implement could have been adopted to minimise it. The court was of the view that, if a culture is developed in which employees expect that, as a matter of routine, managers will check to see that there has been deletion of data, which has been held outside its usual secure repository, by those with whom it has for the time being been deposited, no employee could be justified in thinking that checking the deletion displayed any lack of trust. It would merely be the employer instituting, maintaining and operating safe and proper systems of checking as normal. The court, however, accepted that the risk mitigated by such a system would be the inadvertent retention of information and that, on its own, such a system would not prevent an individual determined to do so from

27 [2017] EWHC 3113 (QB), at [92] to [93], and [95].
28 [2017] EWHC 3113 (QB), at [113] to [114].

copying the data to some other medium; and that, in this particular case, by the time it would have been appropriate to have conducted a check on deletion, the likelihood is that the information had already been copied. Thus, notwithstanding that the court considered Morrisons in this respect to have failed to discharge its duty to take appropriate organisational measures to guard against unlawful disclosure and/or data loss, to the extent that Morrisons fell short of the seventh data protection principle in this respect, the failure neither caused nor contributed to the disclosure that occurred.[29]

Other control issues

7.10 As regards the other control issues, the court held that no one in employment at Morrisons knew, nor ought to have known, that Mr Skelton bore a grudge against Morrisons and was not to be trusted with data; and that to have managed and mentored Mr Skelton within the six-month life of the warning he received in respect of the white powder incident was unrealistic and mischaracterised the life of the warning. Mr Leighton's email of the data bouncing back involved no action by Mr Skelton himself and did not indicate that Mr Skelton was any more or less of a risk than the risk implicit in the original decision to use Mr Skelton as a human conduit for the transmission of data to KPMG. The bounced email carried no implications as to the subsequent security of the data, especially where there were encrypted USB sticks available to transfer data by another means. Additionally, there was no breach of the seventh data protection principle by using a USB stick to transfer the data to Mr Skelton as the use caused no relevant harm – it did not cause or contribute to the disclosure which later occurred – and it was understood that it was permissible to use such a device for transferring a large quantity of data internally from one secure site to another.[30]

Bluecoat server and TOR network

7.11 The court heard evidence that Morrisons' Bluecoat server keeps a record of every website request made and maintains a list of restricted websites whereby, if a request is made for access to a restricted site, the system blocks that access. The TOR network is listed on the Bluecoat server as a restricted site, so it would not have been possible for Mr Skelton to access the TOR website itself from which to download software needed to run the TOR network from his work laptop; and, even if it were possible to access the site, Mr Skelton would not have had sufficient administrator access rights to enable him to install the software onto his laptop. Consequently, the court found the suggestion that Morrisons should have actively monitored internet searches by employees inconsistent with the practice adopted by other large companies. It observed that it would be impracticable, invasive and disproportionate to do this on a routine basis, in particular because it would involve searching against individuals' usage by reference to a number of terms which, in respect of 'TOR', could have produced

29 [2017] EWHC 3113 (QB), at [115] to [121].
30 [2017] EWHC 3113 (QB), at [97], [98], and [111] to [112].

a plethora of innocuous results, such as 'history', 'actor', 'factory' etc. Even if a search had been conducted and shown that Mr Skelton had searched for information about the TOR network, that would not in itself have indicated his unsuitability to be a recipient of payroll data for onward transmission. As an internal IT auditor, it might be thought to be a legitimate part of his role, or mere curiosity. In any event, for practical purposes, such a search was unnecessary as the server blocked access to undesirable material, thus access to dubious websites was restricted by an automatic filter. The court also found that, even if there had been a failure to detect Mr Skelton's internet search usage, given Mr Skelton's careful planning of the crime, such a failure was unlikely to have prevented the data disclosure that occurred.[31]

In light of the above, the court concluded that Morrisons did not know, nor ought it reasonably to have known, that Mr Skelton posed a threat to the employee database, and that, save in one respect, there were no control mechanisms which Morrisons ought to have applied in respect of Mr Skelton which were not appropriately applied; that one respect was in relation to the deletion of data but, in this case, if appropriate measures had been applied, any reasonable measure that might have been implemented would not have prevented Mr Skelton's criminal misuse of the employee data.[32]

Therefore, there was no primary liability resting on Morrisons under any of the DPA 1998, the common law of misuse of private information, or an equitable action for breach of confidence: if Morrisons was liable, it was vicariously or not at all.[33]

'True vicarious liability'

7.12 Turning then to the issue of vicarious liability, the court held that this case concerned 'true vicarious liability'. This is where one party without personal fault is held responsible in law for wrongs committed by another.[34] The court confirmed that, unless a statute providing for liability expressly or impliedly indicated otherwise, a party may be held vicariously liable for a breach of statutory obligations for which that party could not itself be held directly liable. Therefore, even though Mr Skelton became a data controller of the data in his own right when he disclosed it, provided that such disclosure was sufficiently closely connected to his discharge of the functions assigned to him, his autonomous status as a data controller did not exclude vicarious liability on the part of Morrisons for his breaches of statutory duty under the DPA 1998 in respect of that data. Whereas, to the contrary, consistent with the intention of greater security and protection of the data subject, is to impose the obligations of a data controller upon such an employee (making them liable personally, as he would not otherwise be merely qua employee) whilst retaining the employer's

31 [2017] EWHC 3113 (QB), at [99] to [110].
32 [2017] EWHC 3113 (QB), at [123].
33 [2017] EWHC 3113 (QB), at [126].
34 [2017] EWHC 3113 (QB), at [129].

vicarious liability for their wrongdoing where it is appropriate to do so. Thus, two parties are then potentially responsible in law.[35]

Therefore, finding that the potential for vicarious liability was not excluded in this case, the court said that there was no doubt that the relationship between Morrisons and Mr Skelton was such that vicarious liability might apply, as employment is the most common relationship between the person at fault and the person who, though not at fault, is also to be held liable in law in addition to the party at fault.[36]

Course of employment

7.13 In respect of the question as to the 'course of employment', the court referred to the two-stage test outlined at paragraphs 44 and 45 of the *Mohamud* case (see above) and adopted that approach, noting that, since that case had been decided, its approach had been applied by the courts on a number of occasions.[37] After considering the arguments of both parties,[38] the court made the following factual findings:[39]

> '184. First, I reject Ms Proops' argument that the disclosure on the web of the payroll data was disconnected by time, place and nature from Skelton's employment. I find, rather, that as Mr Barnes submitted there was an unbroken thread that linked his work to the disclosure: what happened was a seamless and continuous sequence of events. My reasons for this are first that in October, prior to knowing he was again to be a conduit for payroll data between PeopleSoft and KPMG, Skelton showed signs of interest in the TOR network. When he knew (on 1 November) that he was indeed to be the go-between, he obtained the mobile phone he was later to use just for making the criminal disclosures. He brought in a personal USB stick to work and copied payroll information to it in mid-November. Lying low for a while after that was necessary to create an appearance of separation and to avoid suspicion falling on him too readily. He again investigated TOR in December; adopted the user name and date of birth of a colleague to draw the blame onto him when setting up an account from which to upload the payroll data to the web; sent data to a web-sharing web-site in January, and either because that did not excite any great immediate interest, or because he had planned in advance to cause the maximum embarrassment to Morrisons immediately prior to the announcement of their financial results, sent the anonymous letters he did to three newspapers in March 2014. These actions were in my view all part of a plan, as the research and careful attempts to hide his tracks indicate. As I have already noted (para 22 above) this is precisely the same view as that taken by HHJ Thomas QC when sentencing Skelton. This was no sequence of random events, but an unbroken chain beginning even before, but including, the first unlawful act of downloading data from his personal work computer to a personal USB stick.

35 [2017] EWHC 3113 (QB), at [142] to [144] and [154] to [156].
36 [2017] EWHC 3113 (QB), at [129] and [131].
37 [2017] EWHC 3113 (QB), at [135] to [138].
38 [2017] EWHC 3113 (QB), at [163] to [182].
39 [2017] EWHC 3113 (QB), at [184] to [187].

185. Second, I find that Morrisons deliberately entrusted Skelton with the payroll data. It was not merely something to which work gave him access: dealing with the data was a task specifically assigned to him. Associated with this, I find that in his role with Morrisons, day in and day out, he was in receipt of information which was confidential or to have limited circulation only: and he was appointed on the basis that this would happen, and he could be trusted to deal with it safely. Morrisons took the risk they might be wrong in placing the trust in him.

186. Third, his role in respect of the payroll data was to receive and store it, and to disclose it to a third party. That in essence was his task, so far as the payroll data went: the fact that he chose to disclose it to others than KPMG was not authorised, but it was nonetheless closely related to what he was tasked to do.

187. Fourth, it follows from these findings that when Skelton received the data, though covertly intending to copy it for misuse, he was acting as an employee, and that the chain of events from then until disclosure was unbroken. The fact that the disclosures of 12 January were made from home, by use of his personal equipment, on a Sunday did not disengage them from his employment.'

The court also stated that, in terms of the act being one of 'retributive justice' arising out of a grudge, it must be right, as Lord Toulson had noted in the *Mohamud* case, that the motive of the employee was beside the point – for criminal motives or deliberate dishonesty do not convert an act from one in respect of which there would have been vicarious liability into one in respect of which there would not. The court did say, however, that, viewed broadly, the significance of a personal grudge may be to bring into the work environment factors which belong elsewhere, so as to make it clear that the only relationship between the tort and work is that the workplace happens to be where it is committed, when it might just as well have been elsewhere. That, however, did not apply in this case where the grudge was work-related, the central relationship with which it was concerned was that of Mr Skelton with his employer, and its commission was entirely dependent upon the field of activities assigned to him by that employer.[40]

The court acknowledged the traction in the argument that finding that Mr Skelton's actions were in the course of his employment, and thus Morrisons were vicariously liable, would amount to the court facilitating a criminal's objective in harming his employer, which the court should set its face against. The court noted that, although benefit is no longer critical to an evaluation as to whether a relevant tortious act fell within the course of employment, it remained important. The act in this case was taken to deliberately harm, rather than benefit, Morrisons. Although the principal aim may have been to hurt Morrisons, the method harmed the interests of individuals. The court noted that, in the cases where vicarious liability had been established, the actions of the wrongdoer were always liable to do serious damage to their employer's business, reputation, livelihood and continued viability. Therefore, the court concluded that the issue is not so much at whom the conduct was aimed, but rather upon whose shoulders it is just for the loss to fall. The court approved the broad view of the scope of employment taken

40 [2017] EWHC 3113 (QB), at [190].

in the *Mohamud* case, stating that it was notable that Lord Toulson had explained that the cases in which liability had been upheld were those where the employee misused their position in a way which injured the claimant, and that it was just that the employer who selected them and put them in that position should be held responsible. The court noted that the *Mohamud* case had put great weight on 'enterprise risk', ie that a business or enterprise should be held responsible for the materialisation of the risks associated with their business/enterprise, and added to this, stating that, in theory, an employer also has the right to control. An employer, in general, remains responsible for what work is done, where and when, under what systems and with what equipment, and who the clients or customers are to be. Therefore, an employer could theoretically place a would-be tortfeasor who is an employee in a position where they could not so easily commit the tort, and design systems to prevent it occurring which the employee could be directed to observe.[41]

The court also noted that Morrisons were more likely to have the means to compensate the victims than Mr Skelton and could be expected to have insured against that liability, even if breaches of data security may not historically have been a mainstream risk.[42]

Therefore, it followed from the court's findings that the tort was committed as a result of activity being taken by an employee on behalf of the employer – in the sense of his being chosen to handle the data, with a view to the employer's interests in completing an audit – such that Mr Skelton's employee activity, viewed broadly, could be seen as part of the business activity of the employee, even though he chose to abuse his position. Morrisons, by employing Mr Skelton to carry on the activity, created the risk of the tort committed by him; and Mr Skelton was, to a greater or lesser degree, under the control of the employer.[43]

Having made these findings, the court held that there was a sufficient connection between the position in which Mr Skelton was employed and his wrongful conduct, put into the position of handling and disclosing the data as he was by Morrisons, albeit it was meant to be to KPMG alone, to make it right for Morrisons to be held vicariously liable for a breach of duty under the DPA 1998, misuse of private information and/or breach of the duty of confidence. Mr Skelton's role was to handle the payroll data, receive it, store it for a while, transfer it to others and then delete it and, all bar the last, he did just that. The court held that that was sufficient to draw a close link with his employment, within the principles set out in the *Mohamud* case and exemplified in case law; and, although Morrisons were one target of his actions, it was the court's view that Morrisons should be liable vicariously for the wrongs that Mr Skelton did to the claimants.[44]

41 [2017] EWHC 3113 (QB), at [192] to [193].
42 [2017] EWHC 3113 (QB), at [194].
43 [2017] EWHC 3113 (QB), at [194].
44 [2017] EWHC 3113 (QB), at [195] to [196].

The court did note, however, that, where the issue is the identification of the field of activities of an employee, that is not necessarily to be answered by identifying the obligations that are an adjunct to those activities, and are not activities in themselves, which do not in themselves constitute duties specifically entrusted to the employee in question.[45]

Additionally, Langstaff J, troubled by the submission that the wrongful acts of Mr Skelton were deliberately aimed at the party whom the claimants sought to hold responsible, such that his conclusion on vicarious liability may have rendered the court an accessory in furthering Mr Skelton's criminal aims, granted leave to Morrisons to appeal the conclusion as to vicarious liability.[46]

The decision of the Court of Appeal[47]

7.14 Morrisons did appeal the High Court's decision to the Court of Appeal, submitting that they could not be vicariously liable for Mr Skelton's wrongful acts because they did not occur during the course of his employment.

The court, first finding that the DPA 1998 did not exclude the application of vicarious liability, nor did it exclude causes of action for misuse of private information and breach of confidence and/or the imposition of vicarious liability for breaches of the same,[48] dismissed the appeal and found that Morrisons were vicariously liable.

The court noted that vicarious liability is highly fact specific[49] and, in respect of the test propounded by Lord Toulson in the *Mohamud* case, held that Langstaff J's findings at paragraphs 185 and 186 as to the 'field of activities' that had been entrusted by Morrisons to Mr Skelton (see para **7.13** above) were plainly correct.[50] Thus, the tortious acts of Mr Skelton in sending the claimants' data to third parties were, in the court's view, within the field of activities assigned to him by Morrisons.[51]

In terms of the second part of that test – the sufficiently close connection test – the court considered 'the careful and detailed findings' by Langstaff J at paragraph 184 (see para **7.13** above) to be a complete answer to this question, and entirely agreed that Mr Skelton's actions constituted a 'seamless and continuous sequence' or 'unbroken chain' of events.[52]

45 [2017] EWHC 3113 (QB), at [196].
46 [2017] EWHC 3113 (QB), at [199].
47 *Wm Morrison Supermarkets plc v Various Claimants* [2018] EWCA Civ 2339.
48 [2018] EWCA Civ 2339, at [48] to [60].
49 [2018] EWCA Civ 2339, at [5].
50 [2018] EWCA Civ 2339, at [63].
51 [2018] EWCA Civ 2339, at [72].
52 [2018] EWCA Civ 2339, at [73] to [74].

Therefore, the court agreed with Langstaff J that Morrisons were vicariously liable for the torts committed by Mr Skelton against the claimants, and it dismissed the appeal.[53]

In terms of the point which persuaded Langstaff J to grant Morrisons permission to appeal – namely, the motive of Mr Skelton being to harm his employer rather than to achieve some benefit for himself or to inflict injury on a third party, and thus the imposition of vicarious liability on Morrisons in these circumstances may render the court an accessory in furthering Mr Skelton's criminal aims – the court did not accept that there was an exception to the 'irrelevance of motive', as stated by Lord Toulson in the *Mohamud* case, where the motive is, by causing harm to a third party, to cause financial or reputational damage to the employer.

The decision of the Supreme Court

7.15 The five Supreme Court justices unanimously held (with Lord Reed providing the lead judgment) that Mr Skelton was 'not engaged in furthering his employer's business when he committed the wrongdoing in question. On the contrary, he was pursuing a personal vendetta, seeking vengeance for the disciplinary proceedings some months earlier'. Accordingly, Morrisons was held to not be vicariously liable for his conduct.

The Supreme Court held that the Court of Appeal had misinterpreted the key case law concerning vicarious liability and that the reason why Mr Skelton acted wrongfully was 'highly material'. In coming to its decision, the Supreme Court considered the issue of vicarious liability afresh and applied the test of Lord Nicholls in *Dubai Aluminium* in that the lower courts should have considered whether Mr Skelton's 'wrongful disclosure may fairly and properly be regarded as done by him while acting in the ordinary course of his employment', taking into account whether the action taken 'was so closely connected with acts he was authorised to do'. When considering previous case law, the Court alighted on Lord Toulson's observations in *Mohamud* and observed that that case did not make motive irrelevant.

However, the Supreme Court did not find that the DPA, either expressly or impliedly, stated that vicarious liability could not be imposed upon an employer for the breach of an employee's statutory obligations under the DPA 1998 as a data controller. Lord Nicholls' statement in the case of *Majrowski v Guy's and St Thomas' NHS Trust* [2007] 1 AC 224 was pertinent, where he held 'unless the statute expressly or impliedly indicates otherwise, the principle of vicarious liability is applicable where an employee commits a breach of a statutory obligation sounding in damages while acting in the course of his employment'.

53 [2018] EWCA Civ 2339, at [79].

The judgment held that simply because Mr Skelton's employers had given him the task of collating such personal data, and therefore the opportunity to commit the wrongdoing, was not sufficient to warrant the imposition of vicarious liability.

The Supreme Court, though, has not changed the law with regard to vicarious liability or made it less likely for employers to be found vicariously liable for the acts of their employees when acting in the course of their employment. In fact, the Supreme Court reinforced, with reference to numerous cases including *Mohamud* and *Bellman v Northampton Recruitment Ltd* [2018] EWCA Civ 2214, [2019] 1 All ER 1133, that, when an employee is acting in connection with his employer's business, however wrongly he or she might be doing so, the employer can be held vicariously liable. Thus the Supreme Court affirmed the decision in *Mohamud* that found the employer liable for the assault of a customer by one of its employees as 'it was in connection with the business in which he was employed to serve its customers'. In the present case, by contrast, Mr Skelton was not acting in any way in connection with his business and was purely serving his own needs. A useful illustration of the Supreme Court's reasoning is found in its observation where it states: 'Perhaps unsurprisingly, there does not appear to be any previous case in which it has been argued that an employer might be vicariously liable for wrongdoing … designed specifically to harm the employer'.

Accordingly, unless an employer can show that its employee was acting purely for his or her own benefit and was not connected with his or her employer's business, there is a strong possibility it will still be found vicariously liable for the wrongdoing of its employee. What this decision clearly shows is that each case will turn on its own specific facts relating to the tasks that the employee is authorised to carry out, the manner in which he or she carries them out, the motive that he or she has when carrying them out, and the level of protection of relevant data.

The above is important to bear in mind in the data protection context, when considering that the Supreme Court found that there is nothing in the DPA 1998 that prevents vicarious liability of an employer, even when its employee faces statutory liability under the DPA 1998. Although the judgment did not consider the Data Protection Act 2018 and the GDPR, it is likely that the same principles will apply.

VICARIOUS LIABILITY AND CYBER LITIGATION

7.16 Notwithstanding the decision of the Supreme Court, the *Morrisons* case in the Court of Appeal was the first successful 'group action' in England and Wales for a data breach. The Supreme Court decision does not avail organisations from being held vicariously liable for their employee's misuse of data, despite the fact that the organisations themselves are compliant with data protection legislation, and have appropriate technical and organisational measures in place designed to protect the data that they hold. The *Morrisons* case is about the motives of the employee.

Thus, data protection has a wide reach, and organisations are likely to feel somewhat vulnerable and at the mercy of their employees acting within their field of activities, which will potentially engender a lack of trust between organisations and their employees.

In terms of what this case means for cyber litigation, the publicity surrounding this case, combined with the publicity surrounding the EU General Data Protection Regulation[54] ('GDPR') and the actions of the Information Commissioner's Office ('ICO') under it, have increased public awareness of data protection issues and the value of data. Therefore, there may be an increase in civil claims from employees, customers etc in the event of a data breach and, if the breach affects a large number of individuals, there could be a Group Litigation Order ('GLO'), resulting in organisations being ordered to pay large amounts in damages.

Additionally, under the GDPR, any person who has suffered material or non-material damage as a result of an infringement of the GDPR has the right to receive compensation from the controller or processor for the damage suffered.[55] Section 168(1) of the Data Protection Act 2018 ('DPA 2018') provides that non-material damage includes distress. Although Article 82(3) of the GDPR provides that a controller or processor will be exempt from liability if it proves that it is not in any way responsible for the event giving rise to the damage, given the 'enterprise risk' doctrine relied on in the *Mohamud* and *Morrisons* cases, the courts might be likely to find that, by employing an individual who misused their position, organisations are responsible for the event giving rise to the damage as they employed an individual, the risk of an employee misusing their position is 'one of life's unavoidable facts',[56] and that risk materialised. Therefore, it may be even easier for claims to be brought against organisations and, where there are a large number of claimants, meeting such claims is potentially going to become expensive.

Thus, the decision on vicarious liability in the *Morrisons* case is potentially going to lead to an increase in the amount of cyber litigation being brought, together with an increase in the number of individuals involved in such litigation and the quantum in damages that will need to be paid.

It is also possible to see, given the reasoning of the High Court as adopted by the Court of Appeal, that it may not only be misuse of information for which organisations may be held vicariously liable. It is possible that they may also be held vicariously liable in respect of cyber-assisted and/or cyber-dependent crimes committed by their employees.

54 Regulation (EU) 2016/679.

55 GDPR, Article 82(1).

56 *Mohamud v Wm Morrison Supermarkets plc* [2016] UKSC 11, at [40].

WHAT CAN COMPANIES AND CORPORATES DO TO PROTECT THEMSELVES?

Protecting against employee's actions

7.17 If an employee abuses or misuses their position, what can a company do? As Lord Toulson said in the *Mohamud* case, the risk of an employee misusing their position is 'one of life's unavoidable facts'.[57] However, companies can ensure that they have appropriate technical and organisational measures in place designed to protect the data that they hold. If they have any concerns about the trustworthiness of any of their employees, or come to believe or reasonably suspect that an employee poses a threat to the security and/or processing of data, they can facilitate a change in role and/or seek to limit that employee's access to personal and/or sensitive data. The same is also true if an employer comes to believe or reasonably suspect that an employee cannot be trusted to continue, or poses a threat in respect of continuing, in their role and, where an employer has serious concerns, they may look to try and terminate the employment.

In terms of whether a company should seek to closely monitor their employees and their actions, the level of monitoring required in order to prevent an employee misusing their position is likely to be such that it is not only impracticable, but also disproportionately intrusive, and thus amounts to an unlawful interference with employees' rights to privacy and family life. Additionally, close monitoring is likely to result in a toxic work environment, and engender an atmosphere of lack of trust between employers and employees.

Companies should, however, seek to introduce a culture of data protection, and educate their employees about the importance and need for it. Thus a clear understanding of what is expected and what will be done to check adherence and compliance will be established. Companies should seek to create a 'working together to protect' culture, thereby seeking employee investment in the organisation's efforts.

However, the above would only mitigate the risk of an employee accidentally abusing or misusing their position, rather than protecting against an intentional abuse. In that respect, there is very little that organisations can do to protect themselves against an employee's intentional abuse or misuse of their position.

Protecting against vicarious liability

7.18 Given that it is difficult for organisations to protect themselves against deliberate actions by an employee, companies may seek to protect themselves from being held vicariously liable for their employee's actions by expressly prohibiting certain actions. Due to the strict-liability nature of vicarious liability, merely prohibiting conduct within the sphere of employment will not be

57 *Mohamud v Wm Morrison Supermarkets plc* [2016] UKSC 11, at [40].

sufficient to defeat a claim of vicarious liability. Only a prohibition that limits the sphere of employment may affect the application of vicarious liability, as that may mean that the employee's actions are not sufficiently connected with their employment.[58]

However, being a form of strict liability that is fact specific, there is no 'one size fits all' method for companies to protect themselves against vicarious liability. Indeed, in some cases, there may be no way for companies to protect against the potential of being held vicariously liable, and so the best course of action may be to seek a way to mitigate the effects of being held so liable.

Indeed, employers having insurance to cover a finding of vicarious liability is what was anticipated by the High Court and the Court of Appeal in the *Morrisons* case.

In the High Court proceedings, in response to submissions on behalf of Morrisons that a finding of vicarious liability would be visiting 'excessive liability' on an innocent data controller, and that the possibility of 'eye-watering liability' may impose enormous pressure on a data controller to limit the presence of human agency, even where it plays an important role in an effective and efficient operation, Langstaff J stated:[59]

> 'These *in terrorem* arguments are almost certainly overstated: I note that I have not been referred to a single case in which it is said that vicarious liability had overwhelmed a company. I have no doubt this is because many commercial entities will cover the potential losses by appropriate insurance within the ordinary course of trading. […]'

When the same arguments were put before the Court of Appeal, it was no more sympathetic:[60]

> '77. Ms Proops submitted that, given that there are 5,518 employees who are claimants in the present case, and the total number of employees whose confidential information was wrongly made public by Mr Skelton was nearly 100,000, this illustrates how enormous a burden a finding of vicarious liability in the present case will place on Morrisons and could place on other innocent employers in future cases. These arguments are unconvincing. As it happens Mr Skelton's nefarious activities involved the data of a very large number of employees although, so far as we are aware, none of them has suffered financial loss. But suppose he had misused the data so as to steal a large sum of money from one employee's bank account. If Morrisons' arguments are correct, then (save for any possible claim against the bank) such a victim would have no remedy except against Mr Skelton personally. Yet this hypothetical claimant would, as it seems to us, be in essentially the same position as Mrs Lloyd in *Lloyd v Grace, Smith.*
>
> 78. There have been many instances reported in the media in recent years of data breaches on a massive scale caused by either corporate system failures or

58 *Ilkiw v Samuels* [1963] 1 WLR 991.

59 *Various Claimants v Wm Morrison Supermarkets plc* [2017] EWHC 3113 (QB), at [159].

60 *Wm Morrison Supermarkets plc v Various Claimants* [2018] EWCA Civ 2339, at [77] to [78].

> negligence by individuals acting in the course of their employment. These might, depending on the facts, lead to a large number of claims against the relevant company for potentially ruinous amounts. The solution is to insure against such catastrophes; and employers can likewise insure against losses caused by dishonest or malicious employees. We have not been told what the insurance position is in the present case, and of course it cannot affect the result. The fact of a defendant being insured is not a reason for imposing liability, but the availability of insurance is a valid answer to the Doomsday or Armageddon arguments put forward by Ms Proops on behalf of Morrisons.'

However, if vicarious liability can attach in respect of the malicious, dishonest and/or criminal misuse or abuse of an employee's position, given that there is a risk that every single employee could misuse or abuse their position (as per Lord Toulson in the *Mohamud* case), insurance companies may not be willing to insure against such risks. And this may especially be so if GLOs and representative party actions are going to become an increasingly frequent visitor to the High Court (see further **Chapter 6**) and huge amounts are awarded in damages. Therefore, insurance may not provide the relief/protection that the courts expect as, following the decision of the Court of Appeal and its implications, companies may not be able to obtain such insurance.

That said, in response to the submission on behalf of Morrisons that to hold data controllers vicariously liable for the actions of their employees, in the absence of any culpable default on their part, would potentially expose them, unjustly, to enormously burdensome group litigation and claims out of all proportion to the value of the claims of the individual data subjects concerned,[61] the High Court stated:[62]

> '[...] since this is by agreement of both Counsel the first case in a period of very nearly 20 years since the Act came into force to raise the question whether there is vicarious liability at all under the Act for the actions of an employee in deliberately misusing the data with which he was entrusted, it seems unlikely that the Doomsday scenarios postulated by Morrisons will occur. This is without yet factoring in both an absence of such cases in respect of the 1984 statutory predecessor of the 1998 Act, and the likely relatively modest award of damages in the event of a finding of liability: I suspect that in many cases the liability may be within the means of an ordinary tortfeasor to satisfy, but, if not, though in a group action affecting a very large number of employees the total sum may certainly be significant, it seems unlikely that the amounts payable would equate, for instance, with those that might be contemplated in respect of a product liability claim asserted by a cohort of injured customers.'

This indication by the High Court, that the award of damages for vicarious liability in a group litigation claim in these circumstances would be relatively modest, may give insurers the confidence to provide vicarious liability insurance to companies. However, as vicarious liability is fact specific, and in the *Morrisons* case there was no financial loss suffered, an award may not be so modest in a

61 *Various Claimants v Wm Morrison Supermarkets plc* [2017] EWHC 3113 (QB), at [147].
62 *Various Claimants v Wm Morrison Supermarkets plc* [2017] EWHC 3113 (QB), at [159].

case with different facts or where financial or other loss occurred. Consequently, despite the indications of the High Court, insurers may still be wary of insuring companies against vicarious liability on the basis of an employee's malicious, dishonest and/or criminal misuse or abuse of their position. They may also be wary on the basis that it may be difficult to recover any payouts by way of subrogation against the employee.

Therefore, companies should remember that, as vicarious liability does not replace the liability of the primary wrongdoer, they may be able to seek an indemnity or contribution from the employee to recover the losses resulting from being held vicariously liable for that employee's actions. A claim may be brought for contribution under section 1 of the Civil Liability (Contribution) Act 1978, and the employer will be able to recover an amount that, having regard to the extent of the employee's responsibility for the damage in question, is just and equitable.[63]

Additionally, as an act giving rise to vicarious liability may be a breach of an employee's employment contract, an employer may have the option of claiming damages for the entire loss under a breach of contract claim, thereby avoiding the need to rely on the Civil Liability (Contribution) Act 1978.[64]

However, as one of the rationales for vicarious liability is so that liability is borne by a defendant with the means to compensate those who have been caused harm, companies might find, especially in cases where GLOs have been granted, that an employee's means are insufficient to meet an indemnity or contribution claim, or a claim for breach of contract. What recourse then do innocent companies have? The answer is, in the author's opinion, very little.

63 Civil Liability (Contribution) Act 1978, s 2(1).
64 *Lister v Romford Ice & Cold Storage Co Ltd* [1957] AC 555 (HL).

Chapter 8

Evidential Considerations

This chapter examines some of the evidential considerations that cyber litigation gives rise to, specifically:

- the challenges in evidence gathering in cases where material is held on computers and other electronic storage devices:
  - lawfully obtaining electronic material;
  - Article 8 privacy and family life considerations in respect of electronic material; and
  - obtaining evidence from overseas; and
- the challenges faced once electronic material has been obtained:
  - maintaining the integrity of material;
  - accessibility of material;
  - admissibility of material; and
  - the retention of material.

INTRODUCTION

8.1 In a similar way to jurisdiction in cyber litigation (see **Chapter 5**), there are no special rules or principles of evidence that govern cyber litigation: statutory and common law principles continue to apply as normal in cases concerning or involving technology.

There are, however, specific challenges in evidence gathering in cyber litigation, particularly in terms of lawfully obtaining evidence that is stored on computers and other electronic storage devices, whether the material is protected by Article 8 privacy and family life rights, and obtaining evidence and material that is held overseas.

Not only that but, once the material has been obtained, there are then further considerations as to maintaining the integrity of the material, accessing the material, the admissibility of any material obtained, and the retention of the material.

The development of new technologies is such that it is giving rise to situations where technology, as opposed to humans, handles and reviews evidence. For example, artificial intelligence ('AI') is being used to conduct/assist disclosure and document review. Technology is also affecting the reliance that can be placed on certain types of evidence. For example, sender spoofing and deepfakes call into question evidence that is regularly relied on in criminal trials. The use of AI in disclosure and case decision making, sender spoofing and deepfakes is considered in some detail at paragraphs **2.59** to **2.61** and, as such, will not be repeated here.

This chapter examines some of the evidential considerations that cyber litigation gives rise to, specifically the challenges faced in evidence gathering and the challenges faced once material has been obtained.

WHAT ARE THE SPECIFIC CHALLENGES IN EVIDENCE GATHERING IN CYBER LITIGATION?

Lawfully obtaining electronic material

8.2 Obtaining material, particularly that which is held on computers or other electronic storage devices, can be complex. Not only can such devices hold huge amounts of data but, unless access is voluntarily provided, there is a risk that individuals obtaining and accessing such material (particularly law enforcement officers) could be subjected to arguments of having committed an offence under section 1 of the Computer Misuse Act 1990 ('CMA 1990') (unauthorised access to computer material) or section 3 of the Investigatory Powers Act ('IPA 2016') (offence of unlawful interception) and that the material has been illegally obtained.

Additionally, given the huge amounts of data that such devices hold, there is a risk that, in obtaining such material, parties will also obtain material that they are not entitled to, for example:

- that which is not relevant to the investigation or matter;
- that which falls outside the specifics of the power or warrant providing for the acquisition of the material; or
- protected materials (such as legally privileged material, excluded material and special procedure material).

How do law enforcement officers and other parties go about obtaining material from electronic devices and avoid accusations of having obtained the material illegally? What is the position in relation to protected materials and materials that they are not entitled to?

Police powers – general powers of entry, search and seizure

Statutory powers

8.3 Entry to search for documentation or material is outside the scope of the statutory pre-arrest powers of entry and search provided for by section 17 of the Police and Criminal Evidence Act 1984 ('PACE 1984').

However, section 18(1) of PACE 1984 provides that, following arrest for an indictable offence, the police may enter and search any premises occupied or controlled by the person under arrest if they have reasonable grounds for suspecting that there is evidence on the premises that relates to that offence, or to some other indictable offence which is connected with or similar to the offence for which the person has been arrested. The police may seize and retain anything that they find pursuant to such a search.[1] The power conferred by section 18(1) is only a power to search to the extent that is reasonably required for the purposes of discovering such evidence.[2] It is worth noting that, as section 18(1) requires the premises to be occupied or controlled by the person under arrest for the indictable offence, corporate premises are outside the scope of the section 18 powers of entry, search and seizure.

In addition to the power to seize material pursuant to a section 18(1) search,[3] under section 19 of PACE 1984, the police may seize anything on the premises if they have reasonable grounds for believing that:

- it has been obtained in consequence of the commission of an offence and it is necessary to seize it in order to prevent it being concealed, lost, damaged, altered or destroyed;[4] or
- it is evidence in relation to an offence which they are investigating or any other offence and it is necessary to seize it in order to prevent the evidence being concealed, lost, altered or destroyed.[5]

Where the police have reasonable grounds for believing that material is evidence in relation to an offence which they are investigating or any other offence, or it has been obtained in consequence of the commission of an offence, and such a request is necessary in order to prevent the material being concealed, lost, tampered with or destroyed, the police may require that any information which is stored in any electronic form and is accessible from the premises be produced in a form in which it can be taken away and in which it is visible and legible or from which it can readily be produced in a visible and legible form.[6]

Note that no power of seizure authorises the seizure of an item which the police have reasonable grounds for believing to be subject to legal professional privilege.[7]

Warrants under PACE 1984

8.4 Where the above statutory powers are inadequate in providing a basis for the entry and search of premises, and the seizure of computers and other electronic devices, the police must apply to the court under section 8 of

1 PACE 1984, s 18(2).
2 PACE 1984, s 18(3).
3 PACE 1984, s 19(5).
4 PACE 1984, s 19(2).
5 PACE 1984, s 19(3).
6 PACE 1984, s 19(4).
7 PACE 1984, s 19(6).

PACE 1984 for a warrant to enter and search for material. A warrant will only be issued if the court is satisfied that the following criteria are all satisfied:[8]

- an indictable offence has been committed;
- there is material on the premises (be that specific premises ('specific premises warrant') or all premises occupied or controlled by a person specified in the application ('all premises warrant')) which is likely to be of substantial value (whether by itself or together with other material) to the investigation of the offence;
- the material is likely to be relevant evidence (ie anything that would be admissible in evidence at a trial for the offence);
- it does not consist of or include items subject to legal privilege, excluded material or special procedure material; and
- it is not practicable to communicate with any person entitled to grant entry to the premises or, although it is practicable to communicate with a person entitled to grant entry, it is not practicable to communicate with a person entitled to grant access to the evidence; or entry to the premises will not be granted unless a warrant is produced; or the purpose of a search may be frustrated or seriously prejudiced unless a constable arriving at the premises can secure immediate entry to them.

For an 'all premises warrant', the police must also satisfy the court that:[9]

- there are reasonable grounds for believing that, due to the particulars of the offence, it is necessary to search premises occupied or controlled by the person in question which are not specified in the application order to find material that is likely to be of substantial value to the investigation; and
- it is not reasonably practicable to specify in the application all the premises which the person in question occupies or controls and which might need to be searched.

The police may seize and retain anything for which a search warrant has been authorised.[10]

Where the material is or might be excluded or special procedure material, the police will need to apply for a special procedure warrant under section 9 of, and Schedule 1 to, PACE 1984 (see para **8.23** for further discussion of this material and special procedure warrants).

In applying for a warrant, there is a duty of full disclosure, and omitting any relevant material that would have reasonably led the court to refuse the application will result in the warrant being defective and quashed. Additionally, if the terms of a warrant are not adhered to, or the correct procedure is not followed, the search will be unlawful, and any material obtained under it will need to be returned.

8 PACE 1984, s 8(1), (3) and (4).
9 PACE 1984, s 8(1B).
10 PACE 1984, s 8(2).

Specific cyber-assisted crimes warrants

8.5 Specific entry and search warrants can be applied for in relation to certain specific serious crimes, such as drug offences and terrorism. With technology being increasingly used to commit or assist in the commission of serious crimes (see **Chapter 2** for a full overview and analysis of cyber-assisted crimes), some of these warrants deserve brief mention:

- Section 66 of the Serious Organised Crime and Police Act 2005 enables an officer to apply for a warrant to enter and seize documents not produced pursuant to a disclosure notice (or where it is impractical or prejudicial to an investigation to serve such a notice).
- Under the Terrorism Act 2000:
  - Section 42 permits an officer to apply for a warrant to search premises for a person liable to arrest under section 40(1)(b) of the Act, ie that they are suspected of being concerned in the commission, preparation or instigation of acts of terrorism.
  - Paragraph 1 of Schedule 5 enables a constable to apply for a warrant to search premises and anyone found there for the purposes of a terrorist investigation.
  - Paragraphs 2 and 2A of Schedule 5 permit a warrant for entry, search and seizure of material that may be relevant to terrorist investigations.
  - An order under paragraph 5 of Schedule 5 may require a specified person: to provide to a constable any material that he has in his possession for the purposes of seizure and retention; to give the constable access to the material; and to state to the best of his knowledge the location of the material to which the application relates.
  - Paragraph 11 of Schedule 5 permits a warrant to enter and seize relevant excluded or special procedure material (see para **8.23** for an explanation of this material) required for the investigation of terrorist cases.
- Section 28 of the Terrorism Act 2006 enables a constable to apply for a warrant to enter and search any premises, and seize any terrorist publications.
- Section 17 of the Crime (International Co-operation) Act 2003 provides that, pursuant to a request for assistance received from overseas authorities, a constable may apply for a warrant to enter and search any premises, and to seize and retain any evidence for which he is authorised to search.

Specific statutory power of seizure – Criminal Justice and Police Act 2001

8.6 The Criminal Justice and Police Act 2001 ('CJPA 2001') assists in the lawful acquisition of material held on computers and other electronic storage devices, as it entitles law enforcement officers to seize computers and other electronic storage devices, despite the fact that they may contain material that they are not entitled to seize under the powers listed in Part 1 of Schedule 1 to the CJPA 2001 – for example, because the computer or other electronic storage device contains material that is both within and outside the terms of a warrant.

Section 50(1) of the CJPA 2001 provides that:[11]

> 'Where–
>
> (a) a person who is lawfully on any premises finds anything on those premises that he has reasonable grounds for believing may be or may contain something for which he is authorised to search on those premises,
>
> (b) a power of seizure to which this section applies or the power conferred by subsection (2) would entitle him, if he found it, to seize whatever it is that he has grounds for believing that thing to be or to contain, and
>
> (c) in all the circumstances, it is not reasonably practicable for it to be determined, on those premises–
>
> (i) whether what he has found is something that he is entitled to seize, or
>
> (ii) the extent to which what he has found contains something that he is entitled to seize,
>
> that person's powers of seizure shall include power under this section to seize so much of what he has found as it is necessary to remove from the premises to enable that to be determined.'

Section 50(2) provides that:[12]

> 'Where–
>
> (a) a person who is lawfully on any premises finds anything on those premises ("the seizable property") which he would be entitled to seize but for its being comprised in something else that he has (apart from this subsection) no power to seize,
>
> (b) the power under which that person would have power to seize the seizable property is a power to which this section applies, and
>
> (c) in all the circumstances it is not reasonably practicable for the seizable property to be separated, on those premises, from that in which it is comprised,
>
> that person's powers of seizure shall include power under this section to seize both the seizable property and that from which it is not reasonably practicable to separate it.'

The matters that need to be taken into account in considering whether or not it is reasonably practicable for something to be determined on the premises, or for something to be separated from something else, are:[13]

(1) how long it would take to carry out the determination or separation on those premises;

11 CJPA 2001, s 50(1).
12 CJPA 2001, s 50(2).
13 CJPA 2001, s 50(3).

(2) the number of persons that would be required to carry out that determination or separation on those premises within a reasonable period;

(3) whether the determination or separation would (or would, if carried out on those premises) involve damage to property;

(4) the apparatus or equipment that it would be necessary or appropriate to use for the carrying out of the determination or separation; and

(5) in the case of separation, whether the separation would be likely, or if carried out by the only means that are reasonably practicable on those premises would be likely, to prejudice the use of some or all of the separate seizable property for a purpose for which something seized under the power in question is capable of being used.

It should be noted that the above is an exhaustive list of factors to be considered.[14]

There is a duty imposed on the person in possession of material seized under these powers to ensure that an initial examination of the property is carried out as soon as reasonably practicable after the seizure, in order to determine what falls within the search power and can be retained.[15]

Serious Fraud Office

8.7 Section 2(3) of the Criminal Justice Act 1987 ('CJA 1987') grants the Serious Fraud Office ('SFO') a compulsory power that requires the person under investigation or any other person to produce at such place as specified in the notice, and either forthwith or at such time as may be specified, any specified documents which appear to relate to any matter relevant to the investigation, or any documents of a specified description which appear to so relate. Where any such documents are so produced, the SFO may take copies or extracts from them, and/or require the party producing them to provide an explanation of any of them.

Where there are reasonable grounds for believing that a person has failed to comply with an obligation to produce documents under a section 2(3) notice, it is not practicable to serve a section 2(3) notice, or the service of such a notice might seriously prejudice the investigation, the SFO may seek a warrant for a constable to enter and search the premises where the material is reasonably believed to be, and to take possession of any documents appearing to be documents of the description specified in the information or to take any steps which may appear necessary for preserving them and preventing interference with them.[16]

14 CJPA 2001, s 50(3).
15 CJPA 2001, s 53.
16 CJA 1987, s 2(4)–(5).

Information Commissioner's Office

8.8 The Information Commissioner's Office ('ICO') may obtain electronic material in three ways:

(1) through an Information Notice;

(2) through an Assessment Notice; or

(3) through a warrant issued under Schedule 15 to the Data Protection Act 2018 ('DPA 2018').

Information and Assessment Notices

8.9 An Information Notice requires a controller or processor to provide the ICO with information that it reasonably requires in order to carry out its functions under data protection legislation.[17] The issuing of an Information Notice is subject to the restrictions outlined in section 143 of the DPA 2018, and the Information Commissioner may seek a court order to compel a person to comply with an Information Notice.[18]

An Assessment Notice requires a controller or processor to permit an assessment of whether they have complied, or are complying, with the data protection legislation.[19] An Assessment Notice can, amongst other things:

- require a controller or processor to permit the Information Commissioner to enter specified premises;
- direct the Information Commissioner to specified documents, equipment or material;
- provide the Information Commissioner with an explanation of such documents, equipment or material; and
- make people available for interview.[20]

As with Information Notices, there are certain restrictions on Assessment Notices, which are outlined in section 147 of the DPA 2018. For example, the Information Commissioner may not give an Assessment Notice to a controller or processor with respect to the processing of personal data for journalistic, academic, artistic or literary purposes; and a notice cannot compel the disclosure of legally privileged material.

A person or organisation that has received an Information or Assessment Notice may appeal to the Information Tribunal[21] if they believe that the ICO has breached its Regulatory Action Policy in issuing such notices.[22]

17 DPA 2018, s 142(1).
18 DPA 2018, s 145.
19 DPA 2018, s 146(1).
20 DPA 2018, s 146(2).
21 DPA 2018, s 162.
22 https://ico.org.uk/media/about-the-ico/documents/2259467/regulatory-action-policy.pdf.

Warrants for entry and inspection

8.10 The ICO can apply to the court for a warrant to enter and inspect premises if:

- there are reasonable grounds for suspecting that a controller or processor:
  - has failed, or is failing, to comply with its obligations under the General Data Protection Regulation[23] and/or the DPA 2018, or
  - is committing or has committed an offence under the DPA 2018, and there are reasonable grounds for suspecting that evidence of the failure or commission of the offence is to be found on specified premises or capable of being viewed using equipment on such premises;[24] or
- a controller or processor has failed to comply with requirements imposed by an Assessment Notice.[25]

To grant a warrant, the court must be satisfied that:[26]

- the ICO gave seven days' written notice to the occupier demanding access to the premises; access to the premises was unreasonably refused or the occupier unreasonably refused to comply with a request by the ICO; the occupier has been notified of the application for the warrant and has had an opportunity to be heard by the judge; and
- compliance with the conditions listed above would defeat the object of entry to the premises; or
- the ICO requires urgent access to the premises.

A warrant issued under Schedule 15 will authorise the ICO to enter the premises, search the premises and inspect, examine, operate and test any equipment found on the premises which is used or intended to be used for the processing of personal data.[27]

Where the warrant is issued in relation to non-compliance or commission of an offence, the warrant must also authorise the ICO to:[28]

- inspect and seize any documents or other material found on the premises which may be evidence of the failure or offence;
- require any person on the premises to provide, in appropriate form, a copy of information capable of being viewed using equipment on the premises which may be evidence of the failure or offence;

23 Regulation (EU) 2016/679.
24 DPA 2018, Sch 15, para 1.
25 DPA 2018, Sch 15, para 2.
26 DPA 2018, Sch 15, para 4.
27 DPA 2018, Sch 15, para 5(1).
28 DPA 2018, Sch 15, para 5(2).

- require any person on the premises to provide an explanation of any document or other material found on the premises and of any information capable of being viewed using equipment on the premises; and
- require any person on the premises to provide such other information as may reasonably be required for the purposes of determining whether the controller or processor has failed or is failing to comply with its obligations under the GDPR and/or DPA 2018.

Where the warrant is issued in relation to failure to comply with an Assessment Notice, the warrant must also authorise the ICO to:[29]

- inspect and seize any documents or other material found on the premises which may enable the ICO to determine whether the controller or processor has complied or is complying with the data protection legislation;
- require any person on the premises to provide, in an appropriate form, a copy of information capable of being viewed using equipment on the premises which may enable the ICO to make such a determination;
- require any person on the premises to provide an explanation of any document or other material found on the premises and of any information capable of being viewed using equipment on the premises; and
- require any person on the premises to provide such other information as may reasonably be required for the purposes of determining whether the controller or processor has complied or is complying with the data protection legislation.

The ICO's powers to inspect and seize material do not extend to being able to seize material which is protected by legal professional privilege.[30]

Investigatory Powers Act 2016

8.11 The IPA 2016 provides four methods by which law enforcement agencies can obtain electronic material:

- targeted interception of communications;
- targeted acquisition and retention of communications data;
- targeted equipment interference; and
- bulk interception, acquisition, equipment interference and personal dataset warrants.

Each of these will be addressed in turn.

29 DPA 2018, Sch 15, para 5(3).
30 DPA 2018, Sch 15, para 11.

Targeted interception of communications[31]

8.12 This involves obtaining a warrant from the Secretary of State[32] to acquire the content of communications, either whilst the communication is still transmitting or is present on a server.

A targeted interception warrant may only be granted if:

- it is necessary;
- it is proportionate;
- satisfactory arrangements are in place in terms of safeguards relating to disclosure; and
- the decision to issue the warrant has been approved by a Judicial Commissioner.[33]

The grounds on which such a warrant may be deemed necessary are:[34]

- in the interests of national security;
- for the purpose of preventing or detecting serious crime; or
- in the interests of the economic well-being of the UK, so far as those interests are also relevant to the interests of national security (but note that the warrant will only be considered necessary in the interests of the economic well-being of the UK if the information that it is considered necessary to obtain is information relating to the acts or intentions of persons outside the British Isles).

Only the following bodies can apply for an interception warrant:

- Her Majesty's Revenue and Customs ('HMRC');
- the Ministry of Defence;
- the Metropolitan Police;
- Police Services Scotland and Northern Ireland;
- the Security Service ('MI5');
- the Secret Intelligence Service ('MI6');
- Government Communications Headquarters ('GCHQ'); and
- the National Crime Agency ('NCA').[35]

31 IPA 2016, Parts 1 and 2.
32 IPA 2016, s 19(1).
33 IPA 2016, s 19(1).
34 IPA 2016, s 20(2) and (4).
35 IPA 2016, s 18(1).

Targeted acquisition and retention of communications data[36]

8.13 This involves obtaining information that relates to communications, such as discovering the parties to, and the timing of, an electronic communication. No warrant is required in order to obtain communications data: access is authorised by the Investigatory Powers Commissioner ('IPC') or a 'designated officer'.[37] The bodies that may authorise access to communications data includes those that may apply for an interception warrant, plus additional bodies such as local authorities.[38]

Where the authorisation to obtain communications data is to be granted by the IPC, the IPC will only do so where it is satisfied that:[39]

- it is necessary to obtain the communications data for a specified purpose, namely:
  - in the interests of national security;
  - for the applicable crime purpose, ie the purpose of preventing or detecting serious crime;
  - in the interests of the economic well-being of the UK, so far as those interests are also relevant to the interests of national security;
  - in the interests of public safety;
  - for the purpose of preventing death or injury or any damage to a person's physical or mental health, or of mitigating any injury or damage to a person's physical or mental health;
  - to assist investigations into alleged miscarriages of justice; or
  - to assist in identifying a person or obtaining information about a person's next of kin, or about the reasons for a person's death or condition, where that person has died or is unable to identify themselves because of a physical or mental condition;
- it is necessary to obtain the data for the purpose of a specific investigation or a specific operation or for the purposes of testing, maintaining or developing equipment, systems or other capabilities relating to the availability or obtaining of communications data; and
- the conduct authorised by the authorisation is proportionate to what is sought to be achieved.

The same criteria apply in relation to an authorisation being sought from a designated officer, save that only the first three 'necessary purposes' apply in those cases.[40]

36 IPA 2016, Parts 3 and 4.
37 IPA 2016, ss 60A and 61.
38 IPA 2016, ss 70 and 73.
39 IPA 2016, s 60A(1) and (7).
40 IPA 2016, s 61(1) and (7).

A telecommunications operator may be required to retain communications data for up to one year so that it is available for collection/inspection upon service of the requisite request.[41] Thus the IPA 2016 can require communication service providers to retain UK internet users' internet connection records, which includes the websites visited, for a year. Such retention notices are authorised by the Secretary of State, provided that the decision to give the notice has been approved by a Judicial Commissioner.[42] A retention notice will only be authorised if it is necessary and proportionate for a specified purpose, namely:[43]

- in the interests of national security;
- the applicable crime purpose;
- the interests of the economic well-being of the UK, so far as those interests are also relevant to the interests of national security;
- the interests of public safety;
- for the purpose of preventing death or injury or any damage to a person's physical or mental health, or of mitigating any injury or damage to a person's physical or mental health; or
- to assist investigations into alleged miscarriages of justice.

Targeted equipment interference[44]

8.14 This involves obtaining a warrant from the Secretary of State or law enforcement chief to lawfully interrogate personal equipment in order to access and acquire private information held on it. Such a warrant may only be obtained by the intelligence services and law enforcement officers.[45]

A targeted equipment interference warrant may only be granted if:

- it is necessary;
- it is proportionate;
- satisfactory arrangements are in place in terms of safeguards relating to disclosure; and
- the decision to issue the warrant has been approved by a Judicial Commissioner.[46]

Where such a warrant is sought from the Secretary of State, the grounds on which the warrant may be deemed necessary are:[47]

41 IPA 2016, s 87(3).
42 IPA 2016, s 87(1).
43 IPA 2016, ss 87(1)(a), (10A), (10B) and 263(1).
44 IPA 2016, Part 5.
45 IPA 2016, ss 102(1) and 106(1).
46 IPA 2016, s 102(1).
47 IPA 2016, s 102(5) and (6).

- in the interests of national security;
- for the purpose of preventing or detecting serious crime; or
- in the interests of the economic well-being of the UK, so far as those interests are also relevant to the interests of national security (but note that the warrant will only be considered necessary in the interests of the economic well-being of the UK if the information that it is considered necessary to obtain is information relating to the acts or intentions of persons outside the British Isles).

Where such a warrant is sought from a law enforcement chief, only the 'necessity' ground of preventing or detecting serious crime applies.[48]

Bulk interception, acquisition, equipment interference and personal dataset warrants[49]

8.15 Bulk interception, acquisition and equipment interference warrants can only be applied for by the intelligence services,[50] and can only be granted by the Secretary of State if:[51]

- the warrant is necessary:
  - in the interests of national security;
  - for the purpose of preventing or detecting serious crime; or
  - in the interests of the economic well-being of the UK, so far as those interests are also relevant to the interests of national security (but note that the warrant will only be considered necessary in the interests of the economic well-being of the UK if the information that it is considered necessary to obtain is information relating to the acts or intentions of persons outside the British Isles).
- the conduct authorised by the warrant is proportionate to what is sought to be achieved by that conduct;
- each of the specified operational purposes is a purpose for which the examination of intercepted content or secondary data obtained under the warrant is or may be necessary, and the examination of intercepted content or secondary data for each purpose is necessary on any of the grounds on which the warrant is considered to be necessary;
- satisfactory arrangements in terms of safeguards relating to disclosure are in force in relation to the warrant; and
- the decision to issue the warrant has been approved by a Judicial Commissioner.

48 IPA 2016, s 106(1)(a).
49 IPA 2016, Parts 6 and 7.
50 IPA 2016, ss 138(1), 158(1) and 178(1).
51 IPA 2016, ss 138, 158 and 178.

In relation to bulk interception and bulk equipment interference warrants, there are also the additional requirements that the main purpose of the warrant is the interception of overseas-related communications and the obtaining of secondary data from such communications[52] or obtaining overseas-related communications, overseas-related information or overseas-related equipment data[53] (respectively).

If data is obtained via a bulk equipment interference warrant, a targeted examination warrant will be required in order to access and examine any information relating to individuals in the UK.[54]

Sections 204 and 205 of the IPA 2016 allow the intelligence services to apply to the Secretary of State for a warrant to retain and examine personal data (within the same meaning as the DPA 2018) relating to a number of individuals ('bulk personal datasets') – for example, registers and electoral rolls. Section 199 provides that the intelligence services retain a bulk personal dataset when 'a majority of the individuals are not, and are unlikely to become, of interest to the intelligence service in the exercise of its functions'. Thus the IPA 2016 permits the intelligence services, with the oversight contained within the Act, to retain personal data in relation to large groups of people who are unrelated to any intelligence activity.

Regulation of Investigatory Powers Act 2000

8.16 Chapter II of Part I of the Regulation of Investigatory Powers Act 2000 ('RIPA 2000') provides for the acquisition and disclosure of 'communications data', which is defined as:[55]

- any traffic data comprised in or attached to a communication (whether by the sender or otherwise) for the purposes of any postal service or telecommunication system by means of which it is being or may be transmitted;
- any information which includes none of the contents of a communication (apart from any information falling within the bullet point outlined above) and is about the use made by any person:
  - (i) of any postal service or telecommunications service; or
  - (ii) in connection with the provision to or use by any person of any telecommunications service, of any part of a telecommunication system; or
- any information not falling within the above two bullet points that is held or obtained, in relation to persons to whom he provides the service, by a person providing a postal service or telecommunications service.

52 IPA 2016, s 138(1)(a).
53 IPA 2016, s 178(1)(a).
54 IPA 2016, s 99(9).
55 RIPA 2000, s 21(4).

Such communications data may only be acquired if it is necessary:[56]

- in the interests of national security;
- for the applicable crime purpose, ie the purpose of preventing or detecting serious crime, or of preventing disorder;
- in the interests of the economic well-being of the UK, so far as those interests are also relevant to the interests of national security;
- in the interests of public safety;
- for the purpose, in an emergency, of preventing death or injury or any damage to a person's physical or mental health, or of mitigating any injury or damage to a person's mental health; or
- for any purpose which is specified by an order made by the Secretary of State.

Thus, investigation authorities may use Chapter II of Part I of RIPA 2000 to serve notices on internet service providers requiring them to disclose identified communications data, such as IP addresses or other data relating to email accounts.

Police Act 1997

8.17 Section 93(1) of the Police Act 1997 ('PA 1997') permits the authorisation of covert entry into, and interference with, property or 'wireless telegraphy' by the police, HMRC and other law enforcement agencies. Under section 93(1A), officers are permitted to covertly enter premises to maintain or retrieve any equipment, apparatus or device, the placing or use of which has been authorised by the PA 1997 or by Part II of RIPA 2000 (or under an equivalent Act of Scottish Parliament).

Computer Misuse Act 1990

8.18 Section 10 of the CMA 1990, as amended by section 44 of the Serious Crime Act 2015, provides that section 1 of the CMA 1990 does not prejudice the operation of any enactment relating to powers of inspection, search or seizure, or of any other enactment authorising conduct, and that the withholding of consent to law enforcement officers accessing any program or data will not make their access unauthorised under section 1.

Therefore, even if consent is withheld, provided that they are acting under a statutory power relating to inspection, search or seizure, law enforcement officers can access material held on computers, servers etc and not be guilty of an offence under section 1 of the CMA 1990, and so it cannot be argued that any material so obtained was obtained illegally.

56 RIPA 2000, s 22(2) and (2A).

Telecommunications (Lawful Business Practice) (Interception of Communications) Regulations 2000

8.19 The Telecommunications (Lawful Business Practice) (Interception of Communications) Regulations 2000[57] ('the Telecommunications Regulations 2000') provide that a system controller (which includes an employer) may, or may give express consent to others to, intercept communications in the course of their transmission by means of a telecommunication system which is provided for use wholly or partly in connection with the business, for the purpose of:[58]

- monitoring or keeping a record of communications:
  - to establish the existence of facts, ascertain compliance with regulatory or self-regulatory practices or procedures, or to ascertain or demonstrate the standards which are or ought to be achieved;
  - in the interests of national security (in which case, only certain specified public officials may make the interception);
  - to prevent or detect crime;
  - to investigate or detect unauthorised use of the telecommunication systems; or
  - to secure, or as an inherent part of, effective system operation;
- monitoring received communications to determine whether they are business or personal communications; and
- monitoring communications made to anonymous telephone helplines.

References to 'a business' include references to activities of a government department, of any public authority, or of any person or office holder on whom functions are conferred by or under any enactment.[59]

Such interceptions are only authorised under the Telecommunications Regulations 2000, however, if the employer has made all reasonable efforts to inform potential users that interceptions may be made[60] and if the interception is effected solely for the purpose of monitoring or keeping a record of communications relevant to the business.[61]

Therefore, employers may monitor and keep records of their employees' communications and, given the increased risk of Group Actions and vicarious liability in respect of data breaches (see **Chapters 6** and **7** onwards for more details), employers might seek to make increasing use of the authorisation

57 SI 2000/2699.
58 Telecommunications Regulations 2000, reg 3(1)(a) and (2)(b).
59 Telecommunications Regulations 2000, reg 2(a).
60 Telecommunications Regulations 2000, reg 3(2)(c).
61 Telecommunications Regulations 2000, reg 3(2)(a).

provided under the Telecommunications Regulations 2000 in order to protect themselves against, and mitigate, such risks.

Search and seizure orders (Anton Piller orders)

8.20 Search and seizure orders are a mandatory interim injunction that requires a defendant to allow the claimant's representatives to enter the defendant's premises and search for, copy, and remove and retain documents, information and material. The purpose is to preserve evidence where it is believed that a defendant would otherwise destroy it in contravention of a court order for the delivery up or preservation of documents, or to preserve property which is (or may be) the subject of an action, or as to which a question arises in an action.[62]

In terms of cyber litigation, claimants might look to search for, copy, and remove and retain digital data by way of search and seizure orders. Consequently, companies' entire servers and other digital devices may be imaged under such orders.

Search and seizure orders are not, however, intended to be a way of obtaining evidence, nor a way of enforcing disclosure obligations. Therefore, once an image of digital data is taken, so that the documents are preserved and safe from the risk of destruction, claimants should not be permitted to undertake a search of that image without further application to the court under the disclosure regime. Consequently, a search and seizure order will allow no more than the imaging of digital data.[63]

Protected material

8.21 As outlined at paragraph **8.2** above, there are specific categories of material that parties are not, as a general rule, entitled to seize, despite the fact that they fall within the body of material that has been lawfully obtained under one of the powers/orders etc outlined above.

Material subject to legal professional privilege

8.22 Legally privileged material consists of:[64]

- communications between a lawyer and their client, or any person representing their client, made in connection with the giving of legal advice to the client;
- communications between a lawyer and their client, or any person representing their client, or between a lawyer or their client or any such representative

62 Civil Procedure Act 1997, s 7.

63 *A v B; Hewlett Packard Enterprise Co v Manchester Technology Data (Holdings) Ltd* [2019] EWHC 2089 (Ch) at [25] to [26].

64 PACE 1984, s 10(1).

and any other person, made in connection with or in contemplation of legal proceedings and for the purposes of such proceedings. The dominant purpose of the communications must be the contemplation of legal proceedings;[65] and

- items enclosed with or referred to in such communications and made in connection with the giving of legal advice or in connection with, or in contemplation of, legal proceedings and for the purpose of such proceedings.

Parties are not entitled to such material unless the privilege is waived, or it is determined that the material is not, in fact, privileged.

It should be noted that items held with the intention of furthering a criminal purpose are not items subject to legal professional privilege ('LPP') ('the crime/fraud exception').[66]

Where entire computers, servers and other electronic storage devices are seized or accessed, there is a risk of seizing legally privileged material. Consequently, there should be a procedure in place for conducting an LPP review.

> Case Study
>
> In *A v B; Hewlett Packard Enterprise Co v Manchester Technology Data (Holdings) Ltd*[67] (see para **9.12** for a full discussion of this case), the High Court suggested that one option might be for defendants, through their solicitors, to be provided with an opportunity to review the data first, in order to remove privileged material.[68]
>
> Alternatively, independent lawyers can be appointed to conduct an LPP review.[69]

Excluded material and special procedure material

8.23 Excluded material includes:

- personal records acquired or created in the course of any trade, business, profession or other occupation, and which are held subject to an express or implied undertaking to hold them in confidence or subject to a restriction on disclosure or an obligation of secrecy contained in any enactment;[70] and

65 *Director of the Serious Fraud Office v Eurasian Natural Resources Corporation Ltd* [2018] EWCA Civ 2006.
66 PACE 1984, s 10(2).
67 [2019] EWHC 2089 (Ch).
68 [2019] EWHC 2089 (Ch), at [48].
69 *R (Tchenguiz) v Director of the Serious Fraud Office* [2012] EWHC 2254 (Admin).
70 PACE 1984, s 11(1)(a) and (2).

- journalistic material, whether documents or other records, which is held subject to an undertaking, restriction or obligation of confidence, and has been continuously so held since it was first acquired or created for the purposes of journalism.[71]

Personal records are documentary or other records concerning any identifiable individual (whether living or dead), and which relate to:

- physical or mental health;
- spiritual counselling or assistance given or to be given; or
- counselling or assistance given or to be given for the purposes of personal welfare, whether by a voluntary organisation or any individual who is responsible for the individual's personal welfare.[72]

Thus, medical records are excluded material.

Special procedure material is material which is not legally privileged material or excluded material but which has been acquired or created in the course of any trade, business, profession or other occupation. It is held subject to an express or implied undertaking to hold it in confidence or subject to a restriction on disclosure or an obligation of secrecy contained in any enactment.[73] Journalistic material, other than excluded material, is also special procedure material.[74]

Excluded material and special procedure material may only be accessed by the police under a special procedure warrant obtained pursuant to Schedule 1 to PACE 1984.[75] In order to obtain a special procedure warrant, the police must apply to a judge and prove that one of the access conditions listed at paragraphs 2 and 3 of Schedule 1 to PACE 1984 has been satisfied:

- *Excluded material*: but for section 9(2) (providing that an Act passed before PACE 1984 which authorised a search of premises for the purpose of a criminal investigation by virtue of an issue of a warrant ceases to have effect so far as it relates to the authorisation of searches for LPP, excluded or special procedure material), a search for the material could have been authorised by a warrant under an enactment other than Schedule 1 and the issue of such a warrant would have been appropriate ('the second set of access conditions').[76]
- *Special procedure material*:
  - an indictable offence has been committed; the material is likely to be of substantial value and relevant evidence; other methods have been tried without success or have not been tried because they were

71 PACE 1984, s 11(1)(c) and (3).
72 PACE 1984, s 12.
73 PACE 1984, ss 14(1)(a), (2) and 11(2)(b).
74 PACE 1984, s 14(1)(b).
75 PACE 1984, s 9(1).
76 PACE 1984, Sch 1, para 3.

bound to fail; and it is in the public interest that the material should be produced or access given to it ('the first set of access conditions');[77] or

- but for section 9(2) (see above), a search for the material could have been authorised by a warrant under an enactment other than Schedule 1 and the issue of such a warrant would have been appropriate ('the second set of access conditions').[78]

Where there is a reasonable belief that excluded or special procedure material may be present on computers and other electronic storage devices, law enforcement applicants must ensure that they comply with Schedule 1 in applying for a special procedure warrant, that they give full and frank disclosure, and that the terms of any warrant so granted are appropriately drafted and complied with; otherwise, the warrant and any subsequent search and seizure may be quashed as being unlawful and failing to comply with the requirements of PACE 1984.

Case Study

In *R (on the application of S) v Chief Constable of the British Transport Police*[79] the claimants, who were a solicitor and two solicitors' firms, applied for judicial review of the Crown Court's decision to grant the Chief Constable of the British Transport Police search warrants in respect of their premises.

F and L were solicitors' firms; S was a partner at F. A client of F was being investigated by the police on suspicion of conspiring to steal rail track. He and S attended the police station, where the police made it clear that they regarded evidence from mobile telephones as important to the investigation. When the police searched the client for his mobile telephone, they discovered that it was in S's briefcase.

The police applied to the Crown Court for a warrant under section 9 of and Schedule 1 to PACE 1984 to search S's home address for 'laptops, mobile phones and SIM cards' in connection with offences of 'attempting to pervert the course of justice' and 'concealing criminal property'. The warrant was issued, identifying the 'material likely to be relevant evidence' as being 'a mobile telephone and a laptop computer'. The police executed the warrant and seized S's mobile telephone and a laptop computer. Before the search was completed, S was arrested on suspicion of having been party to a conspiracy to pervert the course of justice.

The client engaged a different law firm, L, and the police applied for warrants to search the premises of both F and L. The material sought was 'S's "in custody" notebook/solicitor pad and any directly associated

77 PACE 1984, Sch 1, para 2.
78 PACE 1984, Sch 1, para 3.
79 [2013] EWHC 2189 (Admin).

documentation relating to [the client]' and, in their information, the police stated that they would search F first, and only search L if the material could not be found at F. They also stated that they would have a member of the Solicitor Regulation Authority ('SRA') present, and Independent Counsel to review any material for LPP.

The warrants were granted and, when they were executed, were accompanied by a 'Details of Request' document which requested not only the 'in custody' notebook/solicitor pad and directly associated documentation, but also the case file and associated documents relating to the client. The warrant was executed at F first but, because Independent Counsel wanted time to carefully consider the documentation and felt that he could not do so at the premises, it was bagged and sealed and taken away. No member of the SRA was present. The warrant was then executed at L, despite the police not knowing whether or not the material seized from F contained the relevant material. Independent Counsel viewed an electronic document, after which he advised the police that there was nothing to seize.

The Administrative Court (Aikens LJ and Silber J) held that all three warrants must be quashed:

1. The warrant in relation to S's home address showed a total disregard for the Schedule 1 statutory requirements, as the information set out the terms of Schedule 1 verbatim without any statement of facts or matters on which the assertions were said to be made.[80]

2. The first set of access conditions were the only ones that could have been relevant in the circumstances for the warrant in relation to S's home address, but those conditions were not satisfied, because there were no reasonable grounds for believing that there was special procedure material that did not include excluded material. The material stored on S's mobile telephone and laptop would have included records in the form of emails, documents and text messages which would have been acquired in the course of S's occupation as a solicitor, and any such material would have been held in confidence. Accordingly, that material would fall within the definition of 'special procedure material', but it could possibly comprise excluded material, and so the first set of access conditions were not satisfied.[81]

3. It was also highly likely that the material would include items which were subject to LPP, and would thus fall outside the definition of 'special procedure material'. As such, the first set of access conditions, which pertain to obtaining special procedure material

80 [2013] EWHC 2189 (Admin), at [51] and [54].
81 [2013] EWHC 2189 (Admin), at [56] to [57].

only, could not be used to obtain a warrant to search for and gain access to LPP material.[82]

4. An applicant for a warrant has to give full and frank disclosure, and it was quite clear from the 'Details of Request' document that the purpose of the warrant to search F's office was beyond that which was expressly stated in the warrant. Accordingly, given the terms of section 15(1) of PACE 1984 (search warrants – safeguards), the issue of the warrant had been unlawful and it had to be quashed.[83]

5. The seizure and removal of the client file from F, without reliance upon section 50 or 51 of the CJPA 2001, went beyond that which was authorised and so must be unlawful.[84]

6. The written information provided that there was a condition precedent to searching L's premises; namely, that the police would first consider if all the documents for which the warrant applied were at F's premises and, if not, only then execute the warrant at L. At the time when the warrant for the search of L's premises was executed, the officers did not know whether the material they had seized from F contained the material for which the warrant applied – it had been seized to be examined by Independent Counsel later. Therefore, the condition precedent for the execution of the warrant against L had not be fulfilled when the warrant was executed.[85]

Where material is stored in any electronic form and a special procedure warrant requires a person to produce or give access to such material, that person must produce the material in a form in which it can be taken away and in which it is visible or legible, or from which it can readily be produced in a visible and legible form, or give access to the material in a form which is visible and legible.[86]

In terms of the process for applying for a special procedure warrant, the application may be made ex parte, unless it relates to material that consists of or includes journalistic material, which must be made inter partes.[87]

Failure to comply with a special procedure warrant effectively constitutes contempt of the Crown Court.[88]

82 [2013] EWHC 2189 (Admin), at [58].
83 [2013] EWHC 2189 (Admin), at [78] to [80].
84 [2013] EWHC 2189 (Admin), at [88].
85 [2013] EWHC 2189 (Admin), at [99] to [101].
86 PACE 1984, Sch 1, para 5.
87 PACE 1984, Sch 1, para 7.
88 PACE 1984, Sch 1, para 7.

Privacy

8.24 In obtaining material, regard must be had to whether obtaining it breaches an individual's right to privacy and right to a family life under Article 8 of the European Convention on Human Rights ('ECHR').

> Case Study
>
> In *Barbulescu v Romania*[89] the applicant worked for a private company. At the employer's request, he set up an instant messaging account to respond to customer enquiries. The employer's internal regulations prohibited personal use of computers, and the applicant was aware of those regulations. The applicant was informed by the employer that his messenger account had been monitored and was required to explain why he had used the internet for personal purposes. He initially stated that he had used the messenger account for work-related purposes only, but was later given a transcript of personal messages that he had sent on the account. The employer dismissed him, and the domestic courts upheld his dismissal.
>
> The applicant alleged that the monitoring of his communications had breached his rights under Article 8 of the ECHR and that the domestic authorities had failed to protect those rights.
>
> The Grand Chamber of the European Court of Human Rights upheld the applicant's complaint.
>
> First, the court found that Article 8 did apply in these circumstances. The messaging service at issue was a form of communication enabling individuals to lead a private social life, and the sending and receiving of communications was covered by the notion of 'correspondence', even if they were sent from an employer's computer. Although the applicant had been informed of the ban on personal internet use, the domestic court had not ascertained whether the applicant had been informed of the monitoring of his communications before it began, and the court found that it did not appear that he had been so informed. Consequently, it was open to question whether the employer's regulations had left the applicant with a reasonable expectation of privacy; but, in any event, an employer's instructions could not reduce private social life in the workplace to zero, even if respect for private life and the privacy of correspondence were restricted insofar as necessary. Therefore, Article 8 applied in the circumstances.[90]
>
> The court held that, as the monitoring had been undertaken by a private company, it could not be regarded as 'interference' with the applicant's right by a state authority. However, the employer's action had been upheld by the national courts. Accordingly, the complaint should be examined from the standpoint of the state's positive obligation to uphold ECHR rights, rather than its negative obligation to refrain from breaching rights.[91]

89 61496/08; [2017] 9 WLUK 42 (ECtHR (Grand Chamber)).
90 61496/08, at [74] to [80].
91 61496/08, at [109] to [111].

In certain circumstances, the state's positive obligation in protecting an applicant's right to respect for private life and correspondence in the context of employment were not adequately fulfilled, unless it secured respect for private life in the relations between individuals by setting up a legislative framework taking into consideration the various interests to be protected in a particular context. Labour law left room for negotiation between the parties to the employment contract, and few states had explicitly regulated the exercise by employees of their right to respect for their private life and correspondence in the workplace. Accordingly, states had to be granted a wide margin of appreciation in assessing the need to establish a legal framework governing the conditions in which an employer could regulate electronic or other communications of a non-professional nature by its employees in the workplace. However, that discretion could not be unlimited, and states should ensure that employers' monitoring measures had adequate safeguards against abuse. The following factors were relevant in considering the proportionality and procedural guarantees of employers' monitoring measures:

- whether the employee had been notified of the possibility of monitoring;
- the extent of the monitoring;
- whether the employer had given legitimate reasons for the monitoring;
- whether a monitoring system based on less intrusive methods than directly accessing communications would have been possible;
- the consequences of the monitoring for the employee; and
- whether the employee had been provided with adequate safeguards.[92]

In terms of compliance with Article 8 in the present case, the court had to determine whether the national authorities had struck a fair balance between the applicant's right to respect for his private life and correspondence and the employer's interests. Although the domestic courts had found that the applicant had had prior notification of the employer's policy, they had not determined whether he had been notified, in advance, of the possibility of monitoring measures. To qualify as prior notice, the warning had to be given before the monitoring was initiated. The courts had not examined the scope of the monitoring or the degree of intrusion. Nor did it appear that they had sufficiently assessed whether there were legitimate reasons for the monitoring. They had not sufficiently examined whether less intrusive methods could have been used, and they had not determined the point at which the employer had accessed the relevant content. Consequently, the domestic authorities had not struck a fair balance between the competing interests, and the court found that Article 8 had been breached.[93]

92 61496/08, at [115] to [122].
93 61496/08, at [127] to [141].

The boundaries of Article 8 considerations in the workplace were further considered in *Libert v France*[94] which held that, although individuals can engage in a private life in the workplace using technology provided by their employers, such an allowance is not unfettered, and employers will be permitted to access such 'private' material in certain circumstances.

Case Study

A French national railway employee was suspended following an accusation by a fellow employee, and then reinstated when the proceedings were discontinued a few months later. During the period of his suspension, his work computer had been seized, and it was discovered that the applicant had stored pornography on his work computer in a file entitled 'personal data'. Indeed, he saved all of his work to this same file. He was dismissed from his position following a disciplinary hearing, and he subsequently brought proceedings claiming that he had been dismissed without genuine or serious cause. Those proceedings were dismissed, and the applicant appealed, submitting that there had been a violation of Article 8 of the ECHR.

The European Court of Human Rights found that, unlike in *Barbulescu v Romania,* the SNCF (the French national railway) was a public authority and, as such, the complaint must be analysed on the basis of a state's positive obligations under Article 8. Consequently, interference violates Article 8 unless it:

- is in accordance with the law;
- pursues one or more of the legitimate aims referred to; and
- is necessary in a democratic society to achieve the aim or aims concerned.[95]

'In accordance with the law': the court observed that the Court of Cassation had already held at the material time that, save in a case of serious risk or in exceptional circumstances, an employer could only open files identified by an employee as personal and stored on the hard disk of their work computer in the employee's presence or after they had been duly called for. The Court of Cassation had added that folders and files created by an employee using the computer supplied by their employer for work purposes were presumed to be professional documents, unless the employee had identified them as personal, and so the employer could therefore have access to them in the employee's absence. Accordingly, the court concluded that, at the material time, positive law had already allowed the employer, within the said limits, to open files stored on an employee's

94 588/13, 22 February 2018.
95 588/13, at [37] to [42].

work computer, and it therefore accepted that the interference complained of by the applicant had a legal basis and that positive law contained adequate provisions specifying the circumstances and conditions in which such a measure could validly be regarded as 'in accordance with the law'.[96]

'Legitimate aim': the court did not accept that the interference was with the legitimate aim of preventing crime, as the opening of the files was not done in the context of the criminal proceedings brought against the applicant, and at no stage of the domestic proceedings had it been considered that the contents of the files might constitute a criminal offence. However, the court did acknowledge that the interference was intended to safeguard the protection of the 'rights of others': in this case, those of the employer, who may legitimately wish to ensure that employees are using computer facilities placed at their disposal for the purpose of carrying out their duties in line with their contractual obligations and the applicable regulations. The court went on to reiterate its observation in *Barbulescu v Romania* that the employer has a legitimate interest in ensuring the smooth running of the company, and that this can be done by establishing mechanisms for checking that its employees are performing their professional duties adequately and with the necessary diligence.[97]

'Necessary': the court observed that the domestic courts properly assessed the applicant's allegation of a violation of Article 8, and found their decision to have been based on relevant and sufficient grounds. The entire hard disk, which is by default named 'D:/data' and traditionally used by staff to store work documents, had been renamed 'D:/personal data', and an employee could not use the whole hard disk, which was supposed to record professional data, for private use. The generic term 'personal data' did not explicitly designate elements related to private life, and the term 'fun' did not necessarily confer a private designation on the file. The SNCF's Charter specifically stated that 'private data' must be clearly identified as such, ie by being labelled 'private'. The applicant's dismissal was not disproportionate, given his massive breach of the SNCF's Code of Professional Conduct and its internal rules, which provided that staff were required to use the computer facilities supplied to them for exclusively professional purposes, with the occasional private use being merely tolerated.

Thus, the court confirmed the employer's power to access the file, and it upheld the dismissal, stating that there had been no violation of Article 8 of the ECHR.

96 588/13, at [44].
97 588/13, at [45] to [46].

Evidence abroad

8.25 Where evidence, whether stored on a computer or other electronic device or otherwise relating to a 'cyber' case, is held outside England and Wales, law enforcement agencies and parties face additional challenges in the pursuit of cyber litigation. What can parties do in order to obtain material that is held overseas and which is needed for cyber litigation?

Obtaining evidence from abroad in criminal 'cyber' cases

8.26 Obtaining evidence from abroad in criminal cases is dealt with through a Mutual Legal Assistance Treaty ('MLAT'), which is governed by the Crime (International Co-operation) Act 2003 ('CICA 2003').

The procedure for requesting material from abroad is set out in section 7 of the CICA 2003, under which prosecuting authorities have to apply to a court within England and Wales for a Letter of Request ('LoR') to be sent to the relevant jurisdiction,[98] or a designated prosecutor can send a LoR of their own volition.[99] Where the request relates to information on banking transactions, the LoR must state the grounds on which the person making the request considers the evidence specified in it to be relevant for the purposes of the investigation.[100] This will be particularly pertinent in money laundering and terrorist financing cases, breach of financial sanctions, blackmail via ransomware etc.

The requisite pre-conditions for obtaining a LoR are that an offence must have been committed or there are reasonable grounds for suspecting that an offence has been committed, and proceedings in respect of the offence have been instituted or the offence is being investigated.[101]

LoRs are submitted and approved by courts or central governments in the place where the evidence is located,[102] and so can take months, if not longer, to be processed and answered.

It should be noted that any evidence obtained pursuant to a LoR cannot, without the consent of the appropriate overseas authority, be used for any purposes other than that specified in the request; and, where the evidence is no longer required for that purpose, it must be returned to the appropriate overseas authority, unless the authority indicates that the material need not be returned.[103]

98 CICA 2003, s 7(1)–(4).
99 CICA 2003, s 7(5).
100 CICA 2003, s 7(7).
101 CICA 2003, s 7(1) and (5).
102 CICA 2003, s 8(1).
103 CICA 2003, s 9(2) and (3).

US-UK Bilateral Data Access Agreement

8.27 In relation to evidential requests for electronic data from the United States ('US'), UK law enforcement agencies will no longer have to resort to the MLAT process and submit LoRs.

In March 2018, the US passed the Clarifying Lawful Overseas Use of Data Act ('the CLOUD Act'),[104] which allows the US to enter into executive agreements with foreign governments in order to facilitate law enforcement access to electronic data. These executive agreements remove LoRs from the data request process, so signatory countries can directly request data and records from US-based providers.

On 3 October 2019, the US and the UK signed the first CLOUD Act Executive Agreement: the US-UK Bilateral Data Access Agreement ('the US-UK Agreement').[105] The intention is that the US-UK Agreement will allow law enforcement agencies in either country to 'demand electronic data regarding serious crime, including terrorism, child sexual abuse, and cybercrime, directly from tech companies based in the other country, without legal barriers'.[106]

A 'serious crime' is one that is punishable by a maximum term of imprisonment of at least three years,[107] and a data request in respect of such crimes can be made to any private entity that provides the public with the ability to:

- communicate;
- process or store computer data; or
- process or store electronic or wire communications, traffic data or metadata pertaining to such communications and subscriber information (including name, address, length and type of service, subscriber number or identity (including assigned network address and device identifiers), telephone connection records, records of session times and durations, and means of payment)[108]

Thus, a wide range of data can be sought under the US-UK Agreement, and be sought from entities such as Apple, Facebook and WhatsApp, which have been notoriously difficult to get information from in the past. The US-UK Agreement came into force in April 2020, and there is enormous value in law enforcement agencies now being able to obtain this data directly from the source company

104 www.justice.gov/dag/page/file/1152896/download.

105 https://assets.publishing.service.gov.uk/government/uploads/system/uploads/attachment_data/file/836969/CS_USA_6.2019_Agreement_between_the_United_Kingdom_and_the_USA_on_Access_to_Electronic_Data_for_the_Purpose_of_Countering_Serious_Crime.pdf.

106 www.justice.gov/opa/pr/us-and-uk-sign-landmark-cross-border-data-access-agreement-combat-criminals-and-terrorists.

107 Agreement between the Government of the United Kingdom of Great Britain and Northern Ireland and the Government of the United States of America on Access to Electronic Data for the Purpose of Countering Serious Crime ('the US-UK Agreement'), Article 1(14).

108 US-UK Agreement, Article 1(3), (7) and (15).

as, not only will it assist in the fight against cyber-assisted and cyber-dependent crimes, but it will also dramatically reduce the time that investigations take.

In order to avail themselves of the US-UK Agreement, UK law enforcement authorities need to apply to the court for an overseas production order under the Crime (Overseas Production Orders) Act 2019 ('COPOA 2019'). Section 4 sets out the conditions for granting an application, namely that:

- there are reasonable grounds for believing that all or part of the electronic data specified in the application is likely to be of substantial value to the proceedings or investigation;
- there are reasonable grounds for believing that all or part of the electronic data specified in the application is likely to be relevant evidence in respect of the offence alleged; and
- there are reasonable grounds for believing that it is in the public interest for the electronic data to be produced.[109]

Once an overseas production order has been granted, and the relevant UK 'designated authority' has reviewed the order and certified that it complies with the US-UK Agreement, it will issue it to the relevant US provider to comply with. The US provider may challenge the order[110] but, unless it does so, it will need to comply with the order and provide the requested information directly to the UK 'designated authority'.

One thing to note about the US-UK Agreement is that it is bilateral, so UK corporates are also subject to it and will find themselves the direct recipients of requests from US law enforcement agencies. As such, they may want to seek advice and guidance on how to comply with and/or challenge such electronic data requests.

For further details and an analysis of the US-UK Agreement, see paragraph **2.58**.

Obtaining evidence from abroad in civil 'cyber' cases

8.28 In civil cases, the procedure to be followed in respect of obtaining evidence from abroad is found in Part 34 of the Civil Procedure Rules ('CPR') and Practice Direction 34A, and is governed by Regulation (EC) 1206/2001[111] and the Evidence (Proceedings in Other Jurisdictions) Act 1975.

109 COPOA 2019, s 4(5)–(7).

110 US-UK Agreement, Article 5(11)–(12), and COPOA 2019, s 7.

111 Council Regulation (EC) 1206/2001 of 28 May 2001 on cooperation between the courts of the Member States in the taking of evidence in civil or commercial matters (the 'Taking of Evidence Regulation').

Where a party wishes to take a deposition from a person who is out of the jurisdiction and not in a Regulation State, ie they are outside a European Union ('EU') Member State, they must apply to the High Court for an order for the issue of a LoR to the judicial authorities of the country in which the proposed deponent is.[112] The LoR may request the judicial authority to take the evidence of the proposed deponent, or arrange for it to be taken.[113] The application for an order for the issue of a LoR should be made by application notice in accordance with Part 23 of the CPR,[114] and must include:[115]

- a draft order;
- a draft LoR in the form set out in Annex A to Practice Direction 34A;
- a statement of the issues relevant to the proceedings;
- a list of questions or the subject matter of questions to be put to the person to be examined;
- a translation of the above, unless English is one of the official languages of the country where the examination is to take place or a practice direction has specified the country as a country where no translation is necessary; and
- an undertaking to be responsible for the Secretary of State's expenses.

Where a party wishes to take a deposition from a person who is in another Regulation State, the court may order the issue of a request to a designated court ('the requested court') in the Regulation State in which the proposed deponent is.[116] An application to the court for such an order should be made by application notice in accordance with Part 23 of the CPR,[117] and the party who is seeking the order must file:[118]

- a draft Form A, as set out in the annex to the Taking of Evidence Regulation;
- a translation of the form, unless English is one of the official languages of the Regulation State where the examination is to take place, or the Regulation State has indicated that English is a language which it will accept;
- an undertaking to be responsible for costs sought by the requested court in relation to:
  - fees paid to experts and interpreters; and
  - where requested by that party, the use of special procedures or communications technology; and
- an undertaking to be responsible for the court's expenses.

112 CPR, r 34.13(1) and (1A).
113 CPR, r 34.13(2).
114 CPR, PD 34A, para 5.2.
115 CPR, r 34.13(6)-(7); CPR, PD 34A, para 5.3.
116 CPR, r 34.23(1)–(2).
117 CPR, PD 34A, para 10.2.
118 CPR, r 34.23(3)–(4).

Alternatively, Article 17 of the Taking of Evidence Regulation permits the court where proceedings are taking place to take evidence directly from a deponent in another Regulation State, provided that the evidence is given voluntarily without the need for coercive measures; and so the court may make an order for the submission of a request to take evidence directly in accordance with Article 17.[119] An application for such an order must be made by application notice in accordance with Part 23 of the CPR,[120] and the party seeking the order must file:[121]

- a draft Form I, as set out in the annex to the Taking of Evidence Regulation;
- a translation of the form, unless English is one of the official languages of the Regulation State where the examination is to take place, or the Regulation State has indicated that English is a language which it will accept; and
- an undertaking to be responsible for the court's expenses.

WHAT ARE THE SPECIFIC EVIDENTIAL CHALLENGES ONCE MATERIAL HAS BEEN OBTAINED?

Maintaining the integrity of material

8.29 Where material has been obtained from computers and other electronic storage devices, there is a need to maintain the integrity of that material in order to ensure that investigations are not criticised, to prevent cases collapsing and to ensure that evidence is admissible.

Therefore, over the years, best practice guidance has been issued to law enforcement agencies in an attempt to reduce attacks on the integrity of material obtained.

Case Study

In 2003, the Association of Chief Police Officers ('ACPO') issued guidelines entitled 'Good Practice Guide for Computer Based Electronic Evidence'.[122] The guidelines were aimed at investigators, evidence recovery staff, those attending crime scenes or making initial contact with victims, and external consultant witnesses. The guidelines also dealt with procedures for obtaining evidence from mobile telephones and hand-held personal computers.

Although ACPO as an organisation no longer exists, the four principles set out in these ACPO guidelines are still followed today, particularly by

119 CPR, r 34.23(5).

120 CPR, PD 34A, para 10.6.

121 CPR, r 34.23(4) and (6).

122 www.7safe.com/docs/default-source/default-document-library/acpo_guidelines_computer_evidence_v4_web.pdf.

police officers and other investigators, as they encapsulate practical advice and best practice in collecting and presenting digital material:

- Principle 1: No action taken by law enforcement agencies or their agents should change data held on a computer or storage media which may subsequently be relied upon in court.
- Principle 2: In circumstances where a person finds it necessary to access original data held on a computer or on storage media, that person must be competent to do so and be able to give evidence explaining the relevance and the implications of their actions.
- Principle 3: An audit trail or other record of all processes applied to computer-based electronic evidence should be created and preserved. An independent third party should be able to examine those processes and achieve the same result.
- Principle 4: The person in charge of the investigation (the case officer) has overall responsibility for ensuring that the law and these principles are adhered to.

The guidelines make it clear that, in order to comply with these principles, wherever practicable, an image should be made of the entire target device, although partial or selective file copying may be considered as an alternative in certain circumstances (for example, where the amount of data to be imaged makes it impracticable).

The guidelines also set out what records should be kept, urge caution on what should and should not be seized, and outline best practice in terms of evidence recovery.

Despite being aimed at criminal investigations and investigations by other law enforcement agencies, there is no reason why similar principles should not apply in civil cases where a party obtains a data image under a search and seizure order and obtains a court order permitting the interrogation of that image.

Accessibility of material

8.30 Law enforcement agencies can often find that material seized is encrypted, and so legislation and technology are used to defeat encryption and view protected information.

Disclosure notices

8.31 Part III (sections 49–56) of RIPA 2000 deals with data protected by encryption.

Section 49 sets out the powers of law enforcement agencies when encrypted information is obtained or otherwise seized or intercepted. It allows a notice requiring disclosure of the encryption key to be served on someone reasonably suspected to be in possession of the key, provided that the disclosure requirement is proportionate and in the interests of national security, for the purpose of preventing or detecting crime or in the interests of the economic well-being of the UK. A further pre-condition is that it must also not be reasonably practicable to obtain possession of the encrypted information in an intelligible form without the disclosure notice.

Section 50 sets out the effect of a notice imposing a disclosure requirement, and a knowing failure to comply with a section 49 notice is a criminal offence under section 53. Section 54 creates an offence of tipping-off, which may be committed where the section 49 notice contains a provision requiring the person to whom the notice is given, and every other person who becomes aware of it or of its contents, to keep secret the giving of the notice, its contents and things done in pursuance of it.

A section 49 disclosure notice can only be sought in relation to encrypted material that has come into the possession of a relevant person by means of the exercise of a statutory power to seize, detain, inspect, search or otherwise to interfere with documents or other property.[123] Therefore, it will not be appropriate in all circumstances.

'Cyber kiosks'

8.32

Case Study

From 20 January 2020, Police Scotland began using 'cyber kiosks', which allow officers to bypass encryption and read personal data from certain digital devices without using a password.[124]

The purpose of the 'cyber-kiosk' is to identify whether or not a device contains any evidential data, so it will only be used in cases where the evidential relevance of a device is unknown. If the triage process shows that the device does not contain anything of evidential relevance, it will be returned to the owner. However, if the device is shown to contain material of evidential relevance, it will be submitted for normal processing.

The intention is that only mobile telephones and tablets will be submitted to the 'cyber-kiosk' triage process.

123 RIPA 2000, s 49(1).

124 www.publictechnology.net/articles/news/scottish-police-get-green-light-use-encryption-busting-'cyber-kiosks'.

For further details and a more in-depth analysis of 'cyber-kiosks', see paragraph **2.57**.

Quantum computing

8.33 If quantum computing proves to be viable as anticipated, it will likely have a significant disruptive effect on security systems that rely on traditional assumptions about the complexity of certain critical operations.

For example, a large amount of encryption relies on the fact that, if you have the product of two prime numbers, working out those two prime numbers, when they are unknown to you, is mathematically hard. It is anticipated that quantum computing could make such mathematical processes easy. This will have dramatic knock-on effects, both in the world of cyber-assisted and cyber-dependent crimes, and also in the world of cyber investigations, as it may mean that certain types of encryption are defunct.

Admissibility of material

Intercept evidence

8.34 Section 56(1) of the IPA 2016 provides that, in legal proceedings or an inquiry held under the Inquiries Act 2005, no evidence may be adduced, question asked, assertion or disclosure made, or other thing done which discloses, in circumstances from which its origin in interception-related conduct may be inferred, any content of an intercepted communication or any secondary data obtained from a communication. Additionally, it is also impermissible to adduce, ask questions about, make assertions or a disclosure which tends to suggest that any interception-related conduct has or may have occurred or may be going to occur.

These prohibitions apply not only to intercept evidence obtained under the IPA 2016, but also to intercept evidence obtained under legislation prior to the IPA 2016 coming into force (for example, intercept evidence obtained under RIPA 2000 and the Interception of Communications Act 1985).[125]

Schedule 3 to the IPA 2016 sets out the various exceptions to the section 56 prohibitions.

Unlawfully obtained material

Discretion to exclude evidence

8.35 Section 78 of PACE 1984 provides that, in criminal proceedings, a judge has a discretion to exclude evidence if, having regard to all the circumstances,

125 IPA 2016, s 56(4).

including the circumstances in which the evidence was obtained, admission of the evidence would have such an adverse effect on the fairness of the proceedings that the court ought not to admit it. The exercise of the discretion should take into account an assessment of the admission of the evidence, any bad faith and/or any deliberate breach of the law.

Thus, a failure by law enforcement agencies to obtain the necessary authorisations, warrants etc in order to obtain and access material stored on a computer or other electronic device might mean that any such material so obtained will be excluded and cannot be relied upon.

Stay of proceedings

8.36 Where the conduct of law enforcement agencies is such that it constitutes bad faith, rather than merely excluding evidence, the entire proceedings may be stayed as an abuse of process.

> Case Study
>
> In *R v Redmond*[126] the applicant had been convicted of drugs offences on evidence obtained by undercover police officers who had recorded conversations in person and on the telephone with him in Spain and Ireland. The applicant argued that the police had undertaken a deliberate course of conduct that was intended to bypass Spanish and Irish law and procedure. He argued that this conduct ought to justify a stay of the proceedings as an abuse of process.
>
> The Court of Appeal held, dismissing the renewed application, that, even if the judge had been in error in concluding that there had been no breach of Spanish and Irish law, his decision to permit the prosecution to proceed was within his lawful discretion. Evidence obtained unlawfully was not automatically inadmissible, and it would not necessarily be unfair for it to be considered by a jury. Although the unlawful obtaining of evidence was an important factor, the crucial issue was whether the Crown had knowingly abused its executive powers, ie whether the officers had acted in bad faith.

Secondary evidence of privileged material permissible

8.37 In terms of civil proceedings, *Calcraft v Guest*[127] has long settled the law on the ability of another party to the proceedings to use privileged documents which have come into their possession.

126 [2006] EWCA Crim 1744.
127 [1898] 1 QB 759.

Case Study

In *Calcraft v Guest* the Court of Appeal (Lindley MR, Rigby and Vaughan Williams LJJ) held that, although privilege is not lost in respect of documents which are obtained illegally, this does not preclude secondary evidence as to their contents being admissible within the civil jurisdiction.

Quoting Parke B in *Lloyd v Mostyn*,[128] the Court of Appeal concurred with the proposition that:[129]

> 'Where an attorney intrusted confidentially with a document communicates the contents of it, or suffers another to take a copy, surely the secondary evidence so obtained may be produced. Suppose the instrument were even stolen, and a correct copy taken, would it not be reasonable to admit it?'

A party cannot benefit from unlawfully obtained evidence

8.38 Whilst *Calcraft v Guest* remains a correct statement of the law (ie secondary evidence of privilege material is permissible within civil proceedings), the courts are holding that parties to civil proceedings should not benefit from unlawfully obtained evidence.

Case Study

In *Dubai Aluminium v Al Alawi*,[130] the claimant sought damages against a former employee for breach of contract, and to recover an unquantified sum in secret commissions. The claimant was granted relief to preserve the defendant's assets.

The defendant sought to discharge these orders on the basis that the agents who had been employed by the claimant to investigate his finances had acted unlawfully in obtaining the evidence used to support the applications. He also sought an order requiring disclosure of the reports and other documents relating to the investigation of his financial affairs carried out by the claimant's agents.

The claimant accepted that the documents were relevant and discoverable, but resisted discovery on the ground of LPP.

Rix J held that LPP did not apply to these documents because:[131]

> '[…] it seems to me that criminal or fraudulent conduct for the purposes of acquiring evidence in or for litigation cannot properly escape the

128 152 ER 558.
129 *Calcraft v Guest* [1898] 1 QB 759, at 764.
130 [1999] 1 WLR 1964.
131 [1999] 1 WLR 1964, at 1969.

consequence that any documents generated by or reporting on such conduct and which are relevant to the issues in the case are discoverable, and fall outside the legitimate area of legal professional privilege.'

In granting the defendant's application, Rix J said:[132]

> '[…] criminal or fraudulent conduct undertaken for the purposes of litigation falls on the same side of the line as advising on or setting up criminal or fraudulent transactions yet to be undertaken, as distinct from the entirely legitimate professional business of advising and assisting clients on their past behaviour, however iniquitous.'

The judge also held that, in cases where criminal or fraudulent conduct has been undertaken for the purposes of acquiring evidence for litigation, there is always the sanction of prosecutions or civil suits, and that those must always remain the primary sanction for any breach of the criminal or civil law.[133]

The Court of Appeal adopted a similar position, ie that a party should not benefit from unlawfully obtained evidence, in *Imerman v Tchenguiz*.[134]

Case Study

In *Imerman v Tchenguiz*, the Court of Appeal (Lord Neuberger MR and Moses and Munby LJJ) was required to determine whether an injunction, preventing the use of material obtained in breach of confidence, had been properly imposed.

The material had been obtained from a work computer database by an employee who was related to a party petitioning for divorce.

Neuberger MR, in dealing with the wrongful and potentially unlawful obtaining of confidential documents said (at para 103):

> '[…] the fact that accessing the documents can be said to have been to protect Mrs Imerman's rights can scarcely be said to render it "in the public interest", even if it was done with a view to exposing, or preventing, Mr Imerman's anticipated wrongful concealment of assets.'

He continued (at para 146) that:

> 'Mrs Imerman should not be entitled to benefit in any way from the wholesale, wrongful, and possibly criminal, accessing and copying of Mr Imerman's confidential documents, particularly as she could have been expected to apply for a peremptory order.'

132 [1999] 1 WLR 1964, at 1970.
133 [1999] 1 WLR 1964, at 1969.
134 [2010] EWCA Civ 908.

Article 6 fair trial rights

8.39 Consideration always needs to be given to the way in which material was obtained, and whether that impacts on the use to which it may be put – specifically, in criminal proceedings, whether relying on the material obtained would affect an individual's fair trial rights under Article 6 of the ECHR.

> Case Study
>
> In *R v Director of the Serious Fraud Office ex p Smith*[135] the applicant chairman and managing director of a company was charged as follows: that, between 1 January 1985 and 29 April 1991, he had knowingly been a party to the carrying on of the business of the company with intent to defraud its creditors, contrary to section 458 of the Companies Act 1985. He was cautioned. On 7 May he was admitted to bail. The Director of the SFO formed the opinion that the matter was appropriate for investigation by procedures under the CJA 1987 and, on 24 June, she served a notice on the applicant under section 2(2) of the CJA 1987 requiring him to attend for interview at her offices and answer questions or otherwise furnish information.
>
> The House of Lords (Lord Templeman, Lord Bridge, Lord Ackner, Lord Lowry and Lord Mustill) held that the plain intention of the CJA 1987 was that the Director of the SFO's compulsory section 2 powers should not end when the person under investigation was charged. Accordingly, an individual could be compelled to answer questions and no fresh caution was required.[136]

The above case was in relation to the SFO's powers under section 2(2) of the CJA 1987 – compulsory powers to answer questions or furnish information – but there would seem to be no reason why the House of Lords' reasoning should not also apply to notices under section 2(3) (see para **8.7** above).

Therefore, an individual charged may still be compelled to provide documentation under a section 2(3) notice.

It is generally accepted, however, that material obtained through compulsion cannot then be used against an individual within criminal proceedings, as this would interfere with an individual's right to a fair trial as protected by Article 6 of the ECHR. In *Beghal v Director of Public Prosecutions*,[137] the Court of Appeal (Gross LJ, Swift J, Foskett J) indicated, obiter, at paragraph 138, that 'it is fanciful to suppose that permission would be granted in criminal proceedings for such admissions to be adduced in evidence'.

135 [1993] AC 1.
136 [1993] AC 1, at [44].
137 [2013] EWHC 2573 (Admin).

In *Re L-R (Children)*,[138] the Court of Appeal (McFarlane LJ, Rafferty LJ, Kitchen J) considered section 98 of the Children Act 1989. This section provides that, in proceedings for an order under Part IV or V, no person will be excused from giving evidence on any matter or answering any question put to them in the course of giving their evidence on the ground that doing so might incriminate them or their spouse or civil partner of an offence. The court identified that such material is often disclosed to criminal prosecutors, notwithstanding the protection provided by the terms of section 98(2) (that a statement or admission made in such proceedings will not be admissible in evidence against the person making it or their spouse or civil partner in proceedings for an offence other than perjury).[139]

Despite these comments of the Court of Appeal, it is highly unlikely that a prosecuting authority would seek to rely on inculpatory material obtained by means of compulsory powers at trial. If they did, the trial judge retains a discretion, under section 78 of PACE 1984, to exclude this material.

Retention of material

Material seized under the Criminal Justice and Police Act 2001

8.40 As outlined at paragraph **8.6** above, section 53 of the CJPA 2001 imposes a duty on the person in possession of material seized under section 50 to ensure that an initial examination of the property is carried out as soon as reasonably practicable after the seizure, in order to determine what falls within the search power and can be retained. Anything that does not fall within that power must be separated from the rest of the seized property and returned as soon as reasonably practicable after the examination.

Additionally, section 54 of the CJPA 2001 places an obligation to return LPP material, and section 55 requires the return of excluded and special procedure material where its retention is not authorised. However, the retention of excluded or special procedure material may be authorised where there are reasonable grounds for believing that it was obtained in consequence of the commission of an offence, or that it is evidence in relation to any offence, and it is necessary for it to be retained in order to prevent its being concealed, lost, damaged, altered or destroyed.[140]

Therefore, in general, law enforcement officers may not retain any LPP or non-relevant general or protected material from computers and other electronic storage devices that they have seized, and must return such material within a 'reasonably practicable' time following the examination. It should be noted, however, that what constitutes a 'reasonably practicable' time is likely to differ

138 [2013] EWCA Civ 1129.
139 [2013] EWCA Civ 1129, at [12] to [14].
140 CJPA 2001, s 56(2)–(3).

between law enforcement agencies and individuals and/or organisations, and it may not be uncommon for the examination of devices and subsequent return of devices and material to take months, if not years.

Material seized under an ICO warrant for entry and inspection

8.41 Paragraph 10(4) of Schedule 15 to the DPA 2018 provides that anything seized by the ICO under a warrant issued pursuant to Schedule 15 may be retained for so long as is necessary in all the circumstances.

GDPR and the DPA 2018

8.42 Article 5(1)(e) of the GDPR provides that personal data must be kept in a form which permits identification of data subjects for no longer than is necessary for the purposes for which the personal data is processed. Personal data may be stored for longer periods insofar as the personal data will be processed solely for archiving purposes in the public interest, scientific or historical research purposes or statistical purposes in accordance with Article 89(1), subject to implementation of the appropriate technical and organisational measures required by the GDPR in order to safeguard the rights and freedoms of the data subject.

Part 3 of the DPA 2018 implements the 'Law Enforcement Directive'.[141] Section 39 of the DPA 2018 provides that the fifth data protection principle in relation to law enforcement processing is that personal data processed for any of the law enforcement purposes (the prevention, investigation, detection or prosecution of criminal offences or the execution of criminal penalties, including the safeguarding against and the prevention of threats to public security)[142] must be kept for no longer than is necessary for the purpose for which it is processed, and that appropriate time limits must be established for the periodic review of the need for the continued storage of personal data for any of the law enforcement purposes. However, where the controller would be required to erase personal data under section 39, but it must be maintained for the purposes of evidence, section 47(2) provides that the controller must, instead of erasing the personal data, restrict its processing.

Thus, law enforcement agencies and parties to civil proceedings must have retention policies that comply with this data protection legislation. Indeed, law enforcement agencies in particular may find themselves facing GLOs or representative party actions if they do not have appropriate retention policies in place and retain personal data for longer than is necessary.

141 Directive (EU) 2016/680 of the European Parliament and of the Council of 27 April 2016 on the protection of natural persons with regard to the processing of personal data by competent authorities for the purposes of the prevention, investigation, detection or prosecution of criminal offences or the execution of criminal penalties, and on the free movement of such data, and repealing Council Framework Decision 2008/977/JHA.

142 DPA 2018, s 31.

Part IV

Remedies and Alternatives to Litigation

Chapter 9

Remedies

This chapter:

- considers the specific criminal and civil remedies that are being, and are likely to be, seen within 'cyber' cases;
- discusses how these criminal and civil remedies are, or may be, applied; and
- discusses how the courts are more likely to adapt current remedies to address 'cyber' cases rather than seeking to develop new cyber-specific remedies.

INTRODUCTION

9.1 With the advent of new technologies and the world's ever-growing reliance on technology, cyber litigation is a growing area for legal disputes, and one that the courts (both criminal and civil) and regulators are increasingly going to see before them. What effective remedies can the courts provide when confronted with cyber-assisted and cyber-dependent crimes, or when parties enter into litigation in respect of 'cyber' matters? Will the well-known and established, tried and tested legal remedies be sufficient to deal with this developing area of litigation?

A full survey of the remedial landscape in England and Wales is outside the remit of this book. However, this chapter considers the specific criminal and civil remedies that are being, and are likely to be, seen within 'cyber' cases, and discusses how they are, or may be, applied. It is also the author's submission that, as the law currently stands, the courts will seek to adapt their current arsenal of remedies to address 'cyber' cases, rather than seeking to develop new cyber-specific remedies.

WHAT CRIMINAL REMEDIES ARE LIKELY TO BE SEEN IN CRIMINAL 'CYBER' CASES?

9.2 The usual remedy provided by the criminal law is prosecution and conviction, resulting in a term of imprisonment, a fine, or both, or a community order. Confiscation proceedings under the Proceeds of Crime Act 2002 ('POCA 2002') may also follow a conviction where a defendant has obtained a benefit from, or in connection with, their criminal conduct.

This will be the usual path for individuals and corporates who commit cyber-dependent and cyber-assisted crimes and, provided that such individuals/corporates can be identified and brought within the jurisdiction, the criminal justice system of England and Wales is well-placed to be able to deal with them (see **Chapter 2** for a full discussion in relation to this).

However, following the UK Jurisdiction Taskforce's ('UKJT') Legal Statement on Cryptoassets and Smart Contracts on 18 November 2019,[1] which stated that cryptoassets are to be treated, in principle, as property, and recent decisions of the High Court holding that cryptoassets are property,[2] particular consideration must now be given to how the criminal justice system will address the issue of restraint and confiscation in respect of cryptoassets.

Restraint and confiscation orders

Restraint orders

9.3 POCA 2002 provides that the Crown Court may make a restraint order prohibiting any specified person from dealing with any realisable property held by them if a criminal investigation has been started and there are reasonable grounds to suspect that the alleged offender has benefited from their criminal conduct, or proceedings have been started and not concluded and there is reasonable cause to believe that the defendant has benefited from their criminal conduct.[3] The purpose is to prevent a person from dissipating or hiding their assets once they know that there is a criminal investigation under way and thus frustrating the power of the court to eventually make a confiscation order (see para **9.4** below).

A restraint order may provide that it applies to all realisable property held by the specified person, whether or not the property is described in the order, and to all realisable property transferred to the specified person after the order is made.[4] Property is defined in section 84 of POCA 2002 as all property, wherever situated, and includes money, all forms of real or personal property, things in action and other intangible or incorporeal property; and 'realisable property' is any free property (that is, property that is not subject to specific types of forfeiture, detention or deprivation orders).[5]

The courts, however, have stressed that restraint orders should not be made lightly. Although there may be a legitimate public interest justifying the making of a restraint order to prevent a person from dissipating or hiding their assets

1 https://35z8e83m1ih83drye280o9d1-wpengine.netdna-ssl.com/wp-content/uploads/2019/11/6.6056_JO_Cryptocurrencies_Statement_FINAL_WEB_111119-1.pdf.

2 *Vorotyntseva v Money-4 Ltd (t/a Nebeus.com)* [2018] EWHC 2596 (Ch); *Robertson v Persons Unknown* Unreported, CL-2019-000444 and *AA v Persons Unknown* [2019] EWHC 3556 (Comm).

3 POCA 2002, ss 40(1)–(2) and 41(1).

4 POCA 2002, s 41(2).

5 POCA 2002, ss 82 and 83.

once they know that a criminal investigation is under way, it does not follow that, if the condition for making an order is satisfied, an order will inevitably be made.[6] The court must be satisfied that there is a real, as opposed to a fanciful, risk that, if a restraint order is not made, the assets in respect of which the order is requested are liable to be dissipated.[7]

Restraint orders can be draconian in their effect, especially if granted during the investigation stage of proceedings. Therefore, section 41(7B) of POCA 2002 provides that, where a restraint order is made during the investigation stage, it must include a reporting requirement, whereby the applicant must report to the court on the progress of the investigation, and the court must discharge a restraint order if a decision to charge is not made in a reasonable time.

Confiscation orders

9.4 Under section 6 of POCA 2002, following a conviction for an offence before a Crown Court, the Crown Prosecution Service or the Serious Fraud Office can apply to the Crown Court for a confiscation order to deprive the defendant of the proceeds of their crime/s.

The court must decide whether the defendant has a criminal lifestyle and, if so, whether they have benefited from their general criminal conduct.[8] The court will find that a defendant has a criminal lifestyle if it is satisfied that:[9]

- the defendant has been convicted of an offence specified in Schedule 2 to POCA 2002;
- the conduct forms part of a course of criminal activity; or
- the offence was committed over a period of least six months and the defendant obtained a benefit of at least GBP 5,000.

Alternatively, if the court decides that the defendant does not have a criminal lifestyle, it must decide whether the defendant has benefited from their particular criminal conduct.[10]

In deciding whether a defendant has benefited from their general or particular criminal conduct, a person benefits from conduct if they obtain property (as per the definition in section 84 of POCA 2002 – see para **9.3** above) or a pecuniary advantage as a result of, or in connection with, the conduct.[11] Additionally, if the court has decided that the defendant has a criminal lifestyle, in deciding whether the defendant has benefited from their general criminal conduct and the benefit obtained from that conduct, the court must also make the four assumptions as to

6 *Director of the Serious Fraud Office v A* [2007] EWCA Crim 1927.
7 *Re B (Restraint Order)* [2008] EWCA Crim 1374.
8 POCA 2002, s 6(4)(a)–(b).
9 POCA 2002, s 75(1)–(4).
10 POCA 2002, s 6(4)(c).
11 POCA 2002, s 76(4)–(5).

the defendant's property as outlined in section 10 of POCA 2002, unless they are demonstrated by the defendant to be incorrect (to the civil standard), or where to apply them would cause a serious risk of injustice.

If the court decides that a defendant has benefited from their general or particular criminal conduct (ie obtained property or a pecuniary advantage as a result of, or in connection with, it), the court must decide the recoverable amount and make a confiscation order requiring the defendant to pay that amount.[12] The recoverable amount is an amount equal to the defendant's benefit from the conduct concerned, which is either the value of the property obtained or a sum of money equal to the value of the pecuniary advantage.[13] However, if the defendant shows that the available amount (the aggregate of the total value of all free property held by the defendant, minus the total amount payable in pursuance of obligations which have priority, and the total value of all tainted gifts) is less than the benefit obtained, the recoverable amount is either the available amount or a nominal amount if the available amount is nil.[14]

In terms of any decisions that the court has to make in respect of whether a defendant has a criminal lifestyle, whether they have benefited from their general or particular criminal conduct, or the recoverable amount, the court must decide the matter on the balance of probabilities.[15]

It is also worth noting that a confiscation order attaches to the individual defendant rather than specific property, and so a defendant does not have to use the assets listed in their section 18 and section 17 statements to meet a confiscation order.

How do restraint and confiscation orders apply to cryptoassets?

9.5 In light of the UKJT's Legal Statement, and the recent decisions of the High Court in *Vorotyntseva v Money-4 Ltd (t/a Nebeus.com)*,[16] *Robertson v Persons Unknown*,[17] and *AA v Persons Unknown*[18] (see paras **9.19**, **9.21** and **9.24** below for a full discussion of these cases), it seems likely that cryptoassets will be treated as property by the criminal courts and thus could be the subject of restraint orders, could represent a person's benefit in confiscation proceedings, and could be an asset that is not only taken into account when calculating the available amount for a confiscation order, but also one that could be used to meet a confiscation order. Consequently, the criminal justice system, law enforcement authorities and practitioners will need to consider the practicalities of restraint and confiscation proceedings in this new era of cryptoassets before engaging in such proceedings.

12 POCA 2002, s 6(5).
13 POCA 2002, s 76(5) and (7).
14 POCA 2002, s 7(1)–(2).
15 POCA 2002, s 6(7).
16 [2018] EWHC 2596 (Ch).
17 Unreported, CL-2019-000444.
18 [2019] EWHC 3556 (Comm).

Restraining cryptoassets

9.6 If cryptoassets are to be the subject of a restraint order, so as to prevent the cryptoassets being dealt with, courts and prosecutors will likely have to consider serving a copy of the restraint order on any cryptoasset exchange providers where the suspect/defendant may have an exchange wallet/s. How will law enforcement authorities ascertain which cryptoasset exchange providers need to be served with the order? Once a restraint order is granted, will a suspect/defendant be compelled to reveal all the exchanges where they have exchange wallets?

Cryptoassets as a benefit from criminal conduct: determining the benefit amount

9.7 Where a defendant has obtained cryptoassets as a result of, or in connection with, their criminal conduct, those cryptoassets will represent that defendant's benefit from their criminal conduct. How are law enforcement authorities to determine whether or not defendants have obtained cryptoassets as a result of, or in connection with, their criminal conduct, and how are cryptoassets to be valued so as to determine the defendant's benefit amount?

Starting with the determination of cryptoassets as a benefit from criminal conduct, unless obtaining cryptoassets forms the basis of the substantive charge, or the defendant is upfront and honest about having obtained cryptoassets as a result of, or in connection with, their criminal conduct, determining whether a defendant has so obtained cryptoassets is going to be incredibly difficult, given their pseudonymous nature. Where it is suspected that defendants have obtained cryptoassets as a result of, or in connection with, their criminal conduct, law enforcement authorities will likely have to engage in an investigation to determine whether or not this is the case. This might require serving disclosure notices on cryptoasset exchange providers and, potentially, blockchain tracing exercises. Will such tracing exercises be outsourced, or will law enforcement agencies need to look to build their own in-house teams of cryptoasset analysts? Will new legislation be required in order to compel defendants to reveal their cryptoasset holdings for the purpose of confiscation proceedings?

Moving on to valuing cryptoassets in order to determine the benefit amount, section 79 of POCA 2002 provides the basic rule for deciding the value at any time of property held by a person, and states that its value is the market value of the property at that time.[19]

In terms of determining the value of property obtained as a result of, or in connection with, criminal conduct, recourse must also be had to section 80 of POCA 2002, which provides that the value of the property at the material time

19 POCA 2002, s 79(1)–(2).

(the material time being the time that the court makes its decision in respect of the confiscation order)[20] is the greater of:[21]

- the value of the property at the time the person obtained it, adjusted to take account of later changes in the value of money; or
- the value at the material time (as above) of:
  - if the person holds the property obtained, that property;
  - if the person holds no part of the property obtained, any property which directly or indirectly represents it in his hands; or
  - if the person holds part of the property obtained, that part of the property and any property which directly or indirectly represents the other part in his hands.

Given the volatility of the market value of cryptoassets, obtaining cryptoassets as a result of, or in connection with, criminal conduct seems to be a very risky endeavour, as the determined benefit amount under a confiscation order could be astronomical.

It should also be borne in mind that, where a defendant is not upfront and honest about obtaining cryptoassets as a result of, or in connection with, their criminal conduct, if law enforcement agencies obtain evidence within six years of the date of conviction about the defendant having so acquired cryptoassets, they can apply to the court under section 21 of POCA 2002 for a reconsideration of the benefit amount.[22] In such circumstances the court must make a new calculation of the defendant's benefit,[23] and what was a reasonable benefit amount could suddenly become astronomical.

Where the benefit amount under the new calculation exceeds the previous benefit amount, the court must make a new calculation of the recoverable amount and, if that newly calculated recoverable amount exceeds the amount to be paid under the confiscation order, the court may vary the confiscation order and substitute the recoverable amount for one that it believes is just.[24]

Ascertaining a defendant's assets in confiscation proceedings and the available amount

9.8 Cryptoassets are growing in popularity, and are popular with individuals who operate within the criminal sphere. However, they are generally pseudonymous and difficult to trace. Therefore, in confiscation proceedings, unless a defendant is upfront and honest about their cryptoasset holdings in their section 18 statement, in order to present an accurate statement of information

20 POCA 2002, s 80(1).
21 POCA 2002, s 80(2)–(3).
22 POCA 2002, s 21(1).
23 POCA 2002, s 21(2).
24 POCA 2002, s 21(7).

to the court and accurately calculate the available amount, law enforcement authorities will likely have to engage in an investigation to determine whether or not defendants hold cryptoassets. This might require serving disclosure notices on cryptoasset exchange providers and, potentially, blockchain tracing exercises. Will such tracing exercises be outsourced, or will law enforcement agencies need to look to build their own in-house teams of cryptoasset analysts? Will new legislation be required in order to compel defendants to reveal their cryptoasset holdings for the purpose of confiscation proceedings?

Where defendants hold cryptoassets, they will be taken into account when calculating the available amount for a confiscation order. The rule pertaining to the value of such cryptoassets is as per section 79 of POCA 2002, which provides that 'its value is the market value of the property at that time'.[25] Unlike section 80 of POCA 2002, which refers to the material time being the time that the court makes its decision in respect of the confiscation order,[26] section 79 provides no further clarification as to what is meant by 'at that time'. The volatile nature of the value of cryptoassets means that, overnight during the course of confiscation proceedings, their market value could either sky rocket or plummet. How will confiscation proceedings address such volatility in ascertaining a defendant's available amount?

Additionally, where a defendant acquires cryptoassets following the making of a confiscation order, if the market value of those cryptoassets suddenly rises, the prosecutor may seek a re-calculation of the available amount under section 22 of POCA 2002, and the defendant could be required to pay more under the confiscation order (see para **9.9** below for a full discussion of this point).

Using cryptoassets to meet a confiscation order

9.9 As outlined at paragraph **9.4** above, confiscation orders attach to the individual defendant rather than specific property, and so a defendant does not have to use their assets listed in their section 18 and section 17 statements to meet a confiscation order. Therefore, even though a defendant may have listed cryptoassets as part of their assets, provided that they have other means of meeting the confiscation order, they will not have to use them to meet the confiscation order.

However, defendants may wish to use their cryptoasset holdings to meet confiscation orders.

Although the actual recoverable amount under a confiscation order will be the lesser of the benefit amount and the available amount, practitioners and defendants should be aware that, just because a defendant does not, at the time of the confiscation proceedings, have an available amount to meet a confiscation order for the benefit amount, that does not mean that they will not be required to pay

25 POCA 2002, s 79(2).
26 POCA 2002, s 80(1).

the benefit amount in the future. As outlined at paragraph **9.7** above, the benefit amount under a confiscation order cannot be amended unless there is evidence that was not originally available to the prosecutor.[27] However, the prosecutor can always apply to amend the available amount. Section 22 of POCA 2002 permits the court to vary an existing confiscation order, and will allow the prosecutor to apply to the court for a further payment to be required from the defendant under an existing confiscation order where their available amount has increased since the original order was made.[28] And there is no time limit on applying for such an amendment.

Therefore, where a defendant has cryptoasset holdings which suddenly increase in value, the prosecutor may seek to apply to the court to vary the confiscation order, as the defendant's available amount has increased, thus requiring the defendant to make a further payment.

Consequently, practitioners will need to make their clients aware that meeting a confiscation order may not be the end of the matter where they have cryptoasset holdings, nor indeed will it necessarily be the end of the matter if they subsequently acquire cryptoassets. Therefore, practitioners may wish to advise their clients to meet the confiscation order with their cryptoasset holdings and advise them that they may be required to pay further amounts in the future.

If defendants are going to use cryptoassets to meet a confiscation order, how will that work in practice? Will defendants provide their wallet ID and private key to law enforcement authorities, thereby giving the law enforcement authority control of the cryptoassets? Alternatively, will law enforcement authorities set up their own cryptoasset wallets in order to permit cryptoassets to be used to meet a confiscation order?

Another option might be that, rather than transfer to law enforcement authority wallets, the law enforcement authorities would have accounts and wallets within cryptoasset exchanges to which the transfer is made. This would then potentially facilitate an easier realisation of the fiat value of the cryptoassets.

Alternatively, defendants may have to realise the fiat value of the cryptoassets and then pay the confiscation order in the usual way.

Conclusions on cryptoassets and restraint and confiscation proceedings

9.10 There are several practical questions that arise in relation to restraint and confiscation proceedings in this new era of cryptoassets, and it will not be too long before the courts and law enforcement authorities have to grapple with these questions in order to confiscate a defendant's proceeds of crime. At first blush, it seems that, rather than forcing cryptoassets into the current framework,

27 POCA 2002, s 21(1)(b).

28 POCA 2002, s 22(1)–(4) and (8)–(9).

law enforcement authorities, the legislature and the courts might have to engage with the cryptoasset ecosystem and set up wallets and exchange accounts etc.

It is unlikely that law enforcement authorities currently have individuals with the technical understanding and capabilities required in order for them to properly engage with the world of cryptoassets. However, given the UKJT's Legal Statement and the decisions in the High Court, they are going to have to ensure that they obtain this understanding and capability soon, or else they will not be in a position to address cryptoassets.

WHAT CIVIL REMEDIES ARE BEING SEEN IN CIVIL 'CYBER' CASES?

Injunctions

9.11 Injunctions, which either require a specific act or require refraining from a specific act, are discretionary remedies. They have their origins in equity, and the High Court's jurisdiction to grant interim or final injunctions 'in all cases in which it appears to the Court to be just and convenient to do so' has been set out in section 37(1) of the Senior Courts Act 1981 ('SCA 1981').

Given the nature of technology and data, and the speed of dissemination, following a malware attack, ransomware attack etc, 'time is of the essence' to protect what has been lost, be that personal data, cryptoassets, confidential designs etc. Thus, in cyber litigation, seeking interim relief tends to be more important than obtaining final relief. The courts are recognising this 'need for speed' in cyber cases, and so the jurisprudence in respect of interim injunctive relief in cyber cases is more developed than that of final relief.

Search and seizure orders (Anton Piller orders)

9.12 Search and seizure orders are a form of mandatory interim injunction that requires a defendant to allow the claimant's representatives to enter the defendant's premises and search for, copy, and remove and retain documents, information and material. The purpose is to preserve evidence where it is believed that a defendant would otherwise destroy it in contravention of a court order for the delivery up or preservation of documents, or to preserve property which is (or may be) the subject of an action, or as to which a question arises in an action.[29]

In light of the UKJT's Legal Statement that, in general, 'cryptoassets have all of the indicia of property' and should therefore 'be treated in principle as property',[30] it appears that, where cryptoassets are the subject of an action, or a question as to them arises in an action – for example, where an action relates to a ransomware attack and a party is seeking to preserve the cryptoassets that

29 Civil Procedure Act 1997, s 7.

30 https://35z8e83m1ih83drye280o9d1-wpengine.netdna-ssl.com/wp-content/uploads/2019/11/6.6056_JO_Cryptocurrencies_Statement_FINAL_WEB_111119-1.pdf.

have been paid before they are dissipated, or protecting cryptoassets in financial settlement proceedings following a divorce – search and seizure orders may be sought in order to preserve them. However, given the draconian nature of search and seizure orders, and the need to show clear evidence that the 'incriminating documents or things' are in the respondent's possession and that there is a 'real possibility' that the respondent may destroy or dispose of the material before an application can be made on notice, the courts may be more inclined to grant freezing orders and proprietary injunctions as a more appropriate interim remedy in such cases (see paras **9.18–9.22** and **9.23–9.25** below).

In addition to the potential for search and seizure orders being made in respect of cryptoassets, in an increasingly digital age, and in the realms of cyber litigation, claimants might be looking to search for, copy, and remove and retain digital data by way of search and seizure orders. Thus companies' entire servers and other digital devices may be imaged under search and seizure orders. Search and seizure orders are not intended to be a way of obtaining evidence or enforcing disclosure obligations, but the searching of material imaged under a search and seizure order might have such an effect by the backdoor.

Case Study

In *A v B; Hewlett Packard Enterprise Co v Manchester Technology Data (Holdings) Ltd*[31] the court considered the proper approach to the inspection and interrogation of imaged digital data obtained under a search and seizure order; specifically, whether the claimant or the defendant would be first entitled to inspect and interrogate the data. The court stated that:

> 'The ability to take a computer image is far quicker, far easier and far less labour intensive than a document by document inspection and copying. That operates in the interests of a claimant who can preserve material more easily, and it operates in the interests of the defendant in that the search can be less physically intrusive in terms of the occupation of its premises and engagement with its computers. It is a natural evolution from the original processes given the new technology which allows it to be done efficiently, and is an easier preservation mechanism for the greater quantity of the digital documentation which now exists when compared with the earlier days of Anton Piller orders. However, that sort of evolution does not necessarily have to carry with it the ability for a searching claimant, as a matter of course, itself to embark on the next phase, which is inspecting the contents of the resulting images.'[32]

After considering the nature of a search and seizure order, the court went on to hold that, once an image of digital data is taken, the documents imaged are preserved and safe from the risk of destruction, and it is that purpose which the order was primarily intended to meet. It is not necessary to carry out any searching or identification for that purpose; the image is safe. Any

31 [2019] EWHC 2089 (Ch).
32 [2019] EWHC 2089 (Ch) at [20].

searches carried out in relation to imaged documents cannot be justified on the footing that it is necessary for the preservation of those documents, and the court held that it could see no justification for a search of those documents being, as a general rule, carried out by the claimant and/or at that stage, ie following the execution of a search and seizure order. Thus, if there was to be an inspection of a digital image by a claimant at that stage of the proceedings, it needed to be justified as a separate exercise and analysed in terms of the disclosure jurisdiction. If anything, search and seizure orders are ancillary to disclosure, because they enable documents to be preserved for that purpose, but without necessarily determining who should do the disclosure.[33] Therefore, a search and seizure order allows no more than the imaging of digital data.

The decision as to whether to allow a claimant to inspect and interrogate imaged data first has, like any other disclosure dispute, to be dealt with on the basis of the particular facts, and the factors to consider will include the following:[34]

- The order will have been obtained in the first place on the basis of a strong prima facie case of not only the dishonesty of the defendant but also the propensity of the defendant to cover his or her tracks by destroying evidence. That may mean that the defendant should not necessarily be trusted to carry out the disclosure (inspection) exercise properly, though this factor may be seriously ameliorated by the defendant's solicitors being involved in the process.
- It may be the case that, as a matter of practicality, the relevance of some important documents may be honestly missed by the defendant's solicitors.
- It may be the case that urgency justifies the claimant carrying out the search. For example, it might be necessary, as a matter of urgency, to follow property, or to identify other wrongdoers in a supply chain, and it may be the case that having the defendant's solicitor carry out the search will not fulfil that need.
- It may be that the application of search terms can narrow the field to such an extent that the exercise becomes akin to the more familiar one of compelling disclosure of a class of documents, not all of which may be relevant, but which can be searched by the receiving party for relevance.
- It may be that the resources available to the claimant are greater than those available to the defendant (particularly in a lot of intellectual property cases, where the claimant is likely to be a well-heeled organisation), so that it makes practical sense, in order to further the overriding objective, to allow the claimant to go first, though this must not be allowed to become a charter for the well-heeled to get an advantage over others merely by virtue of being better-heeled.

33 [2019] EWHC 2089 (Ch) at [25] to [26].
34 [2019] EWHC 2089 (Ch) at [30].

- On the other side of the argument is the very important factor, which must not be lost sight of, that the whole exercise (including the order itself) is a highly intrusive one, and any digital image of the kind in issue in these cases is likely to contain irrelevant material which is private and confidential (if not privileged) and which should not, if it can be avoided, be seen by the claimant at all.

Where a claimant is allowed to inspect and interrogate imaged data first, such an inspection is likely to be subject to the right of the defendant, through their solicitors, to review the data first in order to remove privileged material. Additionally, where a claimant is to run keywords over a data image, they should inform the defendant of the keywords that they are proposing to use, so that the defendant has an opportunity to raise any objections.[35]

Where the claimant is not allowed to inspect and interrogate the imaged data first, and the defendant conducts the disclosure exercise, it would be advisable for both parties to establish the mechanism by which documents deemed to be relevant, disclosable etc by the defendant are to be identified, so that they can be retrieved from the imaged data by the claimant. Alternatively, the defendant could simply provide the material to the claimant. However, neither one of these scenarios would alleviate a claimant's concerns as to the destruction of evidence: if the claimant cannot view the image/can only release material from the image, then the defendant could easily destroy evidence, and the claimant would never know unless the data image was reviewed in its entirety. Therefore, the more advisable course of action for a claimant who has obtained a data image under a search and seizure order would be to apply to the court for an order under CPR rule 31.5(7)(f) for early disclosure that is to be carried out on the defendant's material by the claimant.[36]

Springboard injunctions

9.13 Springboard injunctions have their origins in commercial confidentiality. They were traditionally sought in cases where confidential plans were published and, as it was no longer possible to grant relief to restrain breach of confidence, an injunction was granted to deprive the wrongdoer of the fruits of his wrongdoing prior to the determination of the issue at trial (hence the term 'springboard injunction'). They have since been applied in the employment sphere, preventing former employees from using confidential information to gain a head start and unlawfully competing with their former employers prior to the trial of the issues.

Given that springboard relief is to prevent a defendant from benefiting from an unfair commercial advantage or an unlawful head start which has been wrongly achieved, it is easy to see how springboard injunctions could be an effective interim remedy in cyber cases. They could be used in cases of theft, hacking or

35 [2019] EWHC 2089 (Ch) at [48].
36 [2019] EWHC 2089 (Ch) at [22] and [45].

the publication of confidential designs, patents, specially designed software code, malware etc, or when a company's technical expert goes to work for a competitor.

The scope and ambit of interim springboard injunctions was considered by the Court of Appeal in *Forse & Others v Secarma Ltd and Others*.[37]

> Case Study
>
> Secarma is a cyber security company which alleged that a number of former Secarma employees and directors acted in breach of their post-termination restrictions by seeking to procure key employees of Secarma to join their new employer, Xcina, and build up a competing cyber security business. The individuals and Xcina were alleged to be liable to Secarma for the tort of conspiracy to injure by unlawful means. Secarma successfully obtained an interim springboard injunction at first instance, which prohibited the individuals and Xcina from doing a number of things damaging to Secarma's business and was intended to prevent Xcina from benefiting from the commercial advantage that Secarma claimed Xcina had wrongly achieved from the alleged conspiracy. A number of the individuals, who had not entered into covenants with Secarma restricting the business that they could conduct or the employment that they could undertake after leaving Secarma, and Xcina appealed against the injunctions. The appeal was dismissed, save to the extent that particular aspects of the injunction were too wide in scope.
>
> In terms of the scope and ambit of springboard injunctions generally, the court held, reaffirming *Roger Bullivant v Ellis*,[38] that springboard injunctions must be no greater in scope and for no greater period than is reasonable to remove the unfair competitive advantage secured by the defendant. Thus, it follows that an interim springboard injunction effectively delivers to a claimant, in advance of the trial, all or part of the substantive relief which they seek. At the same time, it operates in restraint of a defendant's freedom to trade or carry on business or to deploy their skills, and such an injunction may also have consequences for the defendant as regards third parties, whether employees or others, if the defendant is precluded from continuing to honour commitments to such third parties. For those reasons the court held that, save only where the time gap between the application for interim relief and the trial is insignificant, the approach in *Lansing Linde Ltd v Kerr*[39] should be applied on applications for an interim springboard injunction: namely, that the court must consider the prospects of the claimant succeeding at trial, and assess and take into account the strength of each side's case, both as regards liability and also the length of time during which any unfair advantage from the springboard will continue.[40]

37 [2019] EWCA Civ 215.
38 [1987] FSR 172.
39 [1991] 1 WLR 251.
40 [2019] EWCA Civ 215 at [30], [34] and [57].

Given that the strength of each side's case will be considered at the interim application stage, parties should not underestimate the importance of having documentary evidence, particularly contemporaneous evidence of the alleged wrongdoing, to show the likelihood of their case succeeding at trial. A party applying for an interim springboard injunction should also assist the court by providing evidence of market conditions to enable the court to estimate the reasonable period for which the relief is required – for example, how easy or difficult it is to recruit replacements; how easy or difficult it would be to recreate similar software and/or designs; or how long it had taken the defendant to secure the advantage that it gained etc. They should also ensure that the injunction applied for goes no wider than is necessary to remove the unfair advantage or head start secured by the defendant.

Practitioners should also note the message of Underhill LJ in his short, concurring judgment. Having noted his surprise that the application proceeded on the basis that a trial could not take place before April 2019, which was four months after the date of the application for the springboard injunction, he also stated that he was surprised that this late trial date was because the claimant had said that it could not be properly prepared by the earlier date offered by the court. Underhill LJ went on to say that:

> 'In a case where a defendant is subject to an interim injunction of a kind which is of its nature damaging to its business claimants may reasonably be expected to pull out all the stops.'[41]

Website blocking injunctions

9.14 Website blocking injunctions are injunctions granted by the High Court against service providers, forcing them to block or impede access to various websites. Although website blocking injunctions have their origin in copyright infringement cases, the courts have extended their application to trade mark infringement cases, and the reasoning of the Supreme Court means that they can be applied for in all other cases where any other rights are infringed by a website.

Copyright infringement

9.15 Section 97A of the Copyright, Designs and Patents Act 1988 ('CDPA 1988') permits a copyright owner to seek an injunction from the High Court against service providers who have actual knowledge of another person using their service to infringe copyright, which forces the service provider to block or impede access to websites that are infringing the copyright owner's copyright.[42]

Unlike the other remedies for copyright infringement under the CDPA 1988, the copyright owner does not need to identify the individuals responsible for the

41 [2019] EWCA Civ 215 at [72].
42 CDPA 1988, s 97A(1).

infringement in order to obtain a website blocking injunction under section 97A: they merely need to identify the websites involved in infringing their copyright. Consequently, copyright owners need to be proactive in identifying websites that infringe their copyright, and the courts have stated that it will be the copyright owners' responsibility to accurately identify the Internet Protocol ('IP') addresses and Universal Resource Locators ('URLs') that need to be notified to the service provider.[43]

In terms of the costs of complying with website blocking injunctions, unless there are good reasons for a different order, an innocent service provider is entitled to be indemnified by the rights-holder against the costs of complying with a website blocking injunction.[44]

> Case Study
>
> In *Cartier International AG and Others v British Telecommunications Plc and Another*[45] the claimants designed, manufactured and sold luxury goods under well-known trade marks. The defendants, five internet service providers ('ISPs'), provided networks by which subscribers could access content on the internet; they did not provide or store content, were not in a position to monitor it, and had no contractual relationship with the operators of websites accessed through their networks. However, their networks enabled the sellers of infringing goods to reach customers.
>
> Website blocking injunctions were made pursuant to section 37(1) of the SCA 1981 and Article 11 of Directive 2004/48 (the Enforcement Directive),[46] which required the ISPs to block, or attempt to block, access to certain websites selling counterfeit copies of the claimants' goods.
>
> In making the injunctions, the High Court required the ISPs to bear the costs of the litigation and of complying with the injunctions. The Court of Appeal upheld those decisions. The ISPs appealed to the Supreme Court against the costs orders, the issue being who should pay the cost of implementing a website blocking injunction obtained against an innocent intermediary to prevent its facilities being used for illegal purposes.
>
> The Supreme Court held that, in principle, rights-holders should indemnify 'legally innocent' service providers (ie those that are 'mere conduits') against their reasonable compliance costs. It said that different considerations may apply to service providers who are engaged in caching

43 Arnold J in *Twentieth Century Fox Film Corp v British Telecommunications plc (No.2)* [2012] 1 All ER 869, at [12].

44 *Cartier International AG and Others v British Telecommunications Plc and Another* [2018] UKSC 28, at [31].

45 [2018] UKSC 28.

46 Directive 2004/48/EC of the European Parliament and of the Council of 29 April 2004 on the enforcement of intellectual property rights.

and hosting, as per Articles 13 and 14 of the E-Commerce Directive 2000,[47] because these operations involve a greater degree of participation in the infringement, which is more likely to infringe laws protecting intellectual property rights if the Article 13 and 14 conditions of immunity are not satisfied (see para **9.27** below in relation to the conditions of immunity under Article 14). This will, however, depend on the precise facts and on the relevant provisions of the intellectual property laws. Consequently, without more, the mere fact that the immunities of intermediaries under Articles 13 or 14 of the E-Commerce Directive 2000 are conditional on active steps being taken against the infringer in certain circumstances is not enough to require a court to make such intermediaries pay the costs of compliance. Therefore, unless there are good reasons for a different order, an innocent service provider is entitled to be indemnified by the rights-holder against the costs of complying with a website blocking injunction.[48]

Trade mark infringement

9.16 There is no similar statutory provision that corresponds with section 97A of the CDPA 1988 and explicitly permits a website blocking injunction to be sought in relation to trade mark infringement.

However, in *Cartier International AG v British Sky Broadcasting Ltd*, the High Court,[49] and subsequently the Court of Appeal,[50] held that website blocking injunctions could be sought in cases of trade mark infringement. In this case, website blocking injunctions had been made against ISPs, requiring them to block customer access to websites advertising and selling counterfeit copies of the trade mark owners' goods.

At first instance, Arnold J held that the court's ability to grant an injunction is unlimited, albeit that, as a matter of practice, the court exercises its discretion in accordance with fairly well-settled principles. However, he noted that those principles are not immutable, and evolve over time as the court has faced new circumstances.[51] Therefore, the court's jurisdiction to grant injunctions under section 37 of the SCA 1981 is broad, and that jurisdiction can be exercised in new ways.[52] Accordingly, not only did the court have jurisdiction to grant a website blocking injunction against an ISP in a trade mark case, but there was also a principled basis upon which the court may exercise that jurisdiction. Therefore,

47 Directive 2000/31/EC of the European Parliament and of the Council of 8 June 2000 on certain legal aspects of information society services, in particular electronic commerce, in the Internal Market (Directive on electronic commerce).

48 *Cartier International AG and Others v British Telecommunications Plc and Another* [2018] UKSC 28, at [31] to [37].

49 [2014] EWHC 3354 (Ch).

50 [2016] EWCA Civ 658.

51 [2014] EWHC 3354 (Ch) at [104].

52 [2014] EWHC 3354 (Ch) at [107].

on a purely domestic interpretation of section 37 of the SCA 1981, the court had jurisdiction to grant the orders sought.[53]

In case he was wrong about this, Arnold J went on to consider whether section 37 of the SCA 1981 should be interpreted, by virtue of the *Marleasing* principle (that is, a domestic court of a Member State must interpret its national law so far as possible in light of the wording and purpose of the Directive in question), in accordance with the third sentence of Article 11 (Injunctions) of the Enforcement Directive[54] ('Member States shall also ensure that rightholders are in a position to apply for an injunction against intermediaries whose services are used by a third party to infringe an intellectual property right') as conferring such a power. He held that section 37 should be so interpreted, so that rights-holders were entitled to apply for an injunction against intermediaries whose services were used by a third party to breach an intellectual property right.[55]

Having established that the court had the power to grant a website blocking injunction in a trade mark infringement case, Arnold J considered whether that power was unfettered or whether threshold conditions had to be met before the power could be exercised. At paragraph 141 of his judgment, he held that similar threshold conditions to those required for a website blocking injunction in copyright infringement cases applied, namely:

(1) the ISPs must be intermediaries within the meaning of the third sentence of Article 11 of the Enforcement Directive;

(2) either the users and/or the operators of the website must be infringing the claimant's trade marks;

(3) the users and/or the operators of the website must use the ISPs' services to do that; and

(4) the ISPs must have actual knowledge of this.

In the circumstances, these four threshold conditions were found to be met, and so the court was able to exercise its power to grant website blocking injunctions.

The court (partially adopting counsel's submissions) then went on to identify the following criteria that must be considered, over and above the threshold conditions, in deciding whether or not to grant a website blocking injunction. In order to grant a website blocking injunction:[56]

(1) the relief must be necessary;

(2) the relief must be effective;

(3) the relief must be dissuasive;

53 [2014] EWHC 3354 (Ch) at [110] to [111].
54 Directive 2004/48/EC of the European Parliament and of the Council of 29 April 2004 on the enforcement of intellectual property rights.
55 [2014] EWHC 3354 (Ch) at [132].
56 [2014] EWHC 3354 (Ch) at [158] and [191].

(4) the relief must not be unnecessarily complicated or costly;

(5) the relief must avoid barriers to legitimate trade;

(6) the relief must be fair and equitable and strike a 'fair balance' between the applicable fundamental rights;

(7) the relief must be proportionate; and

(8) the relief should be applied in such a manner as to provide safeguards against its abuse.

It is also relevant to consider the substitutability of other websites for the Target Websites.[57]

Having considered these criteria, the High Court granted the website blocking injunctions sought, and the ISPs appealed the grant of these injunctions to the Court of Appeal. The Court of Appeal dismissed the appeal, holding that the courts have shown themselves ready to adapt to new circumstances by developing their practice in relation to the grant of injunctions where it is necessary and appropriate to do so to avoid injustice, and so the preferable analysis of the court's jurisdiction to grant injunctions involves a recognition of the great width of those equitable powers, an historical appraisal of the categories of injunctions that have been established, and an acceptance that, pursuant to general equitable principles, injunctions may be issued in new categories when this course appears appropriate.[58]

In terms of the court's power to grant a website blocking injunction in a trade mark case, the Court of Appeal said that the logically anterior question to Arnold J's consideration of the matter was whether Article 11 of the Enforcement Directive provided a further basis for developing the practice of the court, as opposed to merely providing an interpretation tool for section 37 of the SCA 1981.[59] The Court of Appeal held that Article 11 did indeed provide a basis for extending the practice of the court to grant injunctions against intermediaries where their services have been used by a third party to infringe a registered trade mark. The court stated that there was no dispute that ISPs were intermediaries within the meaning of Article 11 and that, accordingly, the courts must now recognise, pursuant to general equitable principles, that granting website blocking injunctions to protect against an infringement of a trade mark is one of the new categories of case in which the court may grant an injunction when it is satisfied that it is just and convenient to do so.[60]

In relation to Arnold J's conclusions as to the interpretation of section 37 in light of the *Marleasing* principle, the court felt that it was more appropriate to consider whether Article 11 provided a further basis for developing the practice

57 [2014] EWHC 3354 (Ch) at [190].
58 [2016] EWCA Civ 658 at [46] and [54].
59 [2016] EWCA Civ 658 at [56].
60 [2016] EWCA Civ 658 at [65] and [66].

of granting injunctions. However, the court held that, had it been necessary to do so, it would have been appropriate to adopt a conforming interpretation of section 37. As section 37 provides that an injunction may be granted in all cases where it is just and convenient to do so, the court saw no difficulty in construing these words in such a way as to include the grant of an injunction in an appropriate case against an intermediary whose services are used by a third party to infringe a registered trade mark.[61]

Thus, even though the Court of Appeal considered the lower court's interpretation point and found that it had been decided correctly, that was not the basis on which it determined that the website blocking injunctions had been properly granted: Article 11 of the Enforcement Directive provided the basis for developing the court's practice to grant injunctions.

The Court of Appeal did, however, endorse the threshold conditions, as propounded by Arnold J, to be met before a court could exercise its discretion to grant a website blocking injunction in a trade mark infringement case,[62] and, in general, approved his analysis of the principles to be taken into account when deciding whether or not to exercise the power to grant a website blocking injunction. Thus the court dismissed the appeals of the ISPs, and determined that the court has the power to grant website blocking injunctions in trade mark infringement cases.

Other rights

9.17 The ISPs appealed to the Supreme Court on the issue of who should pay the cost of complying with the website blocking injunctions. The Supreme Court gave judgment on this point in June 2018 in *Cartier International AG and Others v British Telecommunications Plc and Another*[63] (see para **9.15** above). However, in that judgment, as well as deciding the costs issue, the Supreme Court agreed with the view expressed by Briggs LJ in his dissenting judgment in the Court of Appeal. It held that, quite apart from the power derived from European law, the website blocking injunctions that had been granted in the case could have been made on the ordinary principles of equity, whereby a court may make an order against a third party to assist those whose rights have been invaded by a wrongdoer and/or to prevent the use of the third party's facilities to commit or facilitate a wrong.[64]

It is interesting to note that, in *Cartier*, it was only the costs of compliance point that was appealed to the Supreme Court: the basis for granting the website blocking injunctions was not an issue on appeal. Consequently, the Supreme Court did not need to comment on it but, as outlined above, it did, saying (at para 7) that:

61 [2016] EWCA Civ 658 at [72].
62 [2016] EWCA Civ 658 at [80] to [81].
63 [2018] UKSC 28.
64 [2018] UKSC 28 at [8] and [15].

> 'Although the terms on which an injunction is granted are discretionary, the current practice has been adopted as a matter of principle and routinely applied. It is therefore necessary on this appeal for us to decide whether the principle is sound. That requires us to examine the legal basis on which website blocking injunctions are made. It is founded partly on domestic and partly on EU law.'

The court then went on to examine the domestic law of equity, and the English court's jurisdiction in certain circumstances to order parties to assist those whose rights have been invaded by a wrongdoer. The court examined the Norwich Pharmacal jurisdiction, stating that the true basis of the court's intervention in such cases is that, once the intermediary has been given notice of the infringement of the claimant's rights, his duty is to stop placing his facilities at the disposal of the wrongdoer. However, this duty to assist is not a legal duty in the ordinary sense of the term, as the intermediary comes under the duty without incurring personal liability. Thus, the duty is said to lie on the court to make an order necessary for the administration of justice, rather than on the respondent to satisfy some right existing in the claimant, and so the court has an equitable jurisdiction to intervene.[65] The court then concluded (at para 15):

> 'Website blocking orders clearly require more than the mere disclosure of information. But I think that it is clear from the authorities and correct in principle that orders for the disclosure of information are only one, admittedly common, category of order which a court may make against a third party to prevent the use of his facilities to commit or facilitate a wrong. I therefore agree with the view expressed by Briggs LJ in his dissenting judgment in the Court of Appeal that the website blocking order made in this case could have been made quite apart from the power derived from European law, on ordinary principles of equity.'

Therefore, this judgment indicated that courts have the power to grant website blocking injunctions in all cases where there is a desire to impede or block access to particular websites that infringe rights, irrespective of the nature of the rights infringed.

This was confirmed in *Nintendo Co Ltd v Sky UK Ltd & Others*,[66] where the High Court explicitly stated that the Supreme Court in *Cartier* had made it clear that the court's jurisdiction to make website blocking injunctions is not limited to cases involving the infringement of intellectual property rights.[67]

Case Study

The *Nintendo* case concerned trade mark infringement and claims for infringement of rights under sections 296 (devices designed to circumvent copy-protection) and 296ZD (devices and services designed to circumvent technological measures) of the CDPA 1988, and it was heard by Arnold J.

65 [2018] UKSC 28 at [10] and [11].
66 [2019] EWHC 2376 (Ch).
67 [2019] EWHC 2376 (Ch) at [36].

The claimants were seeking a website blocking injunction requiring the defendant ISPs to block access by their customers to four websites which were advertising and offering for sale devices that allowed technological protection measures ('TPMs') on the claimants' Nintendo Switch games console to be circumvented and thus allow individuals to make unlicensed copies of the claimants' games.

The court granted the application for the website blocking injunctions.

The court stated that the Supreme Court had made it clear that the court's jurisdiction to make website blocking injunctions is not limited to cases involving the infringement of intellectual property rights, and that the ordinary principles of equity provide the court with the jurisdiction to make an order against a third party to prevent the use of their facilities to commit or facilitate a wrong. The court accepted that it had jurisdiction to grant the injunctions sought on that basis.[68]

The court also agreed that threshold criteria analogous to those confirmed by the Court of Appeal in *Cartier* should apply in cases which are not based on infringement of intellectual property rights, save that it may not be necessary in such cases for the defendants to be intermediaries within the meaning of Article 11 of the Enforcement Directive (although that would usually be the case in website blocking injunctions). The court also agreed that the fourth criterion – that the defendants have actual knowledge (which may be as a result of being notified by the rights-holder) – is a horizontal measure that is not restricted to cases involving intellectual property rights.[69]

In terms of whether an injunction should, in fact, be granted in non-intellectual property rights cases, the same eight criteria over and above the threshold conditions, as outlined in *Cartier*, should be considered. Of these factors, proportionality is the key one, since consideration of the other factors feeds into the proportionality analysis.[70]

Therefore, in light of the *Cartier* and *Nintendo* cases, it seems fairly clearly established that:

(1) The ordinary principles of equity provide the court with the jurisdiction to make a website blocking injunction against an ISP in order to prevent the use of that ISP's facilities to commit or facilitate a wrong.

(2) The following threshold conditions must be met before a court can exercise its jurisdiction to grant a website blocking injunction:

68 [2019] EWHC 2376 (Ch) at [36] and [37].
69 [2019] EWHC 2376 (Ch) at [39].
70 [2019] EWHC 2376 (Ch) at [41] and [42].

(i) the defendants may be intermediaries within the meaning of Article 11 of the Enforcement Directive;

(ii) the users and/or operators of the website are infringing the claimants' rights;

(iii) those users and/or operators are using the defendants' services to infringe those rights; and

(iv) the defendants have actual knowledge of this (which may be as a result of being notified by the rights-holder).

(3) In determining whether or not it should grant a website blocking injunction, the court must consider the following factors over and above the threshold conditions. The injunction must:

(i) be necessary;

(ii) be effective;

(iii) be dissuasive;

(iv) be not unduly costly or complicated;

(v) avoid barriers to legitimate trade;

(vi) be a fair balance between the fundamental rights engaged;

(vii) be proportionate; and

(viii) safeguard against abuse.

(4) Of these criteria, proportionality is the key one, since consideration of the other factors feeds into the proportionality analysis.

Consequently, website blocking injunctions can be sought in all cases where there is a desire to impede or block access to particular websites that infringe rights – for example, because they contain a leak of confidential data, they contain deepfake revenge pornography videos or photographs, or they defame an individual etc.

Freezing orders (including worldwide freezing orders)

9.18 Freezing orders are similar to criminal restraint orders in that they are interim injunctions that restrain a party from disposing of or dealing with their assets. Freezing orders relate to assets within the jurisdiction, whereas worldwide freezing orders relate to a party's assets wherever they are located. The purpose of such an order is to preserve the party's assets and prevent the party from moving, hiding or otherwise unjustifiably dissipating their assets so as to defeat any eventual judgment against them. All types of assets may be frozen, including:

- bank accounts;
- shares;

- motor vehicles; and
- land.

The orders take effect against the party personally, rather than attaching to the assets themselves.

To obtain a freezing order, an applicant must establish:

(1) a good arguable case;

(2) the existence of assets belonging to the respondent;

(3) a real risk (a 'good arguable case')[71] that the respondent will dissipate their assets if the order is not given; and

(4) that the order is just and convenient.

A freezing order will often be served on third parties (for example, banks, solicitors etc), so that they know not to permit any transactions that may contravene the terms of the freezing order.

Can freezing orders be sought in respect of cryptoassets?

9.19 As outlined above, in November 2019 the UKJT delivered its Legal Statement on Cryptoassets and Smart Contracts, stating that, in general, 'cryptoassets have all of the indicia of property' and should therefore 'be treated in principle as property'. This Legal Statement is likely to be persuasive authority for the courts to find that cryptoassets are property (as, indeed, it was in *AA v Persons Unknown*) and thus to grant freezing orders in respect of them.

However, prior to the publication of the UKJT's Legal Statement, the courts had already shown themselves willing, and able, to grant freezing orders in respect of cryptoassets.

Case Study

In *Vorotyntseva v Money-4 Ltd (t/a Nebeus.com)*[72] ('the *Vorotyntseva* case'), which was decided in September 2018 although the judgment was not published until November 2019, the High Court granted freezing orders in respect of Bitcoin and Ethereum. In July 2018, the claimant transferred around GBP 1.5 million of Bitcoin and Ethereum to Nebeus's trading platform on the understanding that Nebeus would hold and deal with the cryptoassets on the claimant's behalf. The purpose of the transaction was to test Nebeus's trading platform. The claimant became concerned that the cryptoassets had been dissipated, and so the claimant's solicitors specifically asked for confirmation that the cryptoassets were

71 *Lakatamia Shipping Co v Morimoto* [2019] EWCA Civ 2203 at [36].
72 [2018] EWHC 2596 (Ch).

still in Nebeus's possession and had not been dissipated. No confirmation was forthcoming, and the claimant brought an application for a freezing order against Nebeus and its directors.

The defendants offered an undertaking to maintain the cryptocurrency pending further order, and they produced emails with screenshots which purported to show the claimant's money still being held by Nebeus. Counsel for the claimant challenged the evidence, asserting that the screenshot relating to the claimant's Bitcoin did not, on its own, confirm that her Bitcoin was indeed still being held by Nebeus; and the screenshot relating to the claimant's Ethereum appeared to have been altered, with the claimant's name having been superimposed on the screenshot.

Despite all possible allowances having been made for the defendants, given the short notice of the application, the court noted that very serious questions arose from the material that had been produced. The court accepted the submissions of Counsel for the claimant concerning the evidence produced by the defendants and that the documents supported the claimant's concern about the risk of dissipation. The court stated that it was satisfied that, on the evidence before it, there was a real risk of dissipation in this case. Consequently, the application for the freezing order was granted.

Therefore this case, together with the UKJT's Legal Statement, indicates that, with the growing popularity of cryptoassets, practitioners and courts should expect to see more applications for freezing orders for cryptoassets in the future. This is especially true, perhaps, in matrimonial financial settlement proceedings, where parties may seek freezing orders to prevent the other party from dissipating assets prior to the final financial settlement.

What needs to be considered when seeking freezing orders in respect of cryptoassets?

9.20 There are, however, several considerations that will need to be taken into account when seeking a freezing order in respect of cryptoassets.

Legal considerations

9.21 Although it did not arise in the *Vorotyntseva* case, and is unlikely to arise in matrimonial financial settlement proceedings, if freezing orders are sought in a broader context (for example, in cases of fraud, blackmail etc), unless the cryptoassets remain in the wallets to which they were initially transferred, the courts may take issue with granting freezing orders against any subsequent 'unknown' wallet holders on the basis that, as they do not know who these individuals are, the court cannot conclude where the balance of convenience lies.

This was one of the issues in *Robertson v Persons Unknown*[73] ('the *Robertson* case') (see para **9.24** below for a full discussion in relation to this case).

> Case Study
>
> In the *Robertson* case, a freezing order for the full amount of Bitcoins stolen was sought against 'persons unknown', some of the Bitcoins having been transferred from the original fraudster's wallet to a subsequent 'unknown' wallet held in a cryptoasset exchange provider.
>
> In considering whether or not to grant the freezing order, the court struggled with the prospect that, in granting the order, it may prevent an entirely innocent party from running their business. It compared the situation before it with other ex parte injunctions where the court is informed of who the individual is, their circumstances etc. In the present case, the court said that it did not even know whether the holder of the 'unknown' wallet was engaged in the fraud, and the court said that its real issue was that it did not know who held the 'unknown' wallet and so it could not weigh up the matter on the balance of convenience.[74]

Even though cryptoasset tracing is possible, it is difficult, and it seems that anyone who has been defrauded of cryptocurrency, unless they obtain a Bankers Trust or other form of disclosure order prior to applying for a freezing order, is going to face the difficulty of not knowing who the wallet holder is and whether they are a 'bona fide purchaser for value without notice'. On that basis, irrespective of the balance of convenience element of granting a freezing order, there may be a question as to whether there is, in fact, a good arguable case against the 'persons unknown', as the 'bona fide purchaser for value without notice' rules provide that a person who buys property in good faith and is not on notice of defects in the transferor's title takes good title.

Freezing orders against 'persons unknown' are not an unknown concept, provided that the respondents are clearly identified,[75] but it is not clear whether, or how, the court considered these authorities in the case of *Robertson*. It may be that each case will depend on the facts, and how the claim form and terms of the order are drafted. However, if individuals will have to identify 'persons unknown' in order to apply for a freezing order, and establish that there is a good arguable case and that the balance of convenience lies in granting the order, the chances of recovering the assets may be greatly diminished.

73 Unreported, CL-2019-000444.

74 'A Bitcoin first? Stewarts obtains asset preservation order over cryptocurrency', Marc Jones and Stefan Edwards, 20 August 2019: www.stewartslaw.com/news/cryptocurrency-bitcoin-asset-preservation-order-stewarts/. Marc Jones represented the claimant in *Robertson v Persons Unknown*.

75 *Bloomsbury Publishing Group Plc v News Group Newspaper Ltd (Continuation of Injunction)* [2003] EWHC 1205 (Ch) and *CMOC v Persons Unknown* [2017] EWHC 3599 (Comm).

The answer, therefore, may be that it would, in these circumstances, be better to apply for a proprietary injunction instead (discussed at paras **9.23–9.25** below), and only resort to freezing orders in respect of cryptoassets when the respondent is a known and named party. Applying for a freezing order may, in fact, be possible after a proprietary injunction, if the terms of that injunction include a provision that information as to the identity and address (and/or any other information) of the wallet holders be provided (as was the case in *AA v Persons Unknown*[76] ('the *AA* case') – see para **9.24** below). Therefore, the most appropriate course of action in cases concerning cryptoassets, where the respondents are unknown, may be to first seek a proprietary injunction including terms as to the provision of information and then, in light of the information provided, seek to apply for a freezing order.

Practical considerations

9.22 In terms of practical considerations in respect of seeking freezing orders against known and named respondents, courts and practitioners will have to consider the practicalities of not only establishing any relevant cryptoasset exchange providers, but also serving the freezing orders on them so that they know not to permit any transactions in respect of those cryptoassets. It may be that disclosure orders need to be sought against respondents to establish the cryptoasset exchange providers, or a search and seizure order sought. Although it is hoped that a cryptoasset exchange provider would cooperate with a freezing order, especially in light of their increased regulation under the Money Laundering, Terrorist Financing and Transfer of Funds (Information on the Payer) Regulations 2017 ('MLR 2017')[77] (as amended by the Money Laundering and Terrorist Financing (Amendment) Regulations 2019 ('MLR 2019'),[78] which transpose the European Union's ('EU') Fifth Anti-Money Laundering Directive),[79] this has yet to be tested.

Additionally, if cryptoassets are, under freezing orders, to become a means of settling monetary compensation claims or part of financial settlements in family proceedings, practitioners (and courts) will need to start thinking about the practicalities of realising or transferring the cryptoassets. It may be that orders will be sought whereby individuals are required to give up control of their cryptoasset wallets, or required to deliver up all devices where the keys are stored. These measures only work, however, if the entirety of the cryptoasset balance within those wallets is required in order to settle the claim. Cryptoassets can be subdivided, so it may be that applicants will have to create their own digital wallets to which the cryptoassets can then be transferred.

76 [2019] EWHC 3556 (Comm) at [81] to [86].
77 SI 2017/692.
78 SI 2019/1511.
79 Directive (EU) 2018/843 of the European Parliament and of the Council of 30 May 2018 amending Directive (EU) 2015/849 on the prevention of the use of the financial system for the purposes of money laundering or terrorist financing, and amending Directives 2009/138/EC and 2013/36/EU.

If that is the case, then the court will need to consider how the transfers will be monitored to ensure compliance. If digital wallets are held by cryptoasset exchange providers, the transaction can occur within the exchange. However, this means that the transaction will not appear on the blockchain: it will be an off-chain transaction. For transactions not related to an exchange wallet, they will appear on the public blockchain, and the transactions are usually included in the next block by a third party miner. Given the highly technical and decentralised nature of cryptoasset transactions, how will courts oversee and monitor compliance? Will this function be outsourced? Will law firms seek (or, indeed, need) to employ their own cryptoasset analysts?

It is currently unclear how any of these practical considerations will be resolved, but both practitioners and courts should begin thinking about them now because, before too long, such transactions will be required in the settlement of claims and matrimonial financial settlement proceedings.

Proprietary injunctions (including asset preservation orders)

9.23 Proprietary injunctions are orders for the interim preservation of assets which are the subject matter of a claim where the applicant has a proprietary or tracing claim, ie the applicant seeks to assert that the assets held by the respondent are, in fact, the applicant's property. In determining whether or not to grant a proprietary injunction, the court will apply the *American Cyanamid Co v Ethicon Ltd*[80] principles:[81]

- first, there must be a serious issue to be tried; and
- secondly, the court must consider whether the balance of convenience lies in granting the relief sought.

The balance of convenience involves consideration of the efficacy of damages as an adequate remedy, the adequacy of the cross-undertaking as to damages, and the overall balance of convenience, including the merits of the proposed claim.

Can proprietary injunctions be sought in respect of cryptoassets?

9.24 Cryptoassets and their status are, again, an area of significant interest to lay persons and practitioners alike when it comes to proprietary injunctions.

Even before the UKJT's Legal Statement on Cryptoassets and Smart Contracts, the courts were finding that cryptoassets were property and that proprietary injunctions could be granted in respect of them.

80 [1975] AC 396.
81 *Poly Peck International PLC v Nadir (Asil) (No 2)* [1992] 4 All ER 769.

Case Study

In the *Vorotyntseva* case (see para **9.19** above), a proprietary injunction was granted as part of the freezing order so as to 'prohibit the disposal of the relevant quantities of Bitcoin and Ethereum'.

The court said that the point in relation to the proprietary order was that the Bitcoin and Ethereum were ultimately said to belong to the claimant, and there was no suggestion that the cryptocurrency did not belong to the claimant. The court also held that there was no 'suggestion that cryptocurrency cannot be a form of property or that a party amenable to the court's jurisdiction cannot be enjoined from dealing in or disposing of it'. As such, the court was satisfied that it could make a proprietary injunction.[82]

The decision of the High Court in the *Vorotyntseva* case is very short, and the basis on which the court held that cryptoassets should be treated as property is not clear, nor is the relationship between the freezing order and the proprietary injunction, nor the court's justification for granting the proprietary injunction. However, as the court stated, this was a very preliminary order, and there was to be a return date. Perhaps the submissions and judgment from that hearing will shed light on these matters.

The *Vorotyntseva* case was not, however, the only time that the courts, prior to the UKJT's Legal Statement, concluded that cryptoassets were property and could be the subject of a proprietary injunction.

Case Study

In the *Robertson*[83] case, the court granted an asset preservation order in respect of Bitcoins that had been stolen from the claimant and transferred to an address that was recognised as a cryptoasset exchange provider. (Note that the judgment in the *Vorotyntseva* case had not been published at the time when this case was heard.)

Following a telephone call, and when he was expecting to make a transfer of 100 Bitcoins to a fund, the claimant received an email requesting a transfer, which he duly made. It transpired that the request was a cloned email and that the Bitcoins had been sent to a hacker's digital wallet. A tracing exercise was conducted by Chainalysis (a blockchain investigations firm), and 80 Bitcoins were traced as having been transferred from the hacker's wallet to a wallet held at Coinbase UK (a cryptoasset digital exchange), 15 to LocalBitcoins.com, and another five to a cold wallet.[84] The claimant

82 [2018] EWHC 2596 (Ch) at [13] and [14].

83 Unreported, CL-2019-000444.

84 'UK High Court ruling over $1 million hack implies Bitcoin is "property"', Robert Stevens, 22 August 2019: https://decrypt.co/8654/british-high-court-decides-bitcoin-counts.

applied for: a freezing order against persons unknown in respect of 100 Bitcoins; an asset preservation order over the 80 Bitcoins in the Coinbase wallet; and a Bankers Trust order to reveal the identity of the wallet holder.

At the first ex parte hearing, Moulder J was not prepared to proceed with the application for the freezing order, on the basis that it was unclear whether the unidentified holder of the cryptoasset exchange wallet was the fraudster or even part of the fraud. Moulder J took the view that the cryptoasset exchange wallet holder could be a perfectly innocent third party and, as such, she was not prepared to make a freezing order against the unidentified wallet holder. Additionally, the court was not satisfied that the balance of convenience and risk of dissipation requirements for a freezing order were satisfied.

However, Moulder J did entertain the claimant's argument that he had a proprietary claim over the 80 Bitcoins, and proceeded on the basis that Bitcoin could be personal property. For the purpose of the proprietary injunction (asset preservation order), Moulder J identified a key issue as being whether legal title remained with the claimant. She noted:

> 'So if this turns out to be an effective transfer of title because it is a personal – an item of personal property with a right of possession, it could have been transferred.'

The judge referred to the conclusion of the Financial Markets Law Committee ('FMLC'), in its report 'Issues of Legal Uncertainty Arising in the Context of Virtual Currencies (July 2016)', that cryptocurrencies may be conveniently understood as a kind of hybrid virtual chose in possession. If that were right, then, as Moulder J observed, the claimant would not have a better title than any recipient of the 80 Bitcoins if the recipient were a bona fide purchaser for value. Equally, sale of goods legislation provides other defences that might enable a recipient of cryptocurrencies to defeat a proprietary claim, but only if cryptocurrencies are treated as choses in possession.

At this point in the hearing, the court skirted, but did not pursue, possibly the most difficult issue that could arise in claims involving cryptocurrencies: what is the law governing the proprietary aspects of dealing with cryptocurrencies? The claimant submitted that Bitcoin are not choses in possession and that, on the basis of *Armstrong DLW GmbH v Winnington Networks Ltd*,[85] for the purpose of advancing a proprietary restitutionary claim and obtaining an interlocutory asset preservation order, it did not matter whether the court treated them as choses in action or some form of other intangible property. Ultimately, the court proceeded on that basis, and granted an asset preservation order preventing any dealings with the 80 Bitcoins or any instructions being given to Coinbase to transfer them.

85 [2012] EWHC 10 (Ch).

The court also made Bankers Trust orders enabling Coinbase to disclose information relating to the account holder.[86]

The status of cryptoassets was once again considered by the courts in the *AA*[87] case. The court this time, however, had the benefit of the judgments in both the *Vorotyntseva* and *Robertson* cases, and the UKJT's Legal Statement, to assist its decision.

Case Study

In the *AA* case, a Canadian insurance company was hacked and the ransomware BitPayer was installed. BitPayer encrypted all of the company's computer systems, and USD 1.2 million in Bitcoins was demanded in order to obtain the decryption tool. The ransom price was reduced to USD 950,000 in Bitcoins and, on 10 October 2019, 109.25 Bitcoins were transferred to the address that had been provided. The decryption tool was received the following day and deployed across the company's systems.

The claimant contacted a specialist company that provides software to track payments of cryptocurrency: Chainalysis. It was discovered that some of the Bitcoins were transferred into fiat currency and that 96 Bitcoins were transferred to an address that was linked to the Bitfinex cryptoasset exchange.

The claimant applied to the High Court for: a Bankers Trust order and/or a Norwich Pharmacal order requiring Bitfinex to provide specified information in relation to the cryptocurrency account holding the 96 Bitcoins; and/or a proprietary injunction in respect of the Bitcoins held in the account; and/or a freezing injunction in respect of the Bitcoins held at the specified account; and consequential orders to serve the same, including alternate service and service outside the jurisdiction. During the course of the hearing, the applications for the Bankers Trust/Norwich Pharmacal order and freezing injunction were adjourned.[88]

In terms of the application for a proprietary injunction, the claims in respect of which relief was being sought were limited to the claims of the insurer in restitution and/or constructive trustee against all of the defendants.[89]

86 'Time to clarify the legal status of cryptocurrencies?', Marc Jones, Stewarts Law LLP, 31 October 2019: www.stewartslaw.com/news/legal-status-of-cryptocurrencies/; and 'A Bitcoin first? Stewarts obtains asset preservation order over cryptocurrency', Marc Jones and Stefan Edwards, 20 August 2019. Marc Jones represented the claimant in *Robertson v Persons Unknown.*

87 [2019] EWHC 3556 (Comm).

88 See paras 44 to 49 of the judgment for the reasoning behind this.

89 [2019] EWHC 3556 (Comm) at [50] to [52].

Turning to the relevant principles in relation to the granting of a proprietary injunction, Bryan J stated that the first and perhaps fundamental question that arose in relation to the claim for a proprietary injunction was whether or not, in fact, Bitcoins are property at all.[90] Noting that it is not a statement of law, the court considered the analysis as to the proprietary status of cryptoassets in the UKJT's Legal Statement. The court stated that the analysis is compelling and that, essentially, and for the reasons identified in the UKJT's Legal Statement, it considered a cryptoasset such as Bitcoin to be property:[91]

> 'They meet the four criteria set out in Lord Wilberforce's classic definition of property in *National Provincial Bank v Ainsworth* [1965] AC 1175 as being definable, identifiable by third parties, capable in their nature of assumption by third parties, and having some degree of permanence. That too, was the conclusion of the Singapore International Commercial Court in *B2C2 Limited v Quoine PTC Limited* [2019] SGHC (I) 03 [142].'

The court was also referred to the cases of *Vorotyntseva* and *Robertson.* The court noted that the authorities do not consider the issue in depth, but in both of them cryptocurrencies were treated as property: in *Vorotyntseva*, a worldwide freezing order was granted in respect of a substantial quantity of Bitcoin and Ethereum; and, in *Robertson*, an asset preservation order was granted over cryptocurrencies.

The court concluded that:

> 'In those circumstances and for the reasons I have given, as elaborated upon in the Legal Statement which [...] I consider to be an accurate statement as to the position under English law, I am satisfied for the purpose of granting an interim injunction in the form of an interim proprietary injunction that crypto currencies are a form of property capable of being the subject of a proprietary injunction.'[92]

The court then turned to the applicable principles in relation to a proprietary injunction, concluding that an injunction could be granted because it was satisfied that:[93]

- there was a serious issue to be tried;
- the balance of convenience lay firmly in favour of granting relief in furtherance of the insurer's claimed proprietary rights;
- damages would not be an adequate remedy in circumstances where the 96 Bitcoins could be dissipated; and
- the insurer had a strong claim to the Bitcoins in question.

90 [2019] EWHC 3556 (Comm) at [55].
91 [2019] EWHC 3556 (Comm) at [56] to [59].
92 [2019] EWHC 3556 (Comm) at [61].
93 [2019] EWHC 3556 (Comm) at [65].

Therefore, in light of the *Vorotyntseva*, *Robertson* and *AA* cases, and the UKJT's Legal Statement, it seems fairly well established, at least for the moment, that cryptoassets constitute property under the law of England and Wales and that proprietary injunctions (as well as freezing orders and search and seizure orders) can be granted in respect of them.

What needs to be considered when seeking proprietary injunctions in respect of cryptoassets?

9.25 Similar considerations to those in relation to freezing orders (see paras **9.20–9.22** above) also apply in relation to seeking proprietary injunctions in respect of cryptoassets.

In the case of proprietary injunctions, and arguably more so than in the case of freezing orders, specific consideration will have to be given to the potential need to seek permission to serve out of the jurisdiction, as well as seeking permission for alternative methods of service.

Both of these issues were considered in the *AA* case,[94] and it is likely that whether or not such permission is granted will depend upon the facts of each case. However, given Bryan J's reasoning at paragraphs 77 and 78 of the *AA* judgment, there may be strong arguments for alternative methods of service in all cases where a proprietary injunction is sought in respect of cryptoassets, since:[95]

- all such applications are likely to be really urgent because of the risk of dissipation;
- the proprietary injunction needs to come to the attention of the cryptoasset exchange provider at the earliest possible opportunity; and
- the cryptoassets belong to a claimant, so it is important that the injunction is placed as soon as possible in order that the claimant's rights are preserved and the risk of the property being moved to an unknown location is minimised.

It must also be considered whether the terms of a proprietary injunction need to include provisions requiring information as to the identity and address (and/or any other information) of the wallet holders to be provided,[96] and, in the event of the substantive claim being found in favour of the claimant, how the realisation and transfer of the cryptoassets are to be effected and monitored.

An additional point to note, from both the *Robertson* and *AA* cases, is the potential need for specialist technical involvement in tracing cryptoassets prior to an application for a proprietary injunction. Given that proprietary injunctions may be the initial recourse in cases of fraud, blackmail etc (as discussed at para **9.21**

94 [2019] EWHC 3556 (Comm) at [67] to [78].
95 [2019] EWHC 3556 (Comm) at [77] to [78].
96 [2019] EWHC 3556 (Comm) at [81] to [86].

above), it seems that blockchain analysis will become a specialist industry, and expert opinion will likely become the norm in such applications and substantive claims.

Contract law remedies

9.26 As already mentioned, on 18 November 2019 the UKJT delivered its Legal Statement on Cryptoassets and Smart Contracts. This stated that, in principle, a smart contract can be identified, interpreted and enforced using ordinary and well-established legal principles.

In light of the UKJT's Legal Statement, all remedies that would be available in the event of a breach of non-smart contract – damages, specific performance etc – should, in theory, be applicable to the breach of a smart contract. How this will work in practice, though, is unclear.

In the situation where an entire contract exists in code, what if a party argues, or both parties argue, that the code does not actually reflect the agreement reached? With a non-smart contract, the court may be asked to rectify the document so that it accurately reflects the intention of the parties and the agreement reached (rectification). In a stand-alone smart contract, it may be possible to rectify the source code; but what about the case where the smart contract uses distributed ledger technology, or the smart contract is included in a blockchain? The immutable nature of a blockchain would potentially mean that rectification was not possible in such circumstances. How do the parties, in that situation, rectify or set aside a smart contract if the blockchain cannot be amended? Would the parties have an action against the software developer who wrote the code? Will software developers who are involved in writing the code for smart contracts be required to (or, indeed, be strongly advised to) take out professional indemnity insurance to protect themselves against such actions?

A further interesting question is who exactly would be responsible for performance under a smart contract? The UKJT's Legal Statement said that the characteristic feature of smart contracts, in their view, is automaticity: a smart contract is performed, at least in part, automatically and without the need for, and in some cases without the possibility of, human intervention. That requires the terms of the contract to be recorded in a computer-readable form, ie in code.[97] In that case, can a party ever be said to have or to have not performed under a smart contract? The performance is automatic, based on the source code, which has been written by a software developer. As the software developer is responsible for the source code, does that then mean that they are responsible for what happens as a result of the source code, ie the performance of the smart contract?

The UKJT's Legal Statement focused mainly on a court interpreting a smart contract, as opposed to what it would, should or could do following that

97 At para 135 of the UKJT Legal Statement.

interpretation. Consequently, there is currently lots of uncertainty as to smart contracts and the court's role in relation to them and their enforcement: unlike cryptoassets, there are yet to be any cases before the courts in respect of smart contracts. It may be that parties to smart contracts will need to ensure that the smart contracts themselves contain remedy provisions, providing for what should happen in the event of breach etc. However, parties to any contract cannot foresee all circumstances which may give rise to a breach of contract, so how then could a smart contract provide for remedies in all circumstances? Would the better course be for the smart contract to provide for the most obvious cases of breach and then, in circumstances outside of that, have recourse to the courts? That, however, does not solve the problem of how that would work in practice.

At the Westminster Legal Policy Forum Keynote Seminar – Legal Technology in the UK – on 2 December 2019, Sir Geoffrey Vos (Chair of the UKJT) gave a talk entitled 'Unlocking the potential of smart contracts'. In it, he said that he was delighted about the UKJT's Legal Statement, and that the UKJT will now ask the Law Commission to consider smart contracts and say whether it thinks any legislation is needed. However, Sir Geoffrey qualified the readiness of smart contracts to be put into practice by saying that the mechanism by which smart contract disputes would be resolved is not yet established. He said that there was 'one further piece in the jigsaw' of smart contracts, and 'that is to crack the way in which disputes about them will be resolved'.

Sir Geoffrey's view was that English law and UK jurisdiction dispute resolution clauses, which would either allow for arbitration or a streamlined online dispute resolution mechanism, should now be created so that programmers can include them in smart financial services contracts. He was of the view that the law of England and Wales was well placed to provide the standard dispute resolution mechanisms for many of the smart contracts that would be entered into globally. However, he also said that the next steps in unlocking the potential of smart contracts will be for courts, judges and lawyers, and that he hoped to 'see the creation of innovative dispute resolution methods that are specially crafted to operate in the smart contract environment'.

With this in mind, and with the potential increase in litigation about smart contracts on the horizon, Sir Geoffrey said that England and Wales need to take advantage of the early opportunity afforded to them by the UKLT's Legal Statement setting out the underlying legal position in respect of smart contracts. He acknowledged that the technical community generally regard lawyers and judges as part of the problem rather than the solution, but emphasised that the legal sector now needs to persuade the technical community that there must always be a clear method of available dispute resolution; not because it is expected that something will go wrong, but in order to give investors the confidence to use smart contracts, which will only be achievable if disputes concerning them can be smoothly and efficiently resolved, and at proportionate cost. Therefore, 'lawyers need to seize the initiative and work alongside the technological community to build a safe crypto-world, where efficient contractual relationships, indelibly recorded on-chain, become the investment method of choice for mainstream financial institutions and retail investors alike'.

In light of Sir Geoffrey's comments, if the mechanism by which smart contract disputes should be resolved is not yet established, the availability and application of remedies following such disputes are not yet established either.

Therefore, despite the UKJT's Legal Statement saying that, in principle, a smart contract can be identified, interpreted and enforced using ordinary and well-established legal principles, perhaps, in light of Sir Geoffrey's comment about creating 'innovative dispute resolution methods that are specially crafted to operate in the smart contract environment', that does not mean that traditional contract law remedies should, or can, apply to smart contracts.

WHAT REMEDIES ARE PROVIDED BY 'REGULATORS' IN 'CYBER' CASES?

Notice and take down requests

9.27 The E-Commerce Directive 2000[98] provides limited liability ('safe harbour provisions') for ISPs when they host material, provided that the ISP does not have actual knowledge or awareness of illegal activity or information, or that the ISP, upon obtaining such knowledge or awareness, acts expeditiously to remove or disable access to the information.[99]

The E-Commerce Directive 2000 was transposed into law in England and Wales by the Electronic Commerce (EC Directive) Regulations 2002,[100] which came into force on 21 August 2002. Regulation 19 of the Electronic Commerce (EC Directive) Regulations 2002 transposes Article 14 of the E-Commerce Directive 2000, and provides corresponding 'safe harbour provisions'. It provides that, where a service provider stores (hosts) unlawful material, it will not be liable for damages, any other pecuniary remedy or any criminal sanction as a result of such storage, provided that it does not have actual knowledge of the unlawful material or, upon obtaining such knowledge, it acts expeditiously to remove or disable access to the material.

These provisions gave rise to notice and take down requests, so that ISPs could avoid liability for illegal activity and information posted to their websites. Note, however, that the hosting exemption only applies in civil proceedings seeking damages or another pecuniary remedy, or in relation to criminal cases: it does not apply in civil proceedings where, for example, a claimant is seeking an injunction, and so the ISP would have to comply with the injunction.

98 Directive 2000/31/EC of the European Parliament and of the Council of 8 June 2000 on certain legal aspects of information society services, in particular electronic commerce, in the Internal Market (Directive on electronic commerce).

99 E-Commerce Directive, Article 14.

100 SI 2002/2013.

A notice and take down request is a procedure for asking an ISP or search engine to remove or disable access to illegal, irrelevant, inaccurate or outdated information. Therefore, it provides a method for: having open source malware (such as Eternal Blue) made inaccessible; removing revenge pornography; removing deepfakes; removing and/or making leaked confidential information inaccessible; or removing material that infringes copyright and/or making it inaccessible etc.

The challenge for ISPs and search engines, however, is creating a process whereby they can evaluate the validity of each notice and take down request without the requests and their individual consideration becoming a bottleneck, and so risk being accused of not acting expeditiously to remove or disable access to the information. There is also a concern over the 'chilling effect' of such notices, where notice and take down requests are used to censor material, criticisms and commentary that individuals feel is objectionable as opposed to illegal, irrelevant, inaccurate or outdated.

Where ISPs do not remove or disable access following a notice and take down request, recourse may be had to the High Court's jurisdiction to grant a website blocking injunction (see paras **9.14–9.17** above).

Brexit will not have an impact on the 'limited liability' provisions in the Electronic Commerce (EC Directive) Regulations 2002 as, by virtue of section 1B(2) of the European Union (Withdrawal) Act 2018 ('EUWA 2018'), EU-derived domestic legislation, as it has effect in domestic law immediately before exit day, continues to have effect in domestic law on and after exit day until the end of the implementation period (11:00pm on 31 December 2020). The EUWA 2018 (as amended by the European Union (Withdrawal Agreement) Act 2020) also provides that EU-derived domestic legislation existing before 'IP completion day' (Implementation Period Completion Day, ie 11:00pm on 31 December 2020)[101] continues to have effect in domestic law on and after 'IP completion day'[102] ('retained EU law'). Therefore, although the Electronic Commerce (EC Directive) Regulations 2002 have been amended for a domestic context by regulation 3 of the Electronic Commerce (Amendment etc) (EU Exit) Regulations 2019,[103] their substance remains the same, and ISPs will continue to have 'limited liability' in respect of hosting illegal content. Thus, notice and take down requests will remain an available remedy.

Information Commissioner's Office

9.28 The Information Commissioner's Office ('ICO') is the UK's independent supervisory/regulatory authority in respect of information rights, and it has dual-

101 European Union (Withdrawal Agreement) Act 2020, s 39(1).

102 EUWA 2018, s 2(1) (prospective), as amended by the European Union (Withdrawal Agreement) Act 2020, s 25(1) (prospective).

103 SI 2019/87.

jurisdiction: not only can it prosecute individuals for 'data crimes' under the Data Protection Act 2018 ('DPA 2018'), but it can also impose civil financial penalties under the DPA 2018 for breaches of the General Data Protection Regulation ('GDPR').[104] Thus, it is a powerful tool in addressing and remedying the unauthorised use of personal data.

'Data crimes' under the Data Protection Act 2018

9.29 The DPA 2018 provides that it is an offence for a person to knowingly or recklessly obtain, disclose, procure the disclosure of, or retain personal data without the consent of the data controller.[105] It is also an offence to sell, or offer to sell, personal data obtained in such circumstances.[106]

The DPA 2018 further provides that it is an offence for a person to knowingly or recklessly re-identify information that is de-identified personal data without the consent of the data controller responsible for de-identifying the personal data,[107] and that it is an offence to process such re-identified personal data.[108] It is also an offence for a data controller or an agent of the data controller to alter, deface, block, erase, destroy or conceal information with the intention of preventing disclosure of all or part of the information that a person would be entitled to receive under a data subject access request.[109]

Prosecutions for these offences may only be instituted by the Information Commissioner, or by or with the consent of the Director of Public Prosecutions.[110] The offence of altering personal data to prevent disclosure to a data subject is a summary-only offence, whereas the other offences are either-way offences. However, all of the offences are only punishable by a fine.[111] Where a person is guilty of an offence under section 170 of the DPA 2018 (unlawfully obtaining etc personal data), the court may order a document or other material to be forfeited, destroyed or erased if it has been used in connection with the processing of personal data and it appears to be connected with the commission of the offence.[112] All of these offences are recordable offences.[113]

The DPA 2018 preserves the status quo from the Data Protection Act 1998 ('DPA 1998'), with a fine being the only remedy in respect of these 'data crimes'. This limited sentencing power under the DPA 1998 was a source of frustration for the Information Commissioner and, as a result, individuals were charged with

104 Regulation (EU) 2016/679.
105 DPA 2018, s 170(1).
106 DPA 2018, s 170(4)–(5).
107 DPA 2018, s 171(1).
108 DPA 2018, s 171(5).
109 DPA 2018, s 173.
110 DPA 2018, s 197(1).
111 DPA 2018, s 196(1)–(2).
112 DPA 2018, s 196(4).
113 DPA 2018, s 199(1).

non-DPA 1998 offences which, although addressing the same criminal actions, attracted custodial sentences.

Case Studies

In *Attorney General's Reference (No 140 of 2004)* (also known as *R v Dickinson (Barry Saul)*)[114] the defendant, who was employed by the DVLA, obtained the names and addresses of vehicle owners who had visited an animal breeding site, and did so without the consent of the data controller. He subsequently disclosed this information to animal rights activists, who used it to harass the individuals. This was an offence contrary to section 55 of the DPA 1998 (the earlier equivalent of the offence under section 170 of the DPA 2018) but, rather than being charged under the DPA 1998, the defendant was charged with misconduct in a public office. He pleaded guilty to the offence and was given a custodial sentence.

Similarly, in September 2018, Mustafa Kasim pleaded guilty to an offence under section 1 of the Computer Misuse Act 1990 ('CMA 1990') in respect of securing unauthorised access to personal data between 13 January and 19 October 2016. He was sentenced to six months' imprisonment, and confiscation proceedings under POCA 2002 were commenced. Mr Kasim worked for the accident repair firm Nationwide Accident Repair Services ('NARS') and accessed thousands of customer records containing personal data, without permission, using his colleague's log-in details to access a software system that estimates the cost of vehicle repairs. He continued to do this after he started a new job at a different car repair organisation which used the same software system. NARS contacted the ICO when they saw an increase in customer complaints about nuisance calls. In its news release, the ICO stated:

> 'The ICO usually prosecutes cases like this under the Data Protection Act 1998 or 2018, depending on the individual case. However, in appropriate cases, it can prosecute under other legislation – in this case s.1 of the Computer Misuse Act 1990 – to reflect the nature and extent of the offending and for the sentencing Court to have a wider range of penalties available.'

The same news report quoted Mike Shaw, the Group Manager Criminal Investigations Team at the ICO, as saying:

> 'People who think it's worth their while to obtain and disclose personal data without permission should think again. Although this was a data protection issue, in this case we were able to prosecute beyond data protection laws resulting in a tougher penalty to reflect the nature of the criminal behaviour. Members of the public and organisations can be assured that we will push the boundaries and use any tool at our disposal to protect their rights.'[115]

114 [2004] EWCA Crim 3525.

115 https://ico.org.uk/about-the-ico/news-and-events/news-and-blogs/2018/11/six-month-prison-sentence-for-motor-industry-employee-in-first-ico-computer-misuse-act-prosecution/.

It should be noted that the fines that can be imposed for these 'data crimes' under the DPA 2018 are unlimited in amount[116] and, given the courts' increasing awareness of the value of personal data, and the level of financial penalties that can be imposed in respect of breaches of the GDPR (for which, see paras **9.30–9.31** below), there may be judicial appetite to impose larger fines for these offences. However, the counter-argument is that, although the fines may be unlimited in theory, in practice the level of the fines will need to take a defendant's means into account. Therefore, in order to reflect the severity of the actions, and to give the court greater sentencing powers, the Information Commissioner may seek to continue to prosecute individuals for non-DPA 2018 offences, such as offences under the CMA 1990 etc. Indeed, Mr Shaw's comment in November 2018 – that the ICO will push the boundaries and use any tool at its disposal to protect people's rights – indicates that this is exactly what the ICO will continue to do.

Therefore, although individuals might believe that they are facing an allegation under the DPA 2018, under which they can only be punished by a fine, they may find themselves facing different charges which could attract custodial sentences, and individuals and corporates should be advised of such.

Enforcement notices and penalty notices for breaches of the GDPR

9.30 Under the GDPR, individuals can seek remedies regarding the processing of their personal data directly from data controllers and data processors. They can request the following:

- the rectification of inaccurate personal data;[117]
- the erasure of personal data;[118] and
- a restriction on the processing of their personal data, including where the accuracy of the data is being contested.[119]

They can also object, at any time, on grounds relating to their particular situation, to the processing of their personal data, where that processing is based on necessity for the performance of a task carried out in the public interest, necessity for the performance of a task carried out in the exercise of official authority vested in the controller, or necessity for the purpose of the legitimate interests pursued by the controller or third party.[120]

There is no obligation on individuals to seek these remedies (or enforce these rights) directly from data controllers or processors, and Article 77(1) of the GDPR provides that, without prejudice to any other administrative or judicial remedy,

116 www.sentencingcouncil.org.uk/about-sentencing/types-of-sentence/fines/.
117 GDPR, Article 16.
118 GDPR, Article 17.
119 GDPR, Article 18.
120 GDPR, Articles 21 and 6(1)(e) and (f).

every data subject has the right to lodge a complaint with a supervisory authority if they consider that the processing of their personal data infringes the GDPR.

The Information Commissioner is the UK's supervisory authority for the purposes of Article 51 of the GDPR. Thus, under Articles 57 and 58 of the GDPR, the ICO is responsible for monitoring and enforcing the GDPR in the UK, and it has investigative, corrective, authorisation and advisory powers in order to help it do so. Schedule 15 to the DPA 2018 makes provision about the ICO's powers of entry and inspection. The ICO's enforcement powers are outlined in Part 6 of the DPA 2018, and they include the power to issue information notices (notices requiring the provision of information),[121] assessment notices (notices requiring submission to an assessment by the ICO of compliance with data protection legislation)[122] and enforcement notices (notices requiring particular steps to be taken or to be refrained from, when the Information Commissioner is satisfied that there is a failure to comply with the GDPR or DPA 2018).[123] Where the Information Commissioner is satisfied that there is a failure to comply with the GDPR or DPA 2018, or a failure to comply with an information, assessment or enforcement notice, the ICO can issue a penalty notice and require the payment of a financial penalty.[124]

Section 157 of the DPA 2018 provides that, in relation to an infringement of a provision of the GDPR, the maximum penalty that may be imposed by the ICO under a section 155 penalty notice is the amount specified in Article 83 of the GDPR. Article 83(2) outlines a number of measures to be taken into account when deciding whether to impose, and the amount of, a fine, and provides that the maximum penalty that can be issued is, depending on the provision infringed, either:

- EUR 10 million or, in the case of an undertaking, up to 2% of the total worldwide annual turnover of the preceding financial year, whichever is higher;[125] or
- EUR 20 million or, in the case of an undertaking, up to 4% of the total worldwide annual turnover of the preceding financial year, whichever is higher.[126]

We saw the ICO beginning to flex its civil financial penalty muscles for breaches of the GDPR in 2019, with the fines that it proposed to impose on British Airways PLC ('BA') and Marriott International, Inc ('Marriott').

121 DPA 2018, ss 142–145.
122 DPA 2018, ss 146–147.
123 DPA 2018, ss 149–153.
124 DPA 2018, ss 155–159.
125 GDPR, Article 83(4).
126 GDPR, Article 83(5).

Case Studies

In relation to BA,[127] in June 2018, BA's network was subject to a 'supply chain attack'. The network was accessed by an attacker using compromised remote access credentials of a user within a third party supplier to BA, which were not subject to multi-factor authentication. Once inside the network, the attacker was able to gain higher levels of access and controls until attaining administrative privileges. This allowed the attacker to alter web forms and redirect customer personal data to a website owned and controlled by the attacker. The attacker's website collected the personal data of approximately 500,000 people, including names, addresses, payment card numbers and CVV numbers. BA did not detect the cyber attack for more than two months, only becoming aware of it after being alerted by a third party. Once aware, BA acted promptly, containing the vulnerability and blocking the URL for the malicious site within two hours, and notified the ICO.

The ICO investigation found that:

- BA had failed to put in place appropriate technical and organisational measures to ensure appropriate security of its customers' data;
- BA ought to have identified the weaknesses in its security measures and resolved them with measures that were available at the time; and
- addressing these security issues would have prevented the cyber attack.

The ICO issued a notice of intention to fine BA GBP 183.39 million in July 2019.[128]

Under paragraph 2(2) of Schedule 16 to the DPA 2018, the ICO has six months to convert a notice of intent into a penalty notice. BA made representations to the Information Commissioner about the notice of intent under paragraph 3(3) of Schedule 16 to the DPA 2018. In December 2019, the ICO and BA agreed that the six-month period would be extended to March 2020. In April 2020, the ICO requested information from BA regarding the impact of COVID-19 on its financial position, and both BA and the ICO agreed to a series of further extensions of the statutory deadline to 30 September 2020.

127 https://ico.org.uk/about-the-ico/news-and-events/news-and-blogs/2020/10/ico-fines-british-airways-20m-for-data-breach-affecting-more-than-400-000-customers/; and the ICO Penalty Notice against British Airways plc: https://ico.org.uk/media/action-weve-taken/mpns/2618421/ba-penalty-20201016.pdf.

128 https://ico.org.uk/about-the-ico/news-and-events/news-and-blogs/2019/07/ico-announces-intention-to-fine-british-airways/.

On 16 October 2020, having considered both the representations from BA and the economic impact of COVID-19 on its business, the ICO finally issued a penalty notice against BA for GBP 20 million.

In relation to Marriott, Marriott acquired the Starwood hotels group in 2016. The Starwood hotels group's systems had been compromised in 2014, but Marriott failed to undertake sufficient due diligence when it bought Starwood, and failed to adequately secure its systems. Consequently, the vulnerability was not discovered until 2018, during which time the customer information of approximately 339 million guests had been exposed. The ICO issued a notice of intention to fine Marriott GBP 99.2 million in July 2019.[129]

Marriott also made representations to the Information Commissioner regarding the notice of intent and, on 12 November 2019, in an ICO Disclosure Log, the ICO stated that the 'Information Commissioner is considering those representations in deciding whether to give a penalty notice, and the amount of the penalty if a penalty notice is given'.[130] The six months for converting the notice of intent into a penalty notice was due to expire in early January 2020 and, on 3 January 2020, Mishcon de Reya published a news item on its website stating that:

> 'The ICO has now informed Mishcon de Reya that such an extension has indeed been agreed, saying "Under Schedule 16 of the Data Protection Act 2018, [both BA and Marriott] and the ICO have agreed to an extension of the regulatory process until 31 March 2020. As the regulatory process is ongoing we will not be commenting any further at this time".'[131]

Further representations were made and, as it did with BA, in April 2020 the ICO also sought information from Marriott regarding the impact of COVID-19. A series of further extensions were agreed and, on 30 October 2020, having considered both the representations from Marriott and the financial impact of COVID-19 on its business, the ICO finally issued a penalty notice against Marriott for GBP 18.4 million.[132]

Although these initial notices of intent made headlines and indicated that the ICO was to be feared as a regulator with substantial financial penalty teeth, this image was somewhat undermined by the first penalty notice that it imposed in respect of a breach of the GDPR.

129 https://ico.org.uk/about-the-ico/news-and-events/news-and-blogs/2019/07/statement-intention-to-fine-marriott-international-inc-more-than-99-million-under-gdpr-for-data-breach/.

130 https://ico.org.uk/media/about-the-ico/disclosure-log/2616398/enq0889841-response.pdf.

131 www.mishcon.com/news/ico-agrees-delay-over-gdpr-fines-with-both-ba-and-marriott.

132 ICO Penalty Notice against Marriott International Inc: https://ico.org.uk/media/action-weve-taken/mpns/2618524/marriott-international-inc-mpn-20201030.pdf.

> Case Study
>
> On 17 December 2019, the ICO issued a penalty notice against Doorstep Dispensaree Ltd for GBP 275,000. The pharmacy, which supplies medicines to customers and care homes, left approximately 500,000 documents (including names, addresses, dates of birth, NHS numbers, medical information and prescriptions belonging to an unknown number of people) in unlocked containers at the back of its premises.[133] It should be noted that the pharmacy, unlike BA and Marriott, did not co-operate with the ICO's investigation, and the summary section of the penalty notice states that 'the Commissioner considers that the Breach was extremely serious, and demonstrates a cavalier attitude to data protection'.[134]
>
> Given this damning conclusion, one might have expected the penalty to be significantly higher than it was. However, the amount of the penalty must be viewed in light of the Information Commissioner's obligation to ensure that any administrative fines issued in accordance with Article 83 of the GDPR are effective, proportionate and dissuasive in each individual case[135] and, as the penalty notice states, 'The Commissioner has taken into account the size of Doorstep Dispensaree and the financial information that is available about the company on the Companies House website, as well as the representations that Doorstep Dispensaree has made to her about its financial position'.[136]

The extended negotiations between the ICO and BA and Marriott, and the 90% and 80% reductions in the final BA and Marriott penalties (respectively), also undermine the image that the ICO set with its notices of intent.

However, when considering the final BA penalty, it is important to note that the ICO used different methods to calculate the figures in the notice of intent and the final penalty notice. The fine proposed in the notice of intent was based on the ICO's Draft Internal Procedure, which provides a guide, by reference to the turnover of the controller, as to the appropriate penalty to be imposed. The ICO did not follow the Draft Internal Procedure when calculating the final BA fine, and the figure in the notice of intent was not taken as the starting point for the ICO's consideration of the penalty, nor did it factor into the consideration. Therefore, although turnover was considered in the calculation of the final penalty, unlike in the notice of intent, it was not used as the starting point to calculate the penalty.[137]

133 ICO Penalty Notice against Doorstep Dispensaree Ltd: https://ico.org.uk/media/action-weve-taken/mpns/2616742/doorstop-mpn-20191217.pdf,.
134 ICO Penalty Notice against Doorstep Dispensaree Ltd, at para 68.
135 GDPR, Article 83(1).
136 ICO Penalty Notice against Doorstep Dispensaree Ltd, at para 69.
137 ICO Penalty Notice against BA, paras 7.60–7.66.

The BA fine and its method of calculation should not, however, necessarily be taken as a sign of things to come regarding how the ICO will calculate financial penalties in the future. The ICO's recent Draft Statutory Guidance[138] uses turnover to calculate the appropriate starting point for a penalty. Therefore, future fines may be of a similar magnitude to the BA notice of intent. However, the Draft Statutory Guidance also says that, where a fine based on turnover exceeds the EUR 10 or 20 million limit, the ICO will cap the fine at the relevant limit. This therefore suggests that the 'whichever is higher' clauses may be meaningless, and that that highest fine that the ICO will impose is, actually, EUR 20 million.

Whilst the first three penalties for breach of the GDPR suggest how seriously the ICO takes its supervisory role and how it will hold individuals and companies to account for their actions, they also suggest that it will be the financial standing of the individual/company that will ultimately determine the amount of the penalty imposed. Therefore, large financially secure corporations, such as BA and Marriott, might be likely to pay more heavily for their breaches, even though those breaches may not be as serious as those committed by smaller organisations, and despite their co-operation with the ICO.

It should be noted that the ICO's authority to impose financial penalties in respect of breaches of the GDPR does not relate to the processing of personal data by a person in the course of a purely personal or household activity.[139] Therefore, the ICO has no jurisdiction over the publishing of personal information as a means of harassment; although recourse could be had to the ICO should a request be made to, for example, the website host where such information was published, to erase that personal data and the host refused to comply.

In such circumstances, ie where a website host refuses to comply with a request to erase personal data, recourse may also be had to the courts. Article 79(1) of the GDPR provides that, without prejudice to any available administrative or non-judicial remedy, including the right to lodge a complaint with a supervisory authority, each data subject has the right to an effective judicial remedy where they consider that their rights under the GDPR have been infringed as a result of the processing of their personal data in non-compliance with the GDPR. Where an individual seeks to enforce their rights by way of the courts, if the court is satisfied that there has been an infringement of an individual's rights, it may make an order to secure the data controller's compliance with the GDPR ('a compliance order')[140] and, where there has been material or non-material damage, the latter of which includes distress, the court may also make an order for compensation.[141]

138 ICO Draft Statutory Guidance on Our Regulatory Action: https://ico.org.uk/media/about-the-ico/consultations/2618333/ico-draft-statutory-guidance.pdf.

139 GDPR, Article 2(2)(c); DPA 2018, s 21(3).

140 DPA 2018, s 167.

141 GDPR, Article 82; DPA 2018, s 168.

Therefore, individuals have three ways of seeking a remedy under the GDPR in respect of the unauthorised processing of their personal data: by making a request to a data controller or processor directly; by lodging a complaint with a supervisory authority; or by seeking a remedy from the courts. It is, however, a complaint to the supervisory authority that is likely to have the most punitive effect on a data controller or processor, given the level of financial penalty that may be imposed.

Enforcement notices and penalty notices for breaches of the UK GDPR

9.31 The ICO's supervisory and regulatory role in relation to the GDPR, and the civil financial penalties that it can impose, is not going to vanish with Brexit.

Although the UK left the European Union ('EU') on 31 January 2020 ('Exit Day'), the Withdrawal Agreement provides for an Implementation Period until 31 December 2020. During the Implementation Period, the GDPR will continue to apply in the UK as if it were a Member State.[142]

The EUWA 2018 (as amended by the European Union (Withdrawal Agreement) Act 2020) provides that EU-derived domestic legislation existing before 'IP completion day' (Implementation Period Completion Day, ie 11:00pm on 31 December 2020)[143] continues to have effect in domestic law on and after 'IP completion day',[144] and that any direct EU legislation (including EU Regulations that are applicable to the UK by virtue of Part 4 (Transition) of the Withdrawal Agreement) operative immediately before 'IP completion day' forms part of domestic law on and after 'IP completion day'[145] ('retained EU law').

Thus, the GDPR will become part of the UK's domestic law following the Implementation Period ('the Retained GDPR').

However, retained EU law, including the Retained GDPR, will contain deficiencies arising out of the UK's exit from the EU, either because provisions relate to reciprocal arrangements or are otherwise redundant upon exit from the EU, or because there are references to EU instruments which are no longer appropriate. Therefore, amendments will need to be made to the Retained GDPR in order to correct these deficiencies, to ensure that the law continues to function effectively following the Implementation Period.

142 Agreement on the Withdrawal of the United Kingdom of Great Britain and Northern Ireland from the European Union and the European Atomic Energy Community (19 October 2019), Part Four, Articles 126 and 127: https://assets.publishing.service.gov.uk/government/uploads/system/uploads/attachment_data/file/840655/Agreement_on_the_withdrawal_of_the_United_Kingdom_of_Great_Britain_and_Northern_Ireland_from_the_European_Union_and_the_European_Atomic_Energy_Community.pdf.

143 European Union (Withdrawal Agreement) Act 2020, s 39(1).

144 EUWA 2018, s 2(1) (prospective), as amended by the European Union (Withdrawal Agreement) Act 2020, s 25(1) (prospective).

145 EUWA 2018, s 3(1)–(2)(a) (prospective), as amended by the European Union (Withdrawal Agreement) Act 2020, s 25(2)(a)–(b) (prospective).

These amendments are made by the Data Protection, Privacy and Electronic Communications (Amendments etc) (EU Exit) Regulations 2019 ('the 2019 Regulations').[146] Subject to a few exceptions, the 2019 Regulations come into force on IP Completion Day[147] and amend the Retained GDPR for a domestic UK context – for example, by using domestic language, transferring functions conferred on the European Commission by the GDPR to the Secretary of State and/or the Information Commissioner, and omitting the provisions regarding co-operation and consistency between Member States. The 2019 Regulations will also amend the Retained GDPR so that it includes not only the GDPR provisions as supplemented by Chapter 2 of Part 2 of the DPA 2018 but also the regime as established by Chapter 3 of Part 2 of the DPA 2018 (currently termed the 'applied GDPR'), which is currently outside the scope of the GDPR. Thus the 2019 Regulations create a new single regime for general processing activities: the UK GDPR.

In almost all other respects, the 2019 Regulations do not substantially amend the Retained GDPR, and so the UK GDPR will maintain the data protection standards for data processing that currently exist in the UK under the GDPR and DPA 2018.[148]

In terms of remedies and penalties, the provisions of the UK GDPR will mirror those of the GDPR (including the Article numbers), albeit that the language will be amended for a UK domestic context, and the monetary penalties will be in GBP rather than EUR. Thus, Article 83 of the UK GDPR will provide that the maximum penalty that can be issued is, depending on the provision infringed, either:

- GBP 8,700,000 or, in the case of an undertaking, up to 2% of the total worldwide annual turnover of the preceding financial year, whichever is higher; or
- GBP 17,500,000 or, in the case of an undertaking, up to 4% of the total worldwide annual turnover of the preceding financial year, whichever is higher.

As can be seen from these provisions, there will be no relaxation in terms of compliance and enforcement after the Implementation Period, and non-compliance will still entail severe penalties.

146 SI 2019/419.

147 Data Protection, Privacy and Electronic Communications (Amendments etc) (EU Exit) Regulations 2019, reg 1(2), as amended by European Union (Withdrawal Agreement) Act 2020, Sch 5, Pt 1, para 1(1).

148 Note, however, that there will be a key difference between the UK GDPR and the GDPR in terms of the rules relating to the cross-border transfer of personal data. This is likely to become an incredibly important area of cyber litigation, but a discussion of this topic is outside the scope of this chapter. For a discussion, see **Chapter 5**.

Increasing the powers of the ICO

9.32 On 8 November 2019, the Information Commissioner opened a consultation on the ICO being granted access to investigation and other associated powers under POCA 2002.[149]

The powers that the ICO is seeking are:

- to apply to the court for restraint orders (under Part 2 of POCA 2002);
- to apply to the court for confiscation orders (under Part 2 of POCA 2002);
- cash seizure, detention and forfeiture from premises (under Part 5, Chapter 3 of POCA 2002);
- asset seizure and forfeiture from premises (under Part 5, Chapter 3A of POCA 2002);
- to undertake investigations (including search and seizure warrants) to support the proceedings sought above (under Part 8 of POCA 2002); and
- access to information relevant to the investigation of money laundering.

The ICO is also seeking relevant authorisation powers that will enable it to exercise the powers outlined above.

The rationale behind the consultation and seeking these powers is that personal data has monetary value and is increasingly being recognised and treated as a commodity which is stolen and traded for financial gain. Although the GDPR introduced financial penalties for civil breaches of the DPA 2018, and criminal offences under the DPA 2018 are now recordable, the only sanction for criminal offences under the DPA 2018 is a fine. Thus, there is an imbalance between the sanctions for civil and criminal breaches of the DPA 2018, which causes disparity between the deterrent and punitive effects of the sanctions.

The powers that the ICO is seeking will enable it to undertake confiscation investigations and apply to the court for restraint of any asset or realisable property when there is evidence to show that a defendant in criminal proceedings has benefited from their conduct. The powers sought in relation to seizure and forfeiture of cash and assets will enable the ICO to investigate and recover items that are derived from or intended for use in criminal conduct. The ICO will also be able to access information relevant to the investigation of money laundering offences, enabling it to respond to the changing nature of criminal activity involving the misuse of personal data, and to engage with other law enforcement agencies more effectively in cases which may involve offences of money laundering.

149 https://ico.org.uk/about-the-ico/ico-and-stakeholder-consultations/ico-call-for-views-on-the-application-for-powers-under-the-poca/.

There are, however, additional practical reasons for the ICO seeking these powers. First, these powers would provide the ICO with a tactical advantage during investigations as, through restraint proceedings, subjects of the investigations would no longer have access to potentially significant sums, alleged to be connected with misconduct, to fund their defence. Secondly, under the UK Government's Asset Recovery Incentivisation Scheme, law enforcement authorities and prosecutors each receive 18.75% of confiscated assets, so it is likely that the ICO would wish to participate in the scheme.[150]

The consultation proposes that there will be one Accredited Financial Investigator based within the ICO's Investigations Department who will consider asset recovery in all cases where offenders have benefited from criminal conduct.

The consultation closed on 6 December 2019. At the time of writing, it is unclear how the ICO is proceeding in light of the responses that it received.

However, this consultation is a clear statement of intent from the ICO in terms of its commitment to, and its strengthening of, its regulatory, investigatory and prosecutorial role. It recognises that there is real value in personal data, and seeks to redress the imbalance between civil and criminal sanctions and provide a deterrent to those who would unlawfully obtain and sell personal data. There is, however, still the potential problem of the anonymity and/or pseudonymity of offenders, and so it will inevitably be easier to investigate and fine corporates who have had their systems hacked etc and failed to keep personal data safe. Therefore, it is likely that, should these powers be given to the ICO, it will not be using them against individuals responsible for the big headline cyberattacks, because the ICO will not be able to identify them. Instead, the powers will more likely be focused on those individuals who commit smaller-scale cyberattacks. Whether that will, in fact, have a deterrent effect on the individuals who commit the bigger cyberattacks in order to obtain and sell personal data will remain to be seen. However, what is clear is that the ICO is seeking to establish and position itself alongside the National Crime Agency and Crown Prosecution Service in the fight against cyber-dependent and cyber-assisted crimes.

SHOULD THE COURTS AND REGULATORS DEVELOP NEW REMEDIES FOR CYBER LITIGATION?

9.33 It is not clear if, or to what extent, the criminal courts and law enforcement authorities have turned their minds to how they are going to deal with particular aspects of cyber litigation, but the civil courts and regulators seem willing (and, in the case of the ICO, eager) to extend the ambit of current remedies in order to provide redress in cyber cases. However, can, or should, the courts and

150 'UK Information Commissioner's Office seeks further criminal powers', Ropes & Gray Alert, 2 December 2019: www.ropesgray.com/en/newsroom/alerts/2019/12/UK-Information-Commissioners-Office-seeks-further-criminal-powers.

regulators seek to provide completely new remedies for cyber disputes, rather than extending the scope of old ones?

The jurisprudence from the civil courts is showing that the courts are ready, willing and able to adapt and develop existing remedies to cyber cases. Website blocking injunctions can be sought to block any website where rights are infringed. Thus, not only can perpetrators of, for example, deepfake revenge pornography potentially be prosecuted under the criminal law, individuals can also have recourse to the civil courts to block access to that material. Proprietary and freezing injunctions can be sought to protect people's cryptoassets where they are the victim of fraud, theft, blackmail etc, and not only can civil claims be brought against the perpetrators, it might also be possible to prosecute them under the criminal law. Therefore, the combination of civil law and criminal law working together, addressing different aspects of cyber cases and cyber litigation, provides an arsenal of remedies.

Admittedly, there are some practical considerations that still need to be addressed, and there will be circumstances where the courts will not be able to provide an adequate remedy. Information, once out in the world, will always be out there, somewhere, and there may be no way to detect where it is or who controls it. Where this is the case, the best that can be done is to mitigate the consequences as far as possible through the remedies available.

Additionally, as can be seen from the above in relation to smart contracts, there may be circumstances where completely new remedies are required: despite the UKJT's Legal Statement, it is difficult to see how traditional contract law remedies could be applied to smart contracts. It is the author's submission, however, that, where new remedies are developed for cyber litigation, they will be heavily based on existing remedies and legal principles, and it will just be their application that will be adjusted for the novel and unique 'cyber' aspects of the cases.

The common law of England and Wales has been adapting and evolving for centuries, meeting and addressing the new technological and social changes that time has thrown at it. In this new dawn of cyber litigation, the courts are showing themselves ready to meet the coming challenges and are adapting their current arsenal of remedies to address cyber cases. As more cyber cases come before the courts, the author believes that, rather than developing new cyber-specific remedies, the current practice and trajectory of adaptation and amendment are likely to continue.

Chapter 10

Alternatives to Litigation

> This chapter considers:
>
> - the options available to law enforcement agencies when they do not want to, or cannot, prosecute individuals and corporates for cyber-assisted and cyber-dependent crimes;
> - the options available to parties who do not want to submit their civil 'cyber' disputes to potentially protracted litigation in the courts; and
> - new forms of dispute resolution which, rather than settling 'cyber' disputes, focus on using 'cyber' and technology in order to resolve ordinary disputes.

INTRODUCTION

10.1 Sometimes, litigation is not the most appropriate way to resolve a 'cyber' case. Prosecutors either cannot, or do not want to, prosecute individuals – for example, young children who have hacked their way into a game – or parties do not want to submit their 'cyber' disputes to potentially protracted court litigation.

There are several options available to law enforcement authorities and parties in such circumstances, and parties to civil 'cyber' disputes need not necessarily be confined to these options: to combat and address a changing cyber world, parties may look to amend and adapt the current options and agree these amended and/or adapted processes in their contracts etc.

Not only are there alternatives to criminal and civil 'cyber' litigation, but technology is also giving rise to new forms of dispute resolution which, rather than focusing on settling 'cyber' disputes, use 'cyber' and technology in order to resolve ordinary, everyday disputes.

WHAT ARE THE ALTERNATIVES TO CRIMINAL PROSECUTIONS IN 'CYBER' CASES?

National Cyber Crime Unit's Prevent programme

10.2 The National Cyber Crime Unit ('NCCU') is part of the National Crime Agency ('NCA'), and is responsible for the NCA's Prevent programme.

The Prevent programme is aimed at preventing young people from getting involved, or becoming more involved, in cybercrime. It specifically focuses on cyber-dependent crimes (or 'pure' cybercrimes) (see **Chapter 2** for a full discussion in relation to these) – for example, gaining unauthorised access into a computer network ('hacking'), developing malware, 'pranking' (remotely accessing a computer and messing around), and carrying out a Distributed Denial of Service ('DDoS') or 'booting' (kicking someone off the internet).[1]

Those conducting the vast majority of low, entry-level cyber-dependent crimes – hacking, booting, pranking – are not your archetypal criminal: they are often children kicking their friends offline during gaming sessions, remotely accessing a friend's computer in order to prank them, or hacking into gaming systems in order to cheat and make progress through a game. At first blush, these may seem like innocuous actions – things that anyone learning to code might do – but they are all offences under the Computer Misuse Act 1990 ('CMA 1990'), and the NCA's concern is that such actions are routes into further criminality. The individuals start with gaming, booting and pranking, and find online gaming communities and forums; they build an online profile, become part of a community, and make online social connections. They have an unfettered ability to learn and develop and, as they do so, they come across other forums and communities that are promoting and encouraging other 'challenges' (eg hacking into a bank's computer network), and there is no online intervention stating that the completion of such 'challenges' are criminal offences.[2]

The NCA lacks the resources to investigate these low, entry-level matters.[3] Even if they did have the resources, prosecution provides its own problems. Putting to one side the question as to whether the prosecution of such matters passes the public interest stage of the Full Code Test (that is, the test that prosecutors must apply when deciding whether or not to prosecute a matter: whether there is sufficient evidence to provide a realistic prospect of conviction (the evidential stage), and whether a prosecution is in the public interest (the public interest stage)), the offenders often have significant mitigation – age, immaturity, lack of awareness of the consequences of their actions – but the sentencing powers lack rehabilitative options. For example, hacking into a United States ('US') bank's computer system 'for fun' could result in extradition to the US and a Federal prison sentence.

The Prevent programme tries to 'deter, divert, degrade and disrupt' young people from cybercrime by encouraging them to look at organisations that can assist them to develop their cyber skills and encouraging them to consider careers in cyber security. By seeking to understand the behaviour and characteristics of individuals committing cyber-dependent crimes, the NCCU tries to identify individuals who are already involved, and possible offenders, so that the Prevent

1 www.nationalcrimeagency.gov.uk/what-we-do/crime-threats/cyber-crime/cyber-crime-preventing-young-people-from-getting-involved.

2 'Cyber Prevent: Deter, Divert, Degrade, Disrupt', Greg Francis, National Crime Agency, presented at the Cambridge Cybercrime Conference, 11 July 2019.

3 'Cyber Prevent: Deter, Divert, Degrade, Disrupt', Greg Francis, National Crime Agency, presented at the Cambridge Cybercrime Conference, 11 July 2019.

team can intervene and give individuals the opportunity to make informed choices and, ultimately, the option of avoiding prosecution.

Under the programme, the NCA has undertaken:[4]

- Cease and Desist visits to individuals that it has identified as being involved in entry-level cyber-dependent crimes. These visits are in order to raise the awareness, both of the individuals and the parents, as to what actions are illegal and the risks and consequences of such actions. By raising awareness, these visits also nullify any mitigation arguments about 'lack of awareness of the consequences of their actions' in a future prosecution.
- An online 'Cyber Choices' campaign, whereby it sought to educate parents, educators and children about the law around using computers online and the opportunities available to those with cyber skills.
- Positive Diversions Workshops, which are intervention days for offenders and possible offenders that outline the cybercrime legislation, the consequences of becoming involved in cybercrime and the educational and employment opportunities that use the same skills.

Part of the Prevent programme seeks to provide education about cybercrime in schools, with lesson plans and interactive games to teach children about the CMA 1990. The programme also tries to encourage the private sector to be socially responsible and to set up local coding clubs and provide employment opportunities for children with cyber skills; the NCA's thinking being that, when these children grow up, they will then choose to join these businesses in the private sector rather than pursuing cybercrime.

The Prevent programme has a noble aim, and the NCA wants to avoid prosecuting children for low, entry-level offences. However, until young people are adequately educated about cybercrime, they are unlikely to become aware of the illegality, risks and consequences of their actions, nor the opportunities that are available to them to hone and employ their skills legally.

Serious Crime Prevention Orders

10.3 Serious Crime Prevention Orders ('SCPOs') were created by Part 1 of the Serious Crime Act 2007 ('SCA 2007') and are a civil injunctive order aimed at preventing serious crime and protecting the public by preventing, restricting or disrupting involvement in serious crime.[5] They can be imposed on individuals

4 'Cyber Prevent: Deter, Divert, Degrade, Disrupt', Greg Francis, National Crime Agency, presented at the Cambridge Cybercrime Conference, 11 July 2019.

5 Explanatory Notes to the SCA 2007, paras 3 and 14: www.legislation.gov.uk/ukpga/2007/27/pdfs/ukpgaen_20070027_en.pdf.

over the age of 18 or corporate entities,[6] and they may also be imposed against officers and employees of entities.[7]

There are two ways in which an SCPO may be imposed:

- on an application to the High Court[8] (which is the main route for obtaining an order);[9] or
- on an application in the Crown Court following a conviction for a serious offence.[10]

As this chapter is concerned with alternatives to litigation, this section will focus on obtaining an SCPO by way of an application to the High Court. It should be noted that the Crown Prosecution Service ('CPS') Guidance on SCPOs states that an SCPO should generally only be made either following a conviction for a serious offence or, following a decision that, applying the Code for Crown Prosecutors, the evidence available does not provide a realistic prospect of conviction or a prosecution would not be in the public interest, for reasons other than the availability of an SCPO. The guidance states that it will usually be in the public interest to prosecute a person for a specified serious crime[11] and, during the passage of the Serious Crime Bill, the government stated that SCPOs were not intended, and would not be used, as a 'soft alternative to prosecution ... there has been much mistaken comment about these orders being a way for law enforcement agencies to get round troublesome prosecutions ... that is not the intention'.[12] However, it should also be noted that, as their name suggests, SCPOs are designed to be preventative as opposed to punitive.

An application to the High Court for an SCPO is governed by Part 77 of the Civil Procedure Rules. In relation to proceedings in England and Wales (the SCA 2007 contains corresponding provisions for applications for SCPOs in Scotland and Northern Ireland), only the Director of Public Prosecutions and the Director of the Serious Fraud Office may make an application for an SCPO,[13] which must be made on notice in order to allow for representations from affected third parties.[14]

An SCPO does not levy financial penalties but may contain such targeted prohibitions, restrictions or requirements as the court considers appropriate for the purpose of protecting the public by preventing, restricting or disrupting involvement in serious crime.[15] Failing to comply with an SCPO is a criminal offence, and a person guilty of such an offence will be liable on summary

6 SCA 2007, ss 5 and 6.
7 SCA 2007, ss 30(3), 31(10) and 32(9).
8 SCA 2007, s 1(1).
9 Explanatory Notes to the SCA 2007, para 54.
10 SCA 2007, s 19(1)–(2).
11 www.cps.gov.uk/legal-guidance/serious-crime-prevention-orders.
12 Baroness Scotland, 7 February 2007, Hansard HL, Volume 689.
13 SCA 2007, s 8.
14 SCA 2007, s 9.
15 SCA 2007, s 1(3).

conviction to a sentence of 12 months' imprisonment, or a fine not exceeding the statutory maximum, or both; and, on conviction on indictment, to five years' imprisonment, or a fine, or both.[16]

What are the conditions for imposing an SCPO?

10.4 The High Court may make an SCPO on an application by the Director of Public Prosecutions or the Director of the Serious Fraud Office if:[17]

> '(a) it is satisfied that a person has been involved in a serious crime (whether in England or Wales or elsewhere); and
>
> (b) it has reasonable grounds to believe that the order would protect the public by preventing, restricting or disrupting involvement by the person in serious crime in England and Wales.'

Section 2(1) of the SCA 2007 provides that a person has been involved in a serious crime in England and Wales if he:

> '(a) has committed a serious offence in England and Wales;
>
> (b) has facilitated the commission by another person of a serious offence in England or Wales; or
>
> (c) has conducted himself in a way that was likely to facilitate the commission by himself or another person of a serious offence in England and Wales (whether or not such an offence was committed).'

A 'serious offence in England and Wales' is an offence specified in Part 1 of Schedule 1 to the SCA 2007, or one which, in the particular circumstances of the case, the court considers to be sufficiently serious to be treated for the purposes of the application or matter as if it were so specified.[18]

Section 2(4) provides that a person has been involved in a serious crime elsewhere than in England and Wales if he:

> '(a) has committed a serious offence in a country outside England and Wales;
>
> (b) has facilitated the commission by another person of a serious offence in a country outside England and Wales; or
>
> (c) has conducted himself in a way that was likely to facilitate the commission by himself or another person of a serious offence in a country outside England and Wales (whether or not such an offence was committed).'

A 'serious offence in a country outside England and Wales' means an offence under the law of a country outside England and Wales which, at the time when the court is considering the application, would be an offence under the law of England and Wales if committed in England and Wales; and either (i) would be an

16 SCA 2007, s 25.
17 SCA 2007, s 1(1).
18 SCA 2007, s 2(2).

offence which is specified in Part 1 of Schedule 1 to the SCA 2007 if committed in or as regards England and Wales; or (ii) is conduct which, in the particular circumstances of the case, the court considers to be sufficiently serious to be treated for the purposes of the application or matter as if it were so specified.[19]

Where a person has been convicted of a serious offence and the conviction has not been quashed on appeal, the High Court *must* find that the person has committed a serious offence; but the court must not otherwise decide that the person has committed the offence.[20] In considering whether the person has facilitated the commission of a serious offence, or conducts himself in a way likely to facilitate the commission of a serious offence, the court must ignore any act that the person can show was reasonable in the circumstances and, subject to this, also ignore their intentions or any other aspect of their mental state at the time.[21]

The High Court applies the civil standard of proof when considering the imposition of an SCPO.[22] However, the Explanatory Notes to the SCA 2007 make reference to *R (McCann) v Crown Court at Manchester*,[23] where the House of Lords held that, although the civil standard of proof would apply in relation to an application for an anti-social behaviour order, the standard is a flexible one, ranging from proof on the balance of probabilities (at the lowest level) to beyond reasonable doubt (at the highest). The House of Lords stated that they would expect a high standard of proof to be applied in relation to anti-social behaviour order applications, particularly in relation to whether a person has acted in an anti-social manner. Paragraph 122 of the Explanatory Notes to the SCA 2007 states that the same principle is likely to apply in relation to applications for SCPOs, and the CPS Guidance on SCPOs says that 'It must be anticipated that the same standard will apply in proceedings for a SCPO, where the consequences may be even more restrictive and severe'.[24]

Whether there are reasonable grounds to believe that the order would protect the public by preventing, restricting or disrupting involvement in serious crime in England and Wales is not an issue of disputed fact, but one of judgement and an assessment of future risk. There must be a real, or significant, risk (as opposed to a bare possibility) that the person will commit, or be involved in, further serious offences.[25]

In considering this question, 'involvement by the person in serious crime in England and Wales' is defined in section 2(3) as any one or more of the following:

> '(a) the commission of a serious offence in England and Wales;
>
> (b) conduct which facilitates the commission by another person of a serious offence in England and Wales;

19 SCA 2007, s 2(5).
20 SCA 2007, s 4(1).
21 SCA 2007, s 4(2)–(3).
22 SCA 2007, ss 35(2) and 36(2).
23 [2002] UKHL 39.
24 www.cps.gov.uk/legal-guidance/serious-crime-prevention-orders.
25 *R v Hancox and Duffy* [2010] EWCA Crim 102 at [9].

(c) conduct which is likely to facilitate the commission, by the person whose conduct it is or another person, of a serious offence in England and Wales (whether or not such an offence is committed).'

What are the 'serious offences' in respect of which an SCPO may be made?

10.5 Part 1 of Schedule 1 to the SCA 2007 lists the 'serious offences in England and Wales' in respect of which an SCPO may be made. It includes the following cyber-assisted and cyber-dependent crimes mentioned in **Chapter 2**:

- drug trafficking;[26]
- slavery;[27]
- terrorism;[28]
- firearms offences;[29]
- money laundering;[30]
- fraud;[31]
- bribery;[32]
- computer misuse;[33] and
- financial sanctions legislation.[34]

It also applies to various offences under the Copyright, Designs and Patents Act 1988 and the Trade Marks Act 1994 (intellectual property),[35] and an offence under section 45 of the Serious Crime Act 2015 (organised crime).[36]

The definition of a 'serious offence' has been extended to include the corresponding inchoate offences,[37] the offence of encouraging and assisting,[38] and offences which fall within the descriptions but were offences under preceding legislation at the time of the conduct concerned.[39]

It is worth repeating here that the offences specified in Part 1 of Schedule 1 to the SCA 2007 are not an exhaustive list, as the High Court may also impose an

26 SCA 2007, Sch 1, Pt 1, para 1.
27 SCA 2007, Sch 1, Pt 1, para 1A.
28 SCA 2007, Sch 1, Pt 1, para 2A.
29 SCA 2007, Sch 1, Pt 1, para 3.
30 SCA 2007, Sch 1, Pt 1, para 6.
31 SCA 2007, Sch 1, Pt 1, para 7.
32 SCA 2007, Sch 1, Pt 1, para 9.
33 SCA 2007, Sch 1, Pt 1, para 11A.
34 SCA 2007, Sch 1, Pt 1, para 13B.
35 SCA 2007, Sch 1, Pt 1, para 12.
36 SCA 2007, Sch 1, Pt 1, para 13A.
37 SCA 2007, Sch 1, Pt 1, para 14.
38 SCA 2007, Pt 2.
39 SCA 2007, Sch 1, Pt 1, para 15.

SCPO if, in the particular circumstances of the case, it considers that an offence is sufficiently serious to be treated, for the purposes of the application, as if it were specified in Part 1 of Schedule 1.[40] Therefore, the extension of SCPOs to serious cyber-assisted and cyber-dependent crimes is something that has already been considered by the legislators, and is a real possibility.

What are the types of provision that may be made by an SCPO and what is the duration of an SCPO?

10.6 An SCPO may contain any such prohibitions, restrictions or requirements, and any such other terms, as the court considers appropriate for the purpose of protecting the public by preventing, restricting or disrupting involvement by the person concerned in serious crime in England and Wales.[41]

Section 5 of the SCA 2007 lists various types of provision that may be made by orders, which include prohibitions or restrictions on, or requirements in relation to:

- financial, property or business dealings or holdings;
- working arrangements;
- the means by which an individual communicates or associates with others, or the person/s with whom he communicates or associates;
- access to premises;
- use of premises or an item;
- travel;
- the provision of goods or services;
- employment of staff; and
- the types of agreement to which such persons may be a party.

An SCPO cannot require a person:

- to answer questions, or provide information, orally;[42]
- to answer questions, or provide information or documents, which are covered by legal professional privilege;[43]
- to produce excluded material as defined by section 11 of the Police and Criminal Evidence Act 1984;[44]

40 SCA 2007, s 2(2)(b).
41 SCA 2007, s 1(3).
42 SCA 2007, s 11.
43 SCA 2007, s 12.
44 SCA 2007, s 13(1)(a).

- to disclose any information or produce any document held by them in confidence by virtue of carrying on a banking business, unless:
  - there is consent from the person to whom confidence is owed; or
  - the order specifically requires disclosure of information or documents of this kind, or it requires disclosure of specified information or documents of this kind;[45]
- to provide information or documents or answer questions if it would involve a disclosure prohibited by another enactment.[46]

SCPOs can only be made for the purpose for which the power was given by statute (ie they are designed to be preventative rather than punitive), and the provisions interfering with a person's freedom must be necessary and proportionate to the risk posed.[47] The provisions must also be enforceable[48] and relate to the specific facts of the case.[49] Prohibitions and restrictions are not limited to England and Wales and can extend outside the jurisdiction,[50] but they must be aimed at preventing, restricting or disrupting involvement in serious crime in England and Wales.[51]

An SCPO must specify when it is to come into force, and when it is to cease to be in force, and it cannot be in force for more than five years.[52] Applications may be made to vary[53] or discharge[54] SCPOs, and an appeal against an SCPO made by the High Court may be made to the Court of Appeal (Civil Division).[55]

Deferred Prosecution Agreements

10.7 Deferred Prosecution Agreements ('DPAs') were created by section 45 of, and Schedule 17 to, the Crime and Courts Act 2013 ('CCA 2013') as a new tool to tackle financial and economic crime.[56] The DPA provisions were brought into force on 24 February 2014 by the Crime and Courts Act 2013 (Commencement No 8) Order 2014.[57]

45 SCA 2007, s 13(2)–(4).
46 SCA 2007, s 14.
47 *R v Hancox and Duffy* [2010] EWCA Crim 102, at [10].
48 *R v Barnes and Orford* [2012] EWCA Crim 2549.
49 *R v Seale* [2014] EWCA Crim 650.
50 SCA 2007, s 5(2).
51 SCA 2007, s 1(3).
52 SCA 2007, s 16(1)–(2).
53 SCA 2007, s 17.
54 SCA 2007, s 18.
55 SCA 2007, s 23.
56 Explanatory Notes to the CCA 2013, paras 9 and 59: www.legislation.gov.uk/ukpga/2013/22/pdfs/ukpgaen_20130022_en.pdf.
57 SI 2014/258.

A DPA is a court-approved agreement between a body corporate, partnership or unincorporated association (not an individual)[58] and a designated prosecutor who is considering prosecuting the entity for one of the economic or financial offences specified in Part 2 of Schedule 17 to the CCA 2013.[59] Under a DPA, rather than being subject to a formal criminal prosecution, the corporate entity agrees to comply with a range of requirements and the prosecutor agrees that, upon approval of the DPA by the court, it will institute but then immediately suspend the criminal proceedings for the alleged offence.[60]

The DPA must specify an expiry date[61] and, if the entity has satisfactorily complied with all the requirements contained in the DPA by that date, the prosecutor will give notice to the Crown Court that it is discontinuing the criminal proceedings[62] and the matter is concluded without prosecution. If, however, during the currency of the DPA the prosecutor believes that the entity has failed to comply with the terms, it can apply to the court to determine, on the balance of probabilities, whether the entity has so failed to comply.[63] If the court makes such a finding, it can invite further agreed proposals to remedy the failure to comply, or it may terminate the DPA.[64] If the DPA is terminated, the prosecutor may apply to have the suspension of the indictment lifted, and the original prosecution proceedings may be commenced against the entity.[65]

Although the CCA 2013 makes provision for the Secretary of State to appoint other designated prosecutors, at present, the only designated prosecutors who can enter into DPAs are the Director of Public Prosecutions and the Director of the Serious Fraud Office.[66] Therefore, DPAs are only currently available to corporate entities being investigated and prosecuted in England and Wales (as opposed to the availability of SCPOs, which have corresponding provisions for Scotland and Northern Ireland).

What are the offences for which a DPA may be entered into?

10.8 Part 2 of Schedule 17 to the CCA 2013 lists the offences for which a DPA may be entered into. It includes the following cyber-assisted crimes mentioned in **Chapter 2**:

- common law conspiracy to defraud;[67]
- theft;[68]

58 CCA 2013, Sch 17, Pt 1, para 4(1).
59 CCA 2013, Sch 17, Pt 1, para 1(1).
60 CCA 2013, Sch 17, Pt 1, paras 1(2) and 2.
61 CCA 2013, Sch 17, Pt 1, para 5(2).
62 CCA 2013, Sch 17, Pt 1, para 11(1).
63 CCA 2013, Sch 17, Pt 1, para 9(1)–(2).
64 CCA 2013, Sch 17, Pt 1, para 9(3).
65 CCA 2013, Sch 17, Pt 1, para 2(3); DPA Code, paras 12.5 and 12.7–12.10.
66 CCA 2013, Sch 17, Pt 1, para 3(1).
67 CCA 2013, Sch 17, Pt 2, para 15.
68 CCA 2013, Sch 17, Pt 2, para 17(a).

- money laundering and terrorist financing;[69]
- fraud;[70]
- bribery;[71] and
- financial sanctions legislation.[72]

The offences for which a DPA may be entered into also include the corresponding inchoate offences,[73] the offence of encouraging and assisting under Part 2 of the SCA 2007,[74] and offences under preceding legislation which correspond to those listed in Part 2 of Schedule 17.[75]

How to enter into DPA negotiations?

10.9 Officially, a DPA can only begin when a designated prosecutor invites a corporate entity under investigation to enter into negotiations to agree a DPA as an alternative to prosecution.[76] In practice, however, corporate entities and their legal representatives can contact the designated prosecutor and propose entering into negotiations to agree a DPA.

In order to enter into DPA negotiations, the designated prosecutor must apply the two-stage test as set out in the Deferred Prosecution Agreements Code of Practice ('DPA Code'),[77] which was issued by the Director of Public Prosecutions and Director of the Serious Fraud Office pursuant to paragraph 6(1) of Part 1 of Schedule 17 to the CCA 2013.[78]

The designated prosecutor must first apply the evidential stage and be satisfied that:

- either the evidential stage of the Full Code Test in the Code for Crown Prosecutors (that is, there is sufficient evidence to provide a realistic prospect of conviction) is satisfied; or:
- if that is not met, there is at least a reasonable suspicion based on some admissible evidence that the company has committed the offence, and there are reasonable grounds for believing that a continued investigation would

69 CCA 2013, Sch 17, Pt 2, paras 23, 27 and 27A.
70 CCA 2013, Sch 17, Pt 2, para 25.
71 CCA 2013, Sch 17, Pt 2, para 26.
72 CCA 2013, Sch 17, Pt 2, para 26A.
73 CCA 2013, Sch 17, Pt 2, paras 28 and 29(a) and (c).
74 CCA 2013, Sch 17, Pt 2, para 29(b).
75 CCA 2013, Sch 17, Pt 2, para 30.
76 DPA Code, para 2.1.
77 DPA Code, para 1.2.
78 www.cps.gov.uk/sites/default/files/documents/publications/dpa_cop.pdf. Note that, on 23 October 2020, the Serious Fraud Office also published its chapter on DPAs from its Operational Handbook in order to offer 'comprehensive guidance on how we approach DPAs, and how we engage with companies where a DPA is a prospective outcome': www.sfo.gov.uk/publications/guidance-policy-and-protocols/sfo-operational-handbook/deferred-prosecution-agreements/.

provide further admissible evidence within a reasonable period of time, so that all the evidence together would be capable of establishing a realistic prospect of conviction in accordance with the Full Code Test.

If the evidential stage is met, the designated prosecutor moves on to the second stage – the public interest test – and must determine whether or not the public interest would be properly served by not prosecuting the entity but by entering into a DPA instead. The more serious the offence, the more likely it is that a prosecution rather than a DPA will be required in order to satisfy the public interest test. Indicators of seriousness include not just the value of any gain or loss, but also the risk of harm to the public, unidentified victims, shareholders, employees and creditors. Seriousness is also indicated by the risk of harm to the stability and integrity of financial markets and international trade, and the impact of the offending in other countries will also be taken into account.[79] A prosecution will usually take place unless there are public interest factors against prosecution which clearly outweigh those tending in favour of prosecution.[80] Paragraphs 2.8.1 and 2.8.2 of the DPA Code outline various additional public interest factors in favour of, and against, prosecution (respectively).

If the designated prosecutor is satisfied that the evidential and public interest stages are met, and that the full extent of the alleged offending has been identified,[81] they may initiate DPA negotiations by way of a formal letter of invitation, which offers the entity the opportunity to enter into DPA negotiations and outlines the timeframe in which it must respond to the invitation.[82] However, even if the test is met, the designated prosecutor is not obliged to invite an entity to enter into DPA negotiations, and an entity is under no obligation to accept such an invitation in the event that it is made.[83] If the entity agrees to engage in DPA negotiations, the designated prosecutor will send a further letter setting out the way in which discussions will be conducted and outlining various undertakings as to confidentiality.[84]

In the event that the test is not met, the designated prosecutor must decide whether to continue with or abandon the criminal investigation and, in the latter case, if the evidential stage has not been met at the conclusion of any DPA negotiations, the prosecutor should consider whether a Civil Recovery Order is appropriate.[85]

What happens during DPA negotiations?

10.10 The DPA negotiations must be transparent and all meetings minuted and agreed. The designated prosecutor must ensure that a full and accurate written

79 DPA Code, para 2.4.
80 DPA Code, para 2.5.
81 DPA Code, para 2.2.
82 DPA Code, para 3.5.
83 DPA Code, para 3.3.
84 DPA Code, paras 3.6–3.11.
85 DPA Code, para 1.7.

record is kept of every key action and event in the negotiation process, including details of every offer or concession made by each party, and the reasons for every decision taken by the prosecutor. The designated prosecutor must also ensure that both parties have obtained sufficient information from each other so that each can play an informed part in the negotiations,[86] and it must always be alive to the potential need to disclose material in the interests of justice and fairness in the particular circumstances of any case.[87]

The negotiation process is intended to create an agreement that contains an agreed statement of facts relating to the alleged offence, outlines the requirements to be imposed on the entity and an expiry date.[88] The requirements must be fair, reasonable and proportionate to the offence.[89] Paragraph 5(3) of Part 1 of Schedule 17 to the CCA 2013 provides a non-exhaustive list of possible requirements that may be imposed under a DPA:

'(a) to pay to the prosecutor a financial penalty;

(b) to compensate victims of the alleged offence;

(c) to donate money to a charity or other third party;

(d) to disgorge any profits made by the entity from the alleged offence;

(e) to implement a compliance programme or make changes to an existing compliance programme relating to the entity's policies or to the training of its employees or both;

(f) to co-operate in any investigation related to the alleged offence;

(g) to pay any reasonable costs of the prosecutor in relation to the alleged offence or the DPA.'

If an entity provides inaccurate, misleading or incomplete information during the negotiations, where it knew or ought to have known that the information was inaccurate, misleading or incomplete, the designated prosecutor may instigate fresh proceedings against the entity for the same alleged offence, notwithstanding any DPA that may have been approved.[90]

After the commencement of negotiations but before the terms of a DPA are agreed, the designated prosecutor must apply to the Crown Court for a preliminary hearing declaration that entering into a DPA with the entity is likely to be in the interests of justice and that the proposed terms are fair, reasonable and proportionate.[91]

86 DPA Code, para 3.4.
87 DPA Code, para 5.2.
88 CCA 2013, Sch 17, Pt 1, para 5(1)–(3).
89 DPA Code, paras 7.2 and 7.5.
90 CCA 2013, Sch 17, Pt 1, para 11(3); DPA Code, para 4.3.
91 CCA 2013, Sch 17, Pt 1, para 7(1).

Approving a DPA and suspending the indictment

10.11 Once the designated prosecutor and entity have agreed the terms of a DPA, and assuming that the court made a declaration on a preliminary hearing during the DPA negotiations, the designated prosecutor must make a further application to the Crown Court for a declaration that the DPA is in the interests of justice and that the terms are fair, reasonable and proportionate.[92] A DPA comes into force when it is approved by the Crown Court by way of such a declaration,[93] and the designated prosecutor must then publish the DPA.[94]

Upon the approval of the DPA by the Crown Court, the designated prosecutor institutes proceedings in respect of the alleged offence by preferring a bill of indictment, thereby by-passing the magistrates' court in the DPA process; and, as soon as the proceedings are initiated in this way, they are automatically suspended.[95] The entity then needs to abide by the terms of the agreement to ensure that it is not prosecuted for the offence.

Civil recovery

10.12 Civil recovery is a form of non-conviction, non-sentence, based asset forfeiture. Under Part 5 of the Proceeds of Crime Act 2002 ('POCA 2002'), an enforcement authority (the NCA, Director of Public Prosecutions, Director of the Serious Fraud Office, Her Majesty's Revenue and Customs or the Financial Conduct Authority)[96] can seek a civil recovery order ('CRO') through civil proceedings before the High Court in order to recover property which is, or represents, property obtained through unlawful conduct.[97] The power to seek a CRO is exercisable in relation to any property, whether or not any criminal proceedings have been brought in connection with the property.[98]

Although notice of CRO proceedings is served on the holder of the property, the civil recovery proceedings are against the property itself and not the individual respondent.[99] Therefore, a person who holds property that is the subject of a CRO application may not be the person who carried out the unlawful conduct.[100]

If a CRO is made, it will vest the recoverable property in a trustee for civil recovery,[101] who acts on behalf of the enforcement authority and must comply

92 CCA 2013, Sch 17, Pt 1, para 8(1)–(2).
93 CCA 2013, Sch 17, Pt 1, para 8(3).
94 CCA 2013, Sch 17, Pt 1, para 8(7)(a).
95 CCA 2013, Sch 17, Pt 1, para 2(1)–(2).
96 POCA 2002, s 2A(2).
97 POCA 2002, s 240(1)(a).
98 POCA 2002, s 240(2).
99 Attorney General Office's Asset Recovery Powers for Prosecutors: Guidance and Background Note 2009 (published 29 November 2012): www.gov.uk/guidance/asset-recovery-powers-for-prosecutors-guidance-and-background-note-2009.
100 Attorney General Office's Asset Recovery Powers for Prosecutors: Guidance and Background Note 2009.
101 POCA 2002, s 266(2).

with any directions given by the authority.[102] The trustee will secure the detention, custody or preservation of the property vested in them by the CRO and, in the case of property other than money, they will, so far as is practicable, realise the maximum value of the property for the benefit of the enforcement authority.[103] The CRO may impose conditions as to the manner in which the trustee may deal with the property for the purpose of realising the value of it.[104]

Civil recovery proceedings are civil litigation, so applications for CROs are governed by the Civil Procedure Rules,[105] and the civil standard of proof (the balance of probabilities) applies.

What is the definition of 'property' and 'recoverable property'?

10.13 Section 316(4) of POCA 2002 provides that 'property' is all property wherever situated and includes:

> '(a) money;
>
> (b) all forms of property, real or personal, heritable or moveable;
>
> (c) things in action and other intangible or incorporeal property.'

'Associated property' means property of any of the following descriptions (including property held by the respondent) which is not itself the recoverable property:[106]

> '(a) any interest in the recoverable property;
>
> (b) any other interest in the property in which the recoverable property subsists;
>
> (c) if the recoverable property is a tenancy in common, the tenancy of the other tenant;
>
> […]
>
> (e) if the recoverable property is part of a larger property, but not a separate part, the remainder of that property.'

Rights under a pension scheme are not to be treated as associated with recoverable property.[107]

As has already been mentioned in earlier chapters (see paras **2.40**, **9.2** and **9.19**), on 18 November 2019, the UK Jurisdiction Taskforce ('UKJT') delivered its Legal Statement on Cryptoassets and Smart Contracts.[108] This stated that

102 POCA 2002, s 267(4).
103 POCA 2002, s 267(3)(a)–(b) and (5).
104 POCA 2002, s 266(8).
105 A claim by an enforcement authority for a CRO must be made using the procedure outlined in Part 8 of the Civil Procedure Rules.
106 POCA 2002, s 245(1).
107 POCA 2002, s 245(3).
108 https://35z8e83m1ih83drye280o9d1-wpengine.netdna-ssl.com/wp-content/uploads/2019/11/6.6056_JO_Cryptocurrencies_Statement_FINAL_WEB_111119-1.pdf.

cryptoassets are to be treated, in principle, as property; and the High Court has held that cryptoassets are property.[109] Following this Legal Statement and case law, civil recovery is likely to be something in the forefront of the minds of enforcement authorities when cryptoassets are, or represent, property obtained through unlawful conduct. Consequently, enforcement authorities are likely to, as a first step in civil recovery proceedings, apply to the High Court for a Property Freezing Order ('PFO') under section 245A of POCA 2002, in order to prohibit persons from dealing with the cryptoassets during the civil recovery investigation. However, the practicalities of pursuing civil recovery in respect of cryptoassets is something that will need to be provided for before PFOs and CROs are realistic options for enforcement authorities (as is discussed further at paras **10.17–10.20** below).

'Recoverable property' is property obtained through unlawful conduct.[110] If the property is disposed of once it has been obtained, the property that represents or replaces the original property is also recoverable property.[111]

What is unlawful conduct?

10.14 Conduct occurring in any part of the United Kingdom ('UK') is 'unlawful conduct' if it constitutes a criminal offence in that part of the UK.[112]

For conduct occurring outside the UK, dual criminality is required: conduct occurring outside the UK will be 'unlawful conduct' for the purpose of civil recovery proceedings if it is a criminal offence in the country in which it occurred and, if it had occurred in a part of the UK, it would also be a criminal offence in that part of the UK.[113]

Section 13 of the Criminal Finances Act 2017 expanded the definition of 'unlawful conduct' to include conduct occurring outside the UK that constitutes or is connected with the commission of a gross human rights abuse or violation which, if it occurred in the UK, would be a criminal offence.[114]

What is the standard of proof in civil recovery proceedings?

10.15 The court must decide, on the balance of probabilities, whether unlawful conduct has occurred.[115] If it is so satisfied, the court must then decide (again,

109 *Robertson v Persons Unknown* Unreported, CL-2019-000444; *Vorotyntseva v Money-4 Ltd (t/a Nebeus.com)* [2018] EWHC 2596 (Ch); and *AA v Persons Unknown* [2019] EWHC 3556 (Comm).
110 POCA 2002, s 304(1).
111 POCA 2002, s 305(1).
112 POCA 2002, s 241(1).
113 POCA 2002, s 241(2).
114 POCA 2002, s 241(2A).
115 POCA 2002, s 241(3)(a).

on the balance of probabilities) whether the property has been obtained by, or in return for, that unlawful conduct.[116]

To prove that property has been obtained through unlawful conduct, it is not necessary to prove the commission of a particular criminal offence by a particular person on a particular occasion: it is sufficient to prove that the property was obtained by or in return for offending of a particular type. Proving that property was obtained through unlawful conduct cannot be done solely on the basis that the person holding the property has no identifiable lawful income to warrant their lifestyle. However, the absence of any evidence from the person to explain their lifestyle, or the giving of a false explanation, will allow the court to infer that the source of the income was unlawful.[117]

If the court is satisfied that the property has been obtained by, or in return for, that unlawful conduct, that property is recoverable property and the court must make a CRO.[118]

Even if a CRO is made, the court may not make provisions in respect of any recoverable property if various conditions are met and it would not be just and equitable to make those provisions.[119] Those conditions are that:[120]

> '(a) the respondent obtained the recoverable property in good faith;
>
> (b) he took steps after obtaining the property which he would not have taken if he had not obtained it or he took steps before obtaining the property which he would not have taken if he had not believed he was going to obtain it;
>
> (c) when he took the steps, he had no notice that the property was recoverable; and
>
> (d) if a recovery order were made in respect of the property, it would, by reason of the steps, be detrimental to him.'

In deciding whether it would be just and equitable to make the provision in the CRO, the court must have regard to the degree of detriment that would be suffered by the respondent if the provision were made and the enforcement authority's interest in receiving the realised proceeds of the recoverable property.[121]

When is civil recovery appropriate?

10.16 Civil recovery is not intended to be an alternative to prosecution: the reduction of crime is, in general, best secured by means of criminal investigations

116 POCA 2002, s 242.
117 *R (on the application of the Director of the Assets Recovery Agency and others) v Green and others* [2005] EWHC 3168 (Admin).
118 POCA 2002, s 266(1).
119 POCA 2002, s 266(3)(a).
120 POCA 2002, s 266(4).
121 POCA 2002, s 266(6).

and criminal proceedings,[122] and individuals and bodies corporate should not be allowed to avoid a criminal investigation and prosecution by consenting to the making of a CRO.[123]

Therefore, civil recovery should only be pursued: when it is not feasible to obtain a conviction; when a conviction is obtained but a confiscation order is not made; or when the public interest would be better served by using civil recovery rather than by seeking a criminal disposal.[124] Additionally, as a conviction is not required for a CRO, civil recovery proceedings will only be initiated where the enforcement authority reasonably believes that the aggregate value of the recoverable property is not less than £10,000.[125]

In determining whether or not it is feasible to obtain a conviction, enforcement authorities will consider factors such as the following:[126]

- whether the only known criminality is overseas, and whether there is extra-territorial jurisdiction to pursue a criminal case in the courts of England and Wales;
- whether there is an identifiable living suspect who is within the jurisdiction or realistically capable of being brought within the jurisdiction;
- whether proceeds of crime can be identified but cannot be linked to any individual suspect or offence;
- whether an investigation has generated sufficient evidence to create a realistic prospect of conviction;
- whether a criminal investigation has been conducted but the prosecuting authority considers that there is insufficient evidence to create a realistic prospect of conviction; and
- whether a prosecution has been conducted but has not resulted in a conviction.

In relation to the final bullet point, it was previously thought that an acquittal in criminal proceedings would not affect a claimant's prospects of successfully bringing a claim for a CRO. However, jurisprudence from the European Court of Human Rights ('ECtHR') may have confused the position, the central question being whether proceedings for a CRO, in circumstances where there has been an acquittal in criminal proceedings on the same facts, would undermine the

122 Attorney General Office's Asset Recovery Powers for Prosecutors: Guidance and Background Note 2009, para 1.

123 Attorney General Office's Asset Recovery Powers for Prosecutors: Guidance and Background Note 2009, para 4.

124 Attorney General Office's Asset Recovery Powers for Prosecutors: Guidance and Background Note 2009, para 1.

125 POCA 2002, s 287(1); Proceeds of Crime Act 2002 (Financial Threshold for Civil Recovery) Order 2003 (SI 2003/175), art 2.

126 Attorney General Office's Asset Recovery Powers for Prosecutors: Guidance and Background Note 2009, para 5.

acquittal and thus breach Article 6 of the European Convention on Human Rights (fair trial rights). Whilst domestic jurisprudence suggests that the domestic courts are unlikely to be sympathetic to such an argument, the position of the ECtHR is less clear, and so there may be scope for such an argument before the end of the year and Implementation Day arrives.[127]

In determining whether the public interest would be better served by using civil recovery as opposed to seeking a criminal disposal, the enforcement authorities will consider factors such as the following:[128]

- whether using non-conviction based powers better meets an urgent need to take action to prevent or stop offending which is causing immediate harm to the public, even though this might limit the availability of evidence for a future prosecution;
- whether it is practicable to investigate those with a peripheral involvement in the criminality, and whether a strategic approach must be taken in order to achieve a manageable and successful prosecution;
- whether civil recovery represents a better deployment of resources to target someone with significant property which cannot be explained by legitimate income; and
- whether the offender is being prosecuted in another jurisdiction and is expected to receive a sentence that reflects the totality of the offending, so the public interest does not require a prosecution in England and Wales.

Civil recovery and cryptoassets

10.17 The UKJT's Legal Statement on Cryptoassets and Smart Contracts (see para **10.13** above) stated that cryptoassets are to be treated, in principle, as property; and the High Court has held that cryptoassets are property. Therefore, PFOs and civil recovery are likely to be something in the forefront of the minds of enforcement authorities when cryptoassets are, or represent, property obtained through unlawful conduct.

Given the relative anonymity of those involved in cybercrime and the pseudonymous nature of cryptoassets, cases and investigations involving these elements might be cases where it is not feasible to obtain a conviction and/or the public interest would be better served by using civil recovery as opposed to seeking a criminal disposal.

However, the practicalities of pursuing civil recovery in respect of cryptoassets is something that will need to be addressed before civil recovery is a realistic option for enforcement authorities.

127 'The impact of an acquittal on civil recovery proceedings', Jonathan Fisher QC, Bright Line Law: https://brightlinelaw.co.uk/the-impact-of-an-acquittal-on-civil-recovery-proceedings/.

128 Attorney General Office's Asset Recovery Powers for Prosecutors: Guidance and Background Note 2009, para 6.

Transferring cryptoassets to a trustee

10.18 If cryptoassets are found to be recoverable property, how will they be transferred to a trustee? Current decryption laws under Part III of the Regulation of Investigatory Powers Act 2000 ('RIPA 2000') only apply to 'protected information' that has come into the possession of an authorised person/body by way of a statutory power or any other lawful means.[129] That situation does not apply to a CRO in respect of cryptoassets, and should not be interpreted as doing so, as cryptoassets are not protected information – they are property and they have not come into the possession of an authorised person/body; that is the point of obtaining a CRO: to recover the property. Therefore, RIPA 2000 is not the appropriate mechanism to compel a holder to provide their wallet ID and private key.

One way might be for the CRO to contain a provision that the holder must provide their wallet ID and private key to the trustee, thereby giving them control of the cryptoassets. That, however, assumes not only that the trustee has a certain level of technical understanding and capabilities in order to interact with the cryptoasset world, but also that all cryptoassets within the wallet are recoverable. What if that is not the case, and recoverable cryptoassets are mixed with non-recoverable cryptoassets? Such non-recoverable cryptoassets would not be 'associated property' under section 245 of POCA 2002 because, despite being rewarded to the same wallet, they are distinct items of property. Section 306(2) of POCA 2002 also provides that only the portion of mixed property which is attributable to the recoverable property represents the property obtained through unlawful conduct. On that basis, the non-recoverable cryptoassets would not represent property obtained through unlawful conduct, and a CRO would not be made in respect of them.

Perhaps the answer is that enforcement authorities will have to set up their own cryptoasset wallets, and trustee wallets, in order to recover cryptoassets, and the CRO could provide for the holder to transfer the recoverable cryptoassets to the trustee wallet.

Alternatively, rather than making a transfer to enforcement authority/trustee wallets, enforcement authorities and trustees may seek to set up accounts within cryptoasset exchanges and then have the transfers made to those wallets, as this would potentially facilitate an easier realisation of the value of the cryptoassets into fiat currency.

Can cryptoassets actually be the subject of a CRO?

10.19 However, the above all pre-supposes that cryptoassets could, in fact, be the subject of PFOs and CROs.

129 RIPA 2000, s 49(1).

PFOs and CROs may not be made in respect of property that is outside the UK,[130] but cryptoassets do not have a situs: they are decentralised and intangible. Therefore, do they (or could they) fall within the civil recovery regime? How should the nature of cryptoassets be reconciled with legislative provisions providing jurisdictional constraints on the application of various types of order etc? Her Majesty's Revenue and Customs ('HMRC') guidance on cryptoasset taxation for individuals[131] states that 'Using the residency of the beneficial owner of the exchange tokens to determine the location [of the exchange token] gives a clear, logical, predictable and objective rule which can be easily applied'. HMRC does not say what is meant by 'residency': whether this is tax residency under the statutory residence test, or residency based on the long-standing principles regarding residence for the purposes of jurisdiction. However, if the question as to the situs of cryptoassets did need to be decided by the courts, it seems likely that they might adopt the residency rule proposed by HMRC, albeit interpreting it as residency based on the principles of residence for the purposes of jurisdiction, as opposed to tax residency. Thus, the residence of the holder/owner of the cryptoassets would determine the location of the cryptoassets and whether they could be the subject of a PFO or CRO. However, until the question of the situs of cryptoassets comes before the courts, it is not clear whether a PFO or CRO (nor, indeed, any other order or legislation with jurisdictional constraints as to their applicability) could be sought in respect of cryptoassets.

Conclusions on cryptoassets and civil recovery

10.20 It is currently unclear how certain practicalities would work in respect of the civil recovery of cryptoassets, and that is assuming that cryptoassets fall within the PFO and CRO regimes in the first place. However, assuming that they do, it seems that, rather than forcing cryptoassets into the current legal framework, enforcement authorities are going to have to engage with the cryptoasset ecosystem, potentially having their own dedicated miners, setting up wallets, exchange accounts etc. It is unlikely that enforcement authorities currently have individuals with the technical understanding and capabilities required in order for them to engage with the world of cryptoassets. However, given the UKJT's Legal Statement that cryptoassets are, in principle, property, and the High Court's recent decisions, enforcement authorities are going to have to ensure that they obtain this understanding and capability soon, or else they will not be in a position to address crimes involving cryptoassets.

Criminal taxation

10.21 Criminal taxation is another non-conviction based power that the NCA may pursue instead of a criminal prosecution.

130 *Serious Organised Crime Agency v Perry* [2012] UKSC 35.

131 www.gov.uk/government/publications/tax-on-cryptoassets/cryptoassets-for-individuals#other-considerations.

Under Part 6 of POCA 2002, the NCA may charge tax on a person's or company's income, profits or gains where it has reasonable grounds to suspect that they arise or accrue from criminal conduct on the part of that person/company or another.[132]

In order to be able to exercise such powers, the NCA must serve a notice on the Commissioners of Inland Revenue specifying the person or company and the period in question, and state that it intends to carry out, in relation to the person or company and in respect of the period, the general Revenue functions that are specified in the notice.[133] It is the serving of the notice on the Commissioners of Inland Revenue that vests the general Revenue functions specified in the notice in the NCA.[134]

Criminal conduct is defined in section 326(1) of POCA 2002 as conduct which constitutes an offence in any part of the UK, or would constitute an offence in any part of the UK if it occurred there.

WHAT ARE THE ALTERNATIVES TO CIVIL ACTIONS IN 'CYBER' CASES?

10.22 The tables below outline the various forms of alternative dispute resolution ('ADR') available in England and Wales, and whether they provide binding or non-binding resolutions/determinations:

Form of ADR	Description
Negotiation	The parties attempt to reach an agreement on the matters in dispute without the assistance of a third party. Discussions are usually on a without prejudice basis.
Mediation	With the assistance of a neutral third party (the mediator), the parties identify the issues in dispute, explore the options for resolution and attempt to reach a settlement.
Executive Tribunal	A panel is made up of senior executives from the disputing parties and an independent chairperson. A representative of each party makes a formal presentation of their case to the panel, who then discuss the dispute with the chairperson acting as a mediator.

132 POCA 2002, s 317(1)–(3).
133 POCA 2002, s 317(2).
134 POCA 2002, s 317(3).

Form of ADR	**Description**
Conciliation	As with mediation, with the assistance of a neutral third party, the parties identify the issues in dispute, explore the options for resolution and attempt to reach a settlement. However, in conciliation, the third party actively assists the parties to settle the dispute by, for example, making suggestions regarding settlement options.
Early Neutral Evaluation	The parties appoint an independent person to provide an opinion on the merits which evaluates the facts, evidence and law relating to a particular issue, or the whole case. The parties then use that opinion to negotiate an outcome (non-binding) or agree in advance that the opinion will settle their dispute (binding).
Expert Determination	An expert is appointed by the parties to determine an issue, and the expert's decision is contractually binding on the parties.
Adjudication	An adjudicator provides a decision on a dispute, and that decision is binding on the parties, subject to an agreement altering its effect or referring the dispute to arbitration or litigation for final determination.
Dispute Review Board	A panel is appointed at the start of a project and deals with disputes as they arise, providing interim binding decisions which can be challenged by arbitration or litigation.
Arbitration	The parties agree to submit the dispute to a private forum where an independent arbitrator makes a binding award to finalise the dispute.
Med-Arb	This is a combination of mediation and arbitration: if mediation fails in whole or on any issue, the parties may agree that the mediator becomes an arbitrator.

Non-Binding ADR Processes Without Third Party Intervention	**Non-Binding ADR Processes With Third Party**	**Binding ADR Processes**
Negotiation	Mediation	Expert Determination
	Executive Tribunal	Early Neutral Evaluation (binding)
	Conciliation	Adjudication (interim binding process)

Non-Binding ADR Processes Without Third Party Intervention	Non-Binding ADR Processes With Third Party	Binding ADR Processes
	Early Neutral Evaluation (non-binding)	Dispute Review Board (interim binding process)
		Arbitration
		Med-Arb (hybrid process)

Some of these ADR processes will be more suitable for 'cyber' disputes than others, and it may be that, in some circumstances, there may be a contractual or other obligation on the parties to use a specified form of ADR. For example, as outlined below, registrants of domain names may need to submit to mandatory ADR processes in relation to particular disputes, and Sir Geoffrey Vos has suggested that lawyers need to work with software developers in order to ensure that smart contracts include jurisdiction and/or dispute resolution clauses, as private international law is not necessarily able to deal with borderless chain contracts.[135]

A detailed review of the above-mentioned ADR processes and their respective advantages and disadvantages is outside the remit of this book. However, many of the general advantages associated with ADR seem to make them perfectly suited for 'cyber' disputes. For example, given the fast-moving pace of technology and the cyber world, and the need for swift resolutions, the time-saving aspects of ADR make it seem like the ideal remedying mechanism for 'cyber' disputes (as opposed to protracted litigation). Additionally, given that 'cyber' is a new and ever-developing area, the flexibility, control and creativity afforded by ADR make it seem particularly suited to 'cyber' disputes.

This flexibility and creativity also mean that parties need not necessarily be limited to the current ADR processes available. To combat and address a changing cyber world, parties may start to look at amending and adapting the current ADR processes, for which parties can make provision by agreeing these amended and/or adapted processes in their contracts etc.

ADR provides a framework within which cyber disputes may be resolved, and lawyers should be alive to the opportunity to amend and adapt this framework to meet their clients' needs in the cyber world. Indeed, following Brexit, more parties might opt for arbitration instead of litigation as the method of determining their disputes, as the legal framework for arbitration and the enforcement of arbitral

135 'Unlocking the Potential of Smart Contracts', Westminster Legal Policy Forum Keynote Seminar: Legal Technology in the UK – New Services, Regulatory Issues, and Impact on the Sector and Consumers, 2 December 2019.

awards is not established by European Union ('EU') law, nor dependent on the UK's membership of the EU;[136] thus, lawyers should be alive to the opportunity that this may present.

'Cyber' disputes being resolved by alternative dispute resolution

The unauthorised use of trade marks in domain names

10.23 In the sphere of domain names and trade marks, registration authorities have created a form of adjudication as a mandatory ADR process in the event of disputes over the registration and use of an Internet domain name.

Uniform Domain Name Dispute Resolution Policy: Administrative Panel

10.24 A generic top-level domain ('gTLD'), such as .com or .net, which contains a recognised trade mark, can be registered with the Internet Assigned Numbers Authority ('IANA'). Those who register with IANA agree to submit to the Internet Corporation for Assigned Names and Numbers' ('ICANN')[137] mandatory ADR procedure, the Uniform Domain Name Dispute Resolution Policy ('UDRP'),[138] in the event of a dispute over the registration and use of an Internet domain name. Proceedings under the UDRP are governed by the Rules for Uniform Domain Name Dispute Resolution Policy ('the Rules of Procedure').[139]

Under the UDRP, a trade mark owner ('the complainant') can obtain the cancellation or transfer of a gTLD domain name[140] that is identical or confusingly similar to their trade mark if the registrant has no rights or legitimate interests in the domain name, has registered the domain name in bad faith and is using the domain name in bad faith.[141]

The dispute is referred to an ICANN-approved administrative dispute resolution service provider ('Provider').[142] The Provider is selected by the complainant,[143] and the complainant and registrant submit their cases and evidence in written, electronic form to the Provider.[144] Once the registrant's Response has been received, the Provider appoints the panel that will decide the dispute ('the Administrative Panel').[145] The Rules of Procedure outline the process for

136 Greg Fullelove, 'Q&A: Arbitration and the video gaming industry', 3 February 2020: www.osborneclarke.com/insights/qa-arbitration-video-gaming-industry/.
137 ICANN is an internationally-organised non-profit organisation set up by the internet community to coordinate areas of responsibilities: www.iana.org/about.
138 www.icann.org/resources/pages/policy-2012-02-25-en – UDRP, paras 1 and 4.
139 www.icann.org/resources/pages/udrp-rules-2015-03-11-en.
140 UDRP, para 3.
141 UDRP, para 4(a).
142 UDRP, paras 4, 4(d) and www.icann.org/resources/pages/providers-6d-2012-02-25-en.
143 UDRP, para 4(d).
144 Rules of Procedure, paras 3 and 5.
145 Rules of Procedure, para 6.

initiating and conducting a proceeding, and for appointing the Administrative Panel.[146]

The Administrative Panel makes its decision within 14 days of its appointment,[147] and decides the complaint on the basis of the statements and documents submitted by the parties, the UDRP, the Rules of Procedure and any rules or principles of law that it deems applicable.[148] In order to obtain the cancellation or transfer of the registrant's domain name, the complainant trade mark owner must prove that each element is present[149] (ie that the registrant's domain name is identical or confusingly similar to their trade mark, and that the registrant has no rights or legitimate interests in the domain name, has registered the domain name in bad faith and is using the domain name in bad faith).[150] Paragraph 4(b) of the UDRP outlines a non-exhaustive list of circumstances that are evidence of the registration and use of a domain name in bad faith, and paragraph 4(c) outlines a non-exhaustive list of circumstances that might demonstrate a registrant's rights to, and legitimate interest in, the domain name.

UDRP proceedings do not prevent the parties from submitting the dispute to a court for independent resolution, either before the UDRP process is commenced or after it has been concluded.[151]

All other disputes regarding a domain name registration are to be resolved between the parties through any court, arbitration or other proceeding that may be available, and not the UDRP process.[152]

Uniform Rapid Suspension System: examination

10.25 ICANN also provides the Uniform Rapid Suspension System ('URS')[153] for domain names registered after 1 January 2013. The URS complements the UDRP, offering a lower-cost, faster path to relief for rights holders experiencing the most clear-cut cases of infringement.[154] Proceedings under the URS are governed by the URS Procedure and the URS Rules.[155]

As with the UDRP, the dispute is referred to an ICANN-approved administrative dispute resolution service provider ('URS Provider').[156] Proceedings are initiated by the complainant electronically filing the complaint outlining the trademark rights and the actions complained of to a URS Provider.[157] The URS Provider

146 UDRP, para 4(e); Rules of Procedure, paras 3–7 and 10–16.
147 Rules of Procedure, para 15(b).
148 Rules of Procedure, para 15(a).
149 UDRP, para 4(a).
150 UDRP, para 4(a).
151 UDRP, para 4(k).
152 UDRP, para 5.
153 See: www.icann.org/resources/pages/urs-2014-01-09-en.
154 www.icann.org/resources/pages/urs-2014-01-09-en.
155 See: www.icann.org/resources/pages/urs-2014-01-09-en.
156 See: www.icann.org/resources/pages/urs-2014-01-09-en.
157 URS Procedure, paras 1.1–1.2 and the URS Rules, para 3.

conducts an initial administrative review for compliance with the filing requirements.[158] Assuming that the filing requirements have been complied with, the URS Provider sends a Notice of Complaint to the registrant, who then has 14 calendar days to electronically file a Response.[159]

The URS Provider will then appoint an Examiner to conduct the URS proceeding and make a determination on the dispute.[160] A determination should be rendered within three business days of submission of the Response, and no later than five days after the Response is filed.[161]

Under the URS, a complainant must prove that:[162]

> '(a) the registered domain name is identical or confusingly similar to a word mark:
>
> > (i) for which the complainant holds a valid registration that is in current use;
> >
> > (ii) that has been validated through court proceedings; or
> >
> > (iii) that is specifically protected by a statute or treaty in effect at the time the URS complaint is filed;
>
> (b) that the registrant has no legitimate right or interest to the domain name; and
>
> (c) that the domain was registered and being used in bad faith.'

Paragraph 1.2.6.3 of the URS Procedure outlines a non-exhaustive list of circumstances that demonstrate bad faith registration and use by the registrant.

There is no discovery or hearing under the URS – the materials submitted with the Complaint and Response serve as the entire record used to make a determination.[163] Consequently, there must be no issue of material fact[164] and the burden of proof upon a complainant is 'clear and convincing evidence'.[165]

If a URS determination is in favour of the complainant, the offending domain name will be suspended for the balance of the registration period and will not resolve to the original website: it will redirect to an information page provided by the URS Provider about the URS.[166] If the determination is in favour of the registrant, the domain name will be unlocked (having been locked by the Registry Operator as part of the URS procedure)[167] and full control of the domain name registration will be returned to the registrant.[168]

158 URS Procedure, para 3.
159 URS Procedure, para 5.1 and the URS Rules, para 5.
160 URS Procedure, paras 7–9 and the URS Rules, paras 6, 8–11 and 13.
161 URS Procedure, para 9.6.
162 URS Procedure, paras 1.2.6.1–1.2.6.3.
163 URS Procedure, para 9.1.
164 URS Procedure, para 8.5.
165 URS Procedure, para 8.2.
166 URS Procedure, para 10.2.
167 URS Procedure, para 4.1.
168 URS Procedure, para 10.5.

Both parties have a right to appeal the URS determination to an Appeals Panel (set up by the URS Provider and governed by the Provider's rules and procedures for appeals) within 14 days of the determination.[169] A URS determination does not preclude any other remedies available, and it does not prejudice a party in any other proceedings.[170]

Dispute Resolution Service Policy: mediation and adjudication by an expert

10.26 Those seeking to register top-level domain names, such as .uk or .de, must similarly submit to mandatory ADR procedures prescribed by the relevant country register. In the UK, Nominet[171] is responsible for the registration of UK and Welsh domains, while EURid is the relevant administrator for the .eu domain.[172]

In the UK, parties must submit to proceedings under Nominet's Dispute Resolution Service ('DRS') Policy[173] if there is a complaint about a name or mark which is identical or similar to a domain name and the domain name is an abusive registration.[174] The DRS Policy differs from the UDRP and URS in that the parties are automatically 'opted-in' to mediation rather than going straight to an adjudication.[175]

A complainant must submit their Complaint and evidence to Nominet through its online electronic form.[176] Assuming that the Complaint complies with the DRS Policy, it will be forwarded to the respondent for a Response. As with the Complaint, the Response and any supporting evidence must be submitted through the online electronic form.[177] The complainant is given a right to Reply to the Response[178] and, within three days of receipt of the Reply, Nominet will begin to conduct mediation.[179]

If the parties do not achieve an acceptable resolution through mediation within ten days, and provided that the complainant pays the applicable fee, Nominet will notify the parties that an Expert will be appointed to adjudicate the dispute.[180] Although the Expert will be informed that mediation occurred, the mediation negotiations are confidential as between the parties and Nominet, and they will

169 URS Procedure, para 12.
170 URS Procedure, para 13.
171 www.nominet.uk.
172 https://eurid.eu/en/.
173 https://media.nominet.uk/wp-content/uploads/2017/10/17150434/final-proposed-DRS-policy.pdf.
174 DRS Policy, paras 2.1, 2.1.1 and 2.1.2.
175 DRS Policy, para 10.
176 DRS Policy, para 4.3.
177 DRS Policy, para 7.3.
178 DRS Policy, para 9.
179 DRS Policy, para 10.1.
180 DRS Policy, para 10.5.

not be disclosed to the Expert, nor will the reason why they failed to resolve the dispute.[181]

The Expert will decide the complaint on the basis of the parties' submissions, and will make their decision within 15 days of their appointment.[182]

The complainant will obtain the cancellation, suspension or transfer of a .uk domain[183] if they can prove, on a balance of probabilities,[184] that:

> '(a) they have rights in respect of a name or mark which is identical or similar to the domain name; and
>
> (b) the domain name, in the hands of the respondent, is an abusive registration.'[185]

A domain name is an 'abusive registration' if it was registered or acquired, or is being used, in a manner which has taken unfair advantage of, or was unfairly detrimental to, the complainant's rights.[186] Paragraph 5.1 of the DRS Policy provides a non-exhaustive list of factors that may be evidence of the domain name being an abusive registration, and there is a rebuttable presumption of an abusive registration where a respondent has been found to have made an abusive registration on three or more occasions over the previous two years.[187] Paragraph 8.1 of the DRS Policy provides a non-exhaustive list of factors that may demonstrate that the domain name is not an abusive registration.

Both parties have a right to appeal the Expert's decision.[188] The operation of the DRS will not prevent the parties from submitting the dispute for resolution by a court[189] but, if simultaneous legal proceedings are brought in respect of the matter, the DRS proceedings will be suspended pending the outcome of those proceedings.[190] This differs from the UDRP and URS, where the suspension of the UDRP and URS proceedings due to simultaneous legal proceedings is at the discretion of the Administrative Panel/Examiner.[191]

Society for Computers and Law Adjudication Scheme

10.27 In October 2019, the Society for Computers and Law ('SCL') launched an alternative contractual dispute resolution procedure for 'technology' disputes: the SCL Adjudication Scheme.[192] The SCL Adjudication Scheme has been

181 DRS Policy, paras 10.2 and 10.6.
182 DRS Policy, paras 18.1 and 18.3.
183 DRS Policy, para 4.3.7.
184 DRS Policy, para 2.2.
185 DRS Policy, paras 2.1.1–2.1.2.
186 DRS Policy, para 1.
187 DRS Policy, para 5.3.
188 DRS Policy, para 20.
189 DRS Policy, para 20.13.
190 DRS Policy, para 25.1.
191 Rules of Procedure, para 18(a) and URS Rules, para 17(a).
192 www.scl.org/adjudicationscheme.

developed to achieve speedy and cost-effective outcomes in any dispute arising from a contract for the provision of technology-related goods and services, including, but not limited to:

- software development contracts;
- outsourcing arrangements;
- systems integration contracts;
- IT consultancy contracts;
- software licensing agreements;
- blockchain/smart contracts; and
- cloud computing contracts.

Recourse to the SCL Adjudication Scheme is voluntary, and may be achieved either by incorporating the SCL Model Adjudication Clauses into contracts or by ad hoc referrals to the SCL Adjudication Scheme.[193] There is no restriction on the size or scope of the technology disputes that may be referred to the SCL Adjudication Scheme, but the matter must be capable of resolution within the maximum three-month back-stop timescale provided for by the SCL Adjudication Rules.[194] Therefore, the SCL Adjudication Scheme may not be appropriate for complex disputes.

The SCL Adjudication Scheme uses expedited timescales, with statements of case being exchanged between the parties within 30 working days from the commencement of the procedure. The process is largely paper-based, with strict limits on the volume (and format) of material that each party may submit.[195] The limited timeframe within which to prepare cases, and limitation on the volume of material that may be submitted, again indicates that the SCL Adjudication Scheme may not be appropriate for complex disputes.

There is a pre-selected panel of Adjudicators, made up of lawyers and non-legally qualified technology specialists, from which an Adjudicator may be chosen for individual adjudications. The panel is set up and maintained by SCL, and all Adjudicators must satisfy the SCL Adjudication Eligibility Criteria.[196] The parties are jointly and severally responsible for the Adjudicator's fees and expenses, which are charged in accordance with the SCL Schedule of Charges.[197]

193 www.scl.org/files/download/1836-SCL%20Adjudication%20Scheme%20Rules%20Version%201.pdf.

194 SCL Adjudication Rules, Rule 30.

195 SCL Adjudication Rules, Rules 18–23.

196 SCL Adjudication Guidance Notes: www.scl.org/files/download/1837-SCLA%20Guidance%20Notes%20-%20FINAL.pdf; SCL Adjudication Rules, Rule 7.

197 SCL Adjudication Rules, Rule 27; www.scl.org/files/download/1834-SCHEDULE%20OF%20CHARGES%20-%20SCL%20Adjudication%20Scheme.pdf.

The scope of the adjudication is the dispute as set out in the Dispute and Response Notices, although it may be modified by the Adjudicator with the agreement of the parties.[198] Unless there is a direction to the contrary, the parties must comply with the Adjudicator's decision immediately on the effective date of the decision, and the successful party is entitled to enforce the award (including on any available expedited basis) under the procedures of the Technology and Construction Court, or in any other suitable court.[199] However, an Adjudicator's decision is only provisionally binding, and parties have six months from the effective date of the decision to reopen the dispute in litigation or arbitration. Until those subsequent proceedings have been concluded, however, the parties must comply with the Adjudicator's decision. If no subsequent proceedings are commenced within the six-month limit, the Adjudicator's decision becomes final and binding for all purposes.[200] Despite the aim of the SCL Adjudication Scheme to achieve speedy and cost-effective outcomes, parties' costs will significantly increase if they reopen the dispute in litigation or arbitration, thus undermining a key aim of the SCL Adjudication Scheme.

Adjudicators are required to conduct adjudications in a timely and cost-effective manner, and avoid unnecessary expense. Parties are required to act in good faith and co-operate throughout the procedure.[201]

The SCL Adjudication Scheme provides a more user-friendly and cost-efficient process than litigation. However, only time will tell whether the technology sector will embrace this form of dispute resolution, and whether it will be suitable for complex disputes.

Information security in alternative dispute resolution procedures: the 2020 Cybersecurity Protocol for International Arbitration

10.28 As can be seen from the above, ADR provides a framework within which cyber disputes may be resolved. However, the ADR processes themselves are becoming more aware and attuned to the need to protect the data and information exchanged during the ADR process and the need for cybersecurity.

On 21 November 2019, the 2020 Cybersecurity Protocol for International Arbitration[202] ('the 2020 Protocol') was released by the ICCA-NYC Bar-CPR Working Group on Cybersecurity in Arbitration. The 2020 Protocol is intended to provide a framework to determine reasonable information security measures for individual arbitration matters, and to increase awareness about information security in international arbitrations.[203] This is not because

198 SCL Adjudication Rules, Rules 14–15.
199 SCL Adjudication Rules, Rule 39.
200 SCL Adjudication Rules, Rules 34, 36 and 38.
201 SCL Adjudication Rules, Rules 16–17.
202 www.arbitration-icca.org/media/14/76788479244143/icca-nyc_bar-cpr_cybersecurity_protocol_for_international_arbitration_-_print_version.pdf.
203 Foreword to the 2020 Protocol.

international arbitrations are particularly vulnerable to cyberattacks, but the high-value, high-stakes nature of disputes means that: a security incident is likely to cause significant loss; the information exchanged in an arbitration is often confidential commercial information and/or regulated personal or other data; and arbitrations are often cross-border in nature. Therefore, there is a need for reasonable information security measures. Additionally, the credibility of any dispute resolution system depends on maintaining a reasonable degree of protection of the information exchanged during the process, with respect to not only the information's confidentiality, but also its integrity and availability.[204]

Due to the highly digitised nature of international arbitrations, the 2020 Protocol focuses on cybersecurity (ie the means employed to maintain the confidentiality, integrity and availability of digital material). However, the guidance applies broadly to all information security measures, including both cybersecurity and physical security, and so covers security for all types and forms of electronic and non-electronic information, whether that be commercial or personal data.

The 2020 Protocol is not intended to, and does not, provide a 'one size fits all' information security solution for arbitrations. One of the core premises of the 2020 Protocol is that reasonable information security measures should be applied to arbitral proceedings, but that the measures that will be reasonable in a particular matter may vary significantly, based on the facts and circumstances of the case as well as evolving threats and technology.[205]

Consequently, the 2020 Protocol outlines 14 Principles that provide high-level guidance on information security measures for arbitration proceedings. These Principles:

- outline the scope and applicability of the 2020 Protocol;[206]
- establish the standard of reasonableness in the adoption of information security measures;[207]
- set out a series of factors to be considered in determining what information security measures are reasonable in a particular matter and how they should be applied;[208]
- provide a series of suggested procedural steps to address information security issues in an individual arbitration;[209] and
- clarify that the 2020 Protocol does not establish liability or a liability standard.[210]

204 Commentary to Principle 1 of the 2020 Protocol.
205 Commentary to Principle 1 of the 2020 Protocol.
206 Principles 1–4 of the 2020 Protocol.
207 Principle 5 of the 2020 Protocol.
208 Principles 6–8 of the 2020 Protocol.
209 Principles 9–13 of the 2020 Protocol.
210 Principle 14 of the 2020 Protocol.

The Principles are supplemented by Commentaries and Schedules, the latter of which provide more detailed guidance on baseline information security practices,[211] the risk factors that can be used to assess the risk profile of the arbitration,[212] examples of specific information security measures and processes that might be adopted,[213] and sample language for addressing information security issues in arbitration agreements, procedural orders and post-arbitration dispute resolution clauses.[214]

The Foreword to the 2020 Protocol states that it will evolve over time to take account of changing technology, new and prevalent cyber threats, new/amended laws/regulations, emerging consensuses, new cybersecurity initiatives by other institutions and practical experience.

Although the 2020 Protocol relates to international arbitrations and has been drafted with international commercial arbitrations in mind, its Foreword states that it may also be a useful reference for domestic arbitration matters.

Given the increasing value of data and information, and the consequences that can flow from the loss of, or unauthorised access to, such data and information – for example, economic loss as a result of commercial or personal information being compromised; the loss of integrity of data; or questions about the reliability and accuracy of data – parties and arbitrators in domestic arbitrations may wish to have recourse to the 2020 Protocol in order to protect the information exchanged during the arbitral proceedings. Indeed, it may be wise for parties to any form of ADR to have recourse to the 2020 Protocol in order to establish and adopt appropriate information security measures.

HOW ARE ORDINARY DISPUTES BEING RESOLVED BY 'CYBER' AND TECHNOLOGY?

10.29 The above has focused on the use of ADR to settle cyber disputes. However, new forms of dispute resolution are on the rise which, rather than settling cyber disputes, focus on using 'cyber' and technology in order to resolve ordinary disputes.

Online dispute resolution

10.30 Technology is already being incorporated into the court system – judges have laptops, iPads are being used instead of traditional paper bundles, there are electronic case portals to which case documents are uploaded etc. These measures have been introduced to make existing court procedures more efficient. Online

211 Schedule A to the 2020 Protocol.
212 Schedule B to the 2020 Protocol.
213 Schedule C to the 2020 Protocol.
214 Schedule D to the 2020 Protocol.

dispute resolution ('ODR') goes a step beyond these technological measures and provides a dispute resolution process whereby the formulation of the solution or remedy is largely enabled by technology, although the ODR platforms generally involve human oversight.

The benefits of ODR are that it could result in substantial costs savings, both for individuals and the court system, and may provide an increasingly accessible, user-friendly justice system.

Several jurisdictions have already introduced ODR platforms.

Case Studies

In the United Arab Emirates ('UAE'), the Dubai International Financial Centre's Small Claims Tribunal ('DIFC Courts SCT') is able to hear claims of up to AED 500,000 (approximately GBP 104,000).[215] The DIFC Courts SCT is located within the DIFC Free Zone and operates under English common law. The DIFC Courts SCT can be used in all commercial contracts, even for entities that operate outside the DIFC and UAE, provided that the DIFC Courts SCT jurisdiction clause appears in the contract or both parties have agreed in writing to use the DIFC Courts SCT. Claimants file their case online, and the defendants are served electronically, either by email or direct instant messaging. The DIFC Courts SCT is a 'lawyer-free' zone, with parties representing themselves, and parties do not need to attend in person: they can appear via the Smart SCT. Thus, the DIFC Courts SCT can be used by parties anywhere in the world.

Abu Dhabi offers a similar ODR platform where English common law is directly applicable: the Abu Dhabi Global Market Courts.[216]

The British Columbia Civil Resolution Tribunal ('CRT') is Canada's first online tribunal.[217] It offers an ODR process for: motor vehicle injury disputes up to CAD 50,000; small claims disputes up to CAD 5,000; strata property (condominium) disputes of any amount; and societies and co-operative associations disputes of any amount. In order for the CRT to have jurisdiction over a dispute, there must be a real and substantial connection between British Columbia and the facts in the dispute. Once the application is accepted, parties can enter into a voluntary negotiation process to talk through the dispute and try to reach an agreement through the confidential negotiation platform. If negotiation does not work (or is not wanted), a case manager will try and assist the parties to reach an agreement (facilitation), and such agreements can be turned into orders and enforced like a court order. If negotiation and facilitation fail, an independent CRT member will make a decision about the dispute, and that decision can be enforced as though it was a court order. The CRT

215 https://sct.difccourts.ae/why-opt-in/.
216 www.adgm.com/adgm-courts/digital.
217 https://civilresolutionbc.ca.

hearings are usually conducted on the papers, with parties uploading their evidence online and submitting their argument in writing, although the CRT has discretion to have a hearing held orally, whether by telephone, video conference or in person.

Hong Kong is also looking to introduce ODR. eBRAM Centre Limited ('eBRAM') is a start-up, not-for-profit organisation that was set up with the support of the Asian Academy of International Law Ltd, the Hong Kong Bar Association, The Law Society of Hong Kong, and Logistics and Supply Chain MultiTech R&D Centre Ltd. eBRAM is developing an ODR platform to support business transactions, in the APEC Region and beyond, by providing a user-friendly and secure online platform for businesses to negotiate contracts and, should the need arise, assist in the resolution of any differences in a fair, cost-effective and secure manner through negotiation, mediation and arbitration. eBRAM is designing its platform making use of emerging technologies including blockchain, artificial intelligence ('AI'), soft robotics and cloud.[218]

A little closer to home, in the UK it is possible to apply for divorce and probate online, and the TeCSA Low Value Dispute ('LVD') Adjudication Service, which applies to claims under construction contracts, was made permanent from 1 January 2020.[219] The LVD Adjudication Service is aimed at giving parties certainty as to the cost of adjudication for claims for fixed amounts of up to GBP 100,000. The LVD Adjudication Service only applies to claims for a liquidated sum and does not apply to claims where damages or loss and expenses are to be assessed, nor does it apply to claims for declarations. However, there is no restriction on the type of financial claims that can be made.

Despite the growing prevalence of ODR platforms, not all online court systems have been a success.

Case Study

The Netherlands' Recherché was set up in 2014 to deal with landlord and tenant disputes, debt and divorce. However, it was shut down in July 2017 as it proved to be financially unsustainable.[220] Following this, Justice42 was created, focusing primarily on the Dutch divorce market.[221] This platform – uitelkaar.nl – has been live since September 2017.[222]

218 http://ebram.org.

219 www.tecsa.org.uk/dispute-resolution/adjudication/low-value-disputes-lvd-adjudication-service/.

220 'Online court won't repeat failure of Dutch model, MoR claims', Michael Cross, The Law Society Gazette, 20 June 2017: www.lawgazette.co.uk/practice/online-court-wont-repeat-failure-of-dutch-model-mor-claims/5061641.article.

221 'Goodbye, Rechtwijzer: hello, Justice 42', Roger Smith, Law, Technology and Access to Justice, 31 March 2017: https://law-tech-a2j.org/advice/goodbye-rechtwijzer-hello-justice42/.

222 https://justice42.com/?lang=en.

Additionally, even though ODR may seem to herald an era of increasingly accessible justice, there are real access to justice concerns. To use ODR, not only does one need consistent and reliable internet access, but the need for basic technology and technical skills to access the ODR platforms may exclude some (potentially, the most vulnerable) individuals from using it. And, as the starting point in most cases is self-representation, this could lead to confusion and injustice as individuals may not have the time, knowledge or capabilities to use ODR platforms effectively.

Alternatives to traditional dispute resolution

10.31 In addition to ODR platforms, technology-powered alternatives to traditional dispute resolution are also beginning to make an appearance. These mostly take the form of private-sector funded dispute resolution platforms that rely on blockchain technology and varying levels of human input. Some utilise 'crowd-sourced justice', whilst others apply AI-based diagnostic tools and predictive forecasting, mostly based on statistical analysis of past court behaviour.[223]

Case Studies

Kleros is a decentralised application that works as a decentralised third party to arbitrate disputes in every kind of contract. It is an opt-in court system, and smart contracts have to designate Kleros as their arbitrator, choose how many jurors and which court will rule on the contract in the event of dispute – for example, a software development court, an insurance court etc. Parties provide electronic evidence of their dispute, which is then circulated to jurors to rule on. 'Jurors' stake pinakion ('PNK'), the token used by Kleros to select jurors, in order to hear and decide on disputes; and the more tokens staked, the more likely someone will be selected as a juror. Once a juror has made their decision, they are rewarded for their work with PNK; and, once all jurors have made a decision, it is relayed to the parties. Thus, Kleros is a form of quasi-judicial online court system that relies on game theoretics and incentives to have jurors rule on cases. The result is a dispute resolution system that renders ultimate judgments in a fast, inexpensive and decentralised way.[224]

Mattereum provides a decentralised dispute resolution and enforcement platform, where claims are resolved by technically competent, independent arbitrators whose decisions are recognised internationally and can be directly enforced in the countries where businesses or assets are located.[225]

223 'Thoughts for the new decade: smart contracts, blockchain and constriction dispute resolution', David Savage, Charles Russell Speechlys: www.charlesrussellspeechlys.com/en/news-and-insights/insights/constuction-engineering-and-projects/2020/smart-contracts-blockchain-and-construction-dispute-resolution/.

224 https://kleros.io/static/whitepaper_en-8bd3a0480b45c39899787e17049ded26.pdf.

225 https://mattereum.com/services/.

CodeLegit, which provides an auditing tool designed to verify the compliance of software code, also provides ready-made smart contracts that include an arbitration clause and the Blockchain Arbitration Library. The triggering of the Blockchain Arbitration Library pauses any further execution of the smart contract, thus allowing the parties to settle their dispute by referring it to Blockchain Arbitration, which operates under the Blockchain Arbitration Rules. CodeLegit is the Appointing Authority of the arbitral proceedings, performing all the administrative work and assigning the arbitrators. The cases are usually heard orally via video conference.[226]

Oath Protocol is a blockchain-based governance protocol that enables the community to resolve on-chain or off-chain disputes. It is modelled on the common law jury system, relies on a large, diverse juror pool and provides an incentive system.[227]

Most of these technology-powered alternatives to traditional dispute resolution remain in beta testing mode and/or development, and there are still a number of technical and legal obstacles to be overcome.[228]

Thus, not only does ADR provide a platform to resolve cyber disputes, but the world of technology is also seeking to adapt established court and ADR principles in order to create quasi-/hybrid dispute resolution models that will more easily resolve all kinds of dispute.

226 http://codelegit.com and https://docs.google.com/document/d/1v_AdWbMuc2Ei70ghITC1mYX4_5VQsF_28O4PsLckNM4/edit.

227 https://icodrops.com/oath-protocol/.

228 'Thoughts for the new decade: smart contracts, blockchain and constriction dispute resolution', David Savage, Charles Russell Speechlys.

Index

[All references are to paragraph numbers]